THE 50 GREATEST
PLAYERS IN BOSTON
RED SOX HISTORY

THE 50 GREATEST PLAYERS IN BOSTON RED SOX HISTORY

Robert W. Cohen

Guilford, Connecticut

Published by Lyons Press
An imprint of The Rowman & Littlefield Publishing Group, Inc.
4501 Forbes Boulevard, Suite 200, Lanham, Maryland 20706
www.rowman.com

Distributed by NATIONAL BOOK NETWORK

Copyright © 2018 by Robert W. Cohen
First Down East Books Hardcover edition 2014
First Lyons Press Paperback edition 2018

British Library Cataloguing in Publication Information available

Library of Congress Cataloging-in-Publication Data
Names: Cohen, Robert W., author.
Title: The 50 greatest players in Boston Red Sox history / Robert W. Cohen.
Other titles: Fifty greatest players in Boston Red Sox history
Description: Guilford, Connecticut : Lyons Press Fish, 2018. | Includes
   bibliographical references and index.
Identifiers: LCCN 2018006172 (print) | LCCN 2018004768 (ebook) | ISBN
   9781608936175 (e-book) | ISBN 9781608939909 (pbk. : alk. paper)
Subjects: LCSH: Boston Red Sox (Baseball team)--History. | Football
   players--Rating of--United States.
Classification: LCC GV875.B62 (print) | LCC GV875.B62 C65 2018 (ebook) | DDC
   796.357/640974461--dc23
LC record available at https://lccn.loc.gov/2018006172

ISBN 978-1-60893-310-5 (cloth: alk paper)
ISBN 978-1-60893-990-9 (paperback: alk paper)
ISBN 978-1-60893-617-5 (e-book)

Printed in the United States of America

This book is dedicated to Red Sox legend Bobby Doerr, whose passing on November 13, 2017, at 99 years of age, saddened baseball fans everywhere.

Contents

THE RANKINGS

Acknowledgments

I would like to express my gratitude to the grandchildren of Leslie Jones, who, through the Trustees of the Boston Public Library, Print Department, supplied many of the photos included in this book.

Special thanks go out to the Boston Red Sox, who generously provided me with several of the pictures contained herein.

I also wish to thank MearsonlineAuctions.com, RMYauctions.com, LegendaryAuctions.com, PristineAuction.com, MainlineAutographs.com, DBSportsMemorabilia.com, 1960sBaseball.com, Keith Allison, Jerry Reuss, Richard Albersheim, Stuart Merle, Ted Straub, and Joe Donovan, each of whom generously contributed to the photographic content of this work.

Introduction

THE RED SOX LEGACY

Founded in 1901 as one of the newly formed American League's eight charter franchises, the team that eventually became known as the Boston Red Sox spent its first seven seasons playing without an official nickname. Although Boston's entry in the infant circuit ended up having various monikers affixed to it during that period, including the Americans, Pilgrims, and Somersets, it wasn't until 1908 that the team officially adopted the nickname "Red Sox." Yet, the absence of a widely accepted appellation did not prevent the team from Boston from establishing itself as one of the junior circuit's most formidable squads, even as ownership of the ball club passed from Charles Somers to John I. Taylor. After finishing second and third in their first two years of existence, the Pilgrims (as they were most often called) captured their first American League pennant in 1903, after which they defeated the favored Pittsburgh Pirates, five games to three, in the first modern World Series. They won the pennant again the following year, although the refusal of the NL champion Giants to play them in the World Series denied them the opportunity to defend their world championship. Legendary pitcher Cy Young, player-manager Jimmy Collins, and slugging first baseman/outfielder Buck Freeman served as the team's most prominent figures during the franchise's formative years.

Boston proved to be far less successful the next several seasons, finishing higher than fourth just once between 1905 and 1911. However, after moving from Huntington Avenue Grounds—a onetime carnival sight—into newly constructed Fenway Park in 1912, the Red Sox began their next period of dominance. Led by hard-throwing right-hander Smoky Joe Wood and Hall of Fame outfielder Tris Speaker, the Red Sox ran away with the American League pennant in 1912, finishing 14 games ahead of the second-place Washington Senators. They then defeated the New York Giants in the World Series, four games to three, to win their second "official" world championship.

The Red Sox failed to repeat as AL champions in either of the next two seasons under new owner Joseph Lannin. But they established themselves as baseball's dominant team from 1915 to 1918, winning three more World Series, with star pitcher Babe Ruth leading them to victory in the 1916 and 1918 Fall Classics.

After experiencing so much success throughout most of the first two decades of the 20th century, the Red Sox entered into a prolonged period of futility shortly after Harry Frazee purchased them from Lannin in 1916. A theatrical producer more concerned with acquiring the funds necessary to finance his other primary interests than putting together a successful baseball team, Frazee ended up auctioning off most of his best players to other clubs, beginning the purging by selling Babe Ruth to the Yankees on December 26, 1919. Boston's subsequent failures, which consequently came to be known as the "Curse of the Bambino," extended from 1919 to 1933, a period during which the Red Sox finished last in the American League nine times.

Things began to improve dramatically for the Red Sox in 1933, when 30-year-old millionaire Tom Yawkey purchased them from Bob Quinn—the team's owner for the previous ten seasons. After building the "Green Monster" in left field as part of Fenway Park's reconstruction, Yawkey set about rebuilding his team. First, he improved the Red Sox pitching staff by acquiring Wes Ferrell from the Cleveland Indians and Lefty Grove from the Philadelphia Athletics. He then traded for shortstop Joe Cronin and slugging first baseman Jimmie Foxx. Yawkey also rebuilt the Red Sox farm system, which soon began producing talented players such as Bobby Doerr, Ted Williams, Dom DiMaggio, and Johnny Pesky.

Before long, the Red Sox became a perennial pennant contender, capturing one league title and finishing second six times between 1938 and 1949. Nevertheless, they always seemed to come up just a bit short. Making their first World Series appearance in 28 years in 1946, the Red Sox fell to the St. Louis Cardinals in seven games, losing the series finale on Enos Slaughter's legendary "mad dash" around the bases. Two years later, the Red Sox failed to earn a return trip to the Fall Classic when the Cleveland Indians defeated them in a one-game playoff. Boston held a one-game lead over New York with just two games left to play the very next year, but again came up short when the Yankees defeated them in the final two games of the regular season.

Boston remained a solid team throughout much of the 1950s, due primarily to the presence of Ted Williams in their everyday lineup. But the Sox found themselves unable to compete successfully after Williams announced his retirement in 1960, compiling a losing record seven straight times from 1960 to 1966.

The emergence of Carl Yastrzemski as a true superstar enabled the Red Sox to finish first in one of the most hotly contested pennant races in baseball history in the "Impossible Dream" season of 1967. However, the Sox again barely missed achieving their ultimate goal, losing the World Series to the Cardinals in seven games.

The Red Sox again came tantalizingly close to ending their world championship drought in 1975, when they came within one game of defeating the Cincinnati Reds in a classic World Series matchup. Tom Yawkey passed away the following year, leaving co-ownership of the club to his widow, Jean, and Haywood Sullivan, who continued to run things until Mrs. Yawkey's death in 1992. Boston returned to the World Series one more time during that period, losing the 1986 Fall Classic in heartbreaking fashion to the New York Mets, after earlier holding a 3–2 lead in a series that became best known for Bill Buckner's fielding error in the 10th inning of Game 6.

Featuring stars such as Wade Boggs, Roger Clemens, Pedro Martinez, Mo Vaughn, and Nomar Garciaparra at different times, the Red Sox made six more postseason appearances between 1988 and 2003, failing to advance beyond the American League Championship Series in any of those campaigns. However, just one year after being eliminated by the Yankees in Game 7 of the ALCS on a home run by light-hitting Aaron Boone, the Red Sox exacted a measure of revenge against their bitter rivals by mounting the greatest comeback in major-league history. Trailing New York three games to none in the 2004 ALCS, Boston swept the final four contests, becoming in the process the first team ever to overcome a 3–0 series deficit. David Ortiz and Johnny Damon supplied much of the offensive firepower during Boston's resurgence, while Curt Schilling provided the pitching heroics. The Red Sox carried their momentum into the World Series, sweeping the St. Louis Cardinals in four straight games, thereby ending 86 years of frustration.

The Red Sox again displayed extraordinary resilience three years later, when they overcame a 3–1 deficit against Cleveland in the ALCS to earn a return trip to the Fall Classic. After outscoring the Indians 30–5 over the final three games of the championship series, Boston swept the overmatched Colorado Rockies in four straight games in the World Series. Although the Red Sox advanced to the playoffs in each of the next two seasons as well, they failed to make it back to the Fall Classic. They subsequently failed to earn a postseason berth from 2010 to 2012, posting an embarrassing 69–93 record in the last of those campaigns. However, the Red Sox returned to the top of the baseball world in 2013, winning 97 games during the regular season, before defeating Tampa Bay in the ALDS, Detroit in the ALCS, and St. Louis in six games in the World Series. Boston subsequently faltered in each of the next two seasons, finishing well out of contention in the A.L. East both years, before capturing the division title in both 2016 and 2017. But the Sox exited the postseason tournament quickly both times, losing to the Cleveland Indians in the divisional round of the playoffs in 2016, before suffering a similar fate at the hands of the Houston Astros this past season.

Nevertheless, Boston's victory in the 2013 Fall Classic marked the eighth world championship in franchise history. The Red Sox have also won a total of 13 pennants. The New York Yankees and Philadelphia/Oakland Athletics are the only American League franchises able to boast more pennants. Meanwhile, only the Yankees, Athletics, and Cardinals have won more world championships.

In addition to the level of success the Red Sox have reached as a team over the years, a significant number of players have attained notable individual honors while playing at Fenway. The Red Sox boast 11 MVP winners, placing them fourth in the American League, behind only the Yankees, Athletics, and Detroit Tigers. They also have featured seven Cy Young Award winners, three Triple Crown winners, 24 batting champions, and 18 home run champions. Meanwhile, 29 members of the Baseball Hall of Fame spent at least one full season playing for the Red Sox. Thirteen of those men are depicted on their Hall of Fame plaque wearing a Red Sox cap.

FACTORS USED TO DETERMINE RANKINGS

It should come as no surprise that selecting the 50 greatest players ever to perform for a team with the rich history of the Boston Red Sox presented a difficult and daunting task. Even after I narrowed the field down to a mere 50 men, I found myself faced with the challenge of ranking the elite players that remained. Certainly, the names of Ted Williams, Carl Yastrzemski, Cy Young, Pedro Martinez, Jim Rice, and Roger Clemens would appear at, or near, the top of virtually everyone's list, although the order might vary somewhat from one person to the next. Several other outstanding performers have gained general recognition through the years as being among the greatest players ever to wear a Red Sox uniform. Wade Boggs, Jimmie Foxx, Bobby Doerr, and David Ortiz head the list of other Red Sox icons.

But, how does one differentiate between the all-around brilliance of Carl Yastrzemski and the offensive dominance of Jimmie Foxx, or the pitching greatness of Pedro Martinez and the extraordinary hitting ability of Ted Williams? After initially deciding who to include on my list, I then needed to determine what criteria I should use to formulate my final rankings.

The first thing I decided to examine was the level of dominance a player attained during his time in Boston. How often did he lead the American League in some major offensive or pitching statistical category? How did he fare in the annual MVP and/or Cy Young voting? How many times did he make the All-Star Team?

I also needed to weigh the level of statistical compilation a player achieved while wearing a Red Sox uniform. Where does a batter rank in team annals in the major offensive categories? How high on the all-time list of Red Sox hurlers does a pitcher rank in wins, ERA, complete games, innings pitched, shutouts, and saves? Of course, I also needed to consider the era in which the player performed when evaluating his overall numbers. For example, modern-day starting pitchers such as Roger Clemens and Pedro Martinez are not likely to throw nearly as many complete games or shutouts as Cy Young, who anchored Boston's starting rotation during the first decade of the 20th century. And slugging designated hitter David Ortiz, who played for the Red Sox from 2003 to 2016, was likely to average more home runs per year than someone like Jim Rice, who had most of his finest seasons for the Red Sox nearly 25 years earlier.

Other important factors I needed to consider were the overall contributions a player made to the success of the team, the degree to which he improved the fortunes of the ball club during his time in Boston, the manner in which he impacted the team, both on and off the field, and the degree to which he added to the Red Sox legacy of winning. While the number of pennants the Red Sox won during a particular player's years with the ball club certainly entered into the equation, I chose not to deny a top performer his rightful place on the list if his years in Boston happened to coincide with a lack of overall success by the team. As a result, the names of players such as Jackie Jensen and Frank Malzone will appear in these rankings.

One other thing I should mention is that I only considered a player's performance while playing for the Red Sox when formulating my rankings. That being the case, the names of great players such as Babe Ruth and Lefty Grove, both of whom had most of their best years while playing for other teams, may appear lower on this list than one might expect.

And, finally, there are the cases of David Ortiz and Manny Ramirez, both of whom tested positive for using performance-enhancing drugs while playing for the Red Sox. While Ortiz and Ramirez clearly earned lofty spots in these rankings with their extraordinary offensive feats, I felt compelled to drop both of them a few notches since they likely accomplished many of the things they did through the use of PEDs.

Having established the guidelines to be used throughout this book, we are ready to take a look at the 50 greatest players in Red Sox history, starting with number 1 and working our way down to number 50.

Ted Williams

Courtesy HeritageAuctions.com

Truth be told, I needed to focus only on numbers 2 through 50 when formulating my rankings since Ted Williams clearly separated himself from
every other Red Sox player with his extraordinary hitting ability. Quite pos-
sibly the greatest hitter in baseball history, Williams compiled an amazing
list of accomplishments over the course of his 19 years in Boston. A six-
time batting champion and two-time Triple Crown winner, Williams posted
a lifetime batting average of .344 and hit 521 career home runs, despite

missing almost five full seasons due to time spent in the U.S. military during World War II and the Korean War.

Yet, Williams spent most of his career sharing a love-hate relationship with the fans of Boston, while simultaneously being vilified by the media. Confident, cocky, stubborn, unyielding, intractable, and fiercely independent, Williams rubbed many people the wrong way—something that didn't seem to bother him in the least. Williams's gruff exterior often made life difficult for him in Boston, preventing him from earning many of the individual accolades that likely would have been bestowed upon him had he been more cooperative with the press. However, the same attributes that made him such a controversial figure also helped make him arguably the greatest hitter who ever lived.

Born in San Diego, California, on August 30, 1918, as Teddy Samuel Williams, Ted Williams eventually had the name on his birth certificate officially changed to Theodore, although his mother and closest friends continued to call him "Teddy." Named after his father, Samuel Stuart Williams, and former U.S. president Teddy Roosevelt, Williams attended Herbert Hoover High School in San Diego, where he excelled in baseball to such a degree that he received offers from the St. Louis Cardinals and the New York Yankees before he even graduated. However, since his mother considered him too young to leave home, Williams signed on instead with the local minor-league team, the San Diego Padres. After honing his skills with the Padres, Williams signed an amateur free-agent contract with the Boston Red Sox in 1936. He spent two years in Boston's minor-league farm system before making his major-league debut on April 20, 1939.

Williams hardly acted like a typical major-league rookie when he joined the Red Sox in spring training that year. Exuding tremendous self-confidence, the cocky 20-year-old surprised many of his teammates with his bold and brazen manner. As Williams prepared for his first batting-practice session with the big club, one of his teammates said to him, "Wait until you see [Jimmie] Foxx hit!" Unimpressed, Williams responded, "Wait until Foxx sees *me* hit!"

Williams's brashness might have annoyed his teammates had he not had the ability to back up his words. Boston's new left fielder had a fabulous rookie season, hitting 31 home runs, scoring 131 runs, batting .327, leading the league with 145 runs batted in and 344 total bases, and finishing fourth in the AL MVP voting. He followed that up with another outstanding performance in 1940, batting .344, driving in 113 runs, and leading the league with 134 runs scored and a .442 on-base percentage. However, the best had yet to come.

After Joe DiMaggio's record-setting 56 consecutive game hitting streak captivated the nation earlier in 1941, Williams took center stage during the season's final few weeks as he strove to become the first man since Bill Terry (1930) to hit .400. Williams entered the final day of the season with a batting average of .39955, which would have been rounded up to .400 had he elected not to play in either game of Boston's season-ending doubleheader against Philadelphia. Offered the option to sit out both games by Red Sox manager Joe Cronin, Williams responded, "If I can't hit .400 all the way, I don't deserve it." In a memorable performance, Williams ended up collecting six hits in eight times at bat over the course of the day, to raise his batting average to .406. No man has batted .400 since. The "Splendid Splinter" also knocked in 120 runs and led the American League with 37 home runs, 135 runs scored, 147 walks, a .553 on-base percentage, and a .735 slugging percentage. He finished second to DiMaggio in the league MVP voting.

Williams had another great year in 1942, leading the league in eight different offensive categories, including home runs (36), runs batted in (137), and batting average (.356), to win his first Triple Crown. Yet, even though the Red Sox finished a very respectable second to the Yankees in the American League standings, Williams failed to win the MVP Award. That honor instead went to New York second baseman Joe Gordon.

There is little doubt that the contentious relationship Williams shared with the baseball writers of the day contributed greatly to the lack of support they showed him at times during the MVP balloting. Moody, hot-tempered, impatient, and somewhat temperamental, Williams alienated himself from the members of the media early in his career, thereby jading their opinion of him throughout the remainder of his playing days. Extremely honest and forthright in his responses to their questions, Williams didn't particularly care how they might react to his answers. The Boston beat reporters, who Williams dubbed the "Knights of the Keyboard," often misinterpreted his self-confidence as arrogance, and they conveyed their feelings toward him to the Boston faithful in their newspaper articles. Before long, Red Sox fans turned against Williams as well, finding particularly objectionable his habit of practicing his swing in the outfield during the opposing team's at-bats. Boston fans believed the sport's greatest hitter didn't pay as much attention to the other aspects of the game as he should have, and they soon took to booing him at every opportunity. Williams responded by refusing to ever again tip his cap to them when they cheered him after hitting a home run.

The adversarial nature of Williams's relationship with the press reached its zenith in 1942, when his request for military deferment drew criticism from the media. However, the writers failed to inform the public that the patriotic Williams hesitated to enter the military only because he represented the sole source of income for his mother, a Salvation Army worker. Williams eventually entered the service in 1943, spending the next three years serving as a pilot in the U.S. Navy.

Johnny Pesky, who spent his first seven big-league seasons playing with Williams in Boston, went into the same training program as his teammate. Pesky later recalled the tremendous acumen Williams displayed during the program: "He mastered intricate problems in 15 minutes which took the average cadet an hour, and half of the other cadets there were college grads."

After serving as a flight instructor at Naval Air Station Pensacola, Williams was stationed in Pearl Harbor awaiting orders to join the China Fleet when the war ended. He last served in Hawaii, before being released from active duty in January of 1946.

Williams showed no signs of rust when he returned to the major leagues in 1946. If anything, his added bulk made him physically stronger. The 6'3" slugger had previously depended primarily on his quick wrists and picture-perfect swing to generate power through the hitting zone. But an additional 10–12 pounds of muscle helped Williams become even more of a power threat. In his first year back, Williams hit 38 home runs, knocked in 123 runs, batted .342, and led the league with 142 runs scored, 156 walks, a .497 on-base percentage, and a .667 slugging percentage. The Red Sox captured their first pennant since 1918, with Williams earning AL MVP honors.

In addition to his quick wrists and classic swing, Williams possessed extraordinary eyesight and exceptional patience at the plate. His thorough knowledge of the strike zone enabled him to produce a nearly three-to-one ratio of walks to strikeouts over the course of his career. In fact, after striking out 64 times as a rookie, Williams never fanned more than 54 times in any other season.

In *The Sporting News Selects 50 Greatest Sluggers*, pitcher Bobby Shantz discussed the dilemma pitchers faced when Williams stepped into the batter's box: "Did they tell me how to pitch to Williams? Sure they did. It was great advice, very encouraging. They said he had no weakness, won't swing at a bad ball, has the best eyes in the business, and can kill you with one swing. He won't hit anything bad, but don't give him anything good."

Meanwhile, legendary Cleveland Indians hurler Bob Feller said in *The Greats of the Game*, "The greatest hitter I ever pitched to was Ted Williams. He could hit anybody. . . . Ted had the great eye and hand coordination. He could make contact. He probably could swing harder and make contact better than anybody I ever knew."

Williams followed up his 1946 MVP performance by winning his second Triple Crown in 1947, leading the league with 32 home runs, 114 RBIs, and a .343 batting average. Yet, Joe DiMaggio edged him out in the MVP voting by a single point since one sportswriter who didn't care much for Williams left the Red Sox slugger completely off his ballot.

Williams had another big year in 1948, topping the junior circuit in five different offensive categories and winning his fourth batting title with a mark of .369. He posted even better overall numbers the following year, when he led the league in eight different departments, including home runs (43), RBIs (159), and runs scored (150). He also finished a close second in the batting race with a mark of .343, coming within a few percentage points of winning his third Triple Crown. With the Red Sox finishing just one game behind the pennant-winning Yankees, Williams walked away with his second MVP trophy.

After starting off the 1950 season well, Williams fractured his elbow crashing into the Comiskey Park wall while catching a deep drive hit by Pittsburgh's Ralph Kiner in the All-Star game. Subsequently forced to sit out more than 60 games, Williams nonetheless concluded the campaign with solid numbers. However, he later admitted that he never fully recovered from the injury, and stated that he felt he never again hit the ball with the same authority as before.

Williams put up good numbers in 1951, batting .318, hitting 30 homers, leading the league in walks, total bases, on-base percentage, and slugging percentage, and surpassing 100 RBIs and 100 runs scored for the final time in his career. But, after appearing in only six games the following year, Williams was recalled for active duty in the Korean War on May 1, 1952. Eight years removed from his last flight, Williams was not particularly happy about being pressed into service in Korea, but he did what he felt was his patriotic duty. He eventually flew 39 combat missions before being pulled from flight status in June 1953 as the result of an inner-ear infection. Williams returned to the Red Sox later that year, batting .407 in his 37 games with the team.

Thirty-five years old at the start of the 1954 campaign, Williams appeared in as many as 130 games in only two of his seven remaining seasons. After missing more than 30 games in 1954 due to a broken collarbone he suffered as the result of diving for a ball in spring training, he missed nearly 60 games in 1955 with an assortment of injuries. Battling various aches and pains over the course of his final five seasons, Williams never again compiled more than 420 official at-bats in a season. Yet, he remained a great hitter to the very end, winning two more batting titles, including leading the league with a mark of .388 in 1957, at the age of 38.

After batting .316, hitting 29 home runs, and knocking in 72 runs in only 113 games and 310 official at-bats in 1960, Williams announced his retirement at the conclusion of the campaign. He ended his career with 521 home runs, 1,839 runs batted in, 1,798 runs scored, 2,654 hits, 2,021 walks, a .344 batting average, a .634 slugging average, and an all-time best .483 on-base percentage. Williams ranks first all-time on the Red Sox in career homers, batting average, slugging average, on-base percentage, and bases on balls.

Stan Musial expressed his admiration for Williams when he stated, "Ted was the greatest hitter of our era. He won six batting titles and served his country for five years, so he would have won more. He loved talking about hitting and was a great student of hitting and pitchers."

Carl Yastrzemski, who claimed the starting left field job in Boston after Williams retired from the game, commented, "They can talk about Babe Ruth and Ty Cobb and Rogers Hornsby and Lou Gehrig and Joe DiMaggio and Stan Musial and all the rest, but I'm sure not one of them could hold cards and spades to Williams in his sheer knowledge of hitting. He studied hitting the way a broker studies the stock market, and could spot at a glance mistakes that others couldn't see in a week."

Following his retirement, the baseball writers elected Williams to the Hall of Fame in his first year of eligibility. In his 1966 induction speech, Williams included a statement calling for the admission into Cooperstown of some of the great Negro League players who never had an opportunity to perform in the majors. Williams stated, "I've been a very lucky guy to have worn a baseball uniform, and I hope some day the names of Satchel Paige and Josh Gibson in some way can be added as a symbol of the great Negro players who are not here only because they weren't given a chance."

Williams started a second career in 1969 as manager of the Washington Senators, serving in that capacity until shortly after the start of the 1972 campaign, when the team became the Texas Rangers. He subsequently made guest appearances from time to time at Red Sox spring training, until he became unable to do so in later years due to failing health. Williams had a pacemaker installed in November of 2000 and underwent open-heart surgery in January of 2001. After suffering a series of strokes and congestive heart failures, he died of cardiac arrest at the age of 83 on July 5, 2002.

Upon learning of his passing, Dale Petroskey, the president of the Baseball Hall of Fame, expressed his admiration for Williams by saying, "Ted's passing signals a sad day, not only for baseball fans, but for every American. He was a cultural icon, a larger-than-life personality. He was great enough to become a Hall of Fame player. He was caring enough to be the first Hall of Famer to call for the inclusion of Negro League stars in Cooperstown. He was brave enough to serve our country as a Marine in not one but two global conflicts. Ted Williams is a hero for all generations."

Pittsburgh Pirates manager Lloyd McClendon discussed what the Boston legend meant to him: "Ted was everything that was right about the game of baseball. If you really think about it, he was everything that is right about this country. It is certainly a sad day for all of us. He is a man who lost five years of service time serving his country. What he could have done with those years in the prime of his life . . . it would be awesome to really put those numbers together. He would have probably been the greatest power hitter of all time."

Ted Williams wrote in his book, *My Turn at Bat*, "A man has to have goals—for a day, for a lifetime—and that was mine, to have people say, 'There goes Ted Williams, the greatest hitter who ever lived.'" Many people feel that Williams reached his ultimate goal.

Courtesy Boston Public Library, Leslie Jones Collection

CAREER HIGHLIGHTS

Best Season

With Williams winning the Triple Crown in both 1942 and 1947, one would naturally assume that one of those years represented his finest season. However, as well as Williams performed in each of those years, particularly in 1942 when he led the American League with 36 home runs, 137 RBIs, 141 runs scored, a .356 batting average, 145 walks, 338 total bases, a .499 on-base percentage, and a .648 slugging average, the "Splendid Splinter" actually had two or three better seasons. The 1957 campaign would certainly have to be considered one of his finest. In addition to winning the batting title with a mark of .388 at 38 years of age, Williams hit 38 homers and topped the junior circuit with a .526 on-base percentage and a .731 slugging average. "Teddy Ballgame" had the most productive season of his career in 1949, when he captured the second of his two MVP trophies by batting .343, leading the league with 39 doubles, a .490 on-base percentage, and a .650 slugging percentage, and also topping the circuit with career-high marks of 43 home runs, 159 runs batted in, 150 runs scored, 162 walks, and 368 total bases.

Yet, 1941 is generally considered to be Williams's signature season. In addition to posting a historic .406 batting average, the "Splendid Splinter" drove in 120 runs, led the American League with 37 home runs, 135 runs scored, and 147 bases on balls, and established career highs in on-base percentage (.553), slugging percentage (.735), and OPS (1.287), topping the circuit in those three categories as well. Williams also struck out only 27 times all year—an amazing accomplishment when it is considered that he also hit 37 homers.

Memorable Moments/Greatest Performances

A number of exceptional performances and memorable moments highlighted Williams's career, the first of which occurred on May 4, 1939, when he led the Red Sox to a 7–6 win over the Tigers in Detroit by hitting two home runs in one game for the first time as a major leaguer. Williams hit one of his homers over the right field roof at Briggs Stadium, making him the first player to accomplish the feat.

Williams hit the longest home run ever hit at Fenway Park on June 9, 1946, driving an offering from Detroit's Fred Hutchinson into the right-center field bleachers, 502 feet from home plate. The blast landed on a fan's straw hat in Section 42, Row 37, Seat 21. Williams put on another power display a little over one month later, leading the Red Sox to an 11–10 victory in the first game of a doubleheader sweep of the Indians on July 14 by homering three times and driving in eight runs. "Teddy Ballgame's" homers included a grand slam, a three-run blast, and a solo shot. Just one week later, Williams led his team to another doubleheader sweep, this time of the visiting St. Louis Browns, by collecting seven straight hits and hitting for the cycle in the nitecap.

Williams homered three times in one game twice in 1957, accomplishing the feat for the first time during a 4–1 victory over the White Sox on May 8. He duplicated his earlier effort on June 13, going deep three times during a 9–2 win over the Indians.

Williams's six hits in eight at-bats on the final day of the 1941 season would have to rank among his most memorable performances as well. After earlier ignoring manager Joe Cronin's suggestion to sit out both ends of the doubleheader to protect his .400 batting average, Williams raised his mark to .406 by collecting four hits in the opener and another two in the nitecap. Reflecting back years later on the events of the day, Williams said on *The Greats of the Game*, "There was no doubt in my mind that I was gonna play. I never even thought about sitting out."

Displaying over the course of his career a penchant for hitting dramatic home runs, Williams hit one such homer on July 8, 1941, winning the annual All-Star game for the American League by homering off Chicago Cubs pitcher Claude Passeau with two men out and two men on in the bottom of the ninth inning. Williams's blast gave the junior circuit a 7–5 victory. He later said on *The Greats of the Game*, "I've always said that home run I hit in the '41 All-Star Game was the biggest thing I had done in a big moment."

Williams also came up big at the 1946 Midsummer Classic, homering twice, collecting four hits, driving in five runs, and scoring four others during a 12–0 AL win at Fenway Park. Williams hit his second homer against Rip Sewell, belting the right-hander's "ephous" (or "blooper") pitch deep into the right field stands.

However, Williams saved arguably the most dramatic home run of his career for his final at-bat. Playing before a sparse turnout at Fenway Park on a cool, dreary late-September afternoon, Williams drove a Jack Fisher offering into the bullpen in right-center field for the 521st and final home run of his storied career. Knowing that Williams intended to retire after the game, the Fenway faithful gave him a standing ovation as he rounded the bases. Williams, who remained true to himself to the very end, revealed years later on *Greatest Sports Legends*, "I thought about tipping my cap to them for one brief moment. But I just couldn't bring myself to do it." He elaborated further on his feelings that day on *The Greats of the Game*, stating, "That ranks with all the thrills I've had in baseball—right close to the top. Eighteen or 20 years before, I made up my mind I'm never gonna tip my cap again, and I never did. But, as I went around those bases, I thought about it. But it never happened. But I can tell you, it wasn't because I didn't think the Boston fans were the greatest. They were the greatest fans in the world. I've always tried to salute them in other ways. If I had to do it over again, I probably would."

NOTABLE ACHIEVEMENTS

- Hit more than 30 home runs eight times, topping 40 homers once (43 in 1949)
- Knocked in more than 100 runs nine times, surpassing 120 RBIs six times
- Scored more than 100 runs nine times, topping 130 runs scored six times
- Batted over .350 five times, surpassing the .400 mark once (.406 in 1941)
- Finished in double-digits in triples twice
- Surpassed 30 doubles eight times, topping 40 two-baggers on four occasions
- Walked more than 100 times on eleven occasions, surpassing 130 bases on balls seven times
- Compiled on-base percentage in excess of .490 nine times, surpassing .500 mark three times
- Posted slugging percentage in excess of .600 on 13 occasions, topping .700 mark three times
- Led AL in home runs four times; RBIs four times; batting average six times; runs scored six times; doubles twice; total bases six times; walks eight times; on-base percentage 12 times; slugging percentage nine times; and OPS 10 times
- Major League Baseball's all-time leader in career on-base percentage (.482)
- Ranks second all-time in Major League Baseball in career slugging percentage (.634) and OPS (1.116)

- Holds Red Sox career records for most home runs (521) and walks (2,021); highest batting average (.344); on-base percentage (.482); slugging percentage (.634); and OPS (1.116)
- Ranks second all-time on Red Sox in runs batted in (1,839); runs scored (1,816); hits (2,654); extra base hits (1,117); doubles (525); and total bases (4,884)
- Holds Red Sox single-season records for most runs scored (150); most walks (162); highest batting average (.406); highest on-base percentage (.553); highest slugging percentage (.735); and highest OPS (1.287)
- Last major-league player to bat over .400
- Two-time Triple Crown winner (1942 and 1947)
- Two-time AL MVP (1946 and 1949)
- Thirteen-time *Sporting News* All-Star selection
- Nineteen-time AL All-Star
- Five-time *Sporting News* Major League Player of the Year (1941, 1942, 1947, 1949, and 1957)
- Member of Major League Baseball's All-Century Team
- Sixth on *Sporting News*'s 1999 list of Baseball's 100 Greatest Players
- 1946 AL champion
- Elected to Baseball Hall of Fame by members of BBWAA in 1966

2

Carl Yastrzemski

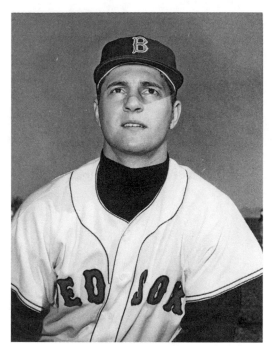

Courtesy LegendaryAuctions.com

Following a legend is never easy. That is something Carl Yastrzemski discovered after he inherited the Boston Red Sox left field job from Ted Williams at the start of the 1961 season. Yastrzemski played well for the Red Sox his first six years in the American League, winning a batting title and being named to three All-Star teams. Nevertheless, his inability to perform at the same lofty level that Williams reached during his remarkable career often left Yastrzemski feeling frustrated, dejected, and reviled. Frequently booed by the Fenway faithful, the young outfielder led a rather turbulent existence his first few years in Boston, failing to gain full acceptance by Red Sox fans until 1967, when he captured the American League Triple Crown and put together one of the finest all-around seasons in league history. From that point on, Yaz reached a level of popularity in Beantown that few other athletes have ever approached.

Born on August 22, 1939, in Southampton, New York, Carl Michael Yastrzemski grew up on his father's potato farm in the small Long Island town of Bridgehampton. As a youngster, Carl played on sandlot baseball teams with his father, Carl Sr., who the younger Yastrzemski always maintained had more ability than himself. After starring in baseball, football, and basketball at Bridgehampton High School, Carl Jr. briefly attended Notre Dame University before leaving school to pursue a professional career in baseball. Courted by several major-league teams, Yastrzemski eventually signed with the Red Sox, who immediately assigned him to Raleigh of the Carolina League. Yastrzemski captured the circuit's batting title in 1959 with a mark of .377, before being promoted to Boston's Triple-A affiliate in Minneapolis the following year. After falling just short of winning his second consecutive batting championship in 1960, Yastrzemski joined the Red Sox for the start of the 1961 campaign.

Yastrzemski placed an immense amount of pressure on himself when he arrived in Boston at the start of the season, stating years later in *Forever Fenway: 75 Years of Red Sox Baseball*, "I think being in Ted Williams' shadow put tremendous pressure on me the first two years. I would have liked to come into the big leagues, been unnoticed and not taken Ted Williams' place, or been called 'the next Ted Williams.' I think it would have made it much easier for me."

Never having failed at any level before, Yastrzemski had a difficult time coping with the initial lack of success he experienced against major-league pitching, later recalling, "I remember I was a scared rookie, hitting .220 after the first three months of my baseball season, and doubting my ability."

Yastrzemski's struggles eventually prompted the Red Sox to summon Williams to work with him. The "Splendid Splinter" helped restore the rookie's shattered confidence, telling him at their first meeting, "I know—I know all about you. Look, kid, don't ever—ya' understand me?—don't ever let anybody monkey with your swing."

Williams's positive reinforcement helped Yastrzemski right himself, and the young left fielder went on to post respectable numbers in his first big-league season, finishing the campaign with 11 home runs, 80 runs batted in, and a .266 batting average. Yaz improved upon those figures in 1962, hitting 19 home runs, driving in 94 runs, scoring 99 others, batting .296, and finishing second in the league with 43 doubles. He won his first batting title the following year, leading the American League with a mark of .321, and also topping the circuit with 183 hits, 40 doubles, 95 walks, and a .418 on-base percentage. Yastrzemski earned his first AL All-Star and *Sporting News* All-Star selections, won his first Gold Glove, and placed sixth in the league MVP voting at season's end.

Yastrzemski continued to play well for the Red Sox in each of the next three seasons, finishing among the league leaders in batting average, doubles, and on-base percentage all three years, earning two more selections to the AL All-Star team, and winning another Gold Glove. In fact, Yaz developed into one of the American League's finest all-around players, displaying good power and a keen batting eye at the plate, while also doing a superb job of playing Fenway's tricky "Green Monster" in left field. Nevertheless, the outfielder often found himself being targeted by the Fenway Faithful for his inability to reach the level of greatness originally predicted for him when he first entered the league. Yastrzemski further antagonized the fans by occasionally demonstrating a lack of concentration on the field, making errors in judgment on the base paths from time to time while also expressing his frustration with his own failures at the plate by failing to run out fly balls or infield groundouts. The Boston fans might have treated Yastrzemski better, though, had they realized that his love and passion for the game caused him to experience these periodic lapses.

Yastrzemski once said, "I think about baseball when I wake up in the morning. I think about it all day, and I dream about it at night. The only time I don't think about it is when I'm playing it."

Boston outfielder Joe Lahoud confirmed Yaz's obsession with the sport when he revealed, "Yaz did it all the time. We'd be on the road and he'd call, 'C'mon, we're going to the ballpark.' I'd say, 'Christ, it's only one o'clock. The game's at seven.' He lived, breathed, ate, and slept baseball. If he went 0 for 4, he couldn't live with it. He could live with himself if he went 1 for 3. He was happy if he went 2 for 4. That's the way the man suffered."

Yastrzemski finally won over the Fenway faithful in 1967, when he led the Red Sox to the American League pennant by putting together a truly remarkable season. After working out feverishly during the offseason and adding nearly 10 pounds of muscle to his frame, the 5'11" Yastrzemski reported to spring training at close to 185 pounds and in the best shape of his life. Although Yastrzemski possessed a fierce swing from the time he first entered the league, his bat appeared to be just a bit quicker, enabling him to pull the ball more regularly, instead of driving it to all fields as he had done in previous years. The change in Yaz's hitting style ended up paying huge dividends, with the 28-year-old outfielder capturing the AL Triple Crown by topping the circuit with 44 home runs, 121 runs batted in, and a .326 batting average. He also led the league with 112 runs scored, 189 hits, 360 total bases, a .418 on-base percentage, and a .622 slugging percentage. In a hotly contested four-team pennant race that went down to the final day of the regular season, Yastrzemski carried the Red Sox on his back down the stretch, batting .523, hitting 5 home runs, knocking in 16 runs, and scoring 14 others over the season's final two weeks. Yaz's heroics enabled Boston to finish just one game ahead of Detroit and Minnesota in the final standings, putting the Red Sox in the World Series for the first time in 21 years. He continued to excel against St. Louis in the Fall Classic, batting .400, with three homers and five RBIs, although the Red Sox ended up losing to the Cardinals in seven games. Yastrzemski's extraordinary performance earned him AL MVP and *Sports Illustrated* magazine's Sportsman of the Year honors at season's end. He also received the Hickok Belt, presented annually to the top professional athlete of the year.

Although Yastrzemski never again reached such heights, he remained one of baseball's very best players from 1968 to 1970. In the first of those campaigns, he hit 23 home runs, drove in 74 runs, scored 90, and led the league with a .301 batting average and a .426 on-base percentage. Despite batting only .255 the following year, Yastrzemski hit 40 homers, knocked in 111 runs, scored 96 others, and won his fifth Gold Glove. He then had a sensational 1970 season in which he placed among the league leaders with 40 home runs, 102 runs batted in, and a .329 batting average. Yaz also topped the circuit with 125 runs scored, a .452 on-base percentage, and a .592 slugging percentage, en route to earning a fourth-place finish in the league MVP voting.

Yastrzemski failed to hit 30 home runs or score 100 runs in any of his 13 remaining seasons. He also batted over .300 just once more and knocked in as many as 100 runs only two more times. Nevertheless, he remained an extremely productive hitter until he finally retired at the conclusion of the 1983 campaign, at the age of 44. In addition to driving in 102 runs in both 1976 and 1977, Yaz surpassed 90 runs scored three more times, leading the league in that category in 1974, when he crossed the plate 93 times. He also used his keen batting eye to consistently finish near the top of the league rankings in on-base percentage. Yaz had his last big year in 1977, batting .296, hitting 28 homers, driving in 102 runs, scoring 99, and winning the last of his seven Gold Gloves for his outstanding play in left field. He spent his final six seasons splitting time between the outfield, first base, and DH spots. By the time he retired, Yastrzemski had amassed 452 home runs, 1,844 runs batted in, 1,816 runs scored, 3,419 hits, 646 doubles, 1,845 walks, and 5,539 total bases, placing him first in Red Sox history in each category except home runs and walks (he trails only Ted Williams and David Ortiz in homers, and he ranks second only to Williams in bases on balls). Yaz also played in more games (3,308), accumulated more plate appearances (13,992), and collected more official at-bats (11,988) than any other Red Sox player. He batted .285 over the course of his career and posted on-base and slugging percentages of .379 and .462, respectively. Some 30 years after he played his last game, Yastrzemski still ranks among Major League Baseball's all-time leaders in games played (second), plate appearances (second), at-bats (third), bases on balls (sixth), hits (ninth), doubles (eighth), and total bases (ninth). He was the first American League player to surpass 3,000 hits and 400 home runs.

Yet, in spite of all his accomplishments, Yastrzemski maintains that he never really enjoyed himself on the ball field, stating years later, "I loved the game. I loved the competition. But I never had any fun. I never enjoyed it; all hard work, all the time."

Courtesy LegendaryAuctions.com

CAREER HIGHLIGHTS

Best Season

Yastrzemski performed exceptionally well in 1970, finishing among the AL leaders with 40 home runs, 102 RBIs, a .329 batting average, 186 hits, and 128 walks. He also topped the circuit with 125 runs scored, 335 total bases, a .452 on-base percentage, and a .592 slugging percentage. Yaz even stole a career-high 23 bases. Nevertheless, there is little doubt that Yastrzemski had his greatest year in 1967, when he led the AL in nine different offensive categories, en route to winning the Triple Crown and capturing league MVP honors. In addition to batting .326, scoring 112 runs, and compiling a .418 on-base percentage, Yaz established career highs in home runs (44), RBIs (121), total bases (360), and slugging percentage (.622). Teammate George Scott, who watched in amazement as Yastrzemski led the Red Sox to the pennant, stated in *Forever Fenway: 75 Years of Red Sox Baseball*, "Yaz had the type of year that every ballplayer dreams of. The guy hit 44 home runs that year, and I can remember 42 of those home runs meant something. They either won ballgames, tied ballgames, or brought us back into the ballgame. He never hit a single home run that year that didn't mean anything. I've never seen any one individual have that type of year that he had in 1967."

Red Sox pitcher Jim Lonborg, who captured AL Cy Young honors in that "Impossible Dream" season of 1967, added, "He [Yaz] had what I consider, in my 15 years of baseball, one of the greatest all-around years, both offensively and defensively."

Memorable Moments/Greatest Performances

Yastrzemski had arguably the greatest day of his career on May 19, 1976, going 4 for 4, with three homers, four RBIs, and four runs scored during a 9–2 win over Detroit at Tiger Stadium. He followed that up the very next day with a three-hit, two-homer, four-RBI performance at Yankee Stadium, leading the Red Sox to an 8–2 victory over the Yankees.

Always an outstanding big-game performer, Yastrzemski batted .455 in the 1975 ALCS, before posting a mark of .310 against the Cincinnati Reds in the World Series. In the one-game playoff against the Yankees for the 1978 AL East title, Yaz homered against Ron Guidry and drove in another run with an RBI single off Rich Gossage. He also captured MVP honors at the 1970 All-Star Game by going 4 for 4 with two walks.

Yastrzemski experienced one of his most memorable moments on September 12, 1979, when he singled off New York's Jim Beattie for his 3,000th career hit during a 9–2 Red Sox win over the Yankees. The safety made Yaz the first American League player to collect 3,000 hits and 400 home runs.

As one might expect, Yastrzemski turned in several of his most memorable performances while leading the Red Sox to the 1967 pennant, playing the best ball of his career during the latter stages of the campaign. Concluding a torrid 12-game stretch during which he batted .523, hit five home runs, knocked in 16 runs, and scored 14 others, Yaz led the Sox to consecutive must-win victories over Minnesota in the final two games of the regular season by going 7 for 8 with 5 RBIs, including a 3-run homer in the first contest. He also snuffed out a Twins rally by throwing out Bob Allison at second base on what looked like a sure double. Yastrzemski continued his extraordinary play against the Cardinals in the World Series, batting .400 and hitting three home runs, including two round-trippers during Boston's Game 2 victory.

NOTABLE ACHIEVEMENTS

- Hit more than 40 home runs three times
- Knocked in more than 100 runs five times
- Scored more than 100 runs twice
- Batted over .300 six times, topping the .320 mark on three occasions
- Surpassed 30 doubles eight times, topping 40 two-baggers on three occasions
- Drew more than 100 bases on balls six times
- Compiled on-base percentage in excess of .400 six times
- Posted slugging percentage in excess of .500 five times, topping .600 mark once (.622 in 1967)
- Led AL in home runs once; RBIs once; batting average three times; runs scored three times; hits twice; doubles three times; total bases twice; walks twice; on-base percentage five times; slugging percentage three times; and OPS four times
- Led AL outfielders in assists seven times and fielding percentage once
- Led AL left fielders in putouts four times
- Ranks among Major League Baseball's all-time leaders in games played (2nd); plate appearances (2nd); at-bats (3rd); hits (9th); extra base hits (13th); doubles (8th); total bases (9th); walks (6th); and runs batted in (14th)

- Holds Red Sox career records for games played (3,308); plate appearances (13,992); at-bats (11,988); hits (3,419); doubles (646); total bases (5,539); RBIs (1,844); and runs scored (1,816)
- Ranks third all-time on Red Sox in home runs (452) and second in bases on balls (1,845).
- First American League player to reach 3,000 hits and 400 home runs
- 1967 Triple Crown winner
- 1967 AL MVP
- 1967 winner of Hickok Belt
- 1970 All-Star Game MVP
- Seven-time Gold Glove winner
- Three-time *Sporting News* All-Star selection (1963, 1965, and 1967)
- Eighteen-time AL All-Star
- 1967 *Sporting News* Major League Player of the Year
- Number 72 on *Sporting News*'s 1999 list of Baseball's 100 Greatest Players
- Two-time AL champion (1967 and 1975)
- Elected to Baseball Hall of Fame by members of BBWAA in 1989

3

Pedro Martinez

Courtesy Boston Red Sox

Pedro Martinez's domination of opposing batters during the offensive-minded period that came to be known as the Steroid Era ultimately enabled him to edge out Roger Clemens and Cy Young for the number three spot in these rankings. Pitching for the Red Sox from 1998 to 2004, Martinez captured one pitcher's Triple Crown, led the American League in ERA four times, topped the junior circuit in strikeouts and winning percentage three times each, and typically compiled an earned run average almost two runs per game below the league norm. Over that seven-year stretch, Martinez posted an overall record of 117–37, for a remarkable .760 winning percentage—the best in franchise history. Meanwhile, his 2.52 ERA as a member of the Red Sox makes him the only hurler since the Dead Ball Era to earn a spot in the team's all-time top 10 in that category. Martinez won two Cy Young Awards while pitching for the Red Sox, placed second in the voting two other times, and finished runner-up in the league MVP balloting in 1999, when he recorded the first of two straight seasons that rank among the greatest ever turned in by an AL hurler. Formulas used by sabermetricians to calculate the effectiveness of players based on different variables have Martinez ranked as one of the two or three greatest pitchers in baseball history. Here, we'll give him the nod over Clemens and Young as the top hurler in Red Sox history.

Born in Manoguayabo, Dominican Republic, on October 25, 1971, Pedro Jaime Martinez came from humble beginnings. Like most houses in Manoguayabo, a small town 30 minutes outside the capital city of his homeland, the Martinez home had dirt floors and a tin roof. Pedro's father, Paolino, one of the most respected pitchers on the island during the 1950s, worked as a janitor, while his mother, Leopoldina, did laundry for other families in town. One of six children, Pedro grew up in a house that included three bedrooms formed by sheets hung from wires.

Seeking to escape his poverty-stricken upbringing, Martinez chose to pursue a career in baseball, signing with the Dodgers as an amateur free agent at the age of 16, in 1988. Despite initial concerns about his size (he began his pro career weighing only 135 pounds), Martinez accelerated through the Los Angeles farm system, excelling against all levels of competition. Opponents marveled at the smooth, compact motion and tremendous arm speed he generated with his small frame. Before long, Martinez earned a promotion to Albuquerque, where he spent the 1992 campaign. The Dodgers called him up in late September, with the 20-year-old right-hander subsequently making two appearances during the season's final week.

After earning a roster spot in spring training the following year, Martinez went on to establish himself as the Dodgers' set-up man over the course of the season. Yet, in spite of the success he experienced in that role, Martinez remained determined to join his older brother Ramon in the team's starting rotation. However, questions surrounding the ability of the 5'10", 175-pound hurler to hold up under the rigors of a 162-game schedule eventually prompted the Dodgers to trade Martinez to the Montreal Expos for standout second baseman Delino DeShields prior to the start of the 1994 campaign.

Martinez gradually developed into one of the National League's finest starting pitchers in Montreal, showing glimpses of the greatness that awaited him by throwing a perfect 9 innings against San Diego on June 3, 1995, before finally surrendering a hit in the bottom of the 10th inning during a 1–0 Expo victory. Martinez posted a combined 38–25 record in Montreal from 1994 to 1996, before having his breakout year in 1997, when he finished 17–8 for a mediocre Expos team. He also struck out 305 batters and led the National League with a 1.90 ERA and 13 complete games, en route to earning his first Cy Young Award. Martinez's 305 strikeouts and 1.90 ERA made him the first right-handed pitcher since Walter Johnson in 1912 to accumulate as many as 300 strikeouts and allow the opposition fewer than 2 runs per 9 innings in the same season.

With free agency looming for Martinez, the Expos traded him to the Red Sox for pitchers Carl Pavano and Tony Armas Jr. in November of 1997. Martinez signed a six-year, $75 million contract with the Sox shortly thereafter, making him the highest paid pitcher in the history of the game at the time. Paying immediate dividends on Boston's huge investment in him, Martinez went 19–7 for the Red Sox in 1998, struck out 251 batters, and posted a 2.89 ERA.

Martinez reached the apex of his career the following year, compiling one of the greatest seasons for a pitcher in baseball history. In addition to leading all American League hurlers with a record of 23–4, 313 strikeouts, and a 2.07 ERA, he allowed only 160 hits and 37 walks in 213 innings of work. Martinez performed so brilliantly that his 2.07 ERA placed him nearly three runs per game below the league average, with New York's David Cone finishing a distant second to him in that category, with a mark of 3.44. Martinez ended up winning the Cy Young Award unanimously and finishing a close second in the league MVP voting. He continued to excel in the postseason, working 17 scoreless innings and allowing only 5 hits, en route to posting victories over Cleveland in the ALDS and New York in the ALCS. His 7-inning, 2-hit, 12-strikeout effort against the Yankees in Game 3 of the ALCS handed the eventual world champions their only loss of the 1999 postseason.

Martinez's ability to excel in such pressure situations provided great insight into his competitiveness and willingness to perform under the spotlight. Former Expos and Red Sox GM Dan Duquette said of Martinez, "He is a fearless competitor who knows how to perform on the big stage, and has terrific charisma."

Mo Vaughn, who played behind Martinez in Boston during the late 1990s, suggested, "He just loves to pitch in front of a packed house, with everyone standing, watching him work."

Among the other qualities that helped make Martinez so devastating were his large arsenal of pitches and his ability to intimidate opposing hitters. Blessed with an outstanding fastball, cutter, curveball, and circle changeup, Martinez had the ability to throw any pitch in any situation. Furthermore, opposing batters often claimed they had a difficult time picking up the ball after Martinez released it from his three-quarter delivery.

At his peak, Martinez consistently reached 95–97 mph on the radar gun with his fastball, prompting former Montreal Expos teammate Larry Walker to comment, "He's so tiny. And I don't know where he gets that speed from. That velocity is amazing."

The combination of his tremendous velocity and devastating changeup made Martinez practically unhittable. Randy Johnson noted, "He's the first person I've ever seen with an above-average fastball and an above-average changeup."

The reputation Martinez developed early in his career as a "headhunter" made him an even more imposing figure on the mound. Martinez never hesitated to let opposing batters know the inside part of the plate belonged to him—a message he delivered frequently and effectively through the years. Jason Giambi suggested, "If you lean over the plate, he'll stick one up your nose."

Lou Piniella, who managed against Martinez as a member of the Mariners, Devil Rays, and Cubs, once claimed, "Some people are a little afraid of Pedro, and that helps him."

Martinez's tendency to throw at opposing hitters precipitated numerous bench-clearing incidents through the years, the most famous of which occurred during Game 3 of the 2003 ALCS against the Yankees. After surrendering a home run to the previous batter, Martinez plunked Yankee outfielder Karim Garcia in the middle of the back with a pitch. After Garcia voiced his objection to the Red Sox right-hander, both benches exchanged pleasantries. New York catcher Jorge Posada yelled a few choice words to Martinez from the Yankee dugout, prompting Martinez to point to his head. Although Martinez later suggested he meant to tell Posada to think rationally, the Yankee receiver believed otherwise, stating that he interpreted the gesture to mean "I'll hit *you* in the head." Both benches emptied and, in the ensuing fray, an angry Don Zimmer lunged at Martinez. The Red Sox hurler then threw the 72-year-old Yankee bench coach to the ground, causing Martinez to subsequently receive considerable criticism from the media.

The aforementioned fracas proved to be just one of many controversies in which Martinez became embroiled during his time in Boston, with virtually all of those highly publicized incidents involving the Yankees. On one occasion, an annoyed Martinez commented on the Red Sox-Yankees rivalry: "I'm starting to hate talking about the Yankees. The questions are so stupid. They're wasting my time. It's getting kind of old. . . . I don't believe in damn curses. Wake up the damn Bambino and have me face him. Maybe I'll drill him in the ass, pardon me the word."

After a Red Sox loss to the Yankees late in the 2004 season, Martinez remarked during a press conference, "They beat me. They're that good right now. They're that hot. I just tip my hat and call the Yankees my daddy." The New York media publicized Martinez's quote heavily, prompting Yankee fans to chant "Who's Your Daddy?" whenever he pitched at Yankee Stadium during the 2004 ALCS.

Through all the controversies, though, Martinez remained a truly great pitcher. After dominating American League hitters throughout the 1999 campaign, he had another remarkable year in 2000. In addition to finishing 18–6, he led the AL with 284 strikeouts, a 1.74 ERA, and four shutouts, en route to capturing his third Cy Young Award. Martinez's 1.74 ERA bettered by nearly two runs per nine innings the mark of 3.70 posted by Roger Clemens, who finished second in the league in that category. Martinez also allowed only 128 hits and 32 walks in 217 innings of work.

After starting off the following season extremely well, Martinez ended up spending much of the year on the disabled list with a rotator cuff injury. Healthy again in 2002, Martinez finished 20–4, with a league-leading 239 strikeouts and 2.26 ERA. Although he continued to take the ball every fifth day for the Red Sox in each of the next two seasons, concerns about his surgically repaired shoulder caused Boston management to place him on a strict pitch-count. Martinez rarely threw more than 100 pitches or went more than 7 innings in either 2003 or 2004. Nevertheless, he remained one of the league's most effective pitchers, striking out more than 200 batters both seasons, compiling a combined record of 30–13, and leading the AL with a 2.22 ERA in 2003. Although Martinez didn't fare particularly well in either of his two starts against New York in the 2004 ALCS, he shared in his teammates' joy when they overcame a three-games-to-none deficit to defeat a stunned Yankee squad and capture the AL pennant. Martinez then threw seven shutout innings against St. Louis in his lone start in the World Series, as the Red Sox ended 86 years of futility by sweeping the Cardinals in four straight games in the Fall Classic.

After becoming a free agent at the end of the year, Martinez reached an agreement with the New York Mets to return to the National League. He had a solid first year in New York, finishing 15–8 with a 2.82 ERA, and

Courtesy Boston Red Sox

bringing a level of respectability to the struggling franchise. Tom Glavine, another member of the Mets' starting rotation in 2005, provided insight into his new teammate's makeup when he said, "Pedro's a great competitor. He stares at hitters and pumps his fist when he pitches, but that's all part of his competitive nature. After the game, he's back to being humble. He's always respectful of his opponents."

However, Martinez didn't experience nearly as much success in his final three years with the Mets. With injuries and advancing age limiting him to a total of only 48 starts and depriving him of his once-blazing fastball, Martinez compiled a composite record of just 17–15 from 2006 to 2008, prompting the Mets to allow him to hit the open market when he once again became a free agent. After sitting out the first half of the 2009 season, Martinez joined the Philadelphia Phillies for the pennant-push, helping his new team repeat as NL champions by going 5–1 down the stretch. With no teams expressing interest in him at season's end, Martinez elected to retire. He concluded his career with a record of 219–100, a 2.93 ERA, a WHIP of 1.054, and 3,154 strikeouts in 2,827 innings pitched—figures that made enough of an impression on the members of the BBWAA that he gained admittance to Cooperstown the first time his name appeared on the Hall of Fame ballot in 2015.. Martinez's .687 winning percentage places him second only to Whitey Ford among all pitchers with at least 200 victories. Meanwhile, in addition to compiling the highest winning percentage in Red Sox history, Martinez holds franchise marks for most strikeouts per nine innings pitched (10.947) and best strikeouts-to-walks ratio (5.447). He also ranks among the franchise's all-time leaders in wins, ERA, WHIP (0.978), strikeouts (1,683), and fewest hits allowed per nine innings pitched (6.791).

Joe Posnanski once wrote in *Sports Illustrated*, "There has never been a pitcher in baseball history—not Walter Johnson, not Lefty Grove, not Sandy Koufax, not Tom Seaver, not Roger Clemens—who was more overwhelming than the young Pedro."

RED SOX CAREER HIGHLIGHTS

Best Season

Although Martinez pitched magnificently for the Red Sox throughout most of his tenure in Boston, he performed particularly well in 1999, 2000, and 2002. In addition to compiling a record of 20–4 in the last of those campaigns, Martinez led all AL hurlers with a 2.26 ERA, 239 strikeouts, and a WHIP of 0.923, en route to earning a second-place finish in the Cy Young voting. Martinez captured Cy Young honors and finished second in the league MVP balloting in 1999, when he led the AL with a 2.07 ERA and established career highs by also topping the circuit in wins (23), winning percentage (.852), and strikeouts (313). However, it could be argued that he pitched even better the following year, even though he won five fewer games. Certainly, Martinez's 18–6 record and .750 winning percentage do not compare favorably to the marks he compiled the previous season (he finished 23–4 in 1999). But the Red Sox were a significantly better team in 1999, recording nine more victories than they posted one year later. It also must be considered that Martinez compiled a lower ERA in 2000 (1.74 to 2.07), threw more complete games (7 to 5), tossed more shutouts (4 to 1), struck out almost as many batters (284 to 313), and posted a better WHIP (0.737 to 0.923). Either season would make a very good choice, but we'll opt here for 2000, since Martinez finished with slightly better overall numbers.

Memorable Moments/Greatest Performances

While Martinez pitched a number of brilliant games during his time in Boston, three efforts in particular stand out as examples of the level of dominance he attained while wearing a Red Sox uniform. He turned in one of his most memorable performances at the 1999 All-Star Game, when, pitching before a packed house at Fenway Park, Martinez thrilled the hometown fans by striking out Barry Larkin, Larry Walker, Sammy Sosa, and Mark McGwire to start the contest. He also fanned Jeff Bagwell in the second inning, thereby whiffing five of the six men he faced, en route to earning game MVP honors.

Facing the Yankees at Yankee Stadium some two months later on September 10, Martinez dominated the eventual world champions, allowing only a home run by New York's Chili Davis during an overpowering 17-strikeout, 1-hit performance that resulted in a 3–1 Red Sox victory. A few weeks later, Martinez strained his back while pitching against Cleveland in Game 1 of the Division Series, leaving the contest with the Red Sox holding a 2–0 lead. The Indians subsequently mounted a comeback against the Red Sox bullpen, eventually winning the game 3–2. The Indians also came out on top in Game 2, before the Red Sox rallied to win the next two contests, thereby evening the series at two games apiece. With Martinez's back still hurting, Boston started Bret Saberhagen in the decisive fifth game in Cleveland. The contest soon evolved into a slugfest, with the Indians holding an 8–7 lead in the fourth inning. Red Sox manager Jimy Williams turned to Martinez in desperation, hoping that his ailing right-hander might stem the tide of the Cleveland onslaught. Unable to throw either his fastball or his changeup with any consistency, Martinez changed speeds and mixed his pitches brilliantly, baffling Cleveland's lineup over six no-hit innings. He finished the game with eight strikeouts, and the Red Sox advanced to the ALCS by scoring five more times to win the contest, 12–8.

NOTABLE ACHIEVEMENTS

- Two-time 20-game winner (1999 and 2002)
- Won at least 18 games two other times
- Compiled ERA below 2.50 five straight times, finishing with a mark under 2.00 once (1.74 in 2000)
- Posted winning percentage in excess of .700 six straight times, compiling mark above .800 twice

- Struck out more than 200 batters six times, surpassing 300k's once (313 in 1999)
- Compiled WHIP below 1.000 four straight times (1999–2002)
- Led AL pitchers in wins once; winning percentage three times; ERA four times; strikeouts three times; shutouts once; and WHIP four times
- Holds Red Sox career records for: highest winning percentage (.760); most strikeouts per nine innings pitched (10.947); and best strikeouts-to-walks ratio (5.447)
- Ranks among Red Sox all-time leaders in: wins (tied-6th); ERA (10th); WHIP (2nd); strikeouts (3rd); fewest hits allowed per nine innings pitched (2nd); and fewest walks allowed per nine innings pitched (6th)
- Holds Red Sox single-season record for most strikeouts (313 in 1999)
- 1999 Triple Crown winner for pitchers
- 1999 All-Star Game MVP
- Finished second in 1999 AL MVP voting
- Two-time AL Cy Young Award winner (1999 and 2000)
- Two-time AL *Sporting News* Pitcher of the Year (1999 and 2000)
- Three-time *Sporting News* All-Star selection (1998–2000)
- Four-time AL All-Star
- 2004 AL champion
- 2004 world champion
- Elected to Baseball Hall of Fame by members of BBWAA in 2015

4

Roger Clemens

Courtesy Jerry Reuss

There will undoubtedly be those Red Sox fans who object to the idea of assigning such a lofty spot in these rankings to Roger Clemens. After all, Clemens spent the second half of his career pitching for other teams, most notably the hated New York Yankees, for whom he worked from 1999 to 2003 and then again in 2007. And, as noted sportswriter Sean McAdam once wrote in the *Providence Journal*, "It's been said before, but it's true: for

Red Sox fans, watching [Roger] Clemens thrive as a Yankee is the equivalent of watching your ex-wife marry your sworn mortal enemy—then live happily ever after." Clemens's reputation in the New England area has been further sullied by his purported use of performance-enhancing drugs for much of his final 11 seasons. Nevertheless, the fact remains that Clemens established himself as arguably baseball's most dominant hurler during his time in Boston, winning three Cy Young Awards and one MVP trophy, and earning five All-Star selections. In his 13 years with the Red Sox, Clemens also struck out more batters (2,590), won more games (192), and threw more shutouts (38) than any other pitcher in franchise history, tying Cy Young for first place in each of the last two categories. And, at least to this point, no evidence has been presented that would suggest any of Clemens's accomplishments as a member of the Red Sox were tainted in any way. Furthermore, even though many Red Sox fans eventually came to view Clemens as an estranged member of their family, "the Rocket," as he came to be known, never forgot his Boston roots, telling ESPN.com in May 2003: "It's never in the past. This town [Boston], this ballpark [Fenway Park], are a part of me. I worked here. I gave my all here. That's the bottom line. That will never change." Therefore, as much as some fans may bristle at the notion of placing Clemens so high on this list, he clearly deserves to be ranked among the team's all-time greats.

Born in Dayton, Ohio, on August 4, 1962, Roger Clemens spent most of his youth in Vandalia, Ohio, before moving with his family to Houston, Texas, at the age of 15. While starring in baseball, football, and basketball at Spring Woods High School, Clemens closely followed the career of his favorite pitcher, Nolan Ryan, after whom he hoped to pattern himself. After graduating from high school, Clemens enrolled at San Jacinto College in Pasadena, Texas, where he spent his freshman year, before transferring to the University of Texas at Austin. Clemens earned All-America honors twice while pitching for the Longhorns, leading them to victory in the 1983 College World Series.

After being selected by the Red Sox in the first round of the 1983 amateur draft with the 19th overall pick, Clemens wasted little time in advancing through their farm system, spending just one year in the minors before making his major-league debut on May 15, 1984. Displaying tremendous potential over the season's final few months, Clemens posted a record of 9–4 and struck out 126 batters in only 133 innings of work. The young right-hander turned in the first truly dominant performance of his career on August 21, when he struck out 15 batters during an 11–1 win over Kansas City at Fenway Park. Unfortunately, shoulder problems forced him to undergo surgery just nine days later, limiting him to only 15 starts and a record of 7–5 in the ensuing campaign.

Still a question mark heading into 1986, Clemens put to rest any remaining concerns about his health by establishing himself as the American League's finest pitcher. In addition to placing second in the league with 238 strikeouts, he led all AL hurlers with a record of 24–4 and a 2.48 ERA, in helping the Red Sox capture their first pennant in 11 years. At one point during the season, Clemens became the first pitcher in major-league history to strike out 20 batters during a nine-inning game. The 24-year-old hurler's brilliant performance earned him league MVP and Cy Young honors. He followed that up with another exceptional year in 1987, compiling a 2.97 ERA, finishing second in the league with 256 strikeouts and 282 innings pitched, and topping the circuit with 20 wins, 7 shutouts, and 18 complete games, en route to winning his second straight Cy Young Award.

Already recognized as the American League's most overpowering pitcher, the 6'4", 220-pound Clemens intimidated opposing batters with his blazing fastball, willingness to throw inside, and fierce competitive spirit. In discussing the ferocious attitude he took with him to the mound before each start, Clemens explained, "Everybody kind of perceives me as being angry. It's not anger . . . it's motivation."

A prototypical power pitcher, Clemens relied primarily on a 98 mph fastball and a hard breaking ball early in his career, although he later developed a slider and a devastating split-finger fastball as well. He also possessed outstanding control and flawless mechanics, which he learned from Tom Seaver, who helped turn him into more of a complete pitcher after he joined the Red Sox during the second half of 1986.

Clemens continued his extraordinary pitching over the next five seasons, winning at least 17 games each year, en route to posting an overall record of 92–50 from 1988 to 1992. In addition to leading the American League in ERA and shutouts in three of those five campaigns, he topped the circuit in strikeouts twice and innings pitched once. Clemens performed particularly well from 1990 to 1992, finishing 21–6 with a league-leading 1.93 ERA in the first of those years, before winning 18 games and leading the league with earned run averages of 2.62 and 2.41 the other two seasons. He earned AL All-Star honors and a top-three finish in the Cy Young voting all three years, capturing the award for the third time in 1991.

Injuries and inconsistency plagued Clemens for much of the next four seasons, causing him to compile an overall record of only 40–39 from 1993 to 1996. And, even though he pitched well during the strike-shortened 1994 campaign, finishing second in the league with a 2.85 ERA, inadequate run support from Boston's mediocre lineup limited him to only 9 wins in his 16 decisions.

Even though Clemens led the American League with 257 strikeouts in 1996, his unimpressive 10–13 record and 3.63 ERA made Red Sox management unwilling to meet his salary demands when he became eligible for free agency at season's end. Believing that the 34-year-old right-hander had already seen his best days, GM Dan Duquette allowed Clemens to sign a four-year, $40 million deal with the Toronto Blue Jays. Clemens left Boston having compiled an overall record of 192–111, along with an ERA of 3.06, a WHIP of 1.158, 100 complete games, 38 shutouts, and 2,590 strikeouts in 2,776 innings of work.

Eager to prove his former employers wrong, Clemens recaptured the fire of his youth after he arrived in Toronto, subsequently putting together two of the finest seasons of his career. He earned Cy Young honors in his first year with the Blue Jays by leading all AL hurlers with a record of 21–7, a 2.05 ERA, 292 strikeouts, and 264 innings pitched. Clemens won his second straight Cy Young and pitcher's Triple Crown the following year by going 20–6, with a 2.65 ERA and 271 strikeouts. Clemens proved to be somewhat less dominant after the Yankees acquired him for David Wells, Graeme Lloyd, and Homer Bush prior to the start of the 1999 campaign, winning a total of only 27 games his first two years in New York. Nevertheless, he helped the Yankees win two world championships, having his best year for them in 2001, when he earned his unprecedented sixth Cy Young Award by finishing 20–3, with a 3.51 ERA and 213 strikeouts.

Clemens continued to pitch effectively for the Yankees through 2003, when, after winning 17 games, he announced his retirement. However, after close friend and former Yankees teammate Andy Pettitte signed as a free agent with the Houston Astros, the 41-year-old Clemens decided to come out of retirement, signing a one-year deal with his adopted hometown team. Clemens ended up spending three years in Houston, pitching extremely well for the Astros and winning his seventh Cy Young Award in 2004, when he finished 18–4, with a 2.98 ERA and 218 strikeouts. Yet, even as his list of career accomplishments continued to grow, Clemens's narcissistic nature became increasingly apparent to the general public. In addition to coming out of retirement no fewer than four times and demanding that he be paid an inordinately high sum of money for appearing in fewer and fewer games each year, Clemens insisted that various perks be included in his contract, one of which made it unnecessary for him to accompany his team on road trips. He again displayed his self-absorbed and avaricious ways on May 6, 2007, when, after retiring for a fourth time, he unexpectedly appeared in the owner's box at Yankee Stadium during the seventh-inning stretch of a game against the Seattle Mariners and announced to the crowd in attendance, "Thank y'all. Well, they came and got me out of Texas, and I can tell you it's a privilege to be back. I'll be talkin' to y'all soon." The Yankees simultaneously announced that they had signed Clemens to a prorated one-year deal worth slightly more than $28 million. Clemens ended up making $18.7 million over the length of the contract, or just over $1 million per start. For their investment, the Yankees received from Clemens a 6–6 record and a 4.18 ERA.

No longer able to hold teams up for ransom, Clemens retired for good at the end of the year. He left the game with an overall record of 354–184, an ERA of 3.12, a WHIP of 1.173, 118 complete games, 46 shutouts, and 4,672 strikeouts in 4,917 innings of work. His 4,672 strikeouts place him third on the all-time list, behind only Nolan Ryan and Randy Johnson. Meanwhile, he ranks ninth all time in career wins. In addition to winning the Cy Young Award seven times, Clemens finished in the top three in the voting three other times. He also earned *Sporting News* Pitcher of the Year honors five times and a total of 11 All-Star nominations.

Unfortunately, most of the things Clemens accomplished after he left Boston later came into question when the Mitchell Report alleged that he used anabolic steroids during the second half of his career. Although Clemens has consistently refuted such charges by stating that he maintained his high level of performance for such a long period of time due to his extensive workout regimen, his former trainer Brian McNamee suggested otherwise, claiming that he injected Clemens with Winstrol on at least three separate occasions between 1998 and 2001. Clemens denied all these allegations under oath before Congress, leading congressional leaders to refer his case to the Justice Department on suspicion of perjury. Although various legal machinations eventually enabled Clemens to be cleared of all charges, he remains guilty in the court of public opinion, causing his career numbers to be tainted in the minds of most people and, at least to this point, keeping him out of the Baseball Hall of Fame.

RED SOX CAREER HIGHLIGHTS

Best Season

Even though Clemens failed to win the Cy Young Award in 1990, it could be argued that he pitched his best ball for the Red Sox that year. In addition to finishing 21–6 with 209 strikeouts, he led all AL pitchers with a

1.93 ERA and four shutouts. Clemens also pitched magnificently in 1987 and 1991, earning Cy Young honors both years. After winning just four of his first 10 decisions in the first of those campaigns, he went 16–3 the rest of the way to finish with a record of 20–9. Clemens also compiled an ERA of 2.97, 256 strikeouts, and a league-leading 18 complete games and seven shutouts. His 18 complete games and 282 innings pitched both represented career highs. Clemens finished 18–10 in 1991, with 13 complete games, and a league-leading 2.62 ERA, four shutouts, 241 strikeouts, and 271 innings pitched. Nevertheless, the 1986 campaign is generally considered to be Clemens's signature season. In addition to leading all AL hurlers with a record of 24–4 and a 2.48 ERA, he struck out 238 batters in 254 innings pitched. Clemens also compiled a league-leading WHIP of 0.969 that represented the finest mark of his career. His fabulous performance earned him AL MVP honors and the first of his record seven Cy Young Awards.

Courtesy rmyauctions.com

Memorable Moments/Greatest Performances

One of only two pitchers in MLB history (Kerry Wood being the other) to strike out 20 batters in a nine-inning game, Clemens amazingly accomplished the feat on two separate occasions. "The Rocket" established a new major-league record on April 29, 1986, when he fanned 20 batters during a 3–1 win over the Seattle Mariners. Clemens's 20 k's surpassed the previous mark of 19 shared by Nolan Ryan, Steve Carlton, and Tom Seaver. Clemens also tied a major-league record by striking out eight consecutive batters at one point during the contest. Red Sox manager John McNamara said afterwards, "I watched perfect games by Catfish Hunter and Mike Witt, but this was the most awesome pitching performance I've ever seen."

Clemens duplicated his earlier effort 10 years later, striking out 20 Detroit Tigers during a 4–0 Red Sox victory on September 18, 1996. Following the contest, Clemens stated, "You can't even count on striking out 20 big-league hitters. I'm just happy to tie it [his own record]. I knew that I had it in the upper teens, but then [Bill] Haselman ran out to the mound to let me know I was near the record. I think that made it more emotional for me. I mean, that's all but seven guys in the game."

Haselman, Clemens's battery-mate during the game, said, "His ball tonight was unbelievable. His two-seamers seemed like they were moving a foot. His splits were moving the same way. He was truly unhittable."

Home plate umpire Tim McClelland added, "That's as dominating as I've seen a pitcher pitch. I've had Randy Johnson with a fastball and slider be dominant, but Roger was throwing a two-seam fastball, a four-seam fastball, a forkball, and slider. He threw four pitches and moved the ball all around."

Meanwhile, Detroit manager Buddy Bell marveled, "The no-hitters I've been involved with and have seen, there's been luck involved. This was just a dominating performance. I think that was the best pitching performance I've ever seen. I don't want to take anything away from those guys [who pitched no-hitters] because that's a great achievement, but this is as good as it gets. I can't imagine anyone having better stuff than that. He was just absolutely outstanding tonight. He would've done that to a lot of teams tonight."

Clemens pitched another memorable game on September 10, 1988, when he threw a one-hitter against the Indians at Fenway Park, defeating Cleveland by a score of 6–0. Clemens allowed just two base-runners the entire game, walking Indians right-fielder Dave Clark in the fifth inning, before losing his no-hitter in the top of the eighth, when Clark blooped a single into short right-center.

NOTABLE ACHIEVEMENTS

- Three-time 20-game winner (1986, 1987, and 1990)
- Won at least 17 games four other times
- Compiled ERA below 3.00 seven times, finishing with a mark under 2.00 once (1.93 in 1990)
- Posted winning percentage in excess of .700 twice, surpassing .800-mark once (.857 in 1986)
- Struck out more than 200 batters eight times
- Threw more than 200 innings eight times, tossing more than 250 innings on five occasions
- Finished in double-digits in complete games five times
- Compiled WHIP below 1.000 once (0.969 in 1986)
- Led AL pitchers in wins twice; winning percentage once; ERA four times; strikeouts three times; shutouts five times; complete games twice; innings pitched once; and WHIP twice
- Struck out 20 batters in one game twice
- Holds Red Sox career record for most strikeouts (2,590)
- Shares Red Sox career record for most wins (192) and shutouts (38)
- Ranks among Red Sox all-time leaders in: innings pitched (2nd); complete games (9th); fewest hits allowed per nine innings pitched (8th); most strikeouts per nine innings pitched (3rd); strikeouts-to-walks ratio (6th); pitching appearances (6th); and games started (2nd).
- 1986 All-Star Game MVP
- 1986 AL MVP
- Three-time AL Cy Young Award winner (1986, 1987, and 1991)
- 1986 Major League Player of the Year
- Two-time AL *Sporting News* Pitcher of the Year (1986 and 1991)
- Three-time *Sporting News* All-Star selection (1986, 1987, and 1991)
- Five-time AL All-Star
- Member of Major League Baseball's All-Century Team
- Number 53 on *Sporting News*'s 1999 list of Baseball's 100 Greatest Players
- 1986 AL champion

5

Cy Young

Courtesy Library of Congress

Already 34 years old when he defected to the newly formed American League in 1901, Cy Young seemed to be approaching the latter stages of his career prior to his arrival in Boston. Having entered the big leagues more than a decade earlier with the National League's Cleveland Spiders, Young already had 286 victories under his belt—more than most pitchers hope to compile in a lifetime. Yet, the legendary right-hander experienced a rebirth in the American League, winning 119 games over the course of the next four seasons, during which time he led his new team to two AL pennants and one world championship. By the time Young left Boston at the conclusion of the 1908 campaign, he had posted 73 more victories, giving him a franchise-record 192 wins. Meanwhile, his career total of 511 victories, which he compiled over the course of 22 big-league seasons, is certain to remain the all-time record as long as baseball is played.

Born in the tiny farming community of Gilmore, Ohio, on March 29, 1867, Denton True Young left school after completing the sixth grade in order to help out on his family's farm. He subsequently competed in many amateur baseball leagues around Gilmore as a teenager, before beginning his professional career in 1889 with the minor-league Canton, Ohio, team of the Tri-State League. It was with Canton that Young acquired his life-long nickname of "Cy," a moniker bestowed upon him by the team's young catcher, who likened the speed of his fastball to that of a cyclone.

After one year at Canton, Young signed with the Cleveland Spiders, who left the American Association for the National League just one year earlier. Young spent the next nine seasons in Cleveland, developing a reputation during that time as one of baseball's finest pitchers. The 6'2", 210-pound right-hander compiled an overall record of 241–135 with the Spiders, winning more than 20 games eight straight times and topping 30 victories on three occasions, including a 36-win 1892 campaign in which he led the league with a .750 winning percentage, a 1.93 ERA, and nine shutouts. Young also threw a career-high 48 complete games and 453 innings that year.

Young continued to excel even after the powers that be moved the pitcher's mound back 5 feet to its present distance of 60 feet, 6 inches from home plate in 1893, relying heavily on his overpowering fastball to compensate for the increased distance. The legendary Honus Wagner, who faced Young regularly during the latter stages of the decade, stated years later that he considered the right-hander's fastball to be the greatest he ever saw, proclaiming, "Walter Johnson was fast, but no faster than [Amos] Rusie. And Rusie was no faster than Johnson. But Young was faster than both of 'em!"

Young joined the St. Louis Perfectos in 1899 when the Spiders' owners gained control of that franchise as well and transferred most of the team's best players to St. Louis as a means of punishing Cleveland fans for their lack of support at the gate. He spent two years in St. Louis, posting an overall record of 45–35, before electing to switch leagues when the Boston Americans offered him a salary of $3,500.

The arrival of Young in Boston and star second baseman Napoleon Lajoie in Philadelphia gave the American League instant credibility. While

Lajoie led the infant circuit in virtually every major offensive category in 1901, Young proved to be equally dominant on the mound, capturing the pitcher's version of the Triple Crown by finishing first among AL hurlers with 33 wins, a 1.62 ERA, and 158 strikeouts. He followed that up with an equally brilliant 1902 campaign in which he compiled a 2.15 ERA, recorded 160 strikeouts, and led the league with 32 wins, 41 complete games, and 385 innings pitched. Young led the Americans (or Pilgrims) to their first of two straight American League pennants the following year by compiling a 2.08 ERA, striking out 176 batters, and finishing first in the circuit with 28 victories, a .757 winning percentage, 34 complete games, 7 shutouts, and 342 innings pitched. He subsequently defeated the Pittsburgh Pirates twice in the first "modern" World Series, helping the Americans capture their first world championship. When they repeated as AL champions the following year, Young once again proved to be a huge contributor, going 26–16, with a 1.97 ERA, 200 strikeouts, 40 complete games, 380 innings pitched, and a league-leading 10 shutouts.

Although Young failed to reach the same level of dominance in any of the next three seasons, he continued to pitch extremely well, surpassing 20 victories once more and posting a sub-2.00 ERA on two occasions. He had another great year in 1908, finishing 21–11, with a 1.26 ERA, 30 complete games, and 299 innings pitched.

Forty-one years of age at the conclusion of the 1908 campaign, Young remained one of the game's top pitchers long after most players entered into retirement. He did so by sharpening his control and compensating for his loss of velocity by developing a pair of curveballs, which he threw from a variety of arm angles. Five times while pitching for the Americans, Young led the league in fewest bases on balls allowed per nine innings, surrendering more than 50 walks in just two of his eight years in Boston. Meanwhile, in discussing the methods he used on the mound to out-think opposing batters, Young later revealed, "If a right-hander crowded my plate, I side-armed him with a curve, and then, when he stepped back, I'd throw an overhand fastball low and outside. I was fortunate in having good speed from over-hand, three-quarter, or side-arm. I had a variety of curves—threw a so-called screwball or in-drop too—and I used whatever delivery seemed best. And I never had but one sore arm."

Although Young credited his off-season practice of chopping wood and doing heavy chores around his farm with keeping him in shape through the years, he placed no special emphasis on his remarkable durability and longevity, stating on one occasion, "It isn't any secret—just outdoor life, moderation, and a naturally good arm. . . . I don't know that I take any better care of myself than any other pitcher does, it just happens, this thing of my lasting. It isn't the result of any system."

In describing the approach he took with him to the mound before each game, Young said, "I never warmed up 10, 15 minutes before a game like most pitchers do. I'd loosen up, three, four minutes . . . five at the outside. And I never went to the bullpen. Oh, I'd relieve all right, plenty of times, but I went right from the bench to the box, and I'd take a few warm-up pitches and be ready. Then I had good control. I aimed to make the batter hit the ball, and I threw as few pitches as possible. That's why I was able to work every other day."

Traded to the Cleveland Naps in 1909, Young had one more solid season left in his aging right arm before Father Time finally began to catch up with him. After winning 19 games and compiling a 2.26 ERA for the Naps in his first year back in Cleveland, Young posted only 10 more victories over parts of the next two seasons, before the Naps traded him back to the National League in 1911. He spent the final two months of his career with the Boston Rustlers, retiring at the conclusion of the 1911 campaign with a career record of 511–316 and an ERA of 2.63. In addition to winning more

Courtesy Library of Congress

games than any other pitcher in major-league history, Young established career records for most games started (815), complete games (749), and innings pitched (7,356). His numbers during his time in Boston include an overall record of 192-112, an ERA of 2.00, 1,341 strikeouts, 2,728 innings pitched, and a franchise-record 0.970 WHIP, 38 shutouts, and 275 complete games.

Following his retirement, Young returned to his farm in Ohio, where he spent the next several years growing potatoes and tending to his sheep, hogs, and chickens. He also served briefly as manager of the Cleveland Green Sox of the outlaw Federal League. Elected to the Baseball Hall of Fame in 1937, Young entered Cooperstown when its doors first opened two years later. He lived until November 4, 1955, passing away from a coronary occlusion at the age of 88. Major League Baseball instituted the pitching award that still bears his name the very next year.

RED SOX CAREER HIGHLIGHTS

Best Season

With the American League featuring many more talented players in 1908 than it did when it first established itself as a separate entity just a few seasons earlier, a strong argument could be made that Young actually pitched his best ball in Boston that year. Although he won "only" 21 games and threw "just" 30 complete games and 299 innings, Young posted a career-best 1.26 ERA and an exceptional WHIP of 0.893, which represented the second-lowest mark of his career. It could also be argued that Young's 1902 performance was his finest as an American Leaguer, since he finished 32–11, with a 2.15 ERA, 176 strikeouts, and a league-leading 41 complete games and 385 innings pitched.

Still, it would be difficult to overlook Young's fabulous 1901 campaign, one in which he led the infant league in five different pitching categories en route to capturing the Triple Crown. In addition to finishing second in the league with 41 starts, 38 complete games, and 371 innings pitched, Young led all AL hurlers with a record of 33–10, an ERA of 1.62, 158 strikeouts, five shutouts, and a WHIP of 0.972. With Boston winning 79 games in 1901, Young posted 42 percent of his team's victories.

Memorable Moments/Greatest Performances

Young's performance against Pittsburgh in the 1903 World Series would certainly have to rank among the highlights of his career. Appearing in four of the eight games and completing all three of his starts, Young helped lead Boston to a five-games-to-three victory by compiling a record of 2–1 and an ERA of 1.85. He also helped his own cause in Game 5 by driving in three runs.

Yet, Young turned in a number of memorable pitching performances during his time in Boston that far surpassed his World Series effort. After losing to the Athletics three days earlier on a one-hitter by Philadelphia staff ace Rube Waddell, Young defeated Waddell and the A's on May 5, 1904, throwing in the process the first perfect game in American League history, and just the third in major-league history. Since Young's perfect game was the first thrown under the modern rules established in 1893, it is generally considered to be the first such effort of the "modern" era. Young's perfect game also ended up being the centerpiece of a record-setting streak during which he set major-league records for the most consecutive scoreless innings pitched and the most consecutive innings pitched without allowing a hit. Although more than one pitcher eventually eclipsed his 45-inning shutout streak, Young continues to hold the record for most consecutive hitless innings, with his mark of 24 ⅓ hitless frames having stood the test of time. Detroit's Sam Crawford finally ended the hitless skein six days later, on May 11, by singling against Young with one man out in the seventh inning. However, Young had the last laugh, continuing his shutout streak by defeating the Tigers 1–0 in 15 innings. Young also pitched extraordinarily well down the stretch of that 1904 campaign, tossing shutouts in his final three starts to enable Boston to edge out New York for the American League pennant.

A little over one year later, on July 4, 1905, Young lost a 4–2 decision to Waddell and the A's, at one point throwing 13 scoreless innings before surrendering a pair of unearned runs in the 20th inning that ended up costing him the game. Going the entire 20 innings without walking a single batter, Young later stated, "For my part, I think it was the greatest game of ball I ever took part in."

On September 9, 1907, Young and Waddell hooked up in another classic pitcher's duel, battling to a standoff in a game that ended in a 13-inning scoreless tie.

Young also pitched a pair of memorable games in 1908, throwing the first of those against Washington on May 30, when only a fifth-inning single by Jerry Freeman prevented him from tossing another perfect game. Exactly one month later, on June 30, Young tossed his third career no-hitter, en route to defeating New York 8–0. He allowed only a walk in the first inning to leadoff batter Harry Niles, who subsequently was thrown out trying to steal second base. Young also tallied three hits and drove in four runs during the contest.

NOTABLE ACHIEVEMENTS

- Two-time 30-game winner
- Won at least 25 games two other times, surpassing 20 victories on two other occasions
- Compiled ERA below 2.00 on five occasions
- Struck out more than 200 batters twice
- Threw at least 30 complete games seven times, topping the 40 mark twice
- Threw more than 300 innings six times
- Tossed 10 shutouts in 1904
- Posted winning percentage in excess of .700 three times
- Compiled WHIP below 1.000 six times
- Led AL pitchers in wins three times; ERA once; strikeouts once; complete games twice; innings pitched twice; shutouts three times; and WHIP four times
- Threw perfect game vs. Philadelphia Athletics on May 5, 1904
- Threw no-hitter vs. New York Highlanders on June 30, 1908
- Holds Red Sox career records for: most complete games (275); best WHIP (0.970); and fewest bases on balls allowed per nine innings pitched (0.986).
- Shares Red Sox career records for most wins (192) and shutouts (38)
- Ranks among Red Sox all-time leaders in: ERA (2nd); strikeouts (5th); innings pitched (3rd); fewest hits allowed per nine innings pitched (9th); strikeouts-to-walks ratio (4th); pitching appearances (8th); and games started (3rd).
- Holds Red Sox single-season records for innings pitched (385 in 1902); games started (43 in 1902); and complete games (41 in 1902)
- Major League Baseball's all-time record-holder for most wins (511); games started (815); complete games (749); innings pitched (7,356); and assists by a pitcher (2,014)
- Holds Major League record for most consecutive hitless innings pitched (24 ⅓ in 1904)
- 1901 Triple Crown winner for pitchers
- Member of Major League Baseball's All-Century Team
- Fourteenth on *Sporting News*'s 1999 list of Baseball's 100 Greatest Players
- Two-time AL champion (1903 and 1904)
- 1903 world champion
- Elected to Baseball Hall of Fame by members of BBWAA in 1937

6

Wade Boggs

Courtesy Boston Red Sox

Rivaling San Diego's Tony Gwynn as the finest scientific hitter of his era, Wade Boggs used his keen batting eye, tremendous bat control, outstanding patience at the plate, and exceptional opposite-field stroke to establish himself as one of the greatest offensive players in Red Sox history. Although he lacked the power of Ted Williams, Carl Yastrzemski, Jim Rice, and other Red Sox sluggers, Boggs proved to be as good a contact hitter as anyone who ever played in Boston, posting a .338 batting average over the course of 11 seasons that only the "Splendid Splinter" himself surpassed. A five-time batting champion, Boggs batted over .350 for the Red Sox in five of six seasons at one point, posting a mark of .325 in his one "off year" during that period. Meanwhile, his tremendous patience at the plate and extraordinary ability to recognize pitches enabled him to compile an on-base percentage in excess of .450 in four of those seasons. By the time Boggs left Boston after the 1992 campaign, he had earned eight All-Star selections, six Silver Sluggers, and four top-10 finishes in the AL MVP voting.

Born in Omaha, Nebraska, on June 15, 1958, Wade Anthony Boggs spent six long years in the minor leagues before finally earning a roster spot on the Red Sox at the start of the 1982 campaign. A 1976 graduate of Plant High School in Tampa, Florida, where he starred as an all-state kicker on the football team, Boggs was originally selected by Boston in the seventh round of the 1976 amateur draft. Although he developed a reputation in the minors as primarily a singles hitter, he later revealed, "I was a home run hitter in high school, but then something happened. The parks just got bigger."

Considered only a marginal prospect by the time he joined the Red Sox in 1982, Boggs split his first season between first and third base, earning increased playing time over the course of the campaign by compiling a lofty .349 batting average in 104 games. His outstanding performance convinced Boston to part with Carney Lansford at season's end, enabling Boggs to lay claim to the starting third base job. Boggs subsequently rewarded the Red Sox by leading the American League with a .361 batting average and a .444 on-base percentage in his first full season. He also knocked in 74 runs and finished among the league leaders with 210 hits, 100 runs scored, and 44 doubles. Yet, Boggs proved to be something of a liability in the field, leading all AL third basemen in errors for the first of two straight times by committing 27 miscues at the hot corner.

After batting .325, collecting 203 hits, scoring 109 runs, and compiling a .407 on-base percentage in 1984, Boggs began an exceptional four-year run during which he led the American League in batting average and on-base percentage each season. In addition to batting over .350 and compiling an on-base percentage in excess of .450 each year, Boggs scored more than 100 runs, amassed more than 200 hits, and accumulated more than 40 doubles all four seasons. He also drove in more than 70 runs and walked more than 100 times in three of the four years. Boggs had his two most productive seasons in 1985 and 1987, batting a career-high .368 in the first of those campaigns, while also knocking in 78 runs, scoring 107, and amassing a career-best 240 hits, en route to earning a fourth-place finish in the AL MVP balloting. Two years later, he batted .363, scored 108 runs, collected 200 hits, and established career highs with 24 home runs, 89 runs batted in, 324 total bases, a .588 slugging percentage, and an OPS of 1.049. In between, Boggs batted .357, knocked in 71 runs, scored 107 others, accumulated 47 doubles and 207 hits, and compiled a league-leading 105 walks and .453 on-base percentage for the 1986 AL champion Red Sox. Boggs also had an exceptional 1988 season, collecting 214 hits and topping the junior circuit with 128 runs scored, 45 doubles, 125 walks, a .366 batting average, a .476 on-base percentage, and a .965 OPS.

Despite posting a batting average of .330, Boggs failed to capture his fifth consecutive batting title in 1989. However, he led the league with 113 runs scored, 51 doubles, and a .430 on-base percentage. By also collecting 205 hits, Boggs became the first American League player to reach the 200-hit plateau seven straight times (Ichiro Suzuki has since surpassed that mark).

Boggs's superb batting eye and exceptional patience at the plate proved to be the keys to the extraordinary success he experienced during his time in Boston. He rarely swung at bad pitches, and he felt extremely comfortable hitting with two strikes on him. In fact, Boggs adopted a two-strike mentality from the time he first stepped into the batter's box, protecting the plate and making use of the entire ball field. Former opposing manager Rene Lachemann once revealed, "I used to tell my pitchers I could get them two strikes on Boggs easy, but, from then on, they were on their own. There's no doubt in my mind that he is the best two-strike hitter in history."

Boggs drove line drives to all parts of the park with his smooth left-handed swing, often taking advantage of Fenway Park's "Green Monster" in left field. He also had the ability to turn on the inside pitch and drive the ball into the right field stands, if the situation happened to call for him to do so.

Boggs's methodical approach to hitting actually represented an extension of his obsessive personality. One of the most superstitious and idiosyncratic players in the history of the game, Boggs awoke at the same time every morning, ate chicken before every game (teammate Jim Rice nicknamed him "Chicken Man"), and took exactly 100 ground balls before each game during infield practice. In preparing for night games, he stepped into the batting cage at precisely 5:17 and ran wind sprints at 7:17. Boggs drew the Hebrew word "Chai" in the batter's box before each at-bat, and he took exactly the same route to and from his position between innings.

Carrying his obsessive nature far beyond the playing field, Boggs admitted to being a "sex addict" during a *20/20* television interview with host Barbara Walters after his longtime extramarital affair with California mortgage broker Margo Adams gained national media attention in 1989.

Boggs also found himself being questioned by some for the manner in which he chose to protect his lead over Don Mattingly in the 1986 batting race by sitting out Boston's final two games. Furthermore, longtime teammate Roger Clemens once described Boggs as "a selfish player," suggesting that the third baseman's individual statistics meant more to him than the success of his team.

Boggs's success on the ball field made it easy for Boston fans and team management to overlook his somewhat eccentric behavior. However, after batting over .300 for the 9th and 10th consecutive times in 1990 and 1991, Boggs posted a mark of only .259 in 1992, prompting the Red Sox to allow him to leave via free agency at season's end. The 34-year-old third baseman subsequently signed with the rival New York Yankees, with whom he experienced an offensive resurgence, compiling batting averages of .302, .342, .324, and .311 the next four seasons, en route to earning All-Star honors each year. He also continued to work extremely hard on improving his defense, eventually earning back-to-back Gold Gloves in 1994 and 1995. After narrowly missing winning the World Series as a member of the Red Sox in 1986, Boggs helped the Yankees capture the world championship

Courtesy mearsonlineauctions.com

10 years later by batting .311 and scoring 80 runs during the 1996 regular season. After the Yankees clinched the Fall Classic by winning Game 6 in New York, Boggs drove a stake through the hearts of Red Sox fans when he celebrated by jumping on the back of a NYPD horse and touring the field with his index finger in the air—despite his self-professed fear of horses.

Boggs spent only one more year in New York before signing with Tampa Bay as a free agent at the conclusion of the 1997 campaign. He remained in Tampa Bay for two years, collecting the 3,000th hit of his career by hitting a home run late in 1999, his final big-league season. He announced his retirement a few weeks later, ending his career with 3,010 hits, 1,513 runs scored, 1,014 RBIs, 118 home runs, 578 doubles, 1,412 walks, a .328 batting average, and a .415 on-base percentage. His numbers with the Red Sox include 2,098 hits, 1,067 runs scored, 687 RBIs, 85 home runs, 422 doubles, 1,004 walks, a .338 batting average, and a .428 on-base percentage. He ranks among the team's all-time leaders in each of those categories, except for home runs and runs batted in.

After retiring as a player, Boggs served as Tampa Bay's hitting coach in 2001. He gained admittance to the Baseball Hall of Fame four years later, being elected by the members of the BBWAA on January 4, 2005, in his very first year of eligibility.

RED SOX CAREER HIGHLIGHTS

Best Season

Boggs posted exceptional offensive numbers from 1985 to 1988, and any of those years would make a good choice. He knocked in 78 runs, scored 107 others, walked 96 times, compiled an on-base percentage of .450, and established career highs with 240 hits and a .368 batting average in the first of those campaigns. Boggs followed that up by collecting 207 hits and leading the league with 105 walks, a .357 batting average, and a .453 on-base percentage in 1986. In addition to amassing 214 hits and topping the junior circuit with 45 doubles, a .366 batting average, and an OPS of .965 in 1988, Boggs established career highs with a league-leading 128 runs scored, 125 bases on balls, and .476 on-base percentage. Nevertheless, I ultimately settled on Boggs's magnificent 1987 campaign in which he scored 108 runs, accumulated 200 hits, walked 105 times, led the league with a .363 batting average and a .461 on-base percentage, and reached career highs with 24 home runs, 89 runs batted in, 324 total bases, a .588 slugging percentage, and a league-leading 1.049 OPS.

Memorable Moments/Greatest Performances

Boggs experienced several memorable moments and reached a number of milestones during his 11 years in Boston. He made the first home run of his major-league career a memorable one, giving the Red Sox a 5–4 win over the Tigers on June 22, 1982, with a game-winning blast in the bottom of the 11th inning.

In 1985, Boggs hit safely in 28 consecutive games, giving him the longest hitting streak in the majors since 1980. Later in the year, during a 7–6 win over Detroit on September 21, he tied Tris Speaker's club mark of 222 hits with a single in the second inning. Three frames later, Boggs passed Speaker and set a new American League record for singles, surpassing the mark previously set by Kansas City's Willie Wilson in 1980. He concluded the campaign with 187 singles, which remained a league record until Seattle's Ichiro Suzuki set a new mark in 2001.

On September 20, 1988, Boggs went 3 for 3 during a 13–2 win over the Toronto Blue Jays, becoming in the process the first 20th-century player to reach the 200-hit plateau six straight times. His three safeties enabled him to separate himself from Philadelphia's Chuck Klein (1929–1933) and Detroit's Charlie Gehringer (1933–1937), who accomplished the feat five consecutive times for their respective teams. Almost exactly one year later, on September 25, 1989, Boggs went 4 for 5 during a 7–4 win over the Yankees, to become the first player in major-league history to surpass both 200 hits and 100 walks in four consecutive seasons. His four hits also gave him seven straight 200-hit campaigns, enabling him to extend his own 20th-century record.

Also an outstanding postseason performer during his time in Boston, Boggs batted .290 against the Mets in the 1986 World Series, .385 against Oakland in the 1988 ALCS, and .438 against the A's in the ALCS two years later, with seven hits in 16 at-bats, including a homer and a double.

NOTABLE ACHIEVEMENTS

- Batted over .350 five times, topping the .320 mark on four other occasions
- Scored more than 100 runs seven times, surpassing 120 runs scored once (128 in 1988)
- Accumulated more than 200 hits seven times, reaching the 240 mark once (1985)

- Topped 40 doubles eight times, surpassing the 50 mark once (51 in 1989)
- Hit more than 20 home runs once (24 in 1987)
- Drew more than 100 bases on balls four times
- Compiled on-base percentage in excess of .400 nine times, surpassing the .450 mark on four occasions
- Posted slugging percentage in excess of .500 once (.588 in 1987)
- Led AL in batting average five times; on-base percentage six times; runs scored twice; hits once; doubles twice; walks twice; and OPS twice
- Led AL third basemen in putouts three times
- Ranks among Red Sox career leaders in batting average (2nd); hits (5th); doubles (5th); runs scored (7th); total bases (7th); walks (5th); on-base percentage (3rd); OPS (9th); games played (8th); plate appearances (8th); and at-bats (8th)
- Holds Red Sox single-season records for most hits (240 in 1985) and most plate appearances (758 in 1985)
- Only 20th-century player to surpass 200 hits seven straight times
- Has highest career batting average (.328) and on-base percentage (.415) of any third baseman in major-league history
- Six-time Silver Slugger winner
- Six-time *Sporting News* All-Star selection
- Eight-time AL All-Star
- Number 95 on *Sporting News*'s 1999 list of Baseball's 100 Greatest Players
- 1986 AL champion
- Elected to Baseball Hall of Fame by members of BBWAA in 2005

7

Jim Rice

Courtesy Legendary Auctions

One of the most dominant hitters of his era, Jim Rice succeeded Ted Williams and Carl Yastrzemski in left field for the Red Sox, giving them their third straight Hall of Fame player at the position. An eight-time All-Star and three-time home run champion, Rice terrorized opposing pitchers from 1975 to 1986, leading all American League batters in homers, RBIs, runs scored, hits, total bases, and slugging percentage during that 12-year period. Rice hit at least 39 home runs and accumulated more than 200 hits three straight times from 1977 to 1979, making him the first player in major-league history to do so. Over the course of those three seasons, he also became just the second player to top the junior circuit in total bases three consecutive times (Ty Cobb was the first). In all, Rice hit more than 20 home runs 11 times and knocked in more than 100 runs 8 times, averaging 29 homers and 106 RBIs during his 12 peak seasons. Yet, in spite of his many accomplishments, it took Rice 15 attempts to gain induction into the Baseball Hall of Fame, with the members of the BBWAA likely forcing him to wait until his final year of eligibility due to the icy relationship they shared with him during his playing days.

Born in Anderson, South Carolina, on March 8, 1953, James Edward Rice grew up in the South when segregation was still the law of the land. As a result, he spent two years at nearby Westside High School, before he was finally permitted to attend the previously all-white T. L. Hannah High as a senior. Rice starred in football, basketball, and baseball in his lone year at T. L. Hannah, after which the Red Sox selected him in the first round of the 1971 amateur draft.

After spending three years competing at the Single-A and Double-A levels, Rice joined Pawtucket, Boston's top farm club, in 1974. He subsequently dominated International League pitching, capturing Rookie of the Year and MVP honors, and winning the Triple Crown by topping the circuit with 25 home runs, 93 RBIs, and a .337 batting average. Summoned to Boston during the latter stages of the campaign, Rice ended up appearing in 24 games for the Red Sox, compiling a batting average of .269, driving in 13 runs, and hitting his first major-league homer.

Boston's crowded outfield situation forced Rice to assume the role of DH throughout most of the first two months of the 1975 season. However, he eventually won the starting left field job, concluding the campaign with 22 home runs, 102 runs batted in, 92 runs scored, and a .309 batting average, en route to earning a third-place finish in the AL MVP voting. He also finished second to teammate Fred Lynn in the Rookie of the Year balloting. Unfortunately, Rice's season came to a premature end on September 21, when a pitch by Detroit's Vern Ruhle broke his left hand, sidelining him for the rest of the year. Unable to participate in the playoffs and World Series, Rice could only watch as the Red Sox dropped the Fall Classic to Cincinnati in seven hard-fought games.

Still on the mend early in 1976, Rice posted relatively modest numbers in his second big-league season, finishing the year with 25 homers, 85 RBIs, 75 runs scored, and a .282 batting average. However, he began to emerge as one of baseball's premier sluggers the following year, when he led the American League with 39 home runs, 382 total bases, and a .593 slugging percentage, while also placing among the leaders with 114 RBIs, 104 runs scored, 206 hits, 15 triples, and a .320 batting average. Rice's exceptional performance earned him All-Star honors for the first time and a fourth-place finish in the league MVP voting.

Rice developed into a one-man wrecking crew in 1978, putting together one of the greatest seasons in Red Sox history. Appearing in all of Boston's 163 games, Rice topped the junior circuit with 46 home runs, 139 RBIs, 213 hits, 15 triples, 406 total bases, a .600 slugging percentage, and an OPS of .970, while also finishing near the top of the league rankings with 121 runs scored and a .315 batting average. Although Ron Guidry also had a fabulous season for the Yankees, who edged out the Red Sox for the AL East title by defeating them in a one-game playoff, Rice easily outpolled him for league MVP honors. Rice followed that up with another extraordinary campaign in 1979, leading the AL with 369 total bases and placing among the leaders with 39 home runs, 130 RBIs, 117 runs scored, 201 hits, 39 doubles, a .325 batting average, and a .596 slugging percentage, en route to earning a fifth-place finish in the MVP balloting.

Standing 6'2" tall and weighing close to 215 pounds, Rice possessed tremendous physical strength, once breaking a bat on a checked swing without even making contact with the ball. His powerful wrists and quick, compact swing enabled him to frequently drive balls off the left field wall at Fenway, or over the screen above the "Green Monster." Yet, the success Rice experienced was not directly tied to the dimensions of his home ballpark, since he hit the ball well to all fields, displaying power from foul line to foul line.

Hall of Fame reliever Rich "Goose" Gossage discussed Rice's intimidating presence in the batter's box when he stated, "I'd be staring him down, he'd be staring right back, and I'm telling you there was no man I wanted to face less than Jim Rice. He was the strongest, toughest guy, most competitive man I ever faced."

Detroit shortstop Alan Trammell also found his knees wobbling every time Rice stepped up to the plate, saying, "He was a man! He got the head of the bat on it; he used a big bat with a huge head, and he didn't get cheated. . . . He hit the ball so hard, as a shortstop, you almost felt like a third baseman because you never felt like you were back far enough."

Meanwhile, even though Rice lacked superior running speed and possessed only marginal instincts in the outfield, he eventually turned himself into a solid defensive player. After spending a significant amount of time at the DH spot in each of his first four seasons, Rice played left field almost exclusively from 1979 to 1987. During that time, he mastered the intricacies of Fenway Park's left-field wall, becoming particularly adept at decoying opposing base-runners, who often found themselves being thrown out at second base after driving balls off the "Green Monster." Rice finished in double-digits in assists on seven occasions, throwing out as many as 21 baserunners in 1983.

A fractured wrist in 1980 and a players' strike in 1981 limited Rice's offensive production somewhat, although he still managed to post decent numbers in each of those seasons. After rebounding in 1982 to hit 24 homers, drive in 97 runs, and bat .309, Rice returned to top form the following year, when he batted .305 and led the league with 39 home runs, 126 RBIs, and 344 total bases.

Rice remained one of the American League's most productive hitters in each of the next three seasons, totaling 75 homers and 335 RBIs from 1984 to 1986, while keeping his batting average close to the .300-mark. However, after driving in 110 runs and batting .324 for the AL champion Red Sox in 1986, Rice found himself unable to sustain a similar level of production in subsequent seasons due to elbow, knee, and vision problems. Reduced to serving as a part-time DH by 1989, Rice engaged in a much-publicized shoving match with 57-year-old manager Joe Morgan after the latter pinch-hit for him with the light-hitting Spike Owen. The Red Sox released Rice at the end of the year after he hit just 3 homers, drove in only 28 runs, and batted just .234 in the 56 games in which he appeared. Rice subsequently announced his retirement, ending his career with 382 home runs, 1,451 RBIs, 1,249 runs scored, 2,452 hits, 373 doubles, a .298 batting average, a .352 on-base percentage, and a .502 slugging percentage. In addition to ranking among the Red Sox all-time leaders in most offensive categories, Rice holds the team's single-season record for most total bases (406 in 1978).

Following his retirement, Rice served the Red Sox as a roving batting instructor from 1992 to 1994, before being assigned the role of hitting coach at the major-league level in 1995. After remaining in that post through 2000, Rice transitioned into the role of instructional batting coach within the Red Sox organization, where he has served since 2001. Since 2003, he has also been employed as a commentator for the New England Sports Network (NESN), where he contributes to the Red Sox pre-game and post-game shows.

Still held in extremely high esteem by the men who competed against him during his playing days, Rice drew praise from former player and executive Tom Grieve, who suggested, "If you had to pick a cleanup hitter who

Courtesy Legendary Auctions

epitomized the role of a guy who hit in the middle of the lineup and got big hits when you needed them, it would have been Jim Rice. He had power to all fields, he was a good hitter, and he hit for average."

CAREER HIGHLIGHTS

Best Season

Rice performed magnificently in 1977 and 1979, hitting 39 home runs, knocking in well over 100 runs, scoring more than 100 times, accumulating more than 200 hits, batting over .320, and leading the league in total bases both seasons. In fact, his .325 batting average and .977 OPS in 1979 proved to be the highest marks of his career. Rice also had a huge year in 1983, concluding the campaign with a .305 batting average and a league-leading 39 homers, 126 RBIs, and 344 total bases. Nevertheless, there is little doubt that Rice had the finest season of his career in 1978, when he captured AL MVP honors by topping the circuit in seven offensive categories, including home runs (46), RBIs (139), hits (213), triples (15), total bases (406), slugging percentage (.600), and OPS (.970). He also batted .315 and scored a career-high 121 runs. Rice's 406 total bases represent the third highest total ever compiled by a right-handed batter in the American League, trailing only the mark of 438 that Jimmie Foxx posted for the A's in 1932, and the figure of 418 that Joe DiMaggio recorded for the Yankees in 1937. He also became just the second AL player to lead the league in both triples and home runs in the same season, and the only player ever to lead the majors in triples, home runs, and RBIs in the same year.

Memorable Moments/Greatest Performances

During a 9–3 win over Kansas City on July 18, 1975, Rice hit one of the longest home runs in Fenway Park history, driving a Steve Busby offering completely out of the ballpark in center field, just to the right of the flag pole. Rice's blast, which Red Sox owner Tom Yawkey later called the longest shot he'd ever seen at Fenway, made him just the sixth player to leave the ballpark in dead center, enabling him to join an extremely exclusive club that included the likes of Hank Greenberg, Jimmie Foxx, and Carl Yastrzemski.

Rice hit three home runs in a game twice for the Red Sox, accomplishing the feat for the first time during an 8–7 loss to Oakland on August 29, 1977. Rice went four for five on the day, with four RBIs and three runs scored. He duplicated his earlier effort exactly six years later, homering three times against Toronto in the second game of a doubleheader split with the Blue Jays on August 29, 1983. Rice's three homers and six RBIs led the Red Sox to an 8–7 win in Game 2, with his two-run shot in the top of the ninth inning providing the margin of victory.

Rice had another memorable day on July 4, 1984, leading the Red Sox to a 13–9 win over Oakland by going 5 for 6, with his grand slam in the bottom of the 10th inning proving to be the decisive blow.

Rice again came up big in the clutch on April 18, 1985, when he gave the Red Sox a 4–3 win over Kansas City by homering with two men out in the top of the 14th inning.

Although Rice struggled against California in the 1986 ALCS, compiling a batting average of just .161 over the course of the seven-game series, he helped the Red Sox come out on top by a score of 8–1 in the decisive seventh contest by delivering a three-run homer in the bottom of the fourth inning. Rice subsequently batted .333 and scored six runs against the Mets in his only World Series appearance.

Yet, Rice performed his most memorable feat during a nationally televised game on August 7, 1982, when he rushed into the stands to help a young boy who had been struck in the head by a line drive off the bat of teammate Dave Stapleton. Contradicting the media's portrayal of him as a surly, unsociable player, Rice literally took matters into his own hands when he left the Red Sox dugout, entered the field boxes along the first base line at Fenway Park, took four-year-old Jonathan Keane in his arms, and carried him onto the field, through the Red Sox dugout, and into the clubhouse, where the bleeding and unconscious youngster could be treated by the team's medical staff. Arthur Pappas, a Red Sox team doctor for over 15 years, said years later in a *Hartford Courant* article that described the incident, "Time is very much a factor once you have that kind of a head injury and the subsequent swelling of the brain. That's why it's so important to get him to care so it can be dealt with. Rice certainly helped him very considerably."

NOTABLE ACHIEVEMENTS

- Hit more than 30 home runs four times, hitting 39 homers three times and 46 homers once
- Knocked in more than 100 runs eight times
- Scored more than 100 runs three times
- Batted over .300 seven times, topping the .320 mark on three occasions
- Surpassed 200 hits four times
- Finished in double-digits in triples twice
- Topped 30 doubles three times
- Surpassed 400 total bases once (406 in 1978)
- Compiled slugging percentage in excess of .500 five times, posting mark of .600 in 1978
- Led AL in home runs three times; RBIs twice; hits once; triples once; total bases four times; slugging percentage twice; and OPS once
- Led AL left fielders in putouts twice; fielding percentage once; and double plays twice
- One of only two players to lead AL in total bases three straight years
- One of only two players to lead AL in triples and home runs in the same season (1978)
- Only player to lead major leagues in triples, home runs, and RBIs in the same season (1978)
- Ranks among Red Sox career leaders in home runs (4th); RBIs (4th); hits (3rd); total bases (3rd); extra-base hits (5th); runs scored (4th); triples (6th); doubles (8th); bases on balls (9th); slugging percentage (9th); games played (4th); plate appearances (4th); and at bats (3rd)

- Holds Red Sox single-season record for most total bases (406 in 1978)
- 1978 AL MVP
- Two-time Silver Slugger winner (1983 and 1984)
- Six-time *Sporting News* All-Star selection (1975, 1977–1979, 1983, and 1986)
- Eight-time AL All-Star
- Two-time AL champion (1975 and 1986)
- Elected to Baseball Hall of Fame by members of BBWAA in 2009

Jimmie Foxx

Courtesy Boston Public Library, Leslie Jones Collection

Jimmie Foxx most certainly would have finished higher in these rankings had he not spent many of his finest seasons with the Philadelphia Athletics. Already recognized as the most feared slugger in the game by the time he joined the Red Sox in 1936, Foxx had previously won three home run titles, one Triple Crown, and two Most Valuable Player Awards while playing for the A's. His prodigious slugging helped lead the Athletics to three straight American League pennants and two world championships between 1929 and 1931, prompting many to refer to him as "the right-handed Babe Ruth."

Still, Foxx clearly accomplished enough during his six-plus years in Boston to earn a top-10 ranking here. In addition to hitting more than 35 home runs and scoring more than 100 runs five straight times for the Red Sox, the slugging first baseman knocked in more than 100 runs six times and batted over .300 on four occasions, with his mark of .349 in 1938 leading the American League. Foxx also hit 50 homers that year and established a team record by driving in 175 runs, en route to capturing AL MVP honors for the third time in his career. Foxx performed at such a high level during his relatively brief time in Boston that he continues to rank among the team's all-time leaders in six different offensive categories, placing second only to Ted Williams in career OPS, on-base percentage, and slugging average.

Born in Sudlersville, Maryland, on October 22, 1907, James Emory Foxx developed the tremendous upper-body strength for which he later became so well noted by doing chores on his father's farm as a youngster. After excelling in both baseball and track and field in high school, Foxx began his professional career with Easton of the Eastern Shore League, where he became former major-league third baseman Frank "Home Run" Baker's protégé. Baker recommended Foxx to his former manager Connie Mack shortly thereafter, leading the Philadelphia Athletics' manager to sign the 17-year-old catcher to a contract in 1925.

After seeing very little action his first three seasons as a backup first baseman, third baseman, and catcher, Foxx finally earned a spot in Philadelphia's starting lineup in 1928. Splitting his time between first and third base, the 20-year-old Foxx appeared in 118 games, batting .327, driving in 79 runs, and scoring 85, in just 400 official plate appearances.

Foxx subsequently became the A's full-time first baseman in 1929, contributing mightily to the three consecutive AL pennants they captured by presenting a fearsome presence in the middle of their batting order. Over the course of those three championship campaigns, Foxx hit a total of 100 home runs, knocked in 394 runs, scored 343, and posted batting averages of .354, .335, and .291.

Although the Athletics failed to repeat as American League champions in 1932, Foxx established himself as baseball's dominant hitter, coming within a few percentage points of winning the Triple Crown by finishing a close second in the batting race with a mark of .364, while also topping the junior circuit with 58 home runs, 169 runs batted in, 151 runs scored, 438 total bases, and a .749 slugging percentage. Foxx's fabulous performance earned him league MVP honors. Foxx repeated as AL MVP in 1933, this time winning the Triple Crown by hitting 48 home runs, driving in 163 runs, and batting .356. He also led the league with 403 total bases and a .703 slugging percentage.

It was during this time that Foxx developed a reputation as one of the game's great sluggers. Possessing incredible physical strength, the 5'11", 190-pound first baseman was perhaps the most muscular player of his era, prompting others to frequently refer to him as "the Beast." With his massive forearms, biceps, and chest, Foxx soon became known for his tape-measure home runs. In Chicago, he hit a ball over the double-decked stands at Comiskey Park, clearing 34th Street. He hit one of the longest balls ever in Detroit, way up into the left field bleachers. Perhaps his most famous home run, though, came at the expense of Lefty Gomez at New York's Yankee Stadium. Foxx hit a long line drive that eventually struck a seat in the deepest part of the upper deck in left-center field. Estimates revealed that the ball would have traveled well over 500 feet had its flight not been interrupted by the shattered seat. A stunned Gomez later commented, "I've developed a deep-rooted hatred for Foxx. He hit two of the longest home runs I've ever seen—and they were both off me."

Foxx's awesome power terrified opposing pitchers. Making him an even more imposing figure at the plate was his practice of cutting off the sleeves on his uniform, which exposed his powerful forearms and biceps for all to see.

Chicago White Sox Hall of Fame pitcher Ted Lyons once commented, "He [Foxx] had great powerful arms, and he used to wear his sleeves cut off way up, and when he dug in and raised that bat, his muscles would bulge and ripple." Lefty Gomez said of his adversary, "He has muscles in his hair."

Foxx continued to excel in Philadelphia, even after team owner and manager Connie Mack sold off most of his best players to other teams. Despite playing without much of a supporting cast, Foxx managed to place among the league leaders with 44 homers, 130 runs batted in, 120 runs scored, and a .334 batting average in 1934. He followed that up with an outstanding 1935 campaign that saw him drive in 115 runs, score 118 others, bat .346, and lead the league with 36 home runs and a .636 slugging percentage. Mack finally decided to part with the one remaining link to Philadelphia's three championship teams when he sold Foxx to the Red Sox prior to the start of the 1936 campaign.

Foxx continued his onslaught on American League pitching in Boston, batting .338 and finishing among the league leaders with 41 home runs, 143 RBIs, 130 runs scored, 105 walks, a .440 on-base percentage, and a .631

slugging percentage in his first year as a member of the Red Sox. Although his batting average slipped to .285 the following year, Foxx remained one of the circuit's most productive hitters, concluding the campaign with 36 homers, 127 RBIs, and 111 runs scored. Foxx then put together one of the most dominant offensive seasons in Red Sox history, earning AL MVP honors in 1938 by hitting 50 home runs, scoring 139 runs, and leading the league with 175 runs batted in, 398 total bases, 119 walks, a .349 batting average, a .462 on-base percentage, and a .704 slugging percentage. Only Hank Greenberg's 58 home runs for Detroit prevented Foxx from winning his second Triple Crown. Foxx's 50 homers made him the first player to surpass that mark with two different teams. He also became the first player in either league to win the MVP Award three times.

Despite missing the final three weeks of the ensuing campaign with appendicitis, Foxx had another great year, driving in 105 runs, scoring 130, batting .360, and leading the league with 35 home runs, a .464 on-base percentage, and a .694 slugging percentage, en route to earning a second-place finish in the AL MVP voting. Foxx spent two more full seasons in Boston, playing second fiddle to Ted Williams in each of those years. Nevertheless, the slugging first baseman remained one of the junior circuit's most potent batsmen, totaling 55 home runs and 224 RBIs in 1940 and 1941, while finishing among the league leaders in on-base and slugging percentage both years.

Even though Foxx was approaching the latter stages of his career by the time Williams joined him in Boston in 1939, he left a lasting impression on the "Splendid Splinter," who ranked his former teammate number three on his all-time list of baseball's greatest hitters in his book *Ted Williams' Hit List*, placing him behind only Babe Ruth and Lou Gehrig (Williams excluded himself from his rankings). In discussing Foxx in his book, Williams stated, "When you talk about power, you start with Foxx and Ruth. . . . If anyone was ever capable of actually tearing the cover off the ball, it would be Double-X [Foxx]."

Williams went on to say, "It sounded like cherry bombs going off when Foxx hit them. Hank Greenberg hit them pretty near as far, but they didn't sound that same way. They sounded like firecrackers when Mantle and Foxx hit them—and I never heard anyone say that about Ruth's or Greenberg's home runs. Foxx and Mantle were two guys from different eras, but I saw quite a bit of them both. I never saw another right-handed hitter, except Mantle and Foxx, really crush the ball—I mean crush it—when he hit it like those guys did."

With Foxx's skills finally beginning to erode, the Red Sox released him early in 1942, after which he spent his three remaining seasons serving as a part-time player for the Chicago Cubs and Philadelphia Phillies. He retired at the conclusion of the 1945 campaign as the second leading home run hitter in baseball history, trailing only Babe Ruth, with 534 round-trippers. He also compiled 1,922 runs batted in, 1,751 runs scored, 2,646 hits, a .325 batting average, a .428 on-base percentage, and a .609 slugging percentage. During his time in Boston, Foxx hit 222 home runs, knocked in 788 runs, scored 721 others, accumulated 1,051 hits, batted .320, compiled a .429 on-base percentage, and posted a .605 slugging percentage. Foxx hit more than 30 homers and knocked in more than 100 runs in 12 straight seasons, from 1929 to 1940. Alex Rodriguez is the only other player in baseball history to accomplish that feat.

Unfortunately, Foxx did not prove to be nearly as successful off the field. He drank heavily, made several poor business decisions, and saw most of the earnings he accumulated during his baseball career disappear. He eventually turned to managing and coaching in the minor leagues to earn a living. He also briefly worked in the Red Sox radio booth. Foxx passed away in July of 1967, at the age of 59, when he choked to death on a piece of meat while dining with his brother.

Years after his passing, Jimmie Foxx remains one of the greatest sluggers in baseball history, and one of the most dominant hitters ever to play the game. John Steadman, sportswriter for the *Baltimore Sun* and formerly with the *Baltimore News American*, once said, "With apologies to Hank Aaron, Willie Mays, Ralph Kiner, and others, Jimmie Foxx was (and still is) the greatest right-handed slugger of all time."

RED SOX CAREER HIGHLIGHTS

Best Season

Although Foxx also had tremendous years for the Red Sox in 1936 and 1939, he clearly had his best season in Boston in 1938. In addition to leading the American League with 175 runs batted in, a batting average of .349, 398 total bases, 119 walks, a .462 on-base percentage, and a .704 slugging percentage, Foxx placed second in the junior circuit with 50 home runs and 139 runs scored. He also finished third with 197 hits.

Memorable Moments/Greatest Performances

Foxx hit a number of tape measure home runs while playing for the Red Sox, with arguably the longest of those coming against the White Sox during a 4–2 loss in Chicago on June 16, 1936. Giving the Red Sox their only two runs of the game with a pair of homers, Foxx cleared the left field roof of Comiskey Park with one of his blasts. The ball, which finally landed on 35th Street, well beyond the confines of Comiskey, ended up traveling an estimated 600 feet. Foxx later stated that he considered it to be the longest home run he ever hit.

Foxx's awesome power instilled fear in opposing pitchers throughout the league, prompting St. Louis hurlers to walk him a major-league record six consecutive times during a 12–8 Red Sox victory over the Browns on June 16, 1938.

Foxx had his most productive day as a member of the Red Sox on September 7, 1938, leading his team to an 11–4 win over the Yankees at Fenway by collecting three hits, hitting a pair of homers, and driving in eight runs during a rain-shortened contest that lasted only five-and-a-half innings. Just three days later, Foxx homered twice in one game for the ninth time in 1938, breaking in the process a single-season record previously held by Babe Ruth and Hack Wilson.

During an 11–8 Red Sox win over the Tigers on May 21, 1940, Foxx tied an American League record by hitting a grand slam home run for the second consecutive day.

Foxx hit one more historic home run for the Red Sox, helping his team defeat the Philadelphia Athletics 10–9 in the first game of a doubleheader on September 24, 1940, by clouting his 500th career homer. The blast allowed Foxx to join Babe Ruth as the only members of the exclusive 500 home run club.

NOTABLE ACHIEVEMENTS

- Hit more than 35 home runs five times, topping 40 homers twice and 50 homers once (1938)
- Knocked in more than 100 runs six times, surpassing 120 RBIs on three occasions
- Scored more than 100 runs five times, topping the 130 mark on three occasions
- Batted over .300 four times, surpassing the .330 mark on three occasions
- Finished in double-digits in triples once (10 in 1939)
- Surpassed 30 doubles four times

- Drew more than 100 bases on balls three times
- Compiled on-base percentage in excess of .400 five times
- Posted slugging percentage in excess of .500 five times, topping the .600 mark three times and the .700 mark once (.704 in 1938)
- Led AL in home runs once; RBIs once; batting average once; total bases once; walks once; on-base percentage twice; slugging percentage twice; and OPS twice
- Led AL first basemen in assists twice and fielding percentage once
- Ranks among Red Sox career leaders in batting average (5th); on-base percentage (2nd); slugging percentage (2nd); OPS (2nd); home runs (9th); and RBIs (8th)
- Holds Red Sox single-season records for most runs batted in (175 in 1938) and most extra-base hits (92 in 1938)
- First major-league player to hit 50 home runs with two different teams
- First major-league player to win three Most Valuable Player Awards
- 1938 AL MVP
- Two-time *Sporting News* All-Star selection (1938 and 1939)
- Six-time AL All-Star
- Number 15 on *Sporting News*'s 1999 list of Baseball's 100 Greatest Players
- Elected to Baseball Hall of Fame by members of BBWAA in 1951

Courtesy Boston Public Library, Leslie Jones Collection

Tris Speaker

Courtesy Library of Congress

Although Tris Speaker is perhaps more closely associated with the Cleveland Indians, he spent his first nine big-league seasons in Boston, serving as the Red Sox starting center fielder in seven of those. During that time, Speaker established himself as an outstanding hitter and base runner, batting over .340, scoring more than 100 runs, and stealing more than 40 bases three times each, while also accumulating more than 45 doubles twice, en route to amassing more two-baggers over the course of his career than any other player in major-league history. As well as Speaker played on offense, though, he developed an even greater reputation for his extraordinary defensive work, eventually gaining general recognition as the finest defensive outfielder ever to play the game. Over the course of 22 major league seasons, Speaker established numerous fielding marks not likely to be broken. In addition to holding the American League record for most career outfield putouts (6,706), he owns the major-league marks for most career outfield assists (449) and double plays (143). Speaker's exceptional all-around play made him the most serious threat to Ty Cobb as the greatest American League player of the Dead Ball Era. Here, it earns him a spot in our top 10.

Born in Hubbard, Texas, on April 4, 1888, Tristram E. Speaker suffered numerous setbacks as a youth that would have derailed the career of a less determined man. After fracturing his right arm in a fall from a horse, the right-handed Speaker had to learn to throw left-handed, which he continued to do throughout his baseball career. A few years later, while playing his only year of college ball for Fort Worth Polytechnic Institute, the 17-year-old Speaker severely injured his left arm in a football accident. Ignoring the suggestion of surgeons, who initially advised amputation, Speaker eventually made a full recovery, enabling him to pursue his dream of playing Major League Baseball.

Speaker got his start in professional ball one year later, playing center field for the Cleburne Railroaders of the Texas League in 1906. After batting .318 for the Railroaders, Speaker was sold to the Boston Red Sox for $800. He made his major-league debut for Boston late in 1907, appearing in only seven games and hitting safely in just 3 of his 19 at-bats, for an extremely unimpressive .158 batting average. Speaker's poor performance prompted the Red Sox to trade him to the Little Rock Travelers of the Southern League in exchange for the use of their facilities for spring training the following year. However, Boston reacquired the 20-year-old outfielder after he batted .350 for the Travelers in 1908. Speaker finished the season with the Red Sox, hitting just .224 in 31 games.

Speaker broke into Boston's starting lineup the following year, batting .309, driving in 77 runs, and accumulating 13 triples—the first of seven consecutive times he finished in double-digits in three-baggers. Speaker also performed brilliantly in center field, leading all American League outfielders with 35 assists and 12 double plays. Duffy Lewis and Harry Hooper joined Speaker in Boston's starting outfield in 1910, subsequently giving the Red Sox arguably the finest outfield trio in the major leagues during the Dead Ball Era. Lewis did an outstanding job of playing Fenway's short left-field wall, while Hooper excelled at covering the ballpark's vast expanse in right. But Speaker surpassed both his outfield mates, serving as the unit's unquestioned leader and playing his position in a bold and brazen manner unmatched by any other outfielder.

Speaker's exceptional speed and uncanny ability to track fly balls enabled him to play an extraordinarily shallow center field. He typically positioned himself a mere 40 or 50 feet behind second base, allowing him to frequently convert line drive singles into outs and throw out runners attempting to advance one base. He even occasionally served as the middleman on double plays. Speaker later gave much of the credit for his outstanding ability to judge fly balls to Cy Young, a member of Boston's pitching staff his first few years with the team. Speaker said, "When I was a rookie, Cy Young used to hit me flies to sharpen my abilities to judge in advance the direction and distance of an outfield-hit ball."

As for Speaker's ability to serve as the captain of Boston's outfield, Duffy Lewis stated, "Speaker was the king of the outfield. . . . It was always 'Take it,' or 'I got it.' In all the years, we never bumped each other."

As Speaker continued to establish himself as baseball's greatest defensive outfielder, he also developed into one of the game's premier hitters. Holding the bat relatively low in order to protect the plate, Speaker didn't hit a lot of home runs. However, he compiled huge sums of doubles and triples. He also rarely struck out, never fanning more than 25 times in any single season. The "Grey Eagle," as he came to be known, followed up his solid 1909 performance with batting averages of .340 and .334 the next two years. Speaker then reached the summit in 1912, earning league MVP honors by topping the junior circuit with 10 home runs, 53 doubles, and a .464 on-base percentage. He also placed among the league leaders with a .383 batting average, 90 runs batted in, 136 runs scored, 222 hits, 52 stolen bases, 329 total bases, a .567 slugging percentage, and an OPS of 1.031. The Red Sox captured the American League pennant and subsequently defeated the New York Giants in the World Series, with Speaker batting .300 during the Fall Classic.

Speaker also performed quite well in each of the next two seasons, posting batting averages of .363 and .338, compiling a career-high 22 triples in 1913, and leading the league with 46 doubles, 193 hits, and 287 total bases the following year. But, when Speaker batted only .322 for the world champion Red Sox in 1915, team president J. J. Lannin angered his center fielder by attempting to reduce his annual salary from $15,000 to $9,000. A war of words ensued, resulting in Speaker eventually being traded to the Cleveland Indians for two players and $55,000. The Indians subsequently increased Speaker's salary to $40,000, making him baseball's highest paid player.

Speaker showed his appreciation to the Indians his first year with them by scoring 102 runs and leading the league with a .386 batting average, 211 hits, 41 doubles, a .470 on-base percentage, and a .502 slugging percentage. He continued to play at an extremely high level in his 10 remaining years in Cleveland, compiling batting averages of .352, .388, .362, .378, .380, .344, and .389 in different seasons, surpassing 100 runs batted in and 200 hits twice each, and topping 100 runs scored on three occasions. Speaker became the only player in baseball history to lead his league in doubles four straight years when he topped the circuit from 1920 to 1923, with totals of 50, 52, 48, and 59, respectively. In the last of those years, he also established career highs by hitting 17 home runs and knocking in 130 runs. In addition to excelling both at the plate and in the field for Cleveland, Speaker served as the team's manager from 1919 to 1926, piloting the Indians to their first world championship in 1920, when he also batted .388, knocked in 107 runs, and scored 137.

Speaker joined the Washington Senators at the conclusion of the 1926 campaign after being implicated in a gambling scandal involving himself and Ty Cobb. Former pitcher Dutch Leonard claimed that both players fixed at least one Cleveland-Detroit game several years earlier, forcing both men to "resign" as managers of their respective teams under a cloud of suspicion. After Leonard refused to appear at the January 5, 1927, hearings to discuss his accusations, Commissioner Landis cleared both men of any wrongdoing and reinstated them to their original teams. Both Cleveland and Detroit subsequently informed their stars that they were free agents who could sign with the team of their choosing. Speaker signed with Washington, while Cobb joined the Philadelphia Athletics.

Speaker played one year in Washington, before spending his final season as a part-time player with Cobb on the Athletics. He retired at the conclusion of the 1928 campaign with a .345 career batting average, a .428 on-base percentage, a .500 slugging average, 3,514 hits, 1,529 runs batted in, 1,882 runs scored, 222 triples, and an all-time record 792 doubles. In addition to amassing more doubles than any other player, Speaker ranks among Major League Baseball's all-time leaders in batting average, triples, hits, and runs scored. His numbers with the Red Sox include 542 RBIs, 704 runs scored, 1,327 hits, 241 doubles, 106 triples, 267 stolen bases, a .337 batting average, a .414 on-base percentage, and a .482 slugging percentage. Speaker ranks among the team's all-time leaders in batting average, on-base percentage, OPS, triples, and stolen bases.

Following his retirement, Speaker remained close to the game for several more years. Before serving as an adviser, coach, and scout for the Indians from 1947 to his death, he briefly managed the Newark Bears of the International League. He also became a part owner of the Kansas City Blues and served for a time as chairman of Cleveland's Boxing Commission. Among his more philanthropic pursuits, Speaker helped found the Cleveland Society for Crippled Children and Camp Cheerful. Speaker gained induction into the Baseball Hall of Fame during the second year of voting, in 1937, becoming just the seventh player to be so honored. He died of a heart attack on December 8, 1958, at the age of 70.

More than half a century after his passing, Tris Speaker is still considered by many baseball historians to be the greatest defensive center fielder in baseball history. Pitcher Smoky Joe Wood, who roomed with Speaker in Boston, said in *The Glory of Their Times*, "Speaker played a real shallow center field and had terrific instincts. . . . Nobody else was even in the same league with him."

Hall of Fame shortstop Joe Sewell, who played with Speaker in Cleveland, stated emphatically, "I played with Tris for seven years. I've seen Joe DiMaggio, and I've seen Willie Mays . . . and all the rest. Tris Speaker is the best center fielder I've seen."

Courtesy Library of Congress

RED SOX CAREER HIGHLIGHTS

Best Season

Even though Speaker also had big years for the Red Sox in 1913 and 1914, the 1912 campaign would have to be considered his finest in Boston. Speaker captured AL MVP honors by batting .383, driving in 90 runs, scoring 136 others, amassing 222 hits, stealing 52 bases, compiling a slugging percentage of .567, and topping the junior circuit with 10 home runs, 53 doubles, and a .464 on-base percentage. In leading the Red Sox to the AL pennant, Speaker set a major-league single-season record by putting together three hitting streaks of at least 20 games. He also became the first major leaguer to surpass 50 doubles and 50 stolen bases in the same season. His 52 steals remained a Red Sox record until Tommy Harper swiped 54 bags in 1973.

Memorable Moments/Greatest Performances

In the second game of a doubleheader with Philadelphia on June 1, 1909, Speaker pulled off an unassisted double play for the first of a major-league record six times by an outfielder. He accomplished the feat a second time less than one year later, on April 23, 1910, snaring a low line drive to short center and beating Philadelphia base-runner Harry Davis back to second base.

Speaker had one of his greatest days at the plate for the Red Sox on June 9, 1912, leading a 9–2 rout of the St. Louis Browns by hitting for the cycle. He had another huge game on June 29, 1915, going 5 for 5 during a 4–3, 10-inning win over the Yankees.

On August 14, 1912, Speaker singled in the first game of a doubleheader with the Browns, thereby extending his hitting streak to 20 games. With Speaker already having put together hitting streaks of 20 and 30 games earlier in the year, the safety made him the only player in major-league history to hit safely in as many as 20 consecutive games three times in the same season.

Two months later, on October 15, 1912, Speaker turned in the only unassisted double play by an outfielder in World Series history, doing so in Game 7 of the Fall Classic against the Giants.

With Game 2 of the 1912 World Series having ending in a tie after being called on account of darkness, the Fall Classic ended up going to eight games. Speaker got perhaps the biggest hit of his Red Sox career in the series finale, tying the game at 2–2 in the bottom of the tenth inning with an RBI single. The Red Sox subsequently added another run, giving them a 3–2 win that made them world champions for the second time.

NOTABLE ACHIEVEMENTS

- Batted over .330 five times, surpassing the .360 mark twice
- Scored more than 100 runs three times, topping 130 runs scored once (136 in 1912)
- Surpassed 200 hits once (222 in 1912)
- Finished in double-digits in triples seven times, topping the 20 mark once (22 in 1913)
- Surpassed 30 doubles four times, topping 40 two-baggers twice and 50 doubles once (53 in 1912)
- Stole more than 30 bases five times, topping 40 thefts three times and 50 steals once (52 in 1912)
- Compiled on-base percentage in excess of .400 six times
- Posted slugging percentage in excess of .500 four times
- Compiled OPS in excess of 1.000 once (1.031 in 1912)
- Led AL in home runs once; hits once; doubles twice; on-base percentage once; and total bases once
- Led AL outfielders in putouts five times; assists three times; and double plays four times
- Ranks among Red Sox career leaders in triples (2nd); stolen bases (2nd); batting average (3rd); on-base percentage (4th); and OPS (8th)
- Holds Red Sox single-season record for triples (22 in 1913)
- Holds major-league records for most career doubles (792); outfield assists (449); and double plays by an outfielder (143)
- Ranks among Major League Baseball's all-time leaders in hits (5th); triples (6th); batting average (6th); on-base percentage (11th); runs scored (12th); and outfield putouts (2nd)
- 1912 AL MVP
- Member of Major League Baseball's All-Century Team
- Number 27 on *Sporting News*'s 1999 list of Baseball's 100 Greatest Players
- Two-time AL champion (1912 and 1915)
- Two-time world champion (1912 and 1915)
- Elected to Baseball Hall of Fame by members of BBWAA in 1937

Bobby Doerr

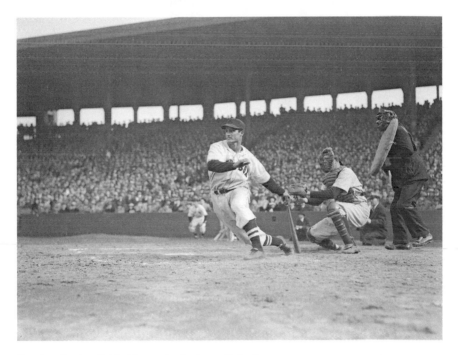

Courtesy Boston Public Library, Leslie Jones Collection

Called "the silent captain of the Red Sox" by his longtime teammate Ted Williams, Bobby Doerr spent his entire career in Boston, leading the Red Sox to one American League pennant and six second-place finishes in his 14 years with them. During that time, Doerr established himself as one of the junior circuit's top run-producers, driving in more than 100 runs on six occasions. He also rivaled Joe Gordon as the finest all-around second baseman of his era, retiring at the conclusion of the 1951 campaign with more career double plays and the highest career fielding percentage of any second sacker in major-league history. And, even though the "Splendid Splinter" overshadowed him throughout virtually his entire career, Doerr earned the respect and admiration of teammates and opponents alike with his solid hitting, outstanding defense, exceptional leadership, and keen sense of fair play. New York Yankee outfielder Tommy Henrich, who spent his 11 years in pinstripes competing against Doerr, once said of his former opponent, "He is one of the few who played the game hard and retired with no enemies."

Born in Los Angeles, California, on April 7, 1918, Robert Pershing Doerr graduated from Los Angeles's Fremont High School in 1936, having begun his professional career two years earlier with the Hollywood Stars of the Pacific Coast League. Doerr remained with the Stars after they moved to San Diego and changed their names to the Padres early in 1936. He signed with the Red Sox later that year after being personally scouted by Hall of Fame second baseman Eddie Collins, who also inked Ted Williams to a contract on the same scouting trip.

Only 19 years old when he broke into the major leagues with the Red Sox in 1937, Doerr spent his rookie season serving primarily as a backup, appearing in only 55 games and accumulating just 147 official at-bats. He became a starter the following year, batting .289, driving in 80 runs, leading the league with 22 sacrifice bunts, and turning 118 double plays at second base—more than any other AL second sacker.

After another solid season in 1939 in which he hit 12 homers, knocked in 73 runs, and batted .318, the 5'11", 175-pound Doerr developed into more of a power hitter in 1940, hitting 22 home runs, driving in 105 runs, and collecting 10 triples, while posting a batting average of .291. He also continued to excel in the field, leading all AL second basemen in putouts and double plays. Doerr earned All-Star honors for the first of four consecutive times the following year by hitting 16 home runs, knocking in 93 runs, and batting .282. He improved upon his overall numbers in 1942, hitting 15 homers, driving in 102 runs, and batting .290, while also compiling the highest fielding percentage of all players at his position for the first of four times.

Initially exempt from military service during World War II due to a perforated eardrum, Doerr remained in Boston in 1943 and 1944, posting a career-high .325 batting average and leading the league with a .528 slugging percentage in the second of those campaigns, before finally being called into duty late in the year. After missing the entire 1945 season, Doerr returned the following year to help lead the Red Sox to their first pennant in 28 years. In addition to hitting 18 home runs, knocking in 116 runs, scoring 95, and batting .271 over the course of that 1946 campaign, Doerr led all American League second basemen in putouts, assists, double plays, and fielding percentage. His outstanding all-around performance earned him a third-place finish in the league MVP voting. Although the Red Sox subsequently lost the World Series to the Cardinals in seven games, Doerr had an exceptional Fall Classic, batting .409, with nine hits, one homer, and three RBIs.

After batting just .258 despite hitting 17 home runs and driving in 95 runs the following year, Doerr returned to top form in 1948, posting a batting average of .285, scoring 94 runs, and finishing among the league leaders with 27 homers, 111 RBIs, and a .505 slugging percentage. He also established a new AL record for second basemen by handling 414 consecutive chances without an error over the course of 73 games, en route to compiling an exceptional .993 fielding percentage that stood as the Red Sox record for second sackers until Mark Loretta surpassed it with a mark of .994 in 2006.

Doerr followed that up with two more outstanding seasons, hitting 18 home runs, driving in 109 runs, and batting .309 in 1949, before compiling a batting average of .294 and establishing career highs with 27 homers, 120 RBIs, and 103 runs scored in 1950. After posting solid numbers over the first four months of the 1951 campaign, Doerr hurt his back while fielding a slow-hit grounder in early August. Failing to show significant improvement during the subsequent off-season, and not wishing to risk more serious injury, the 33-year-old Doerr chose to retire prior to the start of the ensuing campaign. He ended his career with 223 home runs, 1,247 runs batted in, 1,094 runs scored, 2,042 hits, 89 triples, 381 doubles, a batting average of .288, an on-base percentage of .362, and a slugging percentage of .461. Doerr ranks among the Red Sox all-time leaders in most of those categories.

Reflecting back on his playing career, Doerr said years later, "I never did work in the off-season, and I never did play winter ball or anything else. I think it was good for me to get away after a full season. . . . In those days, I don't think anyone ever got too complacent. Even after I played ten years of ball, I still felt like I had to play well or somebody might take my place. They had plenty of players in the minor leagues that were good enough to come up and take your job, and I think that kept us going all of the time. I hustled and put that extra effort in all of the time."

Following his retirement, Doerr spent the next few years working on his farm in Oregon. However, he eventually returned to the Red Sox, serving them as a minor-league scout for nearly a decade, before taking over as first base coach at the major-league level in 1967. Also serving as Boston's unofficial batting instructor that year, Doerr deserves much of the credit for Carl

Yastrzemski's fabulous Triple Crown campaign. Meanwhile, Mike Andrews, who handled second base chores for the Red Sox during that "Impossible Dream" season, expressed his admiration for Doerr when he told the *Boston Herald*'s Steve Buckley, "Bobby Doerr was my mentor. When I was in the minors, I always seemed to improve when he came along. I had so much faith in him that if he told me I'd be a better hitter if I changed my shoe-laces, I'd have done it."

Doerr remained with the Red Sox through the end of 1969, handing in his resignation when manager Dick Williams lost his job. After several years away from the game, Doerr resurfaced in Toronto in 1977, spending the next five years serving as hitting coach for the expansion Blue Jays. Following his stint in Toronto, Doerr left baseball for good, subsequently returning to Fenway only for special occasions, such as the retirement of his jersey number 1 by the Red Sox on May 21, 1988. He also continued to make annual trips to Cooperstown, New York, attending each year's induction ceremonies at the Hall of Fame, which opened its doors to him after a vote by the Veteran's Committee in 1986. Upon the death of former New York Yankees executive and American League president Lee MacPhail in November 2012, Doerr became the oldest living member of the Baseball Hall of Fame, a distinction he held until November 13, 2017, when he passed away at age 99. Upon learning of Doerr's passing, Red Sox owner John Henry issued a statement saying, "Bobby Doerr was part of an era of baseball giants and still stood out as one himself. And, even with his Hall of Fame achievements at second base, his character and personality outshined it all. He will be missed."

CAREER HIGHLIGHTS

Best Season

Doerr had an exceptional year in 1944, when he established career highs with a .325 batting average, .399 on-base percentage, .927 OPS, and a league-leading .528 slugging percentage. His batting average of .325 left him just two points behind the league-leader in that category, Lou Boudreau, who posted a mark of .327 for the Indians. Even though Doerr finished just seventh in the official AL MVP voting, *Sporting News* named him its unofficial winner. However, Doerr missed the final month of the campaign after being called into military duty, limiting him to 15 homers and 81 RBIs.

Doerr earned a third-place finish in the AL MVP balloting in 1946, when he helped lead the Red Sox to the pennant by hitting 18 homers, driving in 116 runs, scoring 95, and batting .271. He also had big years in 1940 (22 homers, 105 RBIs, a .291 average), 1942 (15, 102, .290), 1948 (27, 111, .285), and 1949 (18, 109, .309).

Nevertheless, the feeling here is that Doerr had his finest all-around season in 1950, when he batted .294, compiled an OPS of .886, and established career highs with 27 homers, 120 RBIs, 103 runs scored, 304 total bases, and a league-leading 11 triples. He also led all American League second basemen with a .988 fielding percentage and a career-high 443 putouts.

Memorable Moments/Greatest Performances

On September 17, 1948, Doerr handled 10 chances, setting in the process a new major-league record with 396 consecutive chances without committing an error.

An outstanding hitter as well, Doerr gave the Red Sox a 3–1 victory over the Chicago White Sox on May 6, 1942, by homering twice against Hall of Fame pitcher Ted Lyons. Doerr's second blast served as the game-winner, coming with one man aboard in the bottom of the 10th inning. Doerr also proved to be the hero of the following year's All-Star Game, leading the American League to a 5–3 win over the senior circuit by hitting a three-run homer in the second inning off Mort Cooper of the Cardinals.

Doerr had a pair of huge games for the Red Sox in 1944, with the first of those coming in the second game of a doubleheader split with the Browns on May 17. Although the Red Sox lost the contest by a score of 12–8, Doerr hit for the cycle, going 4 for 5, with two RBIs and three runs scored. Less than two months later, on July 6, Doerr led the Sox to a 13–3 mauling of the Tigers by going 4 for 4, with a double, triple, five RBIs, and three runs scored.

On August 4, 1946, Doerr homered twice and knocked in seven runs during a 9–4 win over the Tigers. He drove in four of those runs with a fifth-inning grand slam.

Doerr hit for the cycle for the second time in his career on May 13, 1947, going 4 for 6, with two RBIs and three runs scored, during a 19–6 win over the Chicago White Sox.

However, Doerr had the biggest game of his career on June 8, 1950, leading the Red Sox to the most lopsided win of the 20th century—a 29–4 pasting of the St. Louis Browns—by hitting three homers and knocking in eight runs.

NOTABLE ACHIEVEMENTS

- Hit more than 20 home runs three times
- Knocked in more than 100 runs six times
- Scored more than 100 runs once (103 in 1950)
- Batted over .300 three times
- Finished in double-digits in triples four times
- Accumulated more than 30 doubles six times
- Compiled slugging percentage in excess of .500 three times
- Led AL in triples once and slugging percentage once
- Led AL second basemen in fielding percentage four times; putouts four times; assists three times; and double plays five times
- Ranks among Red Sox career leaders in: RBIs (6th); runs scored (6th); hits (7th); home runs (8th); triples (4th); doubles (7th); extra-base hits (6th); total bases (6th); walks (7th); games played (6th); plate appearances (6th); and at-bats (6th)
- Ranks fifth all-time among major-league second basemen with 1,507 double plays
- Finished third in 1946 AL MVP voting
- Two-time *Sporting News* All-Star selection (1944 and 1946)
- Nine-time AL All-Star
- 1946 AL champion
- Elected to Baseball Hall of Fame by members of Veterans Committee in 1986

11

David Ortiz

Courtesy Keith Allison

The fact that David Ortiz tested positive for using performance-enhancing drugs shortly after he joined the Red Sox in 2003 subsequently caused many people to question the legitimacy of the numbers he compiled during his time in Boston. However, the slugger's presumed transgression had virtually no effect on the unique relationship that existed between the Fenway Faithful and Ortiz, who remains one of the most popular players ever to don a Red Sox uniform. Ortiz's postseason heroics, which helped lead the Red Sox to three world championships, made him a legendary figure in Boston, prompting team ownership to present him with a plaque in 2005 that proclaimed him to be "the greatest clutch-hitter in the history of the Boston Red Sox." A pretty fair hitter during the regular season as well, Big Papi hit 483 home runs and knocked in 1,530 runs in his 14 years with the Red Sox, placing him second and third, respectively, in team annals. Ortiz also ranks among the club's all-time leaders in runs scored, hits, extra-base hits, doubles, total bases, walks, slugging percentage, and ops. Meanwhile, Ortiz's total of 54 homers in 2006 represents a single-season team record. He also holds Major League records for the most home runs (485), RBIs (1,569), and hits (2,192) by a designated hitter.

Born in Santo Domingo, the capital city of the Dominican Republic, on November 18, 1975, David Americo Ortiz Arias attended Estudia Espallat High School, where he starred in both baseball and basketball. Blessed with outstanding size and quickness, Ortiz did an excellent job at first base for his high school team, while also using his strength, patience at the plate, and quick, powerful hands to excel in the batter's box. After graduating from Estudia Espallat at the age of 17 in 1992, Ortiz signed as an amateur free agent with the Seattle Mariners, who listed him as "David Arias." He retained that moniker until 1996, when, after spending the previous few seasons advancing through Seattle's farm system, he was traded to the Minnesota Twins as the player to be named later in an earlier deal for Dave Hollins. Upon his arrival in Minnesota, he informed the Twins that he preferred to be listed as "David Ortiz."

After spending most of 1997 excelling at all three levels in the minor leagues, Ortiz earned his first big-league call-up in September. Appearing in 15 games for the Twins over the season's final month, he batted .327, knocked in 6 runs, and hit his first home run in the majors. A fractured bone in his right wrist limited Ortiz to only 86 games in 1998. Nevertheless, he managed to hit 9 homers, drive in 46 runs, and bat .277. Ortiz battled injuries and inconsistency at the plate and in the field in each of the next three seasons, before finally settling in as the Twins' full-time DH in 2002. Despite being plagued by knee problems throughout the season, Ortiz concluded the campaign with 20 home runs, 75 RBIs, and a .272 batting average.

With the financially-strapped Twins still unsure of Ortiz's ability to contribute on a regular basis, they released the 27-year-old first baseman/DH when he became eligible for free agency at season's end. Ortiz's close friend Pedro Martinez subsequently lobbied for the free agent's signing in Boston, prompting Red Sox GM Theo Epstein to offer the 6'4", 240-pound Ortiz a one-year deal with a base salary of $1.25 million.

Upon his arrival in Boston, Ortiz thrived as never before, concluding the 2003 campaign with 31 homers, 101 RBIs, a .288 batting average, and a .592 slugging percentage that placed him third in the league rankings. Particularly effective over the course of the season's final 97 games, Ortiz batted .293, hit 29 home runs, and knocked in 82 runs during that span, earning in the process a fifth-place finish in the A.L. MVP voting. Heeding the advice of Red Sox batting coach Ron Jackson, who instructed him to wait a split-second longer at the plate and open his hips slightly when stepping into his swing, Ortiz became far more adept at turning on the inside fastball ù a pitch that gave him trouble earlier in his career. While Ortiz's long arms enabled him to cover the entire plate, his quick hands allowed him to handle the hard stuff inside. He also learned to cut down on his swing with a count of two strikes, taking full advantage of Fenway Park's Green Monster by often lining balls off, and over, the left field wall.

Although Ortiz gave Jackson much of the credit for his increased offensive production, Red Sox teammate Kevin Millar had a different theory, suggesting, "Once he (Ortiz) established himself as an everyday guy, he began to hit. It's not easy to sit in April."

Millar added, "He's always relaxed and at ease."

Meanwhile, closer Keith Foulke noted, "The thing that makes him tough is he's got quick hands; he's on the plate, and he doesn't mind going the other way."

Ortiz also soon emerged as one of the leaders in the Red Sox clubhouse, using his affable nature, positive outlook, and ability to laugh at himself to help galvanize an eclectic mix of personalities that included Nomar Garciaparra, Manny Ramirez, Pedro Martinez, Johnny Damon, and Kevin Millar.

Ortiz followed up his breakout season with an even better 2004 campaign in which he batted .301, scored 94 runs, finished second in the league with 41 homers, 139 RBIs, 351 total bases, and a .603 slugging percentage, and also placed among the leaders with 47 doubles and a .983 OPS, en route to earning his first of five straight All-Star selections, his first of four consecutive Silver Sluggers, and a fourth-place finish in the league MVP balloting. Ortiz continued his torrid hitting in the playoffs and World Series, leading the Red Sox to their first world championship since 1918 by batting .545 against Anaheim in the ALDS, .387 against New York in the ALCS, and .308 against St. Louis in the World Series. The central figure in Boston's stunning comeback against New York in the ALCS, Ortiz hit 3 home runs and drove in 11 runs against the Yankees, winning Games 4 and 5 in walk-off fashion.

Ortiz's success against his team prompted Yankees manager Joe Torre to later say, "He's bulletproof, as far as I'm concerned. Whether there's a left-hander on the mound or a right-hander on the mound, he beats us up pretty good."

Commenting on his teammate's magnificent postseason performance, Pedro Martinez stated, "If he continues to perform the way he's going right now, you can put him right up there with anybody."

Ortiz also drew praise from Curt Schilling, who suggested, "He's confident when other guys are hiding."

Meanwhile, Red Sox outfielder Coco Crisp marveled, "Dang near every time, he comes through for us."

Ortiz had two more monstrous years in 2005 and 2006, concluding the first of those campaigns with 47 home runs, a league-leading 148 RBIs, a batting average of .300, 119 runs scored, a .397 on-base percentage, and a .604 slugging percentage. His extraordinary performance earned him a close second-place finish to Alex Rodriguez in the league MVP voting. Ortiz finished third in the balloting the following year after scoring 115 runs, batting .287, compiling a .413 on-base percentage, posting a .636 slugging percentage, and leading the A.L. with 54 homers, 137 RBIs, 119 walks, and 355 total bases.

Despite playing the entire 2007 season with a torn meniscus in his right knee, Ortiz earned another top-five finish in the MVP voting by hitting 35 home runs, driving in 117 runs, scoring 116 times, batting .332, and leading the league with 111 walks and a .445 on-base percentage. He again came up big in that year's postseason, helping the Red Sox capture their second world championship in four years by hitting 2 homers, knocking in 3 runs, and batting .714 against the Angels in the ALDS, before batting .292 against the Indians in the ALCS and .333 against the Rockies in the World Series.

Although injuries continued to plague Ortiz in each of the next five seasons, he nevertheless managed to appear in the vast majority of Boston's games from 2009 to 2011, averaging 30 homers and 99 RBIs those three years, and compiling a batting average of .309 in 2011. An injury to his right Achilles tendon brought Ortiz's 2012 campaign to a premature end after only 90 games. Yet he still managed to bat .318, hit 23 homers, drive in 60 runs, and score 65 times, in only 324 official at-bats.

Returning to the Red Sox relatively healthy in 2013, Ortiz hit 30 homers, knocked in 103 runs, and batted .309 for a Boston team that compiled the American League's best record during the regular season, earning in the process his ninth All-Star selection, his sixth Silver Slugger, and a 10th-place finish in the A.L. MVP voting. He then helped lead the Sox to their third world championship in 10 years by turning in a memorable performance against the Cardinals in the World Series, homering twice, driving in six runs, and compiling a batting average of .688 during Boston's six-game victory over St. Louis in the Fall Classic.

Ortiz remained one of the junior circuit's most productive hitters over the course of the next three seasons, averaging 37 homers and 113 RBIs from 2014 to 2016. Performing particularly well in the last of those campaigns, the 40-year-old Ortiz earned a sixth-place finish in the MVP balloting by hitting

38 homers, batting .315, and leading the league with 127 RBIs, 48 doubles, a .620 slugging percentage, and an OPS of 1.021.

Nevertheless, Ortiz chose to honor the commitment he made prior to the start of the 2016 campaign to retire at season's end. He ended his career with 541 home runs, 1,768 RBIs, 1,419 runs scored, 2,472 hits, 632 doubles, 19 triples, a batting average of .286, an on-base percentage of .380, and a slugging percentage of .552.

The level of dominance that Ortiz displayed against the Cardinals in the 2013 World Series at 37 years of age, as well as the extraordinary numbers he compiled in his final season at age 40, fueled speculation by some members of the media that the aging slugger, who tested positive for using performance-enhancing drugs earlier in his career, may have resorted to using some form of PEDs again. Still, even after The New York Times reported on July 30, 2009 that the names of Ortiz and then-teammate Manny Ramirez were included on a list of over 100 major league players compiled by the federal government that allegedly tested positive for PEDs during a 2003 survey testing, Ortiz proclaimed his innocence, stating at the time that he was "blind-sided."

Initially declining to comment on the report after discovering his name had appeared on the list, Ortiz said "I'm not talking about that anymore." However, he later relented somewhat, stating, "Today I was informed by a reporter that I was on the 2003 list of MLB players to test positive for performance-enhancing substances."

Ortiz added, "I want to talk about this situation, and I will as soon as I have more answers. In the meantime, I want to let you know how I am approaching this situation. One, I have already contacted the Players Association to confirm if this report is true. I have just been told that the report is true. Based on the way I have lived my life, I am surprised to learn I tested positive. Two, I will find out what I tested positive for. And, three, based on whatever I learn, I will share this information with my club and the public. You know me. I will not hide, and I will not make excuses."

Ten days later, Ortiz held a press conference before a game at Yankee Stadium during which he denied ever buying or using steroids. He suggested that the positive test may have resulted from his use of supplements and vitamins at the time. When asked which supplements he had been taking, Ortiz said he did not know.

Red Sox fans chose to believe Ortiz's explanation; or, at the very least, accept it. However, many others continue to question the veracity of Ortiz's words, causing them to also question the legitimacy of the numbers he posted while playing for the Red Sox. Those numbers include 483 home runs, 1,530 RBIs, 1,204 runs scored, 2,079 hits, 524 doubles, 16 triples, a .290 batting average, a .386 on-base percentage, and a .570 slugging percentage. Ortiz also hit 17 home runs and knocked in 57 runs in 76 postseason games with Boston, causing Red Sox fans to overlook any transgressions he may have committed along the way.

CAREER HIGHLIGHTS

Best Season

Ortiz played his best ball for the Red Sox from 2004 to 2007, surpassing 35 home runs and 100 RBIs in each of those years, while batting over .300 and scoring more than 100 runs three times each. He began his exceptional run in 2004 by batting .301, scoring 94 runs, finishing second in the league with 41 homers, 139 RBIs, 351 total bases, and a .603 slugging percentage, and also placing among the leaders with 47 doubles and a .983 OPS. Ortiz closed out that four-year stretch in 2007 by hitting 35 home runs, driving in 117 runs, scoring 116 times, compiling a .621 slugging percentage, topping the circuit with 111 bases on balls, and establishing career highs with 182 hits, 52 doubles, a .332 batting average, a 1.066 OPS, and a league-leading .445 on-base percentage. Ortiz had a phenomenal 2005 campaign in which he earned a second-place finish in the A.L. MVP voting by batting .300, amassing 180 hits and 40 doubles, placing among the league leaders with 47 home runs, 119 runs scored, 102 walks, a .397 on-base percentage, a .604 slugging percentage, and a career-high 363 total bases, and topping the circuit with a career-best 148 runs batted in. Nevertheless, the feeling here is that Ortiz had his finest all-around season in 2006, when he scored 115 runs, batted .287, compiled a .413 on-base percentage, finished second in the league with a .636 slugging percentage, 85 extra-base hits, and 23 intentional bases on balls, and topped the circuit with 54 home runs, 137 RBIs, 119 walks, and 355 total bases. Ortiz's 54 homers, which established a new single-season franchise record, included three walk-off blasts. Particularly hot during the month of July, Ortiz earned Player of the Month honors by hitting 14 round-trippers.

Memorable Moments/Greatest Performances

Known for his clutch hitting, Ortiz hit a pair of huge home runs during a 10-7, 10-inning victory over the Tigers on August 16, 2005. After tying the game with a one-out solo blast in the top of the ninth inning, Ortiz came through again in the ensuing frame, putting the Red Sox comfortably ahead by hitting a two-out, three-run homer. Ortiz had another big day on July 31, 2006, leading the Red Sox to a 9-8 win over the Indians by driving in

4 runs with a pair of homers, the second of which ended the contest in the bottom of the ninth inning.

Continuing to excel during the latter stages of his career, Ortiz homered twice, doubled, and knocked in six runs during a 10-7 win over the Houston Astros on August 16, 2014.

Ortiz gave the Red Sox a 5-3 win over Baltimore on September 19, 2014, by hitting a two-run homer in the top of the 10th inning.

Ortiz had one of his biggest days at the plate on July 26, 2015, when he led the Red Sox to a lopsided 11-1 victory over the Detroit Tigers by going 4-for-5, with a pair of homers and a career-high seven runs batted in.

Yet, Ortiz will always be remembered most for his extraordinary ability to perform well under pressure during the postseason. He first demonstrated that talent in the 2004 playoffs, leading the Red Sox to a three-game sweep of Anaheim in the ALDS by batting .545, with his 2-run walk-off homer in the bottom of the 10th inning of Game 3 giving Boston an 8-6 win. Ortiz followed that up with a memorable performance against the Yankees in the ALCS, winning Game 4 with a 2-run walk-off homer in the bottom of the 12th inning, and subsequently winning Game 5 with an RBI single in the bottom of the 14th. He also got the Red Sox off to a fast start in Game 7, lining a home run into the right field seats off Kevin Brown in the top of the first inning of a contest the Red Sox eventually won by a score of 10-3. Ortiz concluded the series with 3 homers, 11 RBIs, and a .387 batting average, earning in the process ALCS MVP honors. He subsequently homered once, knocked in 4 runs, and batted .308 against the Cardinals in the World Series.

Ortiz also performed magnificently against the Angels in the 2007 ALDS, batting .714, with 2 homers and 3 RBIs, in leading the Red Sox to a three-game sweep of their overmatched opponents.

Although Ortiz struggled against the Tigers in the 2013 ALCS, compiling a batting average of just .091, he had arguably the biggest hit of the series, tying Game 2 with a grand slam homer off reliever Joaquin Benoit in the bottom of the eighth inning of a game the Red Sox eventually won by a score of 6-5. Ortiz subsequently tormented St. Louis pitchers in the World Series, hitting 2 home runs, driving in 6 runs, batting .688, and posting a remarkable 1.948 OPS, en route to winning Series MVP honors.

Notable Achievements

- Has hit more than 30 home runs seven times, topping 40 homers three times and 50 homers once
- Has knocked in more than 100 runs 10 times, surpassing 120 RBIs on four occasions
- Scored more than 100 runs three times
- Batted over .300 seven times, surpassing the .330 mark once
- Has surpassed 30 doubles eleven times, reaching the 40 mark five times and the 50 mark once
- Has drawn more than 100 bases on balls three times
- Has compiled an on-base percentage in excess of .400 four times
- Has posted a slugging percentage in excess of .500 13 times, topping the .600 mark six times
- Has led AL in home runs once; RBIs three times; doubles once; walks twice; total bases once; extra-base hits three times; on-base percentage once; slugging percentage once; and OPS once
- Ranks among Red Sox career leaders in: home runs (2nd); RBIs (3rd); runs scored (5th); hits (6th); extra-base hits (3rd); doubles (3rd); total bases (5th); walks (4th); slugging percentage (4th); OPS (4th); games played (5th); plate appearances (5th); and at-bats (5th)
- Holds Red Sox single-season record for most home runs (54 in 2006)
- Holds MLB records for most home runs (485), RBIs (1,569) and hits (2,192) by a DH.
- First player ever to hit two walk-off home runs in the same postseason (2004)
- Four-time A.L. Player of the Month.
- Eight-time Edgar Martinez Award winner as the AL's best DH
- Seven-time Silver Slugger winner
- Has finished in top ten in AL MVP voting seven times
- Two-time AL Hank Aaron Award winner
- 2011 ML Roberto Clemente Award winner
- 2004 ALCS MVP
- 2013 World Series MVP
- Named to *Sports Illustrated*'s MLB All-Decade Team in 2009
- Named *Sporting News*'s Designated Hitter of the Decade in 2009
- Five-time *Sporting News* All-Star selection (2004–2007 & 2011)
- Ten-time AL All-Star
- Three-time AL champion (2004, 2007, and 2013)
- Three-time world champion (2004, 2007, and 2013)

Dwight Evans

Courtesy Boston Red Sox

One of the most underrated and overlooked players in Red Sox history, Dwight "Dewey" Evans spent the first half of his career being viewed essentially as a defensive standout with only average offensive ability. Although Evans won three Gold Gloves during his first nine seasons in Boston, he hit more than 20 home runs and batted over .280 just twice, and he never drove in more than 70 runs. The strong-armed right fielder spent most of that time placing a distant third in the Red Sox outfield to sluggers Jim Rice and Fred Lynn, who experienced immediate success when they arrived in Boston in 1975. However, a new batting stance and a different approach at the plate helped Evans eventually evolve into one of the American League's most potent batsmen and finest all-around players. Evans surpassed 20 home runs each year from 1981 to 1989, hitting a total of 256 homers during the decade of the '80s—more than any other player in the junior circuit. He also knocked in more than 100 runs four times, scored more than 100 runs four times, batted over .290 five times, and drew more than 100 bases on balls three times during that stretch, en route to earning two All-Star selections and four top-10 finishes in the league MVP voting. Meanwhile, Evans continued to excel in right field, adding five more Gold Gloves to his collection. By the time Evans left the Red Sox following the 1990 campaign, he ranked among the team's all-time leaders in home runs, RBIs, runs scored, hits, extra-base hits, doubles, walks, and total bases. He also played in more games and had more plate appearances than any other Red Sox player, with the exception of Carl Yastrzemski.

Born in Santa Monica, California, on November 3, 1951, Dwight Michael Evans grew up in Hawaii after his family moved there while he was still an infant. He received little exposure to baseball while living in the "Aloha State," finally developing a passion for the game after he moved with his family to the Los Angeles suburb of Northridge at the age of nine. Evans began taking baseball seriously while attending Chatsworth High School, where he made All-Valley in the San Fernando Valley League as a junior. After Evans earned league MVP honors the following year, the Red Sox selected him in the fifth round of the 1969 amateur draft. Still only 17 years old, Evans spent the next four years advancing through Boston's farm system, before an outstanding performance in 1972 that earned him International League MVP honors prompted the Red Sox to call him up in mid-September. Evans appeared in 18 games over the final three weeks of the season, batting .263, driving in six runs, and hitting his first major-league home run.

The right-handed hitting Evans subsequently found himself platooning much of the time from 1973 to 1975, failing to accumulate as many as 500 official at-bats in any of those seasons, and posting his best offensive numbers in 1974, when he hit 10 home runs, knocked in 70 runs, and batted .281. Yet, he began to develop a reputation for his powerful throwing arm during that time, finishing second among all AL outfielders with 15 assists in 1975. Hall of Famer Rod Carew discussed the degree to which Evans intimidated opposing base runners in *Out by a Step: The 100 Best Players Not in the Hall of Fame*, stating, "You didn't run against him. He made sure you didn't run against him. He dared you to run on him. He came up telling you, 'you go and I got you.' You better make sure rounding second you were 100 percent sure you're gonna make it because, if you're not, he's gonna throw you out."

Evans became a full-time member of Boston's starting outfield in 1976, posting an unimpressive .242 batting average, but hitting 17 homers and earning his first Gold Glove by leading all AL right fielders in assists and fielding percentage. A knee injury kept Evans off the field much of the time in 1977, limiting him to only 73 games, 14 homers, and 36 RBIs. He returned to the lineup the following year to hit 24 home runs and drive in 63 runs, despite batting just .247 and suffering through a poor month of September after being beaned on August 28. Evans posted similar numbers in each of the next two seasons as well, continuing to foster the notion that he had his greatest value to the team as a defender. Don Zimmer, who managed Evans from 1977 to 1980, later said, "When I had Dwight, he was a struggling hitter; always a great right fielder—probably the best that ever played in Fenway Park."

In addition to intimidating opposing runners with his rifle arm, Evans did a superb job of patrolling Fenway Park's vast expanse in right field. He also mastered his home ballpark's tricky right-field corner, often turning apparent doubles into singles. His outstanding defensive work prompted Red Sox legend Johnny Pesky to once say, "Dwight Evans was the best Red Sox right-fielder I ever saw."

However, Evans developed into more of an offensive force in 1981 after he adopted a new approach to hitting. Displaying much more patience at the plate than ever before, Evans established a new career high with 85 bases on balls, even though a players strike shortened the season by seven weeks. He also changed his batting stance, shifting his weight more to his back foot and crouching lower as he awaited the pitcher's offering. Inserted into the number two spot in the Red Sox batting order by new manager Ralph Houk, Evans batted .296, tied for the league lead with 22 home runs, topped the circuit in walks, total bases, and OPS, and also placed among the leaders with 71 RBIs, 84 runs scored, a .415 on-base percentage, and a .522 slugging percentage. Evans continued to play stellar defense in right field as well, earning his fourth Gold Glove. His exceptional all-around performance earned him a third-place finish in the AL MVP voting.

In discussing Evans's improvement as a hitter, Don Zimmer noted years later, "This man's put up some big numbers, and he put them all up after I got fired. Dwight became a real, real good hitter. He turned out to be a heck of a player."

Evans subsequently posted his best numbers to date in 1982, batting .292, driving in 98 runs, topping the circuit with a .402 on-base percentage, and finishing among the league leaders with 32 homers, 122 runs scored, 112 walks, 325 total bases, and a .534 slugging percentage. After injuries caused Evans to have a subpar 1983 campaign, he returned to top form the following year, hitting 32 home runs, knocking in 104 runs, batting .295, compiling an on-base percentage of .388, posting a slugging percentage of .532, and leading the league with 121 runs scored and an OPS of .920. Evans had two more productive seasons in 1985 and 1986, before he began the finest stretch of his career, surpassing 100 RBIs three straight times from 1987 to 1989. He posted his best numbers in the first of those campaigns, finishing the year with 34 home runs, 123 RBIs, 109 runs scored, and a .305 batting average.

Thirty-eight years old at the conclusion of the 1989 campaign, Evans finally began to show signs of aging the following year, when, relegated to DH duties much of the time, he hit just 13 homers, knocked in only 63 runs, and batted just .249. Subsequently granted free agency when the Red Sox declined to re-sign him, Evans joined the Baltimore Orioles, with whom he spent his final year, hitting 6 homers, driving in 38 runs, and batting .270. He retired at season's end with 385 career home runs, 1,384 runs batted in, 1,470 runs scored, 2,446 hits, 483 doubles, a .272 lifetime batting average, an on-base percentage of .370, and a slugging percentage of .470.

Following his retirement, Evans spent a few years working in the Chicago White Sox farm system, before assuming the role of hitting instructor for the Colorado Rockies in 1994. He returned to the Red Sox in 2001, serving them first as a roving instructor, then as hitting coach, and, most recently, as a player development consultant.

Looking back at Evans's playing career, Hall of Famer Paul Molitor stated, "He's probably one of the most underrated players of his time. I don't think people realize the type of career numbers he's been able to put together, kind of getting lost in the middle of being on some teams that had people stealing the headlines. He was just out there being consistent, and he was able to do it for a long time."

RED SOX CAREER HIGHLIGHTS

Best Season

Evans played extremely well in 1982 and 1984, placing among the league leaders in several statistical categories both years. In the first of those campaigns, he hit 32 home runs, knocked in 98 runs, scored 122 others, batted

.292, amassed 37 doubles, walked 112 times, and led the league with a .402 on-base percentage. Two years later, Evans again hit 32 homers and accumulated 37 doubles, drove in 104 runs, batted .295, collected a career-high 186 hits, and topped the circuit with 121 runs scored and an OPS of .920. However, Evans had his finest all-around season in 1987, when he scored 109 runs, led the league with 106 walks, and established career highs with 34 home runs, 123 RBIs, a .305 batting average, a .417 on-base percentage, a .569 slugging percentage, and an OPS of .986, en route to earning a fourth-place finish in the AL MVP balloting.

Memorable Moments/Greatest Performances

Evans had one of his greatest days at the plate on June 28, 1984, hitting for the cycle during an 11-inning 9–6 win over the Seattle Mariners. He went four for seven on the day, driving in three runs and scoring four, with his three-run walk-off homer in the bottom of the 11th inning giving the Red Sox the victory.

Evans achieved a measure of immortality on April 7, 1986, when, on Opening Day at Tiger Stadium, he became the first player ever to hit a home run on the season's first pitch.

However, Evans is remembered most for an extraordinary defensive play he made in the historic sixth game of the 1975 World Series. After coming through earlier in the Fall Classic by tying Game 3 with a dramatic two-run homer in the top of the 9th inning, Evans helped save Game 6 by making a spectacular catch of a Joe Morgan drive to deep right field with a man on first base and the scored tied at 6–6 in the top of the 11th inning. After robbing Morgan of what appeared to be a certain extra-base hit, Evans threw to first base to double up Ken Griffey. Carlton Fisk won the contest in the ensuing frame with one of the most memorable home runs in World Series history.

Evans also came up big in the 1986 World Series, hitting two home runs, knocking in nine runs, and batting .308 against the vaunted pitching staff of the New York Mets.

NOTABLE ACHIEVEMENTS

- Hit more than 20 home runs 11 times, surpassing 30 homers on three occasions
- Knocked in more than 100 runs four times

- Scored more than 100 runs four times
- Batted over .300 once (.305 in 1987)
- Surpassed 30 doubles seven times
- Drew more than 100 bases on balls three times
- Compiled on-base percentage in excess of .400 three times
- Posted slugging percentage in excess of .500 five times
- Led AL in home runs once; runs scored once; walks three times; total bases once; on-base percentage once; OPS twice; and games played twice
- Led AL outfielders in double plays twice and fielding percentage once
- Led AL right fielders in putouts four times; assists three times; double plays three times; and fielding percentage three times
- Ranks third all-time among major-league right fielders with 4,247 putouts
- Ranks among Red Sox career leaders in games played (2nd); plate appearances (2nd); at-bats (2nd); home runs (5th); RBIs (5th); runs scored (3rd); hits (4th); doubles (4rd); triples (8th); extra-base hits (4rd); total bases (4th); and walks (3rd)
- Hit for cycle vs. Seattle Mariners on June 28, 1984.
- Finished third in AL MVP voting in 1981
- Eight-time Gold Glove winner
- Two-time Silver Slugger winner
- Three-time *Sporting News* All-Star selection (1982, 1984, and 1987)
- Three-time AL All-Star (1978, 1981, and 1987)
- Two-time AL champion (1975 and 1986)

Manny Ramirez

Courtesy Keith Allison

Manny Ramirez often exasperated Boston fans and his Red Sox teammates with his obtuse behavior, poor judgment, lack of hustle, and selfish attitude, frequently conducting himself in an unprofessional manner, both on and off the field. Ramirez also displayed a total lack of instincts on the base paths and in the outfield from time to time. Nevertheless, the fact remains that the enigmatic outfielder established himself during his seven-plus years in Boston as arguably the greatest right-handed hitter of his generation, and as one of the best in baseball history. After earlier starring for the Cleveland Indians, Ramirez earned eight consecutive All-Star selections as a member of the Red Sox, surpassing 30 home runs and 100 RBIs six times each, and batting well over .300 on five occasions. Ramirez posted an OPS in excess of 1.000 in five of his seven full seasons in Boston, earning in the process six consecutive Silver Sluggers and five straight top-10 finishes in the AL MVP voting. Only a pair of failed tests for the use of performance-enhancing drugs will likely keep Ramirez out of Cooperstown. However, even though the numbers Ramirez compiled during his time in Boston must subsequently be viewed with considerable skepticism, I found myself unable to completely ignore his extraordinary list of accomplishments. Therefore, Ramirez takes his rightful place among the elite players in Red Sox history.

Born in Santo Domingo, Dominican Republic, on May 30, 1972, Manuel Aristides Ramirez Onelcida moved with his parents to Washington Heights, a predominantly Dominican neighborhood situated in upper Manhattan, at the age of 13. Ramirez honed his baseball skills at George Washington High School, which he attended from 1989 to 1991, playing third base and center field for the school's varsity team when not under suspension for truancy and other academic transgressions. After Ramirez led his high school squad to three straight division championships, the Cleveland Indians selected him in the first round of the 1991 amateur draft with the 13th overall pick. He subsequently advanced rapidly through Cleveland's farm system, making it to the big leagues by September 1993 after being named that season's "Minor League Player of the Year" by *Baseball America* for hitting .433, with 31 home runs and 145 RBIs in 129 combined games at Double and Triple-A. Labeled a "can't miss" prospect when he arrived in Cleveland, Ramirez struggled at first, batting just .170 in 22 games over the final month of the 1993 campaign.

Ramirez began to live up to the hype that preceded him the following year, when he earned a second-place finish in the Rookie of the Year voting by batting .269, hitting 17 homers, and driving in 60 runs, in only 91 games and 290 official at-bats. He developed into a full-fledged star in his sophomore campaign of 1995, earning All-Star honors and his first Silver Slugger by hitting 31 home runs, knocking in 107 runs, and batting .308 for the AL champion Indians.

Ramirez spent the next five years in Cleveland establishing himself as one of the junior circuit's most potent batsmen, compiling more than 30 home runs, 100 RBIs, and a batting average in excess of .300 four times each. He had his two most productive seasons for the Indians in 1998 and 1999, totaling 89 homers, 310 RBIs, and 239 runs scored those two years, while posting batting averages of .294 and .333. His 165 RBIs in 1999 represented the highest single-season total in the major leagues since Jimmie Foxx knocked in 175 runs for the Red Sox in 1938. Ramirez followed that up by hitting 38 home runs, driving in 122 runs, and batting a career-high .351 in 2000. He earned All-Star honors and a top-10 finish in the league MVP balloting all three years.

A free agent at the end of 2000, Ramirez subsequently signed an eight-year, $160 million deal with the Red Sox, with an additional two-year player option. In his first year in Boston, the 29-year-old outfielder paid immediate dividends on the huge investment the Red Sox made in him by batting .306, scoring 93 runs, compiling a .405 on-base percentage, and finishing fourth in the league with 41 home runs, 125 RBIs, a .609 slugging percentage, and a 1.014 OPS, en route to earning the fourth of his 11 straight All-Star selections, the third of his 8 consecutive Silver Sluggers, and a ninth-place finish in the AL MVP voting. Despite missing 39 games with a fractured left index finger in 2002, Ramirez again finished ninth in the MVP balloting after hitting 33 homers, driving in 107 runs, and leading the league with a .349 batting average and a .450 on-base percentage. He posted big numbers again in 2003, concluding the campaign with 37 homers, 104 RBIs, 117 runs scored, a .325 batting average, and a league-leading .427 on-base percentage.

Ramirez made a strong impression on Red Sox fans his first three years in Boston with his superb hitting. In addition to allowing him to make solid contact with even the hardest-thrown fastballs, his extraordinarily quick wrists enabled him to wait longer than most batters before starting his swing, making him an exceptional breaking-ball hitter as well. Ramirez also possessed a keen batting eye, outstanding patience at the plate, and the ability to drive the ball with power to all fields. Red Sox teammate Derek Lowe stated, "I think people on the West Coast don't realize how good he is; how consistent he is." And, even though he rarely received credit for doing so, Ramirez worked as hard as anyone to perfect his swing, constantly studying video and spending hours in the batting cage every day to become one of the game's very best hitters. Curt Schilling said of his former Red Sox teammate, "Physically, he worked his butt off."

Meanwhile, Terry Francona, who managed Ramirez in Boston from 2004 to 2008, revealed to the *Cleveland Plain Dealer* in August of 2013, "Manny was a weird combination. When we'd be at home, I'd always be the first one to the ballpark. But Manny would be in there in the morning lifting. The reason I'd know is because he parked his car right in the middle of the lot so no one else would get in. You'd go into the weight room and the weights were all over the place. Then he'd go home and come back. He worked his butt off. I'm not sure if he wanted people to know that."

Although Ramirez developed a reputation early in his career as a horrific defensive outfielder, he worked hard on improving that aspect of his game as well, eventually turning himself into a proficient left fielder. After leading all AL outfielders with 17 assists in 2005, he finished first among players at his position with a .990 fielding percentage in 2007.

Ramirez, though, had a far more difficult time shaking his reputation as an eccentric, self-indulgent superstar who put himself before his team, and who marched to the beat of his own drummer. Many of Ramirez's teammates professed great fondness for him, with Nomar Garciaparra once saying, "Manny is really a simple person. He works extremely hard. He just wants to play baseball and go home and be with his family. How can you not respect and love a guy like that?" Derek Lowe added, "He's a kid is really what he is. This is how he's been, and probably how he always will be."

Meanwhile, in discussing Ramirez's quirky personality, David Ortiz stated, "He's in his own world . . . on his own planet; totally different human being than everyone else."

However, Ramirez's Red Sox teammates, who jokingly referred to his unconventional behavior as "Manny being Manny," became frustrated with him when he played lackadaisically and conducted himself in a manner detrimental to the rest of the team. Terry Francona stated on one occasion, "There were times when he'd hit a ball and not run. You'd try to stay ahead of him. If you got to a point where he'd beat you to that day off, you might lose him for a week, instead of one day. He was an interesting character, but he could hit, man."

Ramirez's teammates first began to question his dedication to the team in the summer of 2003, when, after begging out of the lineup one day with a case of pharyngitis, he appeared in a bar later that evening with Enrique Wilson of the opposing Yankees. The incident took place shortly after Ramirez told reporters he wouldn't mind playing for the Yankees. The very next day, Ramirez refused to pinch-hit against the Philadelphia Phillies, prompting Red Sox manager Grady Little to bench him.

Ramirez's ill-advised behavior caused Red Sox management to attempt to rid itself of his exorbitant contract by placing him on irrevocable waivers at the end of 2003. But, with no other team willing to absorb Ramirez's $20 million annual salary, he returned to Boston in 2004. Ramirez ended up compiling huge numbers for the Red Sox that year, leading the league with 43 home runs, batting .308, knocking in 130 runs, scoring 108 times, and topping the circuit with a .613 slugging percentage and a 1.009 OPS, en route to earning a third-place finish in the MVP voting. He continued to excel in the postseason, batting .385 against Anaheim in the ALDS, .300 against the Yankees in the ALCS, and .412 against the Cardinals in the World Series. Ramirez followed that up with an equally productive 2005 season, batting .292 and finishing among the league leaders with 45 homers, 144 RBIs, 112 runs scored, a .388 on-base percentage, and a .594 slugging percentage, earning in the process a fourth-place finish in the MVP balloting.

Despite being forced to sit out 30 games in 2006 with tendonitis in his right knee, Ramirez had another outstanding year, concluding the campaign with 35 home runs, 102 RBIs, a .321 batting average, and a league-leading .439 on-base percentage. A strained oblique limited Ramirez to 133 games the following year, causing him to finish the season with only 20 homers, 88 RBIs, and a .296 batting average. Nevertheless, he returned to top form during the postseason, helping the Red Sox win their second world championship in four years by hitting 4 home runs, knocking in 16 runs, and scoring 11 times in their 14 playoff and World Series games.

Ramirez's extraordinary offensive production often forced his teammates and Red Sox management to overlook his somewhat bizarre behavior during the team's successful run that lasted from 2004 to 2007. However, he finally wore out his welcome in 2008, when his dissatisfaction over his contract situation prompted him to behave in a manner that made it impossible for him to remain in Boston any longer. After becoming involved in a heated altercation with teammate Kevin Youkilis in the Red Sox dugout during a June 5 game at Fenway Park, Ramirez physically confronted elderly Red Sox traveling secretary Jack McCormick later in the year when the 64-year-old McCormick failed to fill the outfielder's game-day request for 16 tickets to a game in Houston. Ramirez pushed McCormick to the ground after telling him "Just do your job," prompting the Red Sox to levy a huge fine against the star outfielder. Ramirez further exacerbated his situation by failing to run out several ground balls, sitting out a pivotal contest against the Yankees on July 25, and placing a call from his cell phone while standing in left field during a pitching change at Fenway Park one day.

Left with no other alternative, the Red Sox decided to part ways with Ramirez, who they included in a three-team trade completed just prior to the trade deadline on July 31. The deal, which netted the Red Sox Pittsburgh outfielder Jason Bay, sent Ramirez to the Los Angeles Dodgers, who he subsequently helped advance to the playoffs by hitting 17 home runs, driving in 53 runs, and batting .396 over the season's final two months. Although Ramirez continued to perform well for the Dodgers over the course of the next two seasons, Major League Baseball suspended him for 50 games on May 7, 2009, for violating the Joint Drug Prevention and Treatment Program it established with the Players Association in 2004. It also surfaced that Ramirez previously tested positive for performance-enhancing drugs in 2003. However, he received no penalty for his earlier transgression since MLB had yet to institute a formal policy against steroid users at that time.

After being placed on waivers by the Dodgers late in 2010, Ramirez spent the season's final month with the Chicago White Sox. He subsequently signed with Tampa Bay as a free agent prior to the start of the ensuing campaign, but announced his retirement just five games into the season after reportedly testing positive for using a banned performance-enhancing drug in his spring training drug test. Ramirez later attempted to return to the major leagues, making brief appearances in the farm systems of the Oakland Athletics and the Texas Rangers, before retiring for good after being released by both teams. He ended his career with 555 home runs, 1,831 runs batted in, 1,544 runs scored, 2,574 hits, 547 doubles, a .312 batting average, a .411 on-base percentage, and a .585 slugging percentage. He appeared in a total of 12 All-Star games, earned 9 top-10 finishes in the league MVP voting, and won 9 Silver Sluggers. During his time in Boston, Ramirez hit 274 home runs, knocked in 868 runs, scored 743 times, amassed 1,232 hits, collected 256 doubles, batted .312, compiled a .411 on-base percentage, and posted a .588 slugging percentage. He ranks among the team's all-time leaders in home runs, RBIs, on-base percentage, slugging percentage, total bases, and extra-base hits.

RED SOX CAREER HIGHLIGHTS

Best Season

Ramirez performed brilliantly for the Red Sox in 2002 and 2006, compiling his highest on-base and slugging percentages for them those two seasons. In the first of those campaigns, he hit 33 homers, knocked in 107 runs, scored 84 times, led the league with a .349 batting average and a .450 on-base percentage, and compiled a .647 slugging percentage. Four years later, Ramirez hit 35 homers, drove in 102 runs, scored 79 others, batted .321, compiled a league-leading .439 on-base percentage, and posted a .619 slugging percentage. However, injuries forced him to miss a significant amount of playing time each year, limiting, to some degree, his overall offensive production. Ramirez had an enormously productive year in 2005, when he tied his career high by hitting 45 home runs, knocked in 144 runs, scored 112 others, batted .292, compiled a .388 on-base percentage, and posted a .594 slugging percentage. But he compiled slightly better overall numbers one year earlier, concluding the 2004 campaign with 130 RBIs, 108 runs scored, 44 doubles, a .308 batting average, a .397 on-base percentage, a career-high 348 total bases, and a league-leading 43 homers, .613 slugging percentage, and 1.009 OPS, en route to earning a third-place finish in the AL MVP voting. He continued his exceptional play in the postseason, leading the Red Sox to their first world championship in 86 years by capturing World Series MVP honors. All things considered, Ramirez had his best season for the Red Sox in 2004.

Memorable Moments/Greatest Performances

Ramirez hit two of the longest home runs in the history of Fenway Park during a 9–6 loss to Toronto on June 23, 2001. After hitting a first-inning blast that traveled 463 feet to left-center field, Ramirez homered again in the bottom of the third, with this one traveling 501 feet—just one foot less than the record 502-foot homer Ted Williams hit 55 years earlier.

Ramirez had a pair of five-hit games just a little over a month apart in 2002, collecting five safeties for the first time during a 9–4 victory over Detroit on July 16, before accomplishing the feat again during a 10–9, 10-inning victory over the Angels on August 26. In the second of the two contests, Ramirez homered twice, drove in four runs, and scored three others.

Ramirez delivered the big blow of the decisive fifth game of the 2003 ALDS, hitting a three-run, sixth-inning homer that ultimately gave the Red Sox a 4–3 win over Oakland and a spot in the ALCS. He continued his postseason heroics the following year, compiling a batting average of .350 during the playoffs and World Series, with two home runs and 11 RBIs. Ramirez's homer, four RBIs, and .412 batting average against the Cardinals in the Fall Classic earned him Series MVP honors. Ramirez had another huge postseason in 2007, hitting four home runs, knocking in 16 runs, and batting .348 in Boston's 14 games, as the Red Sox beat the Angels, Indians, and Rockies to win their second world championship in four seasons. His three-run, walk-off homer in the bottom of the ninth inning of Game 2 of the ALDS gave the Red Sox a 6–3 victory over the Angels.

NOTABLE ACHIEVEMENTS

- Hit more than 30 home runs six times, topping 40 homers on three occasions
- Knocked in more than 100 runs six times, surpassing 120 RBIs three times
- Scored more than 100 runs three times
- Batted over .300 five times, topping the .340 mark once (.349 in 2002)
- Collected more than 30 doubles six times, topping 40 two-baggers once (44 in 2004)
- Walked 100 times once (2006)
- Compiled on-base percentage in excess of .400 four times
- Posted slugging percentage in excess of .500 seven times, topping .600 mark four times
- Led AL in home runs once; batting average once; on-base percentage three times; slugging percentage once; and OPS once
- Led AL outfielders with 17 assists in 2005
- Led AL left fielders with .990 fielding percentage in 2007
- Ranks among Red Sox career leaders in home runs (6th); RBIs (7th); on-base percentage (5th); slugging percentage (3rd); OPS (3rd); total bases (10th); and extra-base hits (9th)
- Holds major-league records for most postseason home runs (29) and RBIs (78)
- Ranks third in major-league history with 21 career grand slams
- Finished in top five in AL MVP voting twice (2004 and 2005)
- Six-time Silver Slugger winner (2001–2006)
- 2004 AL Hank Aaron Award winner
- 2004 World Series MVP
- Four-time *Sporting News* All-Star selection (2001, 2002, 2004, and 2005)
- Eight-time AL All-Star
- Two-time AL champion (2004 and 2007)
- Two-time world champion (2004 and 2007)

1 4

Nomar Garciaparra

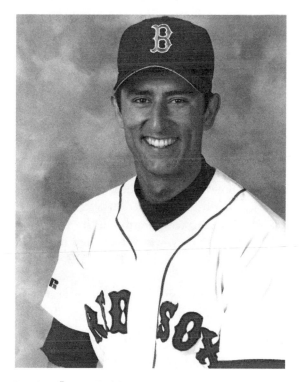

Courtesy Boston Red Sox

Nomar Garciaparra shared something of a love-hate relationship with Red Sox fans during his time in Boston, being treated very much like a hero his first few years in Beantown, before being cast as the scapegoat for the team's problems his final few seasons. Garciaparra established himself as an immediate fan favorite when he arrived in Boston by recording one of the greatest rookie seasons in Red Sox history. He followed that up with three more exceptional years, winning two batting titles and earning AL All-Star honors twice. However, after suffering through an injury-marred 2001 campaign, the hard-hitting shortstop began to draw criticism from Red Sox fans, who found fault with what they perceived to be his lack of mental and physical toughness. Nevertheless, there is little doubt that Garciaparra accomplished enough in his six full seasons with the Red Sox to earn a prominent place in these rankings. In addition to his two batting titles, Garciaparra earned five All-Star selections and five top-10 finishes in the AL MVP voting, placing second in the balloting in his sophomore campaign of 1998. He batted over .300 six times, posting a mark of .372 in 2000 that ranks as the fourth-highest single-season average in club history. Garciaparra also hit more than 30 home runs twice, knocked in more than 100 runs four times, scored more than 100 runs six times, and amassed more than 50 doubles twice, with his 56 two-baggers in 2002 representing the second-highest total ever posted by a Red Sox player.

Born in Whittier, California, on July 23, 1973, Anthony Nomar Garciaparra attended St. John Bosco High School in nearby Bellflower, where he starred in baseball and soccer, and also served as the kicker on the football team. Heavily scouted as a junior, Garciaparra subsequently received scholarship offers from several major universities, including UCLA and Georgia Tech. The Milwaukee Brewers made his decision even more difficult when they selected him in the fifth round of the 1991 amateur baseball draft. However, Garciaparra chose to temporarily put his pro career on hold and enroll at Georgia Tech University, where he ended up earning First Team All-America honors twice and playing for Team USA in the 1992 Olympic Games.

Garciaparra decided to turn pro after his junior year when the Red Sox made him the 12th overall pick of the 1994 amateur draft and offered him a bonus of $895,000 to leave school. He spent the next three years advancing through their minor-league system, finishing out the 1994 campaign at Class-A Sarasota, spending all of 1995 at Class-AA Trenton, and posting exceptional numbers in his 43 games at Triple-A Pawtucket in 1996, after tearing up his knee earlier in the season. Called up by the Red Sox for the final month of the 1996 season, Garciaparra established himself as their shortstop of the future by hitting 4 homers, driving in 16 runs, and committing only 1 error in 24 games.

Garciaparra's arrival in Boston prompted the Red Sox to move John Valentin to second base at the start of the 1997 campaign in order to make room at shortstop for the 23-year-old rookie. With the Red Sox lacking a true leadoff hitter, new manager Jimy Williams also inserted Garciaparra into the number one spot in the batting order. Garciaparra responded by putting up extraordinary numbers for a first-year player, hitting 30 home runs, driving in 98 runs, batting .306, collecting 44 doubles, stealing 22 bases, finishing second in the league with 122 runs scored and 365 total bases, and topping the circuit with 209 hits and 11 triples. Garciaparra's 98 runs batted in established a new major-league record (since broken) for most RBIs by a leadoff hitter. Meanwhile, his 30 homers established a new mark for rookie shortstops. He also excelled in the field, placing second among AL shortstops in assists, while leading all players at his position in putouts and double plays. Garciaparra's fabulous performance earned him All-Star honors, an eighth-place finish in the league MVP voting, and unanimous selection as the AL Rookie of the Year. So impressed with Garciaparra's play was Ted Williams that the latter stated in *Emperors and Idiots: The Hundred Year Rivalry between the Yankees and Red Sox, from the Very Beginning to the End of the Curse*, "He's as good a young player as anyone I've ever seen come into the big leagues. He's tremendous. One of the very best young hitters I ever saw. He's a smart kid, and he knows all about hitting."

After being moved to the middle of the batting order in 1998, Garciaparra teamed up with Mo Vaughn to give the Red Sox one of baseball's most formidable one-two punches. While Vaughn homered 40 times, knocked in 115 runs, and batted .337, Garciaparra placed among the league leaders with 35 home runs, 122 RBIs, 111 runs scored, 195 hits, 8 triples, 353 total bases, a .323 batting average, and a .584 slugging percentage, en route to earning a second-place finish in the AL MVP balloting. Unfortunately, Vaughn's departure at season's end left Garciaparra with very little protection in the Red Sox lineup the following year. The third-year shortstop found himself further handicapped by a wrist injury that plagued him throughout the season's final month. Nevertheless, he managed to hit 27 homers, knock in 104 runs, score 103, and lead the league with a .357 batting average. Garciaparra once again posted exceptional numbers in 2000, concluding the campaign with 21 home runs, 96 runs batted in, 104 runs scored, 51 doubles, and a league-leading .372 batting average, despite missing 22 games due to injury.

Garciaparra's magnificent play during the early stages of his career prompted many astute baseball men to sing his praises. In discussing the young shortstop's hitting, former Yankees star Don Mattingly stated, "He's incredibly strong and has great balance."

Veteran pitcher Aaron Sele chimed in, "What's amazing about Nomar is that, no matter what type of pitch you throw, where you throw it, or when you throw it, he can hit it and hit it hard. He reminds me of Kirby Puckett."

Jason Giambi added, "He's combined incredible physical ability with perfect mechanics—when he's going good, he doesn't miss-hit anything. He's ridiculous."

Meanwhile, Red Sox legend Johnny Pesky said, "The kid's a heck of a lot better player than I was. He comes down here every day like it's the last game he's ever going to play."

The hitting mechanics of which Giambi spoke included a number of idiosyncratic gestures that appeared quite bizarre to others. After each pitch, Garciaparra stepped out of the batter's box, followed an elaborate routine of adjusting his gloves, tapping his bat, adjusting his helmet, and stepping back into the batter's box, where he proceeded to shift his weight from one foot to the other with a series of alternating toe taps. Yet, for all the fidgeting he did between pitches, Garciaparra remained almost motionless once the pitcher began his windup, keeping his head and feet stationary, while shifting his weight slightly onto his back foot.

After four consecutive extraordinarily successful seasons, Garciaparra suffered his first setback in 2001, when a wrist injury forced him to undergo surgery in April that limited him to only 21 games over the course of the campaign. However, he returned to the Boston starting lineup by the start of 2002 to once again post big numbers. Appearing in 156 games for the first of two consecutive seasons, Garciaparra finished the year with 24 homers, 120 RBIs, 101 runs scored, a .310 batting average, 197 hits, and a league-leading 56 doubles. He followed that up in 2003 by hitting 28 home runs, driving in 105 runs, scoring 120 times, accumulating 198 hits, and batting .301.

Yet, even though Garciaparra continued to perform at an extremely high level, Red Sox fans found the precipitous drop in his batting average somewhat disappointing. They became further disenchanted with him as their frustration continued to grow from watching their team consistently finish second in the AL East to the hated Yankees and their star shortstop Derek Jeter, who they came to view as a superior team leader to Garciaparra. The negative feelings toward Garciaparra intensified after he sat out a crucial game at Yankee Stadium in the summer of 2003—one in which Jeter dove headfirst into the stands for a foul ball. To many, Jeter's effort and Garciaparra's absence from the Red Sox lineup summed up the difference between the two players, and the two teams.

After suffering the indignity of watching the Red Sox make a concerted effort to acquire Alex Rodriguez and pursue trade talks that involved himself during the subsequent offseason, Garciaparra missed the first third of the 2004 campaign with a sore Achilles' heel. Adding insult to injury, the Boston media criticized him for what it perceived to be his lack of toughness when he returned to the team. Eligible to become a free agent at season's end, Garciaparra seemed unlikely to return to Boston when his contract expired. A three-game sweep at the hands of the Yankees at the end of June hastened his departure, with the Red Sox electing to send him to the Chicago Cubs as part of a four-team deal they completed just prior to the July 31 trade deadline that netted them first baseman Doug Mientkiewicz and shortstop Orlando Cabrera. Before he left for the Windy City, though, Garciaparra expressed his appreciation to Red Sox fans in a speech to the media.

Plagued by injuries his entire time with the Cubs, Garciaparra remained in Chicago until the end of 2005, when he signed as a free agent with the Dodgers. He spent the next three years in Los Angeles, playing his best ball for the Dodgers in 2006, when he made the All-Star team as a first baseman by hitting 20 homers, knocking in 93 runs, and batting .303. After becoming a free agent again at the end of 2008, Garciaparra signed with the A's, with whom he spent his final season serving primarily as a backup infielder and part-time DH. Granted free agency at season's end, he signed a one-day contract with the Red Sox on March 10, 2010, enabling him to end his career as a member of the team. Garciaparra retired with a lifetime batting average of .313, 229 home runs, 936 RBIs, 927 runs scored, 1,747 hits, a .361 on-base percentage, and a .521 slugging percentage. While playing for the Red Sox, he hit 178 home runs, knocked in 690 runs, scored 709, accumulated 1,281 hits, batted .323, compiled a .370 on-base percentage, and posted a .553 slugging percentage.

Following his retirement, Garciaparra became an analyst at ESPN, appearing on that station's *Baseball Tonight* program and serving as one of the lead analysts on ESPN's coverage of the College World Series. He later joined the television broadcasting crew of the Los Angeles Dodgers, where he has served as a color commentator since 2014.

RED SOX CAREER HIGHLIGHTS

Best Season

Garciaparra performed brilliantly in his rookie campaign of 1997, finishing either first or second in the American League in four offensive categories. In addition to setting new single-season major-league records for most RBIs (98) by a leadoff hitter and most home runs (30) by a rookie shortstop, he broke a couple of long-standing Red Sox rookie records. Garciaparra's league-leading 209 hits established a new mark for Red Sox rookies, surpassing the total of 205 safeties Johnny Pesky posted in 1942. His 365 total

Courtesy Boston Red Sox

bases also eclipsed the mark of 344 that Ted Williams compiled in his rookie year of 1939. Garciaparra also became the first Red Sox player since Jackie Jensen in 1956 to reach double-digits in doubles (44), triples (11), home runs, and stolen bases (22). However, Garciaparra struck out 92 times and walked only 35 times, leaving him with an on-base percentage of .342—a rather mediocre figure for a leadoff hitter. He also posted an OPS of .875 that ranked well below the marks he compiled in some of his other outstanding seasons.

Although Garciaparra scored fewer runs (111) and collected fewer hits (195) in 1998, he posted slightly better overall numbers, concluding the campaign with 35 homers, 122 RBIs, a .323 batting average, a .362 on-base percentage, and an OPS of .946. Remarkably consistent over the course of the season, Garciaparra batted .324 on the road, .322 at home, .320 against lefties, and .324 against righties. Those are the figures that prompted the voters to place him second in the AL MVP balloting.

Garciaparra likely would have compiled the best numbers of his career in 1999 had his performance not been hampered by a wrist injury during the season's final month. Yet he still managed to hit 27 homers, drive in 104 runs, score 103 times, lead the league with a .357 batting average, and post an OPS of 1.022. As things stand, though, Garciaparra had a slightly better year in 2000, concluding the campaign with 21 home runs, 96 RBIs, 104 runs scored, 197 hits, 51 doubles, and career-high marks in walks (61), batting average (.372), on-base percentage (.434), and OPS (1.033). All things considered, Garciaparra had his finest all-around season in 2000.

Memorable Moments/Greatest Performances

Garciaparra put together a number of notable hitting streaks during his time in Boston, establishing an AL rookie record in 1997 by hitting safely in 30 consecutive games, from July 26 to August 29. He also hit safely in 24 straight games in 1998 and 26 consecutive games in 2003.

Garciaparra also had several memorable days at the plate for the Red Sox, with one of those coming on July 16, 1998, when he went 4 for 4, with a homer, two doubles, five RBIs, and three runs scored during a 15–5 win over the Indians. Nearly five years later, on June 21, 2003, he tied a team record by collecting six hits in one game—a 6–5 loss to Philadelphia in 13 innings.

Garciaparra homered three times in one game on two occasions, accomplishing the feat for the first time on May 10, 1999, when he had the most productive day of his career. During a 12–4 win over Seattle, Garciaparra drove in 10 runs, with two grand slams and a two-run homer, becoming in the process the first Red Sox player since Rudy York in 1946 to homer twice in the same game with the bases loaded. Garciaparra further distinguished himself by hitting two of his homers in the same inning, en route to establishing a new major-league record by hitting three home runs in two consecutive innings. Garciaparra had another huge day on July 23, 2002, when he celebrated his 29th birthday by hitting three home runs and driving in eight runs during a 22–4 victory over Tampa Bay in the first game of a day-night doubleheader.

An exceptional postseason player throughout his career, Garciaparra performed particularly well in the 1998 and 1999 playoffs. Although the Red Sox lost the 1998 ALDS to Cleveland in four games, Garciaparra hit three homers, drove in 11 runs, and batted .333. After batting .417, with two homers and four RBIs against the Indians in the 1999 ALDS, Garciaparra homered twice, knocked in five runs, and batted .400 in a losing effort against the Yankees in the ALCS.

NOTABLE ACHIEVEMENTS

- Hit more than 30 home runs twice
- Knocked in more than 100 runs six times, surpassing 120 RBIs twice
- Scored more than 100 runs six times, topping 120 runs scored twice
- Batted over .300 six times, topping the .350 mark twice
- Surpassed 200 hits once (209 in 1997)
- Finished in double-digits in triples twice
- Surpassed 30 doubles six times, surpassing 40 mark four times, and 50 mark twice
- Stole more than 20 bases once (22 in 1997)
- Compiled on-base percentage in excess of .400 twice
- Posted slugging percentage in excess of .500 six times, compiling mark of .603 in 1999
- Led AL in batting average twice; hits once; triples once; and doubles once
- Led AL shortstops in putouts once and double plays once
- Ranks among Red Sox career leaders in: batting average (4th); slugging percentage (5th); and OPS (6th)
- Ranks among Red Sox career leaders in batting average (4th); slugging percentage (5th); OPS (6th); and extra-base hits (10th)
- Holds major-league record for most home runs (3) in consecutive innings of one game
- Holds major-league record for most home runs by a rookie shortstop (30)
- Holds Red Sox rookie records for most hits (209) and most total bases (365)
- Hit three home runs in one game twice (vs. Seattle Mariners on May 10, 1999 & vs. Tampa Bay Rays on July 23, 2002).
- 1997 AL Rookie of the Year
- Finished second in 1998 AL MVP voting
- 1997 Silver Slugger winner
- Two-time *Sporting News* All-Star selection (1997 and 1999)
- Five-time AL All-Star

1 5

Joe Cronin

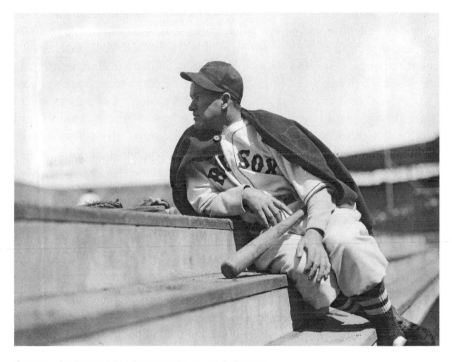

Courtesy Boston Public Library, Leslie Jones Collection

Ironically dealt to the Red Sox from the Washington Senators by his own uncle-in-law, Joe Cronin subsequently spent the next 25 years of his Hall of Fame career in Boston. Doubling as Red Sox player/manager from 1935 to 1944, the star shortstop assumed a less active role after he announced his retirement early in 1945, choosing instead to pilot the team strictly from the dugout. Cronin remained Red Sox manager until he succeeded Eddie Collins as the team's general manager at the conclusion of the 1947 campaign.

He continued in that post through mid-January 1959, when he was elected president of the American League, a position he held for the next 15 years. Although Cronin did a creditable job as Boston's manager and general manager, he made his greatest impact on the field, earning AL All-Star honors five times and two top-10 finishes in the league MVP voting, en route to helping the Red Sox finish second in the standings in three of his seven years as their starting shortstop.

Born in the Excelsior district of San Francisco on October 12, 1906, Joseph Edward Cronin attended nearby Sacred Heart Cathedral High School, from which he graduated in 1924. After working briefly as a bank clerk, the 18-year-old Cronin signed a free agent contract with the Pittsburgh Pirates the following year. Slow and clumsy when he first arrived in Pittsburgh in 1926, Cronin spent most of the next two seasons bouncing back and forth between the Pirates bench and the team's minor-league affiliate in Kansas City. He received his first big break when Washington Senators scout Joe Engel saw him playing shortstop at Kansas City. Engel later said, "I knew I was watching a great player. I bought Cronin at a time he was hitting .221. When I told Clark Griffith [owner of the Washington Senators] what I had done, he screamed, 'You paid $7,500 for that bum? Well, you didn't buy him for me. You bought him for yourself. He's not my ballplayer—he's yours. You keep him and don't either you or Cronin show up at the ballpark.'"

Griffith eventually had a change of heart, allowing Cronin to finally join the Senators midway through the 1928 campaign. Assuming the team's starting shortstop job during the season's second half, Cronin batted a mere .242 and committed 16 errors in 63 games. The 22-year-old shortstop's defensive struggles continued the following season when he committed a league-leading 62 miscues. Yet Cronin showed promise at the plate, improving his batting average to .281.

The right-handed hitting Cronin had his breakout season in 1930, batting .346 and finishing among the league leaders with 126 runs batted in, 127 runs scored, 203 hits, and 17 stolen bases. Cronin also improved in the field, reducing his error total to 35, while leading all American League shortstops in assists and putouts. He followed that up with four more extremely productive seasons for the Senators, knocking in more than 100 runs each year, batting over .300 three times, and scoring more than 100 runs once, en route to earning All-Star honors twice and a top-10 finish in the AL MVP voting on three occasions. Cronin's role in Washington expanded in 1933, when he became the team's player/manager. The star shortstop ended up leading the Senators to the American League pennant by batting .309, driving in 118 runs, scoring 89, and topping the circuit with 45 doubles. Only Jimmie Foxx's Triple Crown performance for Philadelphia prevented Cronin from capturing league MVP honors. In addition to finishing second to Foxx in the MVP balloting, Cronin made the first of his seven All-Star game appearances at shortstop for the American League.

Early in 1934, Washington owner Clark Griffith (the same man who once called Cronin a "bum") introduced his young manager to his niece, Mildred Robertson, then a club secretary. Cronin and Robertson were married later that year, which turned out to be the shortstop's final one in Washington. In an ironic twist, Griffith sold his new nephew to the Red Sox for the then-enormous sum of $225,000 at the end of the 1934 season. Yet, even though he parted ways with his newest family member, Griffith arranged for Boston's new player/manager to receive a five-year contract good for $50,000 per year.

Cronin enjoyed playing in his new surroundings, finding Fenway Park's "Green Monster" in left field far more inviting than Griffith Stadium's distant outfield fences. After hitting only 11 home runs in his first two seasons with the Red Sox, Cronin learned how to take better advantage of his new home ballpark's dimensions by becoming more of a pull hitter. Cronin, who never hit more than 13 home runs in any of his seven years with the Senators, hit no fewer than 16 homers from 1937 to 1941. He also accumulated more than 30 doubles in each of those five seasons, batted over .300 four times, knocked in more than 100 runs three times, and scored more than 100 runs twice. After hitting 18 home runs, driving in 110 runs, scoring 102, collecting 40 doubles, and batting .307 in 1937, Cronin hit 17 homers, knocked in 94 runs, scored 98 others, batted .325, and led the league with 51 doubles the following year. He finished seventh in the AL MVP voting both years. Cronin subsequently posted more than 100 RBIs in both 1939 and 1940, also hitting a career-high 24 home runs in the second of those campaigns.

After batting .311, hitting 16 homers, and knocking in 95 runs in 1941, the 35-year-old Cronin took himself out of the starting lineup the following year to make room at shortstop for young Johnny Pesky. Cronin remained an extremely effective bench player for the Red Sox until early in 1945, when he broke his leg, bringing an end to his playing career. Cronin retired from the game with 170 home runs, 1,424 runs batted in, 1,233 runs scored, 2,285 hits, 515 doubles, a .301 lifetime batting average, a .390 on-base percentage, and a .468 slugging percentage. As a member of the Red Sox, Cronin hit 119 homers, knocked in 737 runs, scored 645, collected 1,168 hits, amassed 270 doubles, batted an even .300, compiled a .394 on-base percentage, and posted a .484 slugging percentage.

Serving his team for the first time solely as a manager, Cronin piloted the Red Sox to the American League pennant in 1946, although they ended up losing the World Series to the St. Louis Cardinals in seven games. He moved into the Boston front office two years later, spending the next 11 years running the team as its general manager, and being elected to the Hall of Fame primarily on the merits of his playing career in 1956. Cronin drew considerable criticism during his tenure as Red Sox GM for his apparent lack of interest in integrating the team (he once passed on signing a young Willie Mays, and he never traded for an African American player). The failure of the Red Sox to keep up with the times led to a slow decline in their performance during the 1950s, one that continued well after Cronin left Boston at the end of the 1958 campaign to assume the duties of American League president. (Pumpsie Green coincidentally became the first African American to wear a Red Sox uniform six months after Cronin relinquished his position as club GM.)

Cronin remained AL president for 15 years, presiding over the league's expansion from 8 to 10 teams in 1960, then to 12 teams in 1969, during his two terms in office. In his final year as president, he blocked George Steinbrenner's attempt to lure Dick Williams away from Oakland to be his manager, while simultaneously allowing the Tigers to sign Ralph Houk away from Steinbrenner's Yankees.

After being succeeded as American League president by Lee MacPhail in 1973, Cronin retired to Osterville, Massachusetts, where he spent the next 11 years before passing away at the age of 77 on September 7, 1984.

The many hats Joe Cronin wore during his half-century in baseball have obscured to some extent the degree to which he excelled as a ballplayer. Cronin posted one of the highest career slugging percentages of any shortstop in history, with his 170 home runs surpassing the total compiled by any other player at his position during the first half of the 20th century. Cronin's 1,424 runs batted in and 515 doubles also placed him second only to Pittsburgh Pirates legend Honus Wagner among shortstops during that period.

Longtime Philadelphia Athletics owner and manager Connie Mack once expressed his appreciation for Cronin's playing ability by offering the following response to a question about the shortstop: "Oh my yes, Joe is the best there is in the clutch. With a man on third and one out, I'd rather have Cronin hitting for me than anybody I've ever seen."

RED SOX CAREER HIGHLIGHTS

Best Season

It could certainly be argued that Cronin had his best season for the Red Sox in 1940, since he hit more home runs (24), knocked in more runs (111), and scored more times (104) than in any other year he played in Boston. He also posted a solid .285 batting average, compiled a .380 on-base percentage, and concluded the campaign with a .502 slugging percentage. Yet, even though Cronin hit fewer homers (17), drove in less runs (94), and scored fewer times (98) in 1938, he compiled better overall numbers. In addition to leading the American League with a career-high 51 doubles, Cronin batted .325 and established career highs with 91 walks, a .428 on-base percentage, and a .536 slugging percentage. His OPS of .964 proved to be the highest mark he posted in any of his 20 major-league seasons.

Memorable Moments/Greatest Performances

On May 30, 1938, Cronin squared off against New York Yankees outfielder Jake Powell in one of baseball's more infamous brawls. During the second game of a doubleheader loss to the Yankees at Yankee Stadium, Red Sox pitcher Archie McKain hit Powell in the stomach with a pitch. Powell attempted to exact a measure of revenge against the Boston hurler by charging the mound. However, Cronin intercepted him before he reached McKain, after which he and Powell spent the next two or three minutes slugging it out. After being ejected from the game, Cronin and Powell continued to battle one another in the area beneath the stands, before finally being separated by Yankee players. The league subsequently fined and suspended both players for ten days.

The following year, on July 9, 1939, Cronin helped the Red Sox complete a five-game sweep of the Yankees by driving in runs in both ends of a doubleheader played at Yankee Stadium. By knocking in runs in the 4–3 and 5–3 Red Sox wins, Cronin established a new team record by collecting at least one RBI in 12 straight games.

Cronin had one of his biggest games as a member of the Red Sox on August 2, 1940, leading his team to a 12–9 win over the Tigers by going 4 for 5, hitting for the cycle, and driving in four runs. He had another huge day after he became a part-time player later in his career, hitting a pinch-hit three-run homer in both ends of a doubleheader against the St. Louis Browns on June 17, 1943. Just two nights earlier, Cronin had hit a three-run pinch-hit home run against Philadelphia, giving him three homers in his last four at-bats. He concluded the campaign with 18 hits in 43 pinch-hit appearances, including an AL record five pinch-hit home runs.

Courtesy Boston Public Library, Leslie Jones Collection

NOTABLE ACHIEVEMENTS

- Hit more than 20 home runs once (24 in 1940)
- Knocked in more than 100 runs three times
- Scored more than 100 runs twice
- Batted over .300 six times
- Finished in double-digits in triples once (14 in 1935)
- Accumulated more than 30 doubles six times, surpassing the 40 mark twice and the 50 mark once
- Compiled on-base percentage in excess of .400 five times
- Posted slugging percentage in excess of .500 four times
- Led AL with 51 doubles in 1938
- Ranks eighth in Red Sox history with career on-base percentage of .394
- Hit for cycle vs. Detroit Tigers on August 2, 1940
- Two-time *Sporting News* All-Star selection (1938 and 1939)
- Five-time AL All-Star
- Elected to Baseball Hall of Fame by members of BBWAA in 1956

Babe Ruth

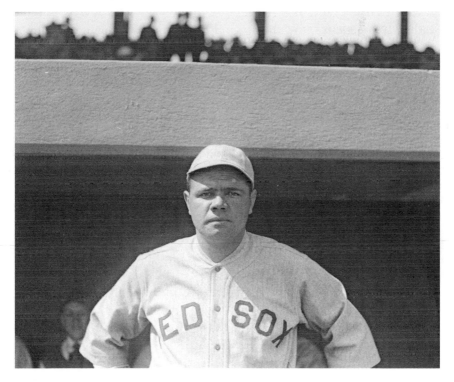

Courtesy Library of Congress

Babe Ruth's name generally elicits thoughts of prodigious slugging and over-whelming offensive production unmatched by any other player in baseball history. Ruth dominated his era from an offensive standpoint more than anyone else who ever played the game. En route to establishing himself as baseball's all-time home run king—a distinction he held for more than half a century—Ruth became the first player to surpass 30, 40, 50, and 60 home runs in one season. He also became the first player to reach the 200, 300, 400, 500, 600, and 700 career home run plateaus. Ruth set numerous other records along the way, including single-season marks for most runs scored, most walks, and highest slugging percentage, and career marks for most walks and highest slugging percentage. Most people also tend to associate Ruth with the New York Yankees, the team he played for when he set all those records. However, prior to joining the Yankees in 1920, Ruth spent six years in Boston, establishing himself during that time as arguably the best left-handed pitcher in baseball. Working almost exclusively as a starting pitcher from 1915 to 1917, Ruth posted an overall record of 65–33, while leading all American League hurlers in ERA, complete games, and shutouts once each. Only the "Bambino's" unprecedented slugging ability prompted the Red Sox to convert him into an outfielder, thereby preventing him from going down as one of the greatest left-handed pitchers ever to perform in the junior circuit. And only the lack of foresight displayed by Red Sox ownership likely prevented Ruth from creating the same dynasty in Boston that he eventually fashioned in New York. Still, Ruth managed to lead the Red Sox to three American League pennants and three world championships during his relatively brief stay in Beantown, earning him a prominent place in these rankings.

Born in Baltimore, Maryland, on February 6, 1895, George Herman Ruth proved to be completely incorrigible while growing up on the streets of Baltimore, spending much of his time in St. Mary's Industrial School for repeatedly running afoul of the law. Raised primarily by his father, a saloon-keeper who frequently took to beating him, Ruth entered St. Mary's at an early age after his parents grew increasingly weary of trying to keep him out of trouble. It was at the boys' home that the gangly and awkward-looking young man learned to harness his great energy and play baseball. Convinced that Ruth had the ability to eventually succeed at the major-league level, Brother Gilbert—the institution's athletic director—released him in 1912 so that he could pitch for the Baltimore Orioles of the International League, after first persuading Baltimore's owner-manager Jack Dunn to become the 17-year-old's guardian. The nickname "Babe" soon became affixed to the rambunctious teenager, who spent the next two years pitching for the Orioles before the Red Sox purchased his contract in 1914. The 19-year-old left-hander made his major-league debut with the team later that year, appearing in four games and winning two of his three decisions. Ruth became a regular member of Boston's starting rotation the following year, compiling a record of 18–8 and an outstanding 2.44 earned run average for the eventual world champions.

Ruth developed into arguably the best left-handed pitcher in baseball in 1916, winning 23 games, completing 23 of his 40 starts, throwing 324 innings, and leading the league with a 1.75 ERA and 9 shutouts. With the Red Sox winning the American League pennant, Ruth subsequently helped them defeat Brooklyn in the World Series by allowing just one run and six hits during a 14-inning, 2–1 complete-game victory in his only start. Ruth had another sensational season in 1917, posting a 2.01 ERA and a league-leading 35 complete games. However, the Babe began to demonstrate over the course of that 1917 campaign that he also handled himself quite well in the batter's box, compiling a .325 batting average in his 123 at-bats.

The Red Sox subsequently decided to expand Ruth's role as a hitter the following year, reducing his number of mound appearances and placing him in the outfield on those days he didn't pitch. Ruth responded by excelling in both areas. In addition to winning 13 of his 20 decisions and compiling an outstanding 2.22 ERA, he batted .300 and led the league with 11 home runs, even though he totaled only 317 official plate appearances. Ruth then helped the Red Sox capture their third World Series in four seasons by defeating Chicago twice in the Fall Classic, en route to extending his consecutive scoreless innings streak in World Series play to 29 ⅔ innings—a mark that stood for 43 years. Although Ruth continued to pitch sporadically in 1919, he spent most of his time in the outfield, batting .322 and leading the American League with 29 home runs, 114 runs batted in, 103 runs scored, a .456 on-base percentage, and a .657 slugging percentage. Ruth's 29 homers established a new major-league record.

Ruth's extraordinary slugging and charismatic personality made him baseball's most popular and recognizable figure, prompting him to demand that Red Sox owner Harry Frazee double his salary to $40,000. However, Frazee, a theatrical producer with many outstanding debts, refused to meet his disgruntled outfielder's demands. More concerned with financing a Broadway show called *No, No, Nanette*, Frazee changed the landscape of baseball forever when he sold Ruth to the New York Yankees for $100,000 in December of 1919.

While it subsequently took the Red Sox another 86 years to win a World Series, Ruth helped the Yankees create baseball's greatest dynasty. Along the way, the "Sultan of Swat" established several records, some of which have yet to be broken. Ruth retired as Major League Baseball's all-time leader in home runs (714) and runs batted in (2,220). He scored 2,174 runs, batted .342, amassed 2,873 hits, walked 2,062 times, and compiled a .474 on-base percentage. Ruth's .690 career slugging percentage remains the highest in baseball history. He surpassed 50 homers on four occasions, with his 60 home runs in 1927 remaining the highest single-season total in major-league history for 34 years. Ruth led the Yankees to seven pennants and four world championships, with his incredible offensive production and larger-than-life personality making him the most recognizable figure in American sports history.

Yet, Ruth's rise to fame began in Boston, and the game's greatest slugger always retained a soft spot in his heart for pitching. Describing years later the feeling he got whenever he took the mound, Ruth stated in *Giants of Baseball*, "As soon as I got out there I felt a strange relationship with the pitcher's mound. It was as if I'd been born out there. Pitching just felt like the most natural thing in the world. Striking out batters was easy."

Meanwhile, legendary manager Leo Durocher, who served as a backup infielder on the Yankees in 1928 and 1929, later said, "There's no question about it, Babe Ruth was the greatest instinctive baseball player who ever lived. He was a great hitter, and he would have been a great pitcher."

Courtesy Library
of Congress

RED SOX CAREER HIGHLIGHTS

Best Season

Even though Ruth pitched brilliantly in 1917 as well, winning 24 games, compiling a 2.01 ERA, throwing 326 innings, and tossing a league-leading 35 complete games, he had his best season on the mound one year earlier. In addition to going 23–12 with 23 complete games and 324 innings pitched in 1916, Ruth led all AL hurlers with a 1.75 ERA and nine shutouts, with the latter mark remaining a league record for lefties until Ron Guidry matched it in 1978. At one point during the season, Ruth tossed 24 consecutive scoreless innings. He also didn't allow the opposition a single home run all year.

After being moved to the outfield prior to the start of the 1919 campaign, Ruth had easily his finest offensive season in Boston, batting .322 and leading the league with 29 home runs, 114 RBIs, 103 runs scored, 284 total bases, a .456 on-base percentage, and a .657 slugging percentage. He also managed to post a record of 9–5 in his 17 mound appearances.

Yet, a strong case could be made that Ruth had his finest all-around season for the Red Sox in 1918. Completing 18 of his 19 starts on the mound, Ruth went 13–7 with a 2.22 ERA. He also played the field in 72 games, concluding the campaign with 66 RBIs, 50 runs scored, 11 triples, 26 doubles, a .300 batting average, a .411 on-base percentage, and a league-leading .555 slugging percentage and 11 home runs.

Memorable Moments/Greatest Performances

During a 4–2 win over the St. Louis Browns on July 21, 1915, Ruth put on display for all to see his tremendous all-around ability. In addition to allowing only five hits and two unearned runs to the Browns, Ruth went four for four, with a home run, two doubles, and three RBIs.

Ruth experienced considerable success in his head-to-head matchups with Washington Senators pitching great Walter Johnson, posting six victories against him before suffering his first defeat. On August 15, 1916, Ruth improved his record to 3–0 against the "Big Train" by outdueling him 1–0 in 13 innings. The following year, on May 7, Ruth again outpitched Johnson, allowing just two singles during a 1–0 Red Sox victory over the Senators. The Babe also knocked in the game's only run with an eighth-inning sacrifice fly.

A little over two months later, on July 11, 1917, Ruth defeated the Detroit Tigers by a score of 1–0, with only Donie Bush's eighth-inning infield single preventing him from tossing a no-hitter. Ruth, who finished the contest by striking out Bobby Veach, Sam Crawford, and Ty Cobb in the bottom of the ninth inning, later called this game his greatest thrill.

Ruth had his greatest day at the plate for the Red Sox on September 5, 1919, going 5 for 6 with a homer, double, four RBIs, and three runs scored during a 15–7 win over the Athletics. Two weeks later, on September 20, he helped the Red Sox celebrate "Babe Ruth Day" at Fenway Park by hitting his 27th home run of the year. The blow tied him with Ned Williamson (1884) for the most home runs in a season in major-league history.

Ruth's extraordinary pitching performances in the 1916 and 1918 World Series also rank among his greatest achievements as a member of the Red Sox. On October 9, 1916, Ruth began his streak of 29 ⅔ consecutive scoreless innings in postseason play by keeping the Brooklyn Robins off the scoreboard over the final 13 frames of a 14-inning, 2–1 Red Sox victory in Game 2 of the Fall Classic. After allowing an inside-the-park home run in the first inning, Ruth surrendered only five more hits, going the distance in his lone start in the series. He continued his exceptional pitching in the 1918 series, winning both his starts against the Chicago Cubs, compiling a 1.06 ERA, tossing a complete-game shutout, and allowing just 13 hits in 17 innings of work. In his three World Series starts with the Red Sox, Ruth compiled a record of 3–0 and a miniscule 0.87 ERA. He threw two complete games and surrendered only 19 hits in 31 innings of work.

NOTABLE ACHIEVEMENTS

- Won more than 20 games twice
- Compiled ERA below 2.00 once (1.75 in 1916)
- Completed more than 20 games twice, surpassing the 30 mark once (35 in 1917)
- Threw more than 300 innings twice
- Led all AL pitchers in ERA once; complete games once; shutouts once; and starts once
- Set World Series record that stood for 43 years by throwing 29 ⅔ consecutive scoreless innings
- Ranks among Red Sox all-time leaders in ERA (5th); winning percentage (5th); complete games (8th); and shutouts (10th)
- Hit more than 20 home runs once (29 in 1919)
- Knocked in more than 100 runs once (114 in 1919)

- Scored more than 100 runs once (103 in 1919)
- Batted over .300 four times
- Finished in double-digits in triples twice
- Drew more than 100 bases on balls once (101 in 1919)
- Compiled on-base percentage in excess of .400 twice
- Posted slugging percentage in excess of .600 once (.657 in 1919)
- Led AL in home runs twice; RBIs once; runs scored once; total bases once; on-base percentage once; and slugging percentage twice
- Set new major-league record with 29 home runs in 1919
- Member of Major League Baseball's All-Century Team
- First on *Sporting News*'s 1999 list of Baseball's 100 Greatest Players
- Three-time AL champion
- Three-time world champion
- Elected to Baseball Hall of Fame by members of BBWAA in 1936

17

Mo Vaughn

Courtesy Boston Red Sox

Extremely popular during his time in Boston, Mo Vaughn gave the Red Sox a powerful bat in the middle of their lineup and an equally powerful voice in their clubhouse in his eight years with the club. Playing for mostly mediocre Red Sox teams from 1991 to 1998, Vaughn hit more than 35 home runs and knocked in more than 100 runs four times each, while also compiling a batting average in excess of .300 on five separate occasions.

The American League's Most Valuable Player in 1995, Vaughn led a team that finished seven games under .500 the previous season to the AL East title by finishing first in the junior circuit in RBIs and placing among the leaders in five other offensive categories as well. Vaughn posted even better numbers the following year, en route to earning a fifth-place finish in the league MVP voting. All the while, the man nicknamed "Hit Dog" continued to exert a tremendous amount of influence on his teammates, constantly exhorting them to do their best, and challenging them when he felt he needed to do so.

Born in Norwalk, Connecticut, on December 15, 1967, Maurice Samuel Vaughn grew up in Dutchess County, New York, where he attended and played baseball for Trinity-Pawling High School. After graduating from Trinity, Vaughn enrolled at Seton Hall University in South Orange, New Jersey, where he spent the next three years starring for the school's baseball team, playing alongside future Red Sox teammate John Valentin. After being named MVP of the 1987 Big East Conference Baseball Tournament, Vaughn garnered 1988 playoff MVP honors while playing for the Wareham Gatemen in the Cape League. He began his pro career the following year after the Red Sox selected him in the first round of the 1989 amateur draft, with the 23rd overall pick.

Vaughn spent less than two full seasons in the minor leagues before making his debut with the Red Sox on June 27, 1991. Seeing significant playing time over the season's final three months, the 23-year-old rookie hit 4 homers, drove in 32 runs, and batted .260 in 74 games. Despite struggling at the plate throughout much of the ensuing campaign, Vaughn gradually established himself as Boston's starting first baseman, finishing the year with 13 homers, 57 RBIs, and a .234 batting average, in 113 games and just over 400 plate appearances.

Vaughn began to mature as a hitter in 1993, when, appearing in all but 10 of Boston's 162 games, he batted .297 and led the team with 29 home runs, 101 RBIs, 86 runs scored, a .390 on-base percentage, and a .525 slugging percentage. He posted outstanding numbers again the following year, concluding the strike-shortened 1994 campaign with 26 homers, 82 RBIs, and a .310 batting average.

With the Red Sox having failed to make the playoffs in each of the four previous years, they desperately needed a leader heading into 1995. While Kevin Kennedy replaced Butch Hobson as manager, Vaughn assumed the mantle of leadership both on the field and in the clubhouse. Establishing himself as one of the American League's most feared batsmen, the 6'1", 235-pound Vaughn hit 39 home runs, scored 98 runs, batted an even

.300, and topped the circuit with 126 runs batted in. Equally important, he became the club's vocal and inspirational leader, providing direction to his teammates, and helping them air out their personal differences. Vaughn's powerful presence helped lead the Red Sox to a record of 86–58 and a first-place finish in the AL East. Although Cleveland's Albert Belle posted more impressive individual statistics over the course of the campaign, the members of the BBWAA acknowledged the overall contributions Vaughn made to his team by naming him the league's Most Valuable Player in an extremely close vote. Vaughn had another big year in 1996, placing among the league leaders with 44 home runs, 143 RBIs, 118 runs scored, 207 hits, and a .326 batting average.

Vaughn's massive frame and fierce countenance made him one of the American League's most intimidating batters. Known for crowding the plate, he stood so close to the dish that his front elbow often appeared to be hovering in the strike zone, practically daring opposing pitchers to throw inside to him. With many hurlers choosing to work him outside instead, Vaughn took advantage by using his left-handed uppercut swing to consistently drive balls off, and over, the "Green Monster" in left field.

In addition to his tremendous offensive production, Vaughn became a fan favorite in Boston due to his willingness to give back to his community and heavy involvement with charitable causes. In March of 1994, he hit a home run in Anaheim, California, for 11-year-old Boston cancer patient Jason Leader. When asked about his kind gesture, Vaughn told a *Forbes* reporter, "All I was doing was a little bit for a young man. I hope it gave him just a little more strength to push on, to keep going." Vaughn also spent a considerable amount of time meeting with groups of inner-city schoolchildren, urging them to stay in school. He further gave of himself by using the proceeds from formal autograph signings to fund cultural outings for poor children.

Vaughn continued his assault on American League pitching in 1997, batting .315, hitting 35 homers, driving in 96 runs, and scoring 91 others, despite missing 21 games after undergoing arthroscopic surgery to repair torn cartilage in his left knee. He followed that up by hitting 40 home runs, knocking in 115 runs, scoring 107 times, and finishing second in the league with a career-high .337 batting average in 1998, en route to earning a fourth-place finish in the MVP balloting.

Unfortunately, the 1998 campaign ended up being Vaughn's final one in Boston. In spite of the tremendous popularity he enjoyed while playing for the Red Sox, the slugging first baseman began to encounter problems in his dealings with Boston management and the local media in his final two years in Beantown. Always one to speak his mind, Vaughn stated on numerous occasions that he felt the conservative Red Sox administration "did not want him around." He also sparred verbally with general manager Dan Duquette and noted *Boston Globe* columnist Will McDonough. Vaughn's situation in Boston grew increasingly tenuous when he received negative publicity for his involvement in a pair of incidents involving strip clubs; first, for allegedly punching a man in the mouth outside of one such club in downtown Cleveland, and, later, for crashing his truck while returning home from a strip club in Providence, Rhode Island. Weary of the constant bickering, the Red Sox made little effort to re-sign Vaughn when he became a free agent at the conclusion of the 1998 campaign, allowing him to sign a six-year $80 million deal with the Anaheim Angels shortly after Cleveland defeated the Red Sox in four games in the ALDS.

Despite beginning his career in Anaheim inauspiciously by badly spraining his ankle when he fell down the visitor's dugout steps attempting to catch a foul pop on his first play of his first game with the Angels, Vaughn hit well in his first two years on the West Coast. After hitting 33 homers, driving in 108 runs, and batting .281 in 1999, he homered 36 times, knocked in 117 runs, scored 93, and batted .272 in the first year of the new millennium. However, a ruptured tendon in his left arm subsequently forced Vaughn to undergo offseason surgery, sidelining him for the entire 2001 campaign. Desperate for a powerful bat in the middle of their lineup, the New York Mets decided to take a chance on Vaughn, acquiring him from the Angels for pitcher Kevin Appier prior to the 2002 season.

Although Vaughn hit 26 homers and knocked in 72 runs in his first year with the Mets, he proved to be a total bust in New York. Tipping the scales at close to 300 pounds throughout most of his tenure with the ball club, Vaughn found his massive frame too much for his aching knees to support. After hitting just .190 in his first 27 games of 2003, Vaughn elected to announce his retirement, concluding his career with 328 home runs, 1,064 RBIs, 861 runs scored, 1,620 hits, a .293 batting average, a .383 on-base percentage, and a .523 slugging percentage. In his eight years with the Red Sox, Vaughn hit 230 home runs, knocked in 752 runs, scored 628, accumulated 1,165 hits, batted .304, compiled a .394 on-base percentage, and posted a .542 slugging percentage.

Following his retirement, Vaughn continued his involvement with worthy causes, purchasing and operating OMNI New York LLC, which has bought and rehabilitated more than 1,000 units of distressed housing in the New York metropolitan area. His company is also involved in projects

Courtesy Boston Red Sox

in Cheyenne, Miami, and Las Vegas and has expressed an interest in the Boston area as well. Vaughn's name gained national attention again in 2007, when it appeared in the Mitchell Report, which revealed that he had purchased HGH in 2001, apparently in an attempt to speed up the recovery process for his injured arm.

RED SOX CAREER HIGHLIGHTS

Best Season

Vaughn had a big year in 1995, capturing AL MVP honors by hitting 39 home runs, leading the league with 126 RBIs, scoring 98 runs, batting .300, compiling a .388 on-base percentage, and posting a .575 slugging percentage. However, he put up even better numbers the following season, when he batted .326 and established career highs with 44 homers, 143 runs batted in, 118 runs scored, 207 hits, 370 total bases, a .420 on-base percentage, and a 1.003 OPS. Vaughn's 44 home runs and 207 hits made him the first major-league player since Jim Rice in 1978 to surpass 40 homers and 200 hits in the same season.

Memorable Moments/Greatest Performances

Vaughn had a number of big days at the plate for the Red Sox, including a pair of three-homer games. He accomplished the feat for the first time on September 24, 1996, leading the Red Sox to a 13–8 win over the Orioles at Fenway by going 4 for 5, with three homers, five RBIs, and three runs scored. Vaughn duplicated his earlier effort by going 4 for 4, with three solo homers, during a 10–4 home win over the Yankees on May 30, 1997.

Vaughn began his final season with the Red Sox in style on April 10, 1998, hitting a walk-off grand slam against Seattle in the bottom of the ninth inning, to give the Red Sox a 9–7 Opening Day victory. Vaughn's blast culminated a memorable comeback by the Red Sox that saw them overcome a 7–2 deficit heading into the final frame.

However, Vaughn saved arguably his greatest performance for the first game of Boston's 1998 ALDS matchup with Cleveland, leading the Red Sox to an 11–3 victory by homering twice, doubling, and knocking in seven runs.

NOTABLE ACHIEVEMENTS

- Hit more than 30 home runs four times, topping 40 homers twice
- Knocked in more than 100 runs four times, surpassing 120 RBIs twice
- Scored more than 100 runs twice
- Batted over .300 five times, topping the .320 mark twice
- Surpassed 200 hits twice
- Topped 30 doubles twice
- Compiled on-base percentage in excess of .400 four times
- Posted slugging percentage in excess of .500 six times
- Led AL in RBIs and plate appearances once
- Led AL first basemen in putouts once and double plays twice
- Ranks among Red Sox career leaders in home runs (7th); on-base percentage (8th); slugging percentage (6th); and OPS (5th)
- Hit three home runs in one game twice (vs. Baltimore Orioles on September 24, 1996 & vs. New York Yankees on May 30, 1997)
- 1995 AL MVP
- 1995 Silver Slugger winner
- 1995 *Sporting News* All-Star selection
- Three-time AL All-Star (1995, 1996, and 1998)

1 8

Carlton Fisk

Courtesy Boston Red Sox

Although he actually played more years in Chicago, Carlton Fisk will always be remembered more for the time he spent in Boston. A New Englander through and through, Fisk was born in Vermont, attended school in New Hampshire, and came up through the Red Sox farm system. He spent his first 10 major-league seasons in Boston, earning seven All-Star selections, three top-10 finishes in the league MVP voting, and one Gold Glove during that time, en route to establishing himself as one of the finest catchers in American League history. By the time Fisk retired in 1993, he had spent more years behind the plate (24) than any other AL receiver, caught more games (2,226) than any other catcher in history, and hit more home runs (351) than any other receiver ever to play the game. Even though most of his records have since been broken, Fisk remains one of only four catchers in baseball history to hit 300 home runs, score 1,000 runs, and drive in 1,000 runs, joining Yogi Berra, Johnny Bench, and Ivan Rodriguez on an extremely exclusive list. In all, Fisk earned All-Star honors 11 times, hit more than 20 home runs eight times, batted over .300 three times, knocked in more than 100 runs twice, and scored more than 100 runs once. Yet, in spite of his outstanding career accomplishments, Fisk will always be remembered most fondly by Red Sox fans for a home run he hit in the 1975 World Series that ended one of the greatest games in the history of the Fall Classic.

Born in Bellows Falls, Vermont, on December 26, 1947, Carlton Ernest Fisk acquired the nickname "Pudge" as a result of the stocky frame he carried with him throughout his youth. After graduating from Charlestown High School in New Hampshire, Fisk attended the University of New Hampshire on a basketball scholarship, hoping to one day fulfill his dream of playing for the Boston Celtics. While still just a sophomore at New Hampshire, though, Fisk was selected by the Red Sox with the fourth overall pick of the 1967 amateur draft. After spending the next three years advancing through Boston's farm system, the 21-year-old catcher received his first major-league call-up late in 1969, appearing in just two games for the Red Sox before being returned to the minors for more seasoning. Fisk split his time in 1970 and 1971 between catching in the minor leagues and fulfilling his military obligations, before finally rejoining Boston toward the end of the 1971 campaign. Playing extremely well for the Red Sox in 14 games, Fisk batted .313 and hit his first two major-league home runs.

His confidence buoyed by his outstanding performance the previous September, Fisk established himself as Boston's starting catcher early in 1972. Starting 129 games behind the plate in his first full season, the 24-year-old receiver helped the Red Sox finish second in the extremely competitive AL East by hitting 22 home runs, knocking in 61 runs, scoring 74, batting .293, and leading the league with nine triples, en route to becoming the first player ever to earn unanimous selection as AL Rookie of the Year. Fisk also finished fourth in the MVP voting, earned All-Star honors, and won the only Gold Glove Award of his career. A fierce competitor with an outspoken nature, Fisk quickly developed into one of Boston's team leaders, expressing at one point during the season his strong belief in always putting forth a 100 percent effort by chastising star outfielders Carl Yastrzemski and Reggie Smith for not hustling. He also did an exceptional job of handling Boston's pitching staff, quickly earning the respect and trust of veteran pitchers such as Luis Tiant, Marty Pattin, Sonny Siebert, and Ray Culp.

Fisk experienced something of a sophomore jinx in 1973, seeing his batting average drop to .246 and striking out a career-high 99 times. Nevertheless, he still managed to hit 26 home runs, knock in 71 runs, and earn his second straight All-Star selection. Injuries derailed Fisk in each of the next two seasons, cutting into his playing time significantly. A foul tip off the bat of Joe Torre in a 1974 spring training game injured his groin, causing him to miss the first three weeks of the season. Fisk then sat out the entire second half of the year with a seriously injured knee suffered during a home-plate collision with Cleveland's Leron Lee. Having recovered from reconstructive knee surgery during the offseason, Fisk missed the first half of the 1975 campaign after having his thumb broken by an errant pitch from Detroit's Fred Holdsworth in spring training. However, the Boston catcher returned to the team in late June to help the Red Sox reach the World Series by batting .331 and driving in 52 runs in 79 games.

The 1975 World Series served as the backdrop for the defining moment of Fisk's Hall of Fame career. Considered by many to be the greatest game in the history of the Fall Classic, Game 6 turned into a see-saw affair that featured several exceptional plays by both teams. With Cincinnati ahead in the series three games to two, the score remained tied 6–6 heading into the bottom of the 12th inning. Leading off the bottom of the frame against Reds hurler Pat Darcy, Fisk drilled the righty reliever's second pitch high and deep down the left field foul line. The image of Fisk jumping up and down as he attempted to wave the ball fair while heading toward first base remains vivid in the mind of every baseball fan who witnessed the event. Fisk's drive struck the foul pole, giving the Red Sox a 7–6 win and forcing a seventh and deciding game that Cincinnati eventually won.

After squabbles with Boston management over a new contract contributed to Fisk having an off year in 1976, he rebounded in 1977 to have arguably his finest all-around season. Starting 149 games behind the plate for the Red Sox, Fisk hit 26 home runs, knocked in 102 runs, batted .315, and established career highs with 106 runs scored and a .402 on-base percentage, en route to earning an eighth-place finish in the league MVP voting. He followed that up with another outstanding performance in 1978, concluding the campaign with 20 homers, 88 RBIs, 94 runs scored, a .284 batting average, and a career-high 39 doubles that placed him second in the league rankings. Although the Yankees ended up defeating the Red Sox in a one-game playoff for the AL East title, Fisk's contributions to Boston over the course of the season earned him a ninth-place finish in the league MVP balloting.

A rib injury limited Fisk to just 91 games in 1979, but he returned to Boston's starting lineup full time the following year to hit 18 homers, drive in 62 runs, and bat .289. However, the 1980 campaign turned out to be his last in Boston. After the Red Sox front office blundered by failing to postmark his new contract in time, Fisk technically became a free agent at the conclusion of the 1980 season. He subsequently signed a $3.5 million deal with the Chicago White Sox, with whom he spent the remainder of his career.

After performing well his first two years in Chicago, Fisk helped lead a young White Sox squad to the first AL West title in franchise history in 1983, with his 26 home runs, 86 RBIs, 85 runs scored, .289 batting average, and tremendous on-field presence earning him a third-place finish in the league MVP voting. Noted for his ability to handle a pitching staff, Fisk took control of Chicago's young crop of hurlers that included AL Cy Young Award winner LaMarr Hoyt. Also notorious for making an inordinate number of trips to the mound over the course of a game, Fisk once prompted opposing manager Bobby Valentine to wonder out loud if the White Sox were being paid by the hour.

Although games that Fisk spent behind home plate may have taken a bit longer to complete, he clearly had a positive effect on the vast majority of pitchers he handled over the course of his career. Fisk served as Chicago's primary catcher when Bobby Thigpen established a new record by recording 57 saves in 1990. He also helped develop Jack McDowell, who won the Cy Young Award in 1993. Luis Tiant, who pitched to dozens of backstops in his day, worked with Fisk in Boston for several seasons. The man known as "El Tiante" said flatly, "He was the best catcher I ever had."

Injuries once again befell Fisk in 1984, limiting him to just 102 games and a .231 batting average, and prompting him to institute a new training regimen that he used the remainder of his career. After adopting a more scientific approach to physical conditioning that included long sessions of weight training, the 6'3", 220-pound Fisk appeared in better shape than ever before when he reported to spring training in 1985. Fully healthy for the first time in years, Fisk appeared in a total of 153 games for the White Sox, 120 of which he started behind home plate. The additional muscle tacked on by the 37-year-old receiver enabled him to establish new career highs with 37 home runs and 107 runs batted in, although he batted just .238. Fisk also stole a career-best 17 bases.

Although he never again put up huge offensive numbers, Fisk remained a productive hitter for most of his final eight seasons in Chicago, enabling him to eventually establish a new home run record for catchers. He also continued to contribute to the White Sox with his deft handling of pitchers and exceptional leadership skills. Admired and respected by teammates and opponents alike for his tremendous pride and work ethic, Fisk drew praise from former White Sox manager Jim Fregosi, who stated, "Pudge works harder than anyone I know, because he sets goals for himself and then follows through. I think he's the ultimate professional."

Fisk's level of professionalism was such that he refused to settle for anything less than a 100 percent effort, even from the opposition. In a highly publicized incident that occurred in May 1990, Fisk screamed at New York Yankees rookie Deion Sanders for failing to hustle to first base on a popup. When Sanders arrived at the plate for his next at-bat, Fisk warned him, "If you don't play it [the game] right, I'm going to kick your ass right here." Following the contest, the veteran catcher scoffed, "Yankee pinstripes, Yankee pride . . . I'm playing for the other team, and it offended me." Sanders ended up apologizing the next day.

In a move that ended Fisk's relationship with the White Sox organization for many years, the team unceremoniously released him midway through the 1993 campaign, just days after he set a new record for most games caught. The day after being released, Fisk and his wife sent a message to the Boston faithful when they hired a plane to tow a banner that read, "IT ALL STARTED HERE. THANKS BOSTON FANS, PUDGE FISK."

Fisk retired after being released by the White Sox, ending his career with 376 home runs, 1,330 runs batted in, 1,276 runs scored, 2,356 hits, a .269 batting average, a .341 on-base percentage, and a .457 slugging percentage. While playing for the Red Sox, he hit 162 home runs, knocked in 568 runs, scored 627 others, amassed 1,097 hits, batted .284, compiled a .356 on-base percentage, and posted a .481 slugging percentage.

The White Sox won their division later that year but refused to allow Fisk to enter the clubhouse to congratulate his former teammates. Their shabby treatment of him prompted Fisk to announce that he wished to be depicted wearing a Red Sox cap on his Hall of Fame plaque after the members of the BBWAA accorded him baseball's greatest honor in 2000. In making his announcement, Fisk, who worked at the time as a special assistant to Red Sox general manager Dan Duquette, proclaimed, "I would like to say that this has always been my favorite hat, and I will be wearing this hat probably for the rest of my career." In a formal ceremony five years later, the Red Sox officially named the left-field foul pole at Fenway Park "the Fisk Pole."

Courtesy Boston Red
Sox

RED SOX CAREER HIGHLIGHTS

Best Season

Remaining healthy throughout the entire 1977 campaign enabled Fisk to compile easily his best overall numbers in his 10 years with the Red Sox. En route to earning *Sporting News* All-Star honors for one of two times, Fisk hit 26 home runs, knocked in 102 runs, batted .315, compiled a .521 slugging percentage, and established career highs with a .402 on-base percentage, 106 runs scored, 169 hits, and 75 walks.

Memorable Moments/Greatest Performances

Fisk had a number of big days at the plate for the Red Sox, with his performance on Opening Day in 1973 heading the list. During a 15–5 pasting of the arch-rival Yankees at Fenway Park, Fisk went 3 for 4, with two home runs, a double, six runs batted in, and four runs scored. Fisk delivered four runs with one swing of the bat—a fourth-inning grand slam off reliever Lindy McDaniel.

Nevertheless, Fisk is remembered equally by the Fenway Faithful for his involvement in a number of notable incidents that took place during his time in Boston. On August 1, 1973, Fisk brawled with Yankee catcher Thurman Munson, his fiercest rival for supremacy among AL catchers throughout the first half of his career. With the Red Sox and Yankees deadlocked at 2–2 in the top of the ninth inning and Munson occupying third base, New York attempted a suicide squeeze. When teammate Gene Michael failed to make contact with the pitcher's offering, Munson tried to knock the ball out of Fisk's glove by barreling into him as he approached home plate. The collision between the two men initiated a 10-minute bench-clearing brawl that resulted in both catchers being ejected. Munson and Fisk held a grudging respect for one another in subsequent seasons, but ill feelings continued to exist between them until the former died in a 1979 plane crash.

Fisk found himself involved in another controversial play in Game 3 of the 1975 World Series, when he contended that Cincinnati's Ed Armbrister interfered with him in front of home plate on an attempted sacrifice bunt. Fisk subsequently made an errant throw to second base, allowing the Reds to eventually push across the winning run in the bottom of the 10th inning.

Still, the most memorable moment of Fisk's career unquestionably took place just a few days later, in Game 6 of that classic 1975 World Series, when Fisk ended the 12-inning marathon and sent the Fenway Faithful home happy by driving Cincinnati reliever Pat Darcy's second pitch off the left field foul pole. Recalling his memorable blast, Fisk noted, "I knew it was gonna go out. It was just a question of it being fair or foul. The wind must have carried it 15 feet toward the foul pole. I just stood there and watched. I didn't want to miss seeing it go out." Fisk added, "And then after that, running around the bases, it was just one of those things. You couldn't believe what happened to you. As I look back on it, it's almost like it happened to somebody else."

NOTABLE ACHIEVEMENTS

- Hit more than 20 home runs four times
- Knocked in more than 100 runs once (102 in 1977)
- Scored more than 100 runs once (106 in 1977)

- Batted over .300 three times
- Surpassed 30 doubles once (39 in 1978)
- Compiled on-base percentage in excess of .400 once (.402 in 1977)
- Posted slugging percentage in excess of .500 five times
- Led AL with nine triples in 1972
- Led AL catchers in putouts twice and assists once
- Ranks second all-time among major-league catchers in home runs (351) and games played (2,226)
- 1972 AL Rookie of the Year
- 1972 Gold Glove winner
- Two-time *Sporting News* All-Star selection (1972 and 1977)
- Seven-time AL All-Star
- 1975 AL champion
- Elected to Baseball Hall of Fame by members of BBWAA in 2000

Dustin Pedroia

Courtesy Keith Allison

The heart and soul of the Red Sox team for most of his career, Dustin Pedroia has established himself during his time in Boston as an exceptional all-around player and a superb team leader. An outstanding hitter with a ferocious swing and surprising power for a man his size, the 5'8", 165-pound Pedroia consistently makes solid contact with the ball, enabling him to annually finish among the league leaders in batting average, hits, and doubles; he has placed in the AL's top-10 in each category five times. A swift and savvy base-runner as well, Pedroia has stolen at least 20 bases four times and scored more than 100 runs on four occasions. Meanwhile, Pedroia's brilliant play at second base has earned him four Gold Gloves and recognition in 2013 as the Wilson AL Defensive Player of the Year.

However, to gauge Pedroia's contributions to the Red Sox merely by listing his accomplishments on the playing field would do him a grave injustice. A consummate team player who cares only about winning, the diminutive second sacker plays the game with an edge, passing on to his teammates a sense of urgency and a spirit of selflessness. Blessed with an energetic and effervescent personality, Pedroia also possesses a tremendous amount of self-confidence and a quick wit—two qualities that make him a natural-born leader and arguably the most beloved man in the Boston clubhouse. Expressing the sentiments held toward Pedroia by most of his Red Sox teammates, David Ortiz once stated, "I love him. I love that guy!"

Born in the agricultural town of Woodland, California, on August 17, 1983, Dustin Luis Pedroia excelled in baseball and football while attending Woodland High School, starting at shortstop for the varsity baseball team and at quarterback for the freshman football squad, before a broken ankle ended his career on the gridiron. Despite earning All-Delta League honors three consecutive times at Woodland High, Pedroia drew little attention from most college and pro scouts since he stood only 5'2" and weighed just 140 pounds as a senior. Finally, though, he received an offer to attend Arizona State University, where he beat out Ian Kinsler for the starting shortstop job as a freshman, prompting the latter to eventually transfer to the University of Missouri.

Pedroia performed exceptionally well over the course of his three years at Arizona State, starting all of the team's 185 games and posting a career batting average of .384. He also contributed greatly to the success of the squad off the field, relinquishing the last two years of his athletic scholarship in order to help the school recruit better pitchers. Believing he had nothing else to prove at the collegiate level after he earned First-Team All-America honors as a junior, Pedroia decided to turn pro when the Red Sox selected him in the second round of the 2004 amateur draft, with the 65th overall pick. After signing with Boston for a $575,000 bonus, he spent the next two years gradually transitioning to second base in the minor leagues, before being called up to Boston for the first time in August of 2006. Pedroia appeared in 31 games during the remainder of the year, hitting his first two major-league home runs, although he struggled terribly at the plate, compiling a batting average of just .191.

Yet, even though Pedroia experienced little success against major-league pitching at first, he never lost confidence in himself, surprising his new teammates with the temerity he displayed as he sauntered around the Red

Sox clubhouse. Believing he belonged with the big club as soon as he arrived in Boston, Pedroia caught some of the team's older veterans somewhat off-guard, with Curt Schilling later saying, "When you meet Dustin for the first time, you kind of step back a little bit."

Before long, though, Pedroia's teammates learned to love him, especially after he beat out Alex Cora for the starting second base job early in the ensuing campaign. After starting off the season slowly, Pedroia went on a 13-game hitting streak that enabled him to earn AL Rookie of the Month honors for May. He continued his hot hitting over the season's final four months, concluding the campaign with a .317 batting average, a .380 on-base percentage, 8 homers, 39 doubles, 50 RBIs, and 86 runs scored, despite playing the final two months of the year with a cracked hamate bone in his left hand. Pedroia's strong performance earned him AL Rookie of the Year honors. Although he subsequently struggled against the Angels in the ALDS, Pedroia came alive against Cleveland in the ALCS, batting .345, with a homer and five RBIs, before homering once and driving in four runs, in helping the Red Sox sweep Colorado in the World Series.

While Pedroia's outstanding play in the field contributed greatly to the success the Red Sox experienced over the course of the season, his confidence also helped restore to the team some of the swagger it lost following the championship campaign of 2004. And teammates and fans alike loved his scrappy style of play and the enthusiasm he brought with him to the ball park each day.

Speaking of his young second baseman, then Red Sox general manager Theo Epstein stated, "He's got great energy and great drive. He likes to prove people wrong."

In describing his style of play, Pedroia said, "I just show up to the yard, work hard, and play as hard as I can."

He added, "I don't like losing at anything. Why should I?"

Meanwhile, in addressing his size, or lack thereof, Pedroia suggested, "Being big has nothing to do with playing baseball. . . . I don't really care what people think. I don't really have to prove anything to anybody. I just have to prove stuff to my teammates."

Pedroia continued to prove that he had the ability to perform at an elite level in his sophomore campaign of 2008, earning AL MVP honors by hitting 17 home runs, knocking in 83 runs, stealing 20 bases, finishing second in the league with a .326 batting average, and topping the circuit with 118 runs scored, 213 hits, and 54 doubles. He also committed only six errors, earning in the process the first of his four Gold Gloves. Pedroia followed that up with another good year in 2009, hitting 15 homers, driving in 72 runs, stealing another 20 bases, batting .296, and leading the league with 115 runs scored.

Unfortunately, a broken bone in his foot limited Pedroia to just 75 games in 2010. However, a return to full health the following year enabled him to bat .307, score 102 runs, and establish career highs with 21 home runs, 91 RBIs, and 26 stolen bases. Pedroia's outstanding performance earned him a ninth-place finish in the league MVP voting. Pedroia missed three weeks in 2012 after tearing the adductor muscle in his right thumb. Nevertheless, he managed to hit 15 homers, drive in 65 runs, score 81 times, steal 20 bases, and bat .290. He displayed his toughness again in 2013, playing the entire year with a torn UCL in his thumb—an injury he suffered when sliding into first base on opening day. Although Pedroia hit only nine home runs as a result, he batted .301, knocked in 84 runs, scored 91 times, amassed 193 hits and 42 doubles, and committed only five errors, en route to earning his third Gold Glove and a seventh-place finish in the MVP balloting. After subsequently helping the Red Sox win their third World Series in 10 years, Pedroia underwent successful thumb surgery in November that enabled him to enter the 2014 campaign fully healthy. However, Pedroia ended up being bitten by the injury bug in each of the next two seasons as well, limiting him to 135 games in 2014 and only 93 contests the following year. Nevertheless, he managed to earn Gold Glove honors for the fourth time in the first of those campaigns by committing only two errors in the field all year long, en route to leading all A.L. second basemen with a career-best .997 fielding percentage.

Healthy again in 2016, Pedroia helped lead the Red Sox to the division title by hitting 15 homers, driving in 74 runs, scoring 105 times, and finishing third in the league with 201 hits and a .318 batting average. But, after undergoing left knee surgery during the subsequent offseason, Pedroia appeared in only 105 games in 2017, as he continued to experience soreness in the affected area. He concluded the campaign with 7 homers, 62 RBIs, 46 runs scored, and 119 hits, giving him career totals of 140 home runs, 724 RBIs, 920 runs scored, and 1,802 hits. Pedroia has also amassed 394 doubles, 15 triples, and 138 stolen bases, compiled a lifetime batting average of .300, posted an on-base percentage of .366, and compiled a slugging percentage of .441. The Red Sox hope that a return to full health in 2018 will allow the 34-year-old Pedroia to add significantly to those numbers over the course of the next few seasons.

In the meantime, Pedroia will likely continue to influence his teammates in a positive way, passing on to them his enthusiasm and passion for the sport, which he revealed when he stated, "I know this sounds like a cliché, but I really don't play for money. I play because I love the game, and because I want to make an impact."

Pedroia will also continue to play the game with a chip on his shoulder, proclaiming, "I'm going to go out there and be who I am, and if you don't like it, then watch somebody else."

CAREER HIGHLIGHTS

Best Season

Pedroia had an outstanding year in 2011, when he batted .307, scored 102 runs, amassed 195 hits and 37 doubles, and established career highs with 21 home runs, 91 RBIs, 26 stolen bases, 86 walks, and a .387 on-base percentage. Nevertheless, he played his best ball for the Red Sox during his MVP campaign of 2008. In addition to hitting 17 homers, driving in 83 runs, stealing 20 bases, and compiling an on-base percentage of .376, he finished second in the league with a .326 batting average, topped the circuit with 118 runs scored, 213 hits, and 54 doubles, and posted a career-high OPS of .869. Pedroia did a little bit of everything for the Red Sox that year, winning the first of his three Gold Gloves and his only Silver Slugger, and even batting cleanup for several games.

Memorable Moments/Greatest Performances

Pedroia hit safely for nearly a month in 2011, putting together a 25-game hitting streak from June 29 to July 28 that represents the longest such streak ever posted by a Red Sox second baseman.

Pedroia put together another impressive hitting streak in 2016, hitting safely in 11 consecutive official trips to the plate from August 25 to August 27, a period during which he singled 10 times, doubled once, walked once, scored twice, and knocked in three runs.

Pedroia had one of his best days at the plate on June 15, 2007, when he helped lead the Red Sox to a 10–2 win over the San Francisco Giants by going 5 for 5, with a homer, double, five RBIs, and two runs scored. However, he turned in his most notable play of the season on September 1, when his diving stop of Miguel Tejada's seventh-inning hard-hit smash up the middle helped preserve fellow rookie Clay Buchholz's no-hitter against Baltimore.

Pedroia again went 5-for-5 during a 13-2 mauling of the Minnesota Twins on July 21, 2016, finishing the game with two doubles, three singles, one RBI, and three runs scored.

Pedroia had a huge series against Cleveland in the 2007 ALCS, batting .345, leading all players with eight runs scored, and helping the Red Sox clinch a spot in the World Series by hitting a two-run homer and a three-run double during Boston's 11–2 win over the Indians in Game 7. He subsequently helped jump-start the Red Sox offense in Game 1 of the World Series by hitting a leadoff homer against Jeff Francis in the bottom of the first inning.

Although the Red Sox failed to repeat as AL champions the following year, losing to Tampa Bay in seven games in the ALCS, Pedroia had a big series against the Rays, batting .346, with three home runs, five RBIs, and nine runs scored.

Pedroia, though, had the greatest day of his career on June 24, 2010, when he went 5 for 5, with three home runs and five RBIs against the Colorado Rockies in a game the Red Sox won 13–11 in 10 innings.

NOTABLE ACHIEVEMENTS

- Has batted over .300 five times
- Has hit more than 20 home runs once (21 in 2011)
- Has scored more than 100 runs four times
- Has surpassed 200 hits twice
- Has surpassed 30 doubles eight times, topping the 40 mark three times and the 50 mark once (54 in 2008)
- Has stolen at least 20 bases four times
- Has led AL in runs scored twice; hits once; and doubles once
- Has led AL second basemen in fielding percentage three times
- Ranks among Red Sox career leaders iin: runs scored (10th); hits (8th); extra-base hits (8th); doubles (6th); total bases (8th); stolen bases (6th); sacrifice flies (6th); plate appearances (9th); and at-bats (9th)
- 2007 AL Rookie of the Year
- 2008 AL MVP
- 2008 Silver Slugger winner
- Four-time Gold Glove winner (2008, 2011, 2013 & 2014)
- 2013 Wilson AL Defensive Player of the Year
- Four-time AL All-Star (2008–2010, 2013)
- Two-time AL champion (2007 and 2013)
- Two-time world champion (2007 and 2013)

Dom DiMaggio

....

Courtesy Boston Public Library, Leslie Jones Collection

The accomplishments of Dominic DiMaggio likely would be better appreciated had the star outfielder not spent virtually his entire career being overshadowed by the American League's two greatest players—big brother Joe and teammate Ted Williams. Yet, even though the youngest DiMaggio brother often found himself taking a backseat to those two great sluggers, he carved out quite a career for himself, earning seven All-Star selections despite missing three of his peak seasons due to time spent in the military during World War II. The owner of the longest consecutive-game hitting streak in Red Sox history, DiMaggio compiled more hits (1,679) than any other major-league player during his 10 full seasons. He also ranked second in runs scored and third in doubles during that time. Meanwhile, even though Dom didn't receive nearly as much publicity as Joe, he eventually surpassed his older brother as the finest defensive center fielder in the American League, establishing himself in 1948 as one of only five outfielders in baseball history to record as many as 500 putouts in a season. Joe, himself, once called his younger brother "the best defensive outfielder I've ever seen."

Born in San Francisco, California, on February 12, 1917, Dominic Paul DiMaggio attended Galileo High School, after which he chose to follow in the footsteps of his older brothers, Vince and Joe, by pursuing a career in Major League Baseball. After turning down an academic and baseball scholarship to Santa Clara College, Dominic joined the Pacific Coast League's San Francisco Seals, for whom he patrolled center field from 1937 to 1939.

With the Red Sox having purchased DiMaggio's contract from the Seals for $75,000 at the conclusion of the 1939 campaign, the 23-year-old outfielder made his major-league debut on April 16, 1940, starting off the season in right field, before claiming the starting center field job later in the year. DiMaggio had a solid rookie season, batting .301, scoring 81 runs, and leading all AL outfielders with 16 assists, even though he appeared in only 108 games. He followed that up with a similarly productive sophomore campaign, batting .283, finishing among the league leaders with 117 runs scored, 37 doubles, and 13 stolen bases, and also placing near the top of the league rankings in outfield putouts and assists, en route to earning his first All-Star selection. DiMaggio made the All-Star team again in 1942, when, in addition to batting .286, he hit a career-high 14 home runs, scored 110 runs, amassed 36 doubles and 8 triples, stole 16 bases, and led all AL outfielders with 439 putouts, 19 assists, and 7 double plays.

The 5'9", 168-pound outfielder soon became affectionately known to his teammates as the "Little Professor" due to his smallish frame, serious expression, and glasses, which he wore to correct his nearsightedness. Meanwhile, DiMaggio earned the admiration of every other Red Sox player with his astute approach to the game, exceptional base-running and defensive ability, and sound fundamental play. He typically batted leadoff for the Red Sox, immediately ahead of Johnny Pesky, who said of his longtime teammate and close friend in *Forever Fenway*, "Dominic DiMaggio was the perfect player—never made a mistake; never missed a sign."

Ted Williams expressed his respect for DiMaggio's ability to perform under pressure when he stated, "If the game was on the line and you needed a clean hit or a hard-hit ball, he was as good as anybody."

DiMaggio even drew praise from Ty Cobb, who once said of the young center fielder, "Dom's a throwback to the kind of players we used to have."

Having established himself as one of the American League's top out-fielders over the course of his first three seasons, DiMaggio subsequently missed the next three years after enlisting in the U.S. Navy during World War II. DiMaggio later revealed, "I had to fight my way into the Navy. They rejected me because of my eyesight, and, for the longest time, I told them I wanted to be in the Navy. I was not about to sit out the war." Despite a 4-F classification, he enlisted at the conclusion of the 1942 campaign, after which he served a three-year stint in the U.S. Navy. While in the service, DiMaggio played for the Norfolk Naval Training Station team in Virginia and saw overseas duty as well.

After being discharged in January of 1946, DiMaggio returned to the Red Sox to help lead them to a record of 104–50 and the American League pennant. He compiled a batting average of .316 in his first year back, knocked in 73 runs, and scored 85 others, en route to earning a ninth-place finish in the league MVP voting and his lone *Sporting News* All-Star selection. DiMaggio posted slightly subpar numbers in 1947, but he rebounded the following season to begin an extremely productive four-year stretch during which he scored well over 100 runs each season and batted over .300 twice. In addition to batting .285 in the first of those campaigns, DiMaggio scored 127 runs and established career highs with 87 RBIs, 40 doubles, 101 walks, and 503 outfield putouts, making him one of a select few to reach the 500 plateau in the last category. He followed that up by batting .307, scoring 126 runs, and walking 96 times in 1949, enabling him to compile an extremely impressive .404 on-base percentage. He also hit safely in 34 consecutive games at one point during the season, establishing in the process an all-time Red Sox record. DiMaggio led the American League in runs scored in each of the next two seasons, crossing the plate 131 times in 1950 and 113 times in 1951. He also topped the circuit with 11 triples and 15 stolen bases in the first of those campaigns, while finishing third in the league with 193 hits and a .328 batting average.

DiMaggio proved to be an exceptional leadoff hitter for Boston during that time, using his solid line-drive swing and keen batting eye to set the table for sluggers Ted Williams and Vern Stephens. In addition to batting over .300 four times during his career, DiMaggio drew at least 90 bases on balls three times, helping him to compile an on-base percentage in excess of .400 on two occasions. He also possessed outstanding speed and marvelous instincts on the base paths, making him a threat to score whenever he reached base.

Injuries and advancing age limited the 35-year-old DiMaggio to just 128 games in 1952. Nevertheless, he still managed to bat .294 and score 81 runs. However, after being benched in favor of Tommy Umphlett by new Red Sox manager Lou Boudreau early in 1953, DiMaggio decided to call it quits, announcing his retirement on May 9, even though he believed he still had one or two more good years left in him. DiMaggio left the game with career totals of 87 home runs, 618 RBIs, 1,046 runs scored, 1,680 hits, 57 triples, 308 doubles, and 750 bases on balls. He compiled a batting average of .298 in his years with the Red Sox, posted a .383 on-base percentage, and compiled a slugging average of .419. DiMaggio ranks among the team's all-time leaders in runs scored, hits, doubles, total bases, walks, plate appearances, and at-bats.

Following his playing career, DiMaggio started a successful company that manufactured upholstery and carpeting for automobiles, which he ran until his retirement in 1983. He also gave a considerable amount of time

Courtesy Boston Public Library, Leslie Jones Collection

to raising millions of dollars for charities in the Boston area. As someone who cared deeply for the plight of his fellow retired players, DiMaggio spent several years donating all the proceeds from his autograph signings to the American Professional Players Association, an organization that helped support older players not covered by a retirement plan.

Dominic DiMaggio lived until the ripe old age of 92, passing away at his home in Marion, Massachusetts, on May 8, 2009, from pneumonia. Upon learning of his passing, Red Sox principal owner John Henry said in a statement, "His loss saddens us all, but his contributions to the glory and tradition of our ball club will forever be etched in the annals of Red Sox history."

DiMaggio's son, who received a great deal of exposure over the years to the sense of friendly competition that existed between his father and his uncle, added, "Dad had a great deal of respect for Uncle Joe and what he did. But he never felt inferior. He was a competitor, and a strong competitor."

CAREER HIGHLIGHTS

Best Season

DiMaggio had very solid years in 1941 and 1942, scoring a total of 227 runs over the course of those two seasons, and establishing career highs with 14 home runs and 16 stolen bases in the second of those campaigns. However, he played his best ball for the Red Sox from 1948 to 1951, posting at least 185 hits, 30 doubles, and 110 runs scored each year. A strong case could be made for DiMaggio's 1948 performance since, in addition to reaching career highs in RBIs (87) and doubles (40), he scored 127 runs and amassed 503 outfield putouts—easily the most in his career. But DiMaggio had his best all-around season in 1950, when he knocked in 70 runs and established career highs with 131 runs scored, 193 hits, 11 triples, a .328 batting average, a .414 on-base percentage, and a .452 slugging percentage. He placed in the league's top-10 in seven offensive categories, topping the circuit in runs scored, triples, and stolen bases (15).

Memorable Moments/Greatest Performances

DiMaggio's Red Sox record 34-game hitting streak certainly has to rank among his greatest achievements. He batted .357 and scored 35 runs during the streak, which lasted from June 26 to August 7, 1949. Ironically, big brother Joe, whose major-league record Dominic found himself chasing, helped end the 34-game streak by making a shoe-top catch of his younger sibling's sinking line drive in the eighth inning of Boston's 6–3 win over New York on August 9. Dom also hit safely in 27 straight games during the 1951 campaign.

DiMaggio demonstrated his ability to perform well under pressure on the final day of the 1948 regular season, when he helped the Red Sox advance to a one-game playoff against the Cleveland Indians for the American League pennant by collecting three hits during a 10–5 win over the Yankees. DiMaggio singled twice, homered, knocked in a run, and scored two others during the contest.

DiMaggio had one of his most productive days on April 30, 1950, scoring five runs in the first game of a doubleheader sweep of the Philadelphia Athletics. During a 19–0 pasting of the A's in the opening contest, DiMaggio went 2 for 3, with two doubles, three walks, two RBIs, and a career-high five runs scored. He also collected two hits in the nitecap.

Two months later, on June 30, 1950, Dominic and his brother Joe made history when they hit home runs in the same game—a 9–6 Yankee win. By doing so, they became just the second pair of brothers on opposing teams to homer in the same game.

DiMaggio also played a pivotal role in the 1946 World Series. After scoring the deciding run in Game 5 to give the Red Sox a 3–2 lead over St. Louis in the Fall Classic, he came up to hit in a crucial late-game situation in the series finale. Stepping up to the plate with the Cardinals holding a 3–1 lead in the top of the eighth inning, and with runners on second and third with two men out, DiMaggio drove the ball off the wall in right-center field, scoring both runners and tying the game at 3. However, he pulled a muscle while rounding first base, prompting Red Sox manager Joe Cronin to remove him from the contest and replace him with Leon Culberson. The Cardinals subsequently took advantage of DiMaggio's absence in the bottom of the frame when Enos Slaughter made his famous "Mad Dash" from first to home on Harry Walker's double to short left-center field. Slaughter's run proved to be the game winner, making the Cardinals world champions. Yet, many argued that DiMaggio would have prevented Slaughter from scoring had he been in the contest, instead of Culberson. DiMaggio himself felt that way, as revealed by David Halberstam, who wrote in his 2003 book, *The Teammates*, "Watching the play had been pure agony for Dominic DiMaggio. . . . His own injury, his own pulled hamstring, Dominic now decided, had been the decisive play of the game."

NOTABLE ACHIEVEMENTS

- Batted over .300 four times
- Scored more than 100 runs six times, topping 120 runs scored on three occasions
- Finished in double-digits in triples once (11 in 1950)
- Surpassed 30 doubles seven times, reaching the 40 mark once (40 in 1948)
- Walked more than 100 times once (101 in 1948)
- Compiled on-base percentage in excess of .400 twice
- Led AL in runs scored twice; triples once; stolen bases once; games played once; and at-bats twice
- Led AL outfielders in putouts twice; assists three times; and double plays twice
- Ranks among Red Sox career leaders in runs scored (8th); hits (10th); doubles (9th); total bases (9th); bases on balls (8th); plate appearances (10th); and at-bats (10th)
- Holds Red Sox record for longest hitting streak (34 games in 1949)
- One of only five major-league outfielders to record as many as 500 putouts in a season (503 in 1948)
- 1946 *Sporting News* All-Star selection
- Seven-time AL All-Star
- 1946 AL champion

Smoky Joe Wood

Courtesy Library of Congress

Smoky Joe Wood never made it into the Baseball Hall of Fame. Even though he posted back-to-back 20-win seasons for the Red Sox in 1911 and 1912, Wood never won more than 15 games in any of his other six years in Boston, concluding his career with a total of only 117 victories. But Wood had one of the greatest seasons of any pitcher in baseball history in 1912, compiling mind-boggling numbers that included a record of 34–5 and a league-leading .872 winning percentage. Only a sore arm that Wood developed the following year likely prevented the flame-throwing 23-year-old right-hander from going down as one of the greatest pitchers of the Dead Ball Era. Walter Johnson, who rivaled Wood as baseball's premier hurler in 1912, is generally considered to be the most dominant pitcher of his time. Yet, when asked if he could throw harder than Wood, Johnson replied, "Listen, my friend . . . there's no man alive that throws harder than Smoky Joe Wood."

Born in Kansas City, Missouri, on October 25, 1889, Howard Ellsworth Wood lived a somewhat nomadic existence during his formative years, spending time in Kansas, Illinois, Colorado, and Pennsylvania, before his family finally settled down in Ness City, Kansas, in 1906. Wood began his professional career one year later, at the age of 17, when he signed as an infielder with the Hutchinson White Sox of the Western Association. After being converted into a pitcher by the pitching-starved White Sox, Wood ended up winning 18 games, earning him a promotion to the American Association's Kansas City Blues. Wood spent most of 1908 in Kansas City, before being purchased by the Red Sox late in the season. He subsequently made just six appearances for Boston over the season's final month, splitting his two decisions, compiling an ERA of 2.38, and completing one of his two starts.

Despite having each of his next two seasons cut short by injuries, Wood pitched effectively after being inserted into the Red Sox starting rotation early in 1909. He concluded his first full season with a record of 11–7, an ERA of 2.18, 13 complete games, and four shutouts. Even though Wood finished just 12–13 in 1910, he placed among the league leaders with a 1.69 ERA and 145 strikeouts.

Fully healthy for the first time in 1911, Wood had his breakout season, placing near the top of the league rankings with 23 wins, an ERA of 2.02, 231 strikeouts, 25 complete games, 276 innings pitched, and five shutouts. He surpassed each of those marks the following year, though, leading all AL hurlers with a record of 34–5, a winning percentage of .872, 35 complete games, and 10 shutouts. He also finished second in the league to Walter Johnson with a 1.91 ERA and 258 strikeouts—an inordinately high number for the Dead Ball Era. Meanwhile, Wood's 344 innings pitched placed him third in the league rankings. Wood punctuated his magnificent campaign by defeating the New York Giants three times in the World Series, twice as a starter and once in relief, in leading the Red Sox to the world championship.

Unfortunately, the 1912 season proved to be Wood's last as a dominant pitcher. He started off the 1913 campaign well enough, posting a record of

11–5 and an ERA of 2.29 through his first 18 starts. But, pitching against the Tigers in Detroit on July 18, he slipped on the wet grass while attempting to field a Bobby Veach infield grounder along the third base line, breaking his thumb in the process. Rushing back from the injury too soon, Wood altered his pitching motion, causing him to hurt his shoulder and depriving him of his once overpowering fastball. Although he pitched effectively the next two seasons whenever he found himself able to take the mound, Wood experienced constant pain in his shoulder and typically had to receive an inordinate amount of rest between starts. Unable to raise his arm for several days after each time he pitched, Wood started a total of only 30 games for the Red Sox in 1914 and 1915. Nevertheless, after posting a record of 10–3 in the first of those campaigns, he finished 15–5 with a league-leading 1.49 ERA the following year.

No longer able to tolerate the pain, Wood elected to sit out the 1916 season, apparently ending his career at only 26 years of age. However, he eventually decided to mount a comeback, persuading the Cleveland Indians to sign him prior to the start of the 1917 campaign. Wood appeared in only five games for the Indians that year, after which he abandoned pitching and moved to the outfield. Always fairly proficient at the plate, Wood spent his final five seasons in Cleveland playing the outfield, usually splitting time in right with the lefty-swinging Elmer Smith. After hitting .366 in a part-time role in 1921, Wood claimed a starting spot the following year, batting .297 and knocking in 92 runs. He retired at season's end after being offered the head coaching job at Yale University, where he remained until 1942. Wood ended his career with 23 home runs, 325 runs batted in, and a .283 batting average. While pitching for the Red Sox from 1908 to 1915, he compiled an overall record of 117–56, along with an exceptional 1.99 ERA. He also completed 121 of his 157 starts, threw 1,416 innings, struck out 986 batters, and tossed 28 shutouts. Wood's 1.99 ERA is the best in Red Sox history. He also ranks among the team's all-time leaders in wins, winning percentage, strikeouts, complete games, and shutouts.

After being relieved of his duties at Yale University in March of 1942, Wood left New England for California, where he opened an extremely successful golfing range with his brother. He eventually returned to the New England area, where he remained a passionate follower of baseball until he passed away on July 27, 1985, at the age of 95, while residing at a convalescent home in West Haven, Connecticut.

Although the relative brevity of Smoky Joe Wood's career prevented him from ever being admitted to Cooperstown, the once-overpowering right-hander left a lasting impression on those who saw him perform. Red Sox teammate Harry Hooper stated in *Baseball: The Biographical Encyclopedia*, "I've seen some pretty fair pitching, but I've never seen anything like Smoky Joe Wood in 1912."

RED SOX CAREER HIGHLIGHTS

Best Season

This was an absolute no-brainer. Wood's 1912 campaign ranks as arguably the greatest ever turned in by any Red Sox pitcher. His total of 34 wins represents a single-season team record, while his 10 shutouts tie him with Cy Young (1904) for the most by any Red Sox hurler. Wood's .872 winning percentage, 258 strikeouts, and 344 innings pitched give him one of the top five single-season marks in each of those categories as well.

Memorable Moments/Greatest Performances

On July 29, 1911, Wood threw the fourth no-hitter in Red Sox history when he defeated the St. Louis Browns 5–0 in the first game of a doubleheader.

Wood also turned in a memorable performance in the 1912 World Series, posting three of Boston's four wins over the New York Giants. After going the distance in winning Games 1 and 4, Wood faltered in Game 7, being knocked out in the second inning after allowing the Giants six runs on seven hits. However, he redeemed himself in the series finale (with Game 2 having ended in a 6–6 tie, the series went to eight games), coming out of the bullpen in the eighth inning and working the final three frames, as Boston defeated New York 3–2 in 10 innings. By striking out 11 batters in his Game 1 win, Wood became the first pitcher to record double-digit strikeouts in a World Series game.

Wood also figured prominently in one of the most highly publicized games of the Dead Ball Era, squaring off against Walter Johnson in a head-to-head matchup of epic proportions. The date was September 6, 1912, and the place was Fenway Park. With the Red Sox bearing down on the AL pennant, they sent their ace to the mound to face Johnson, who earlier in the year had established a new league record by posting 16 consecutive victories. The game took on added significance since Wood entered the contest having won 13 straight games himself. With a capacity crowd in attendance, the two great hurlers matched each other, pitch for pitch, through five scoreless frames. The Red Sox finally broke through against Johnson in the bottom of the sixth, scoring once on back-to-back bloop doubles by Tris Speaker and Duffy Lewis. Wood protected Boston's slim lead the rest of the way, defeating Johnson by a score of 1–0, for his 14th straight win, and his 30th of the season. He tied Johnson's mark nine days later, defeating St. Louis 2–1, before finally seeing his own streak ended with a loss to Detroit on September 20.

NOTABLE ACHIEVEMENTS

- Won more than 20 games twice, surpassing 30 victories once (34 in 1912)
- Compiled ERA below 2.00 three times
- Struck out more than 200 batters twice
- Completed more than 20 games twice, surpassing the 30 mark once (35 in 1912)
- Threw more than 300 innings once (344 in 1912)
- Tossed 10 shutouts in 1912
- Led all AL pitchers in wins once; winning percentage twice; ERA once; complete games once; and shutouts once
- Ranks first all-time among Red Sox pitchers with a career ERA of 1.99
- Ranks among Red Sox all-time leaders in wins (tied-6th); winning percentage (4th); shutouts (3rd); complete games (4th); and strikeouts (9th)
- Holds Red Sox single-season records for most wins (34) and shutouts (10), both in 1912
- Threw no-hitter vs. St. Louis Browns on July 29, 1911.
- Won three games in 1912 World Series
- Two-time AL champion
- Two-time world champion

Luis Tiant

Courtesy Boston Red Sox

One of the most beloved men ever to play for the Red Sox, Luis Tiant resurrected his career in Boston during the 1970s. After earlier starring for the Cleveland Indians, Tiant experienced shoulder problems that seemingly brought his days as a dominant hurler to an end. Unwanted by any other major-league club, the 30-year-old Tiant joined the Red Sox in 1971, after which he discovered the Fountain of Youth. "El Tiante," as he came to be affectionately known, spent the next eight years in Boston, winning a total of 122 games and posting more than 20 victories on three occasions. More than just an outstanding pitcher, Tiant emerged as a cult hero of sorts, thrilling fans with his flamboyant style of pitching and awesome mound presence, and ingratiating himself to his teammates with his affable personality, charm, and keen sense of humor. Fellow Red Sox hurler John Curtis once wrote a newspaper story about trying to explain to his wife why he loved Tiant. Dwight Evans later said, "Unless you've played with him, you can't understand what Luis means to a team."

Born in Marianao, La Habana, Cuba, on November 23, 1940, Luis Clemente Tiant y Vega followed in the footsteps of his father, Luis Eleuterio Tiant, a legendary left-handed pitcher who starred in the Cuban Leagues and American Negro Leagues for 20 years. After traveling to Mexico City with an all-star club to compete in an international tournament at the tender age of 16, the younger Tiant began his professional career two years later, in 1959, with the Mexico City Tigers. Tiant spent two years in the Mexican League, before a recommendation by former All-Star second baseman Bobby Avila prompted the Cleveland Indians to purchase his contract for $35,000 at the conclusion of the 1961 campaign. He spent the next two and a half years advancing through Cleveland's farm system, unable to return home to Cuba at any time due to the heightened tensions that existed between the United States and Fidel Castro's newly established regime in his native land.

Tiant finally made his debut with the Indians on July 19, 1964, tossing a 4-hit, 11-strikeout, 3–0 shutout against the eventual AL champion New York Yankees at Yankee Stadium. He continued to pitch well for the Indians the remainder of the year, finishing the season with a record of 10–4 and an ERA of 2.83. Although Tiant failed to win more than 12 games for the light-hitting Indians in any of the next three seasons, he pitched effectively, compiling an ERA below 3.00 twice. He developed into a star in 1968, concluding what became known as "the Year of the Pitcher" with a record of 21–9, 19 complete games, 264 strikeouts, and a league-leading 1.60 ERA and nine shutouts, en route to earning a fifth-place finish in the AL MVP voting. Tiant pitched the most dominant game of his career on July 3, striking out 19 Minnesota Twins in hurling his team to a 1–0, 10-inning victory.

However, Tiant's career soon took a sudden downturn. After he finished just 9–20 in 1969, the Indians elected to include him in a six-player deal they completed with the Minnesota Twins at season's end. Tiant spent just one injury-marred year in Minnesota, making only 17 starts due to a sore right shoulder, before being released by the Twins early in 1971 after pitching ineffectively during spring training. The Atlanta Braves subsequently signed Tiant to a 30-day trial with their Triple-A minor-league affiliate, but, after they chose not to promote him, he signed with Louisville, Boston's top farm club.

Summoned to Boston on June 3, 1971, Tiant struggled over the final four months of the season, winning only one of his eight decisions while splitting his time between starting and relieving. However, after beginning the ensuing campaign in the bullpen, he emerged as the ace of Boston's staff, finishing the year with a record of 15–6, 12 complete games, six shutouts, and a league-leading 1.91 ERA, en route to earning AL Comeback Player of the Year honors and an eighth-place finish in the league MVP voting. Tiant followed that up with consecutive 20-win seasons, going 20–13, with a 3.34 ERA and 23 complete games in 1972, before posting a record of 22–13, an ERA of 2.92, 25 complete games, and a league-leading seven shutouts in 1974.

In addition to excelling for the Red Sox on the mound, Tiant soon developed into the team's most popular player in the clubhouse. Revered by all his teammates for his sense of humor and self-deprecating manner, Tiant helped create unity on a team previously known for its cliques by making fun of himself and everyone else. He called Carl Yastrzemski "Polacko" and referred to Carlton Fisk as "Frankenstein." A barrel-chested man whose physical appearance suggested he weighed more than he actually did, Tiant often emerged from the shower with a cigar in his mouth, looked at his naked body in the mirror, and declared himself to be a (in his exaggerated Spanish accent) "good-lookeen sonofabeech."

Tiant also earned the respect of his teammates with his ability to perform well under pressure. Manager Darrell Johnson said of his ace right-hander, "If a man put a gun to my head and said I'm going to pull the trigger if you lose this game, I'd want Luis Tiant to pitch that game."

Referred to as "the Fred Astaire of baseball" by Reggie Jackson, Tiant epitomized style and elegance on the mound. After altering his pitching motion early in his career as a way of compensating for a loss in velocity he experienced due to a shoulder blade injury, Tiant employed a delivery in which he turned away from home plate, in effect creating a hesitation pitch. Contorting his body into a seemingly unnatural position, he actually spent more time looking at second base than he did home plate as he prepared to release the ball. Tiant's unusual motion affected the timing of many an opposing batter, helping to explain the extraordinary success he experienced during the second half of his career. He also possessed a varied arsenal of pitches, including a sharp-breaking curveball, which he had the ability to throw from a number of different arm angles. However, Tiant always maintained that the fastball was his favorite pitch, stating on one occasion, "The fastball is the best pitch in baseball. It's like having five pitches, if you move it around."

Hampered by back problems, and burdened by growing concerns over his ailing father, who he hadn't seen since he came to the United States 14 years earlier, Tiant failed to compile the kind of numbers in 1975 that he posted in each of the three previous seasons. Although he finished the year with a record of 18–14 and 18 complete games, his 4.02 ERA represented his highest mark in any full season to that point. However, Tiant's performance improved significantly during the latter stages of the campaign after a plea from representatives of the United States government convinced Fidel Castro to allow Tiant's parents to visit him in Boston. After Tiant greeted his parents at the airport a few days earlier, the Red Sox arranged for them to be introduced to the crowd at Fenway Park on August 26, and for his father to throw out the first pitch. The emotion-filled ceremonies that preceded the contest only added to the level of popularity that Tiant reached with the fans in Boston.

Free of worry for the first time in years, Tiant pitched exceptionally well during the season's final month, going 3–1 with a 1.47 ERA down the stretch. He subsequently carried his momentum into the postseason, nearly pitching the Red Sox to their first world championship in 57 years by defeating Oakland once in the ALCS and Cincinnati twice in the World Series. Tiant's extraordinary performance throughout the postseason prompted Baltimore Orioles staff ace Jim Palmer to say, "You can talk about anybody else on that team [1975 Red Sox] you want to, but, when the chips are on the line, Luis Tiant is the greatest competitor I've ever seen."

Tiant had one more big year for the Red Sox, going 21–12, with a 3.06 ERA and 19 complete games in 1976, before his age finally started to get the better of him. After a subpar 1977 season during which he went 12–8 with a 4.53 ERA, he posted 13 victories and a 3.31 ERA the following year. The Red Sox subsequently offered Tiant just a one-year contract when he became eligible for free agency at season's end, prompting him to sign a two-year deal with the Yankees, who also promised him a scouting position when he retired. Upon learning of Tiant's defection, both Dwight Evans and Carl Yastrzemski expressed their sorrow, with a weeping Yaz stating, "They [Red Sox management] tore out our heart and soul."

Tiant fulfilled the terms of his contract with the Yankees, posting a total of 21 victories in his two years in New York before moving on to Pittsburgh in 1981. Released by the Pirates at the end of the year, Tiant ended his career with the California Angels in 1982. He retired with a career record of 229–172, an ERA of 3.30, 187 complete games, 49 shutouts, and 2,416 strikeouts. In Tiant's eight years with the Red Sox, he went 122–81, with a 3.36 ERA, 113 complete games, 26 shutouts, and 1,075 strikeouts. He

Courtesy Boston Red Sox

ranks among the team's all-time leaders in wins, shutouts, complete games, innings pitched (1,775) and starts (238).

Following his retirement, Tiant spent several years scouting for the Yankees in Mexico. He later became a minor-league coach for the Dodgers and White Sox, before serving as head coach from 1998 to 2001 at the Savannah College of Art and Design. Tiant subsequently rejoined the Red Sox, serving them first as a minor-league pitching coach and, later, as a member of their Spanish broadcasting team.

RED SOX CAREER HIGHLIGHTS

Best Season

Tiant had an outstanding year in 1972, when he finished 15–6 with a league-leading 1.91 ERA. However, he started only 19 games, making another 24 appearances coming out of the bullpen. Tiant also pitched exceptionally well in 1973 and 1976, finishing 20–13, with a 3.34 ERA, 23 complete games, 206 strikeouts, and a league-leading 1.085 WHIP in the first of those campaigns, before going 21–12, with a 3.06 ERA and 19 complete games in 1976. Nevertheless, the feeling here is that Tiant had his best overall season for the Red Sox in 1974, when he finished 22–13, with a 2.92 ERA, 176 strikeouts, 25 complete games, and a league-leading seven shutouts, en route to earning a 4th place finish in the Cy Young voting and an 11th-place ranking in the MVP balloting. Tiant's 22 wins, 25 complete games, and 311 innings pitched all represent career-high marks for him.

Memorable Moments/Greatest Performances

Tiant pitched amazingly well over a period of 10 starts in 1972, compiling a record of 9–1, with six shutouts, nine complete games, and a 0.82 ERA. He began his incredible run with four consecutive shutouts, throwing 40 straight scoreless innings at one point. Included in his streak was a two-hit shutout of the Chicago White Sox on August 19, a game in which he lost his no-hitter with two men out in the eighth inning. With Tiant not having lost a game in nearly two months, Red Sox fans rose to their feet and gave him a standing ovation as he walked to the bullpen to warm up for his start prior to the second game of a twi-night doubleheader against the Orioles on September 20. They subsequently spent most of the evening chanting "Loo-Eee, Loo-Eee, Loo-Eee," as Tiant continued to mow down hitter after hitter. When Tiant came up to bat in the bottom of the eighth inning on his way to another shutout, the crowd again rose to give him an ovation that continued throughout his at-bat, during the break between innings, and throughout the entire top of the ninth. Columnist Larry Claflin wrote in the *Boston Herald* the next morning that he had never heard a sound like it at a game, unless it was "the last time Joe DiMaggio went to bat in Boston." Teammate Carl Yastrzemski said "I've never heard anything like that in my life. But I'll tell you one thing: Tiant deserved every bit of it."

Tiant also turned in a memorable performance on September 16, 1975, when he helped the Red Sox separate themselves from the hard-charging Orioles in the AL East by tossing a five-hit shutout against the Birds, defeating Baltimore ace Jim Palmer by a score of 2–0.

However, Tiant saved his most unforgettable games for the 1975 postseason, getting the Red Sox off to a fast start against Oakland in the ALCS by surrendering just five hits to the three-time defending world champions during a 7–1 Boston victory in Game 1. One week later, he began the 1975 World Series with a 6–0 five-hit shutout of the Cincinnati Reds. Tiant followed that up with a gutsy performance in Game 4, consistently working out of jams and throwing a total of 163 pitches, en route to a complete-game 5–4 win. Tiant faltered somewhat in Game 6, failing to hold an early 3–0 lead, and leaving the contest after the seventh inning with the Red Sox trailing 6–3. However, Bernie Carbo's dramatic three-run homer in the bottom of the eighth tied the score, before Carlton Fisk won the contest with his 12th-inning blast.

Tiant also came up big late in 1978, posting three victories in the season's final nine games, to help force a one-game playoff with the Yankees for the AL East title. Before taking the mound for one of his starts, Tiant stated, "If we lose today, it will be over my dead body. They'll have to leave me face down on the mound."

NOTABLE ACHIEVEMENTS

- Three-time 20-game winner
- Won at least 15 games two other times
- Posted winning percentage in excess of .700 once (.714 in 1972)
- Compiled ERA below 3.00 twice, posting mark below 2.00 once (1.91 in 1972)
- Completed more than 20 games twice
- Threw more than 250 innings four times, topping 300 innings once (311 in 1974)
- Struck out more than 200 batters once (206 in 1973)
- Led AL pitchers in ERA once; shutouts once; and WHIP once
- Ranks among Red Sox all-time leaders in wins (5th); shutouts (4th); strikeouts (7th); complete games (tied-6th); innings pitched (4th); and games started (5th)
- 1972 AL Comeback Player of the Year
- 1975 Babe Ruth Award winner as best postseason performer
- Two-time AL All-Star (1974 and 1976)
- 1975 AL champion

Johnny Pesky

Courtesy Boston Public Library, Leslie Jones Collection

One of the most popular figures in Red Sox history, Johnny Pesky spent more than six decades serving the franchise in one capacity or another, earning in the process the nickname "Mr. Red Sox." After spending the first seven-plus years of his playing career in Boston, Pesky returned to the Red Sox following his retirement to serve them as a manager, broadcaster, coach, and executive at different times. In the process, he witnessed first-hand the exploits of every great player to don a Red Sox uniform since 1940, including the likes of Ted Williams, Carl Yastrzemski, Jim Rice, and Pedro

Martinez. A pretty fair player himself during his time in Boston, Pesky batted over .300 in six of his seven full years in Beantown, leading the American League with more than 200 hits in each of his first three major-league seasons. More than 60 years after he played his last game for the Red Sox, Pesky continues to rank among the team's all-time leaders in batting average and on-base percentage.

Born in Portland, Oregon, on February 27, 1919, John Michael Paveskovich played baseball at Lincoln High School, while also simultaneously performing for several local amateur teams. The son of Croatian immigrants, the young infielder found his name being shortened to "Pesky" by Portland sportswriters, before he ultimately decided to legally change it himself. After being signed by the Red Sox as an amateur free agent in 1940, Pesky spent two years in the minor leagues, posting a batting average of .325 at both his stops, before being called up to the majors at the start of the 1942 campaign.

Appearing in 147 of Boston's 152 games as a rookie, Pesky had an exceptional first season, scoring 105 runs, finishing second in the league to teammate Ted Williams with a batting average of .331, and topping the circuit with 205 hits and 22 sacrifice bunts. He also led all AL shortstops in assists. Pesky's outstanding performance earned him a third-place finish in the league MVP voting.

Apparently well on his way to establishing himself as one of baseball's best middle infielders, Pesky spent the next three years serving in the Navy during World War II, eventually rising to the rank of lieutenant. Following his discharge in 1946, he returned to Boston, where he picked up right where he left off by batting .335, scoring 115 runs, amassing 43 doubles, and leading the league with 208 hits. Pesky posted extremely similar numbers the following year, batting .324, scoring 106 times, and once again topping the circuit in hits, this time with a total of 207. Joe Cronin, who managed the Red Sox during Pesky's first three years in the league, later said, "He was phenomenal in those first three seasons. You couldn't ask for more than he gave."

Bobby Doerr, Pesky's double play partner during that period, expressed his admiration for his teammate when he said, "He's the most dedicated guy I've ever known. The game of baseball is his life. I don't know a single person who loves the game as much."

The Red Sox acquired slugging shortstop Vern Stephens from the St. Louis Browns following the conclusion of the 1947 campaign, prompting them to ask Pesky to move to third base. Pesky handled the switch well, placing second among AL third sackers in assists in his first year at his new position, before leading all league third basemen in putouts, assists, and double plays the following season. He also continued to put up solid offensive numbers each year, batting over .300 and scoring more than 100 runs three more times between 1948 and 1951, while also posting an on-base percentage in excess of .400 in three of those years.

At 5'9" and 168 pounds, Pesky had little power at the plate. Primarily a singles hitter who slapped the ball to all fields, the left-handed hitting Pesky hit only 17 home runs his entire career, hooking several of those around the short right-field foul pole at Fenway Park that correspondingly came to be known as the "Pesky Pole." Pesky's hitting style also made him one of the most difficult men in baseball for opposing pitchers to strike out. In more than 5,500 plate appearances, he fanned a total of only 218 times, never striking out more than 36 times in any campaign. Spending most of his time in Boston batting second in the Red Sox lineup, between Dom DiMaggio and Ted Williams, he later gave those two stars most of the credit for the success he experienced, stating, "I hit behind Dominic DiMaggio, and in front of Ted Williams. I hung on Ted and Dominic's coattails."

Yet, Williams and DiMaggio saw things differently. DiMaggio said in *Forever Fenway*, "John Pesky and I would have a hit-and-run. I think he was the greatest hit-and-run batter that ever put on a uniform."

Meanwhile, Williams suggested, "It didn't take an expert to see he [Pesky] was going to make it real big right from the start with that quick bat, blazing speed, and good glove."

The "Splendid Splinter's" assessment of his teammate and longtime friend actually was a bit out of character for him since the two men shared a unique relationship that author David Halberstam described in 1989 as "a fifty-year marathon of playful insults." Williams gave Pesky the nickname "Needle-Nose" or "Needle" for his most prominent facial feature. The good-natured, self-effacing Pesky didn't mind the moniker in the least, stating on more than one occasion, "They could have called me whatever they wanted. It was just wonderful being in the majors." Pesky also put his nose to good use on the field, flicking it as a way of delivering the hit-and-run sign to DiMaggio. He later joked, "Even a guy with thick glasses like DiMaggio couldn't miss that sign."

With the Red Sox looking to find a regular position for 1950 American League batting champion Billy Goodman, who spent the previous four seasons playing all over the diamond, Pesky became expendable when he started off the 1952 campaign slowly. After posting a batting average of just .149 in 25 games over the first two months of the season, Pesky found himself being included in a huge nine-player trade the Sox completed with Detroit on June 3 that netted them future Hall of Fame third baseman George Kell, among others. Pesky spent the next two years in Detroit, never regaining his earlier form, before being dealt to the Senators midway through the 1954 campaign. He finished out the year in Washington, retiring at season's end with a career batting average of .307, 867 runs scored, 1,455 hits, and a .394 on-base percentage. Pesky's numbers with the Red Sox included 776 runs scored, 1,277 hits, a .313 batting average, and a .401 on-base percentage.

Following his retirement, Pesky signed with the New York Yankees, in whose farm system he began a long and successful coaching career. After coaching at Denver for one year, Pesky managed in the Detroit Tigers minor-league system from 1956 to 1960, and in the Red Sox system in 1961 and 1962. Brought up to manage the big club in 1963, Pesky lasted just two seasons, being fired with two games remaining in the 1964 campaign after finding himself unable to deal with the country-club atmosphere that existed in Boston at that time. Pesky subsequently moved on to Pittsburgh, where he served as a coach with the Pirates in 1965 and 1966, before again returning to Boston, this time as a broadcaster. After six years in the broadcast booth, Pesky returned to the field to serve as first base coach under manager Darrell Johnson in 1975. He spent the next decade serving in that capacity under three different managers until becoming special assistant to the general manager in 1985, and, later, special assignment instructor. After leaving the organization, Pesky remained a loyal follower of the Red Sox, attending the 2004 World Series and subsequently taking part in the Opening Day ceremonies of 2005 in which the members of the team received their World Series Championship rings. In addition to helping Carl Yastrzemski raise the 2004 World Series Championship banner at Fenway Park that day, Pesky had the honor of raising the team's 2007 Championship banner on April 8, 2008. The Red Sox honored his many years of service to the club later that year by retiring his number 6. Johnny Pesky passed away nearly four years later, dying at the Kaplan Family Hospice House in Danvers, Massachusetts, on August 13, 2012, at the age of 92.

Always humble and unassuming, Pesky once said, "I wasn't a great player. I was a decent player. I knew the game, I'd like to think. I know I had a lot of fun."

RED SOX CAREER HIGHLIGHTS

Best Season

Pesky played his best ball for the Red Sox his first three seasons, compiling extremely comparable numbers in each of those campaigns. But, while any of those years would make a good choice, he had his best overall season in 1946. Showing little rust after returning from the war, Pesky scored 115 runs, compiled a .401 on-base percentage, and established career highs with 208 hits, 43 doubles, 265 total bases, a .335 batting average, a .427 slugging percentage, and an OPS of .827. In addition to leading the league in hits, he finished second in runs scored, third in batting average and doubles, fourth in on-base percentage, and sixth in total bases, en route to earning his lone All-Star selection and a fourth-place finish in the AL MVP voting.

Memorable Moments/Greatest Performances

Pesky nearly tied a major-league record by hitting safely in 11 consecutive at-bats during the first week of May 1946. His 11 straight safeties left him just one shy of Pinky Higgins's major-league mark. Pesky continued his hot hitting two days after his streak ended by becoming the first player in American League history to score six runs in one game during a 14–10 victory over the Chicago White Sox on May 8. He went four for five during the contest, with a walk, a double, and two runs batted in.

Pesky also hit well over an extended period during the 1947 campaign, fashioning a 27-game hitting streak that remains one of the longest in Red Sox history.

Yet, ironically, Pesky is perhaps remembered most for a play he didn't make, being victimized by Enos Slaughter on the latter's famous "Mad Dash" around the bases in Game 7 of the 1946 World Series. Slaughter, already in motion when the Red Sox pitcher began his delivery to home plate, never hesitated once Harry Walker delivered his hit to short left-center field. Pesky received the cutoff throw from backup outfielder Leon Culberson with his back to home plate, hesitated for one brief moment to locate Slaughter, and then threw home too late to nab the Cardinals base-runner. Subsequently accused of "holding the ball," Pesky spent the rest of his life fielding questions about the play. However, Cardinals catcher Joe Garagiola later stated on numerous occasions that Slaughter would have scored the winning run with or without any hesitation from Pesky. For his part, Pesky returned home to Portland, Oregon, after the Series and stayed in his house for five weeks before finally coming out. Displaying his characteristic good nature, he told the *Boston Globe* years later, "If you're a palooka, you've got to live with it."

Courtesy Mears Online Auctions

NOTABLE ACHIEVEMENTS

- Batted over .300 six times, surpassing the .330 mark twice
- Scored more than 100 runs six times, topping 120 runs scored once (124 in 1948)
- Surpassed 200 hits three times
- Topped 40 doubles once (43 in 1946)
- Walked more than 100 times twice
- Compiled on-base percentage in excess of .400 four times
- Led AL in base hits three times; sacrifice hits once; and at-bats twice
- Led AL shortstops in assists once (1942)
- Led AL third basemen in putouts once; assists once; and double plays twice
- Ranks among Red Sox career leaders in batting average (9th) and on-base percentage (7th)
- Finished in top five in AL MVP voting twice (3rd in 1942; 4th in 1946)
- Two-time *Sporting News* All-Star selection (1942 and 1946)
- 1946 AL All-Star
- 1946 AL champion

Vern Stephens

Courtesy Boston Public Library, Leslie Jones Collection

Although largely forgotten today, Vern Stephens slugged home runs at a faster pace than any other major-league shortstop prior to the arrival of Ernie Banks in Chicago during the 1950s. A powerfully built right-handed batter, Stephens hit more than 20 homers six times during his career, doing so in each of his first three seasons in Boston, after the Red Sox acquired him for a boatload of players and $375,000 following the 1947 campaign. Inserted immediately behind Ted Williams in the Red Sox batting order, Stephens went on to form one-half of the American League's most formidable one-two punch over the course of the next few seasons, surpassing 30 home runs twice, scoring more than 100 runs three times, and topping the junior circuit in RBIs in both 1949 and 1950. Meanwhile, even though he lacked the range of some of the game's more slightly built shortstops such as Phil Rizzuto, Pee Wee Reese, and Marty Marion, Stephens possessed a much stronger throwing arm, enabling him to lead all players at his position in assists three straight times at one point during his career.

Born in McAllister, New Mexico, on October 23, 1920, Vernon Decatur Stephens eventually settled with his family in Long Beach, California, where he attended Polytechnic High School. A naturally gifted athlete who also played basketball and swam in high school, Stephens later attributed his exceptional upper body strength to swimming. Upon his graduation from Polytechnic, Stephens spent one year at Long Beach Junior College, before his .522 batting average there convinced him to turn pro. After being pursued by the Red Sox and Cleveland Indians as well, Stephens signed with the St. Louis Browns as an amateur free agent in 1938, while still only 17 years of age. Stephens spent the next four years honing his skills in the St. Louis farm system, making such a strong impression on San Antonio manager Marty McManus in 1940 that the former big-league shortstop called him "the best shortstop prospect I have ever seen."

Following a late-season call-up to St. Louis in 1941, Stephens joined the Browns for good the following year, earning the starting shortstop job in spring training. Although the 21-year-old Stephens committed a league-leading 42 errors as a rookie, he excelled at the plate, hitting 14 homers, driving in 92 runs, and batting .294, en route to earning a fourth-place finish in the AL MVP voting.

A knee injury Stephens first suffered in the minor leagues caused him to flunk his army physical, enabling him to continue his professional career while most of the game's best players entered the military to serve in World War II. The young shortstop thrived during the war years, earning three top-10 finishes in the league MVP balloting, topping the junior circuit in home runs and RBIs once each, and leading the Browns to their first and only pennant in 1944, when he hit 20 homers and led the league with 109 runs batted in.

Stephens hardly resembled the prototypical shortstop of his time. Standing 5'10" and weighing 185 pounds, he had a very strong upper body that allowed him to drive balls with power to all fields. A right-handed hitter, he had a spread stance and stood deep in the batter's box. Mark Christman, who shared the left side of the St. Louis infield with Stephens, marveled at his teammate's strength in William Mead's classic book on wartime baseball,

Even the Browns, noting that, even though he played his home games at Sportsman's Park, a notoriously tough park for right-handed hitters, Stephens had the ability to hit the ball onto the pavilion roof in right-center field. And, even though Stephens perhaps lacked the range of some of his contemporaries in the field, his powerful throwing arm enabled him to cut off many balls by playing deeper. In fact, Christman compared Stephens favorably to the Cardinals' Marty Marion in Mead's book, stating that his teammate had, "not as good hands, but he covered as much ground, and he had an arm like a shotgun."

A salary dispute with Browns management at the conclusion of the 1945 campaign prompted Stephens to use the rival Mexican League as a negotiating ploy. However, after signing a five-year, $175,000 contract to play in Mexico, Stephens returned to the United States when the Browns increased their offer. Stephens remained in St. Louis two more years, totaling 29 home runs and 147 RBIs in 1946 and 1947, before the Red Sox took advantage of the Browns' financial woes by offering them nine marginal players and the inordinately large sum of $375,000 for the star shortstop, utility infielder Billy Hitchcock, and pitchers Ellis Kinder and Jack Kramer.

Stephens's arrival in Boston prompted the Red Sox to shift Johnny Pesky to third base, even though prior speculation had the former Browns shortstop manning the hot corner instead. In discussing his shift in positions, Pesky later said, "I knew Stephens was a shortstop, and I was willing to play anywhere. I'd have played right field if that would have let Stephens play. I knew how good a player he was."

Stephens, who led all American League shortstops in assists in his final year in St. Louis, continued that trend, topping all players at his position in assists in each of his first two seasons in Boston as well. Commenting on his new double play partner's fielding skills, Bobby Doerr told *Sport* magazine in 1948, "Stephens is nice to work with, like Pesky. They cooperate on pop flies in the sun, and work with you on other plays. Perhaps the best thing that impresses me about Vern is the speed with which he goes across the bag on double plays."

Stephens made even more of an impact at the plate, helping the Red Sox increase their win total by 13 games with his outstanding offensive production. Finding Fenway Park very much to his liking, he hit 29 home runs, scored 114 runs, and finished second in the league to Joe DiMaggio with 137 RBIs in 1948, en route to earning All-Star honors for the first of four straight times and a fourth-place finish in the AL MVP voting. Stephens followed that up by posting even more impressive numbers in 1949, finishing the year with

39 homers, 113 runs scored, a .290 batting average, and a league-leading 159 runs batted in. He compiled outstanding numbers again in 1950, hitting 30 home runs, finishing second in the league with 125 runs scored, batting .295, and once again topping the circuit in RBIs, this time with a total of 144.

Yet, amazingly, Stephens failed to earn *Sporting News* All-Star honors in any of those seasons, losing out to Cleveland's Lou Boudreau in 1948 and New York's Phil Rizzuto the other two years. While the members of the BBWAA named Boudreau and Rizzuto AL MVP in 1948 and 1950, respectively, it remains something of a mystery as to why Stephens failed to earn a spot on the *Sporting News* All-Star squad the other year, especially when it is considered that his offensive numbers far exceeded those compiled by every other player at his position, and, also, that he led all AL shortstops in assists.

Perhaps at least part of the answer lies in the fact that Stephens occasionally drew criticism for posting those huge offensive totals in Fenway Park. Yet, even though the slugging shortstop undoubtedly benefitted from taking aim at the "Green Monster" in half his games, he still averaged 15 home runs and 67 RBIs *on the road* from 1948 to 1950. He also played solid defense, rarely missed a game, and got along well with his manager and teammates.

Opposing pitchers certainly held Stephens in high esteem, with Ed Rummill quoting Yankee left-hander Ed Lopat in the Fall 1951 issue of *Complete Baseball* as saying, "He's tough, real tough . . . if you throw one to the outside corner, he's liable to hit it down the right field line for two or three bases." Browns right-hander Ned Garver told the same writer, "That Stephens gives me as much trouble as the rest of the Red Sox combined." Jack Kramer added, "Stephens is as strong as [Jimmie] Foxx ever was. I'm convinced of it."

Stephens moved to third when the Red Sox acquired Lou Boudreau from Cleveland prior to the start of the 1951 campaign, leaving Boudreau to split time at shortstop with Johnny Pesky. However, Stephens aggravated his old knee injury during the season, limiting him to only 109 games and 377 official at-bats. Nevertheless, he still managed to hit 17 home runs, drive in 78 runs, and bat an even .300.

Unfortunately, injuries continued to mount for Stephens the following year, enabling him to hit only 7 home runs, drive in just 44 runs, and hit only .254, in fewer than 300 official at-bats. The Red Sox traded Stephens to the Chicago White Sox for three nondescript players at the end of the year, ending his five-year stay in Boston. Stephens subsequently spent his final three seasons serving as a part-time player, splitting his time between the White Sox, Browns, and Orioles (following the Browns to Baltimore, where they changed their name). After being released by the White Sox midway through the 1955 campaign, he signed with the Seattle Rainiers of the Pacific Coast League, where he played through the end of the 1956 season before finally announcing his retirement. Stephens ended his major-league career with 247 home runs, 1,174 runs batted in, 1,001 runs scored, 1,859 hits, a .286 batting average, a .355 on-base percentage, and a .460 slugging percentage. In his five years with the Red Sox, he hit 122 homers, knocked in 562 runs, scored 449, accumulated 721 hits, batted .283, compiled a .364 on-base percentage, and posted a .492 slugging percentage.

Only 35 years old at the time of his retirement, Stephens subsequently turned to golf, which he had taken up during his holdout in 1946. He eventually became one of the best amateurs in the state of California, appearing in numerous Pro-Am tournaments, including the Bing Crosby National at Pebble Beach. Stephens also became a sales representative for several companies, including the Bechtel Corporation at Long Beach, where he suffered a heart attack while lifting a piece of machinery on November 3, 1968. Rushed to the hospital, he died the following day, less than two weeks after celebrating his 48th birthday.

RED SOX CAREER HIGHLIGHTS

Best Season

Stephens played exceptionally well for the Red Sox in both 1948 and 1950, knocking in 137 runs and scoring 114 others in the first of those years, and batting .295, hitting 30 home runs, driving in a league-leading 144 runs, and reaching career-high marks with 125 runs scored, 185 hits, and 34 doubles in 1950. However, he had his best season in 1949, when, in addition to batting .290 and scoring 113 runs, he established career highs with 39 home runs, 101 walks, 329 total bases, a .391 on-base percentage, a .539 slugging average, and a league-leading 159 RBIs. Stephens's 39 homers established a new record for major-league shortstops (later broken by Ernie Banks). Meanwhile, his 159 RBIs, which tie him with Ted Williams for the second-highest single-season total in Red Sox history, remain the standard for players at his position. In fact, no other player surpassed that figure until Manny Ramirez knocked in 165 runs for Cleveland 50 years later.

Memorable Moments/Greatest Performances

Despite being known more for his offense, Stephens entered the record books for his glove work on May 5, 1948, tying a major-league record for shortstops by participating in five double plays during a 4–3 Red Sox victory over Detroit.

However, Stephens experienced the vast majority of his most memorable moments in Boston as a result of his bat. On August 24, 1948, he delivered a two-run homer in the bottom of the ninth inning that gave the Red Sox a 9–8 win over the Cleveland Indians. Just four days later, Stephens went 4 for 4, with two doubles, two RBIs, and one run scored during a 6–2 victory over the Chicago White Sox.

Stephens had another big day at the plate on July 17, 1949, knocking in all four Red Sox runs during a 4–2, 2–1 doubleheader split with the Indians in Cleveland. After going 2 for 3, with a homer, two RBIs, and one run scored in the 4–2 opening game loss, Stephens collected three hits in four times at bat in the nitecap, including a game-winning homer in the top of the ninth inning.

Stephens provided more heroics on August 24, 1950, when his grand slam home run in the bottom of the ninth inning gave the Red Sox a 6–2 win over the St. Louis Browns. He delivered another dramatic home run on May 30, 1951, giving the Red Sox an 11–10 victory in the first game of a doubleheader sweep of the Yankees by homering off Specs Shea in the bottom of the 15th inning.

NOTABLE ACHIEVEMENTS

- Hit more than 30 home runs twice
- Knocked in more than 130 runs three times, surpassing the 150 mark once (159 in 1949)
- Scored more than 100 runs three times, topping 120 runs scored once (125 in 1950).
- Batted .300 once (1951)
- Surpassed 30 doubles twice
- Walked more than 100 times once (101 in 1949)
- Compiled slugging percentage in excess of .500 three times
- Led AL in runs batted in and games played twice each
- Led AL shortstops in assists twice and double plays once
- Ranks tenth all-time on Red Sox with career slugging percentage of .492
- Finished fourth in 1948 AL MVP voting
- Four-time AL All-Star

Jackie Jensen

Courtesy Boston Red Sox

An intense fear of flying, coupled with concerns over his failing marriage, forced Jackie Jensen into premature retirement at the age of 32. Nevertheless, Jensen accomplished enough during his seven seasons in Boston to earn a prominent place in these rankings. One of the finest all-around athletes ever to play for the Red Sox, Jensen possessed power at the plate, speed on the base paths and in the outfield, and a strong throwing arm that enabled him to lead all AL outfielders in assists once and double plays twice. After being acquired by the Red Sox from Washington prior to the 1954 campaign, the right-handed hitting Jensen knocked in 667 runs over the course of the next six seasons—more than any other player in the major leagues. He led the AL in RBIs three times during that period, topped the circuit in stolen bases once, batted over .300 once, and earned league MVP honors in 1958, when he hit 35 home runs, drove in 122 runs, and batted .286. Only Jensen's own insecurities likely prevented him from going down as one of the greatest players in Red Sox history.

Born in San Francisco on March 9, 1927, Jack Eugene Jensen experienced little in the way of stability while growing up on the West Coast. Jensen's parents divorced when he was five, leaving his mother to raise him alone. The fact that Jensen barely knew his father and spent most of his youth moving from one place to another with his financially strapped mother caused him to spend most of his adult life seeking the security of a warm and loving home.

Still, the blond-haired, blue-eyed Jensen seemingly lived a charmed life to most outsiders. After graduating from Technical High School in Oakland, California, where he starred in baseball and football, Jensen served in the Navy near the end of World War II. Following his discharge, he attended the University of California, where he earned consensus All-America honors as a halfback in football, and as a pitcher and outfielder in baseball. After helping California win the inaugural College World Series in 1947, Jensen became the first player in school history to rush for 1,000 yards the following year. Displaying his exceptional all-around ability on the gridiron in California's 1948 season-ending 7–6 victory over Stanford, Jensen rushed for 170 yards, punted once for 67 yards, and converted a late-game 4th-and-31 situation by running for 32 yards on a faked punt. Although California ended up losing the 1949 Rose Bowl to seventh-ranked Northwestern by a score of 20–14, Jensen rushed for a 67-yard touchdown during the contest, en route to earning a fourth-place finish in the Heisman Trophy balloting.

Shortly after completing his junior year in 1949, Jensen left college to sign with the Oakland Oaks of the Pacific Coast League. A few months later, the 22-year-old Jensen married 18-year-old Zoe Ann Olsen, who won 14 national diving championships and a silver medal in the 1948 Olympics. Jensen's string of good fortune continued when the Yankees purchased his and teammate Billy Martin's contracts from Oakland prior to the start of the 1950 campaign.

Frequently referred to as the "Golden Boy" upon his arrival in New York due to his blond hair, good looks, chiseled body, and successful college career, Jensen was initially expected to replace the aging Joe DiMaggio in center field. However, Jensen batted only .171 in a back-up role in his first year with the Yankees. His play improved considerably in 1951, but, with Mickey Mantle joining the Yankees that year as well, Jensen once again found himself on the bench much of the time. The Yankees subsequently included Jensen in a six-player trade they completed with Washington on May 3, 1952, finally giving the young outfielder an opportunity to play. Starting in right field for the Senators in 1952, Jensen hit 10 homers, knocked in 82 runs, scored 83, batted .280, and compiled a league-leading 17 outfield assists, en route to earning the first of his three All-Star selections. Jensen posted extremely similar numbers for Washington the following year, after which the Red Sox acquired him for pitcher Mickey McDermott and outfielder Tom Umphlett.

Far more comfortable playing in the shadow of Ted Williams, Jensen flourished in Boston, batting .276 and establishing new career highs with 25 home runs, 117 RBIs, 92 runs scored, and a league-leading 22 stolen bases in his first year with the Red Sox. He followed that up with three more outstanding seasons, averaging 23 homers, 105 RBIs and 86 runs scored from 1955 to 1957, while posting batting averages of .275, .315, and .281. Jensen performed particularly well in 1955 and 1956, hitting 26 homers, scoring 95 runs, and knocking in a league-leading 116 runs in the first of those campaigns, before driving in 97 runs and batting a career-high .315 in the second.

The Red Sox finished no higher than third in any of Jensen's first four years with them, winning as many as 84 games twice. They continued on a similar path in 1958, posting 79 victories and finishing third in the AL standings. Nevertheless, Jensen captured league MVP honors by hitting 35 home runs, batting .286, scoring 83 runs, topping the circuit with 122 runs batted in, and placing among the leaders with a .396 on-base percentage and a .535 slugging percentage. He had another big year in 1959, hitting 28 homers, driving in a league-leading 112 runs, scoring 101 times, and earning Gold Glove honors for the only time in his career.

Yet, even as Jensen continued to perform at an extremely high level, he lapsed deeper and deeper into an emotional abyss. Plagued throughout his career by a fear of flying, Jensen gradually developed an intense phobia toward air travel as his marriage continued to deteriorate. Red Sox owner Tom Yawkey tried to help Jensen combat his aversion to flying by arranging for therapy treatments. But the sessions proved to be ineffective, with Jensen's condition becoming so bad that he often woke up in the middle of the night shaking and trembling. His teeth chattered on flights, and he frequently had to resort to pills or liquor just to board a plane. Frank Mal-zone and Pete Runnels, two of his closest friends on the team, routinely found themselves hauling an unconscious Jensen aboard team flights. Jensen later stated in an April 12, 1976, *Sports Illustrated* article entitled "A Fear of Flying," "I would be out when they got me to my seat, usually with some sleeping pill. Then, when the engines started, I'd be wide awake and every-body else on the plane would be sound asleep."

Realizing that his psychological problems were likely to bring his play-ing career to a premature end, Jensen said during spring training in 1959, "Well, no matter how lucrative my career may get from here on, I can tell you it won't last one day longer than necessary. Nobody's going to have to rip the uniform off my back. I can hardly wait for the time when I'll be in a position to do that myself."

Jensen decided to end his playing career sooner, rather than later, announcing his retirement from baseball in January 1960. He cited as his pri-mary reasons for leaving the game at the age of 32 his fear of flying and the anxiety he experienced while being separated from his family for long periods of time. In making his announcement Jensen stated, "I have only one life to live, and I'll be happier when I can spend it with my family. Being away from home with a baseball team for seven months a year doesn't represent the kind of life I want, or the kind of life my wife and children want."

Jensen ended up sitting out only one year before attempting a comeback in 1961. However, he failed to regain his earlier form after he returned to the Red Sox, concluding the campaign with just 13 home runs, 66 runs batted in, and a .263 batting average. Furthermore, Jensen cured neither his marriage woes nor his fear of flying during his time away from the game, divorcing his wife a few years later and continuing to experience panic attacks every time he needed to board an airplane. Jensen finally turned to hypnotherapy as a means of alleviating his fears, but he found only marginal comfort from the many sessions he attended.

Weary of the effort he needed to put forth to continue his career, and frustrated with his disappointing performance, Jensen called it quits for good at the end of 1961. He concluded his 11-year playing career with 199 home runs, 929 runs batted in, 810 runs scored, 1,463 hits, a .279 batting average, a .369 on-base percentage, and a .460 slugging percentage. In his seven seasons with the Red Sox, Jensen hit 170 homers, knocked in 733 runs, scored 597 others, accumulated 1,089 hits, batted .282, compiled a .374 on-base percentage, and posted a .478 slugging percentage.

Unable to save his marriage or overcome his fear of flying, Jensen later realized that he made a mistake by retiring as early as he did, stating on one occasion, "Looking back, it was foolish to quit. But I thought it would answer my problems."

Following his retirement, Jensen experienced numerous business failures before becoming sports director at a Reno, Nevada, radio station, and, later, a college football broadcaster for ABC television. He suffered a heart attack at only 42 years of age in 1969, just one year after he divorced his first wife and married Katherine Cortezi, who subsequently brought a sense of stability into his life. After recovering from his near-fatal illness, Jensen went on to coach baseball at the University of Nevada and, also, at his alma mater, the University of California. Jensen suffered another heart attack on July 14, 1982—one that ended up taking his life. He was only 55 years old at the time of his passing.

Some six years earlier, Jensen discussed his premature retirement from baseball in *Sports Illustrated*, telling that publication:

> There is no question I was looking for an excuse to leave the ball club, and I know the fear [of flying] was related to the insecurity of my first marriage. I wanted to go home, but I loved baseball. I got terribly down on myself. I could think about it rationally, ask myself why I couldn't beat this thing. "You don't have to like flying," I'd say to myself. "A lot of people don't but they still fly." But, when the time came, I just couldn't make myself do it. . . . I came to resent myself for behaving in such an infantile way. I know I had another four years that I could've played. The way I was driving in runs, I could have set some records. My only regret is that now I can't hope to be considered for the Hall of Fame.

RED SOX CAREER HIGHLIGHTS

Best Season

Jensen had a big year in 1956, when he hit 20 homers, knocked in 97 runs, and established career highs with 182 hits, a league-leading 11 triples, a .315 batting average, and a .405 on-base percentage. He also performed exceptionally well in 1959, placing among the league leaders with 28 home runs, 101 runs scored, 31 doubles, 20 stolen bases, 88 walks, and a .492 slugging percentage, while earning the only Gold Glove of his career. However, Jensen's MVP campaign of 1958 proved to be the finest of his career. In addition to leading the league with a career-high 122 runs batted in, Jensen finished second in walks (99), fifth in homers (35), doubles (31), and on-base percentage (.396), and sixth in slugging percentage (.535). Jensen's OPS of .931 represented the highest mark of his career.

Memorable Moments/Greatest Performances

Jensen came up big for the Red Sox on September 21, 1954, driving in five of the eight runs they scored during a doubleheader sweep of the Philadelphia Athletics. After giving his team a 4–3 win in the opener by singling home the winning run in the bottom of the 10th inning, Jensen delivered a three-run homer in the nitecap to give the Red Sox another 4–3 victory.

Jensen had the biggest day of his career on August 2, 1956, leading the Red Sox to an 18–3 romp over the Detroit Tigers by knocking in nine runs. Jensen went three for five during the contest, knocking in three runs with a first-inning homer, and driving home another three runs with a bases-loaded triple.

Jensen experienced the greatest power surge of his career from June 27 to July 1, 1958, homering in four straight games. He went 6 for 15 during the streak, with 5 home runs and 11 RBIs.

NOTABLE ACHIEVEMENTS

- Hit more than 20 home runs six straight times, topping 30 homers once (35 in 1958)
- Knocked in more than 100 runs five times, surpassing 120 RBIs once (122 in 1958)
- Scored more than 100 runs once (101 in 1959)
- Batted over .300 once (.315 in 1956)
- Finished in double-digits in triples once (11 in 1956)
- Surpassed 30 doubles twice
- Stole at least 20 bases twice
- Compiled on-base percentage in excess of .400 once (.405 in 1956)
- Posted slugging percentage in excess of .500 once (.535 in 1958)
- Led AL in RBIs three times; triples once; stolen bases once; and sacrifice flies three times
- Led AL outfielders in assists once and double plays twice
- Led AL right fielders in assists twice and fielding percentage once
- 1958 AL MVP
- 1959 Gold Glove winner
- Two-time AL All-Star (1955 and 1958)

Fred Lynn

Courtesy Boston Red Sox

The first player in major-league history to capture Rookie of the Year and MVP honors in the same season, Fred Lynn took the American League by storm in 1975, leading the Red Sox to the pennant by topping the junior circuit in four offensive categories, placing among the leaders in six others, and winning the first of his four Gold Gloves. Lynn continued to shine in his five remaining years in Boston, earning All-Star honors each season, and placing in the top five in the league MVP voting once more. However, the center fielder's all-out style of play ended up hurting him in the long run, forcing him onto the DL any number of times, reducing his speed and ball-hawking ability somewhat, and preventing him from compiling the Hall of Fame type numbers he appeared capable of producing early in his career. With Lynn's period of dominance limited to a few short seasons, the members of the BBWAA never seriously considered him when he became eligible for induction into Cooperstown. Nevertheless, he clearly earned a prominent place in these rankings with his exceptional all-around ability and willingness to make sacrifices for his team. A throwback player with an "old-school" mentality, Lynn believed in always putting forth a 100 percent effort, displaying little regard for his body over the course of his career by crashing into outfield walls and sliding hard into second base to break up potential double plays. Lynn's fearless style of play and strong work ethic made him a fan favorite, not only in Boston, but around the American League. In discussing the manner with which he approached his chosen profession, Lynn said in a 1977 interview, "People are going to say we're in it just for the money, and nothing else. But that's not true. I really like the game. It's more than a job to me. It's a part of me, and has been all my life. I'm happy that I came along when I did and am well paid. But, with me, it's a matter of pride, not money. I enjoy the game."

Born in Chicago, Illinois, on February 3, 1952, Fredric Michael Lynn grew up in Southern California after moving with his family to the suburbs of Los Angeles at the age of one. A three-sport star at El Monte High School, Lynn lettered in baseball, football, and basketball, pitching and playing center field for his school's baseball team and playing on both offense and defense for the football squad. Drafted by the Yankees in the third round of the 1970 amateur draft, Lynn instead elected to enroll at the University of Southern California on a football scholarship. Although he acquitted himself well on the gridiron in his first year at USC, he eventually decided to concentrate solely on baseball, switching his scholarship during his sophomore year. After earning All-America honors in 1972 and 1973 by leading the Trojans to their second and third consecutive NCAA Baseball Championships, Lynn signed with the Red Sox when they selected him in the second round of the 1973 amateur draft. He spent most of 1973 playing for Boston's Double-A affiliate in Bristol, Connecticut, before being promoted to Triple-A Pawtucket, where he helped his new team win the International League playoffs.

After spending virtually all of 1974 with Pawtucket, Lynn earned his first major-league call-up late in the year, compiling a batting average of .419, hitting two homers, and driving in 10 runs over the final two weeks of the campaign. He subsequently claimed the starting center field job early in 1975, being joined in the Boston outfield by fellow rookie and former Pawtucket teammate Jim Rice. With both players excelling throughout the campaign, they soon became known as the "Gold Dust Twins." Rice made his greatest impact at the plate, consistently driving balls off, and over, Fenway's "Green Monster" with his powerful right-handed swing. Meanwhile, Lynn excelled in all phases of the game. A true "five-tool player," Lynn possessed power, speed, and superior defensive ability. Joe Torre stated in *Out by a Step: The 100 Best Players Not in the Baseball Hall of Fame*, "Freddie Lynn to me was a [Don] Mattingly when he first came up—you didn't know how to get him out. He could run—Mattingly couldn't run . . . but Freddie, he was a pretty player to watch. The great swing, hit the ball all over the place, played center field at Fenway and looked so easy doing it."

Lynn ended up hitting 21 home runs, knocking in 105 runs, finishing second in the league with a .331 batting average, and topping the circuit with 47 doubles, 103 runs scored, a .566 slugging percentage, and an OPS of .967, en route to earning AL Rookie of the Year and league MVP honors. An outstanding all-around hitter, Lynn demonstrated right from the start his ability to turn on inside pitches and pull them into the stands in right field. He also used his smooth left-handed swing to frequently drive outside offerings off the left field wall at Fenway.

Yet, Lynn made an equally strong impression with his exceptional fielding ability, displaying outstanding range and instincts in center field, and, also, a strong and accurate throwing arm. Whether robbing an opposing batter of a base hit by diving for a line drive, or reaching over the fence to take away an apparent home run, Lynn proved to be absolutely fearless in the outfield. Reflecting back on the pride he took in his defense in a 2004 interview with Jon Goode at Boston.com, Lynn stated, "I am most proud of the Gold Gloves and really cherished those. I prided myself on defense. When I played basketball and football I always wanted to guard the toughest guy. When I played center field, I felt like I was guarding somebody, and I didn't want any ball to fall in my area. I took it personally when balls would fall in and I didn't catch them."

A true team player as well, Lynn downplayed his personal accomplishments after being named AL MVP in 1975, stating in the *1976 Complete Handbook of Baseball*, "One man doesn't make a team. All the awards are great, but they are secondary to winning. If we didn't win, none of these awards would mean anything."

The Red Sox failed to return to the playoffs in each of the next two seasons, with Lynn missing a significant amount of playing time each year due to injury. Nevertheless, he performed well whenever he found himself able to take the field, batting .314, scoring 76 runs, and stealing a career-high 14 bases in 1976, and hitting 18 homers, driving in 76 runs, and scoring 81 times in 1977, after sitting out the first month of the campaign with torn ligaments in his left ankle.

Healthy again in 1978, Lynn helped Boston post 99 regular-season wins by hitting 22 home runs, knocking in 82 runs, scoring 75, and batting .298, while also winning the first of three consecutive Gold Gloves. However, a one-game playoff loss to the Yankees prevented Lynn and the Red Sox from advancing to the postseason. Although the Red Sox could do no better than third the following year, Lynn had the finest statistical season of his career after spending the entire offseason working out on Nautilus equipment. Lynn concluded the 1979 campaign with 39 home runs, 122 runs batted in, 116 runs scored, and a league-leading .333 batting average, .423 on-base percentage, and .637 slugging percentage. Unfortunately, the injury bug once again bit Lynn in 1980, limiting him to only 110 games. Yet, he still managed to bat over .300 (.301) for the fourth time in six seasons.

When Lynn failed to come to terms on a new contract with Boston at the end of the year, the Red Sox included him in a five-player trade they completed with the California Angels on January 23, 1981, that netted them Joe Rudi, Frank Tanana, and Jim Dorsey. Although Lynn enjoyed playing in his home state, he later expressed his appreciation for the fans of Boston when he said, "They supported you all the time. They were always there and let you know what they were feeling in the good side and the bad side, which was OK. As a player, it keeps you on your toes. You don't ever come to Fenway with a complacent attitude. You come there to play, otherwise they will let you know you are not living up to their expectations, and I liked that."

Lynn remained in California the next four seasons, making the AL All-Star team each year from 1981 to 1983. He played his best ball for the Angels in 1982, concluding the campaign with 21 homers, 86 RBIs, 89 runs scored, and a .299 batting average. Lynn subsequently signed with the Orioles as a free agent prior to the 1985 season, spending most of the next four seasons in Baltimore. Plagued by injuries much of the time in California and Baltimore, Lynn never again ascended to the same heights he reached early in his career with the Red Sox. Nevertheless, he remained an extremely productive player for both teams, surpassing 20 home runs seven straight times from 1982 to 1988. Traded to the Tigers late in 1988, Lynn remained in Detroit through the end of 1989, after which he signed a one-year free-agent deal with the San Diego Padres. He retired after one year in San Diego, concluding his career with 306 home runs, 1,111 RBIs, 1,063 runs scored, 1,960 hits, a .283 batting average, a .360 on-base percentage, and a .484 slugging percentage. During his time in Boston, Lynn hit 124 homers, drove in 521 runs, scored 523 others, accumulated 944 hits, batted .308, compiled a .383 on-base percentage, and posted a .520 slugging percentage.

Following his retirement, Lynn worked as a color commentator for ESPN from 1991 to 1998, doing some College World Series and West Coast MLB games. He also began donating a considerable amount of time to charitable work, including the FACE Foundation, which helps underprivileged families pay for life-saving surgeries for their pets.

Although Lynn ended up playing for five different teams and spent only six of his 16 full major-league seasons in Boston, he considers himself a member of the Red Sox family, stating on one occasion, "I'm a Red Sox. I didn't want to leave the Red Sox. I came up with them and, from 1973 to 1980, I was their property. I thought I'd end up spending my entire career in Boston. It was tough, even though I was going to a great team and playing for a great owner in Gene Autry."

Courtesy Boston
Red Sox

RED SOX CAREER HIGHLIGHTS

Best Season

Lynn had easily his two best seasons in 1975 and 1979, placing in the league's top five in nine different offensive categories both years. In addition to hitting 21 home runs, knocking in 105 runs, batting .331, and compiling a .401 on-base percentage in 1975, Lynn topped the junior circuit with 103 runs scored, 47 doubles, a .566 slugging percentage, and an OPS of .967. Yet, even though the Red Sox won the pennant and Lynn captured AL MVP and Rookie of the Year honors that year, he actually posted significantly better numbers in most categories in 1979, when he established career highs with 39 homers, 122 RBIs, 116 runs scored, 177 hits, 82 walks, 338 total bases, and a league-leading .333 batting average, .423 on-base percentage, .637 slugging percentage, and 1.059 OPS. All things considered, Lynn had the finest season of his career in 1979.

Memorable Moments/Greatest Performances

At one point during his fabulous rookie season of 1975, Lynn reached base safely in 38 consecutive games. Included in his streak was a June 18 effort against the Detroit Tigers that ranks as one of the greatest hitting performances in Red Sox history. In leading his team to a 15–1 victory at Tiger Stadium, Lynn went 5 for 6, with three home runs, a triple, a single, 10 RBIs, and four runs scored. His 16 total bases on the day tied an American League record.

Lynn had another memorable day on May 13, 1980, when he hit for the cycle during a 10–5 Red Sox win over Minnesota at Fenway. In addition to going four for five on the day, Lynn knocked in four runs and scored two others.

An outstanding big-game performer throughout his career, Lynn had an exceptional 1975 postseason, batting .364 and driving in three runs against Oakland in the ALCS, before homering once and knocking in five runs against Cincinnati in the World Series. Although the dramatic home runs hit by Bernie Carbo and Carlton Fisk during the latter stages of Game 6 have become a part of Boston folklore, forgotten by many is Lynn's three-run first-inning blast that gave the Red Sox an early 3–0 lead.

NOTABLE ACHIEVEMENTS

- Hit more than 20 home runs three times, topping 30 homers once (39 in 1979)
- Knocked in more than 100 runs twice
- Scored more than 100 runs twice
- Batted over .300 four times, topping the .330 mark twice
- Surpassed 30 doubles five times, topping 40 mark twice
- Compiled on-base percentage in excess of .400 twice
- Posted slugging percentage in excess of .500 twice, topping .600 mark once (.637 in 1979)
- Compiled OPS in excess of 1.000 once (1.059 in 1979)
- Led AL in batting average once; runs scored once; doubles once; on-base percentage once; slugging percentage twice; and OPS twice
- Led AL center fielders in fielding percentage once and double plays once
- Ranks among Red Sox career leaders in slugging percentage (7th) and OPS (7th)
- Hit three home runs in one game vs. Detroit Tigers on June 18, 1975.
- Hit for cycle vs. Minnesota Twins on May 13, 1980.
- 1975 AL MVP
- 1975 AL Rookie of the Year
- First player to win Rookie of the Year and MVP Awards in the same season (1975)
- Four-time Gold Glove winner
- Three-time *Sporting News* All-Star selection (1975, 1978, and 1979)
- Six-time AL All-Star
- 1975 AL champion

Lefty Grove

Courtesy Boston Public Library, Leslie Jones Collection

One of the greatest pitchers in baseball history, Lefty Grove arrived in Boston in 1934 already having notched 195 victories as a member of the Philadelphia Athletics. Dealt to the Red Sox by the A's in the midst of the Great Depression for financial reasons, the 34-year-old Grove no longer possessed the blazing fastball that made him the sport's most dominant hurler during his time in Philadelphia. In addition to posting an overall record of 195–79 in his nine years with the A's, the lanky left-hander compiled an ERA of

2.88—an exceptional figure when it is considered that the period extending from the 1920s into the early 1930s became known for its tremendous offensive production. Over the course of those nine seasons, Grove led all American League pitchers in wins and winning percentage four times each, ERA five times, and strikeouts a record seven consecutive times, en route to winning two Triple Crowns. Yet, even though Grove lacked his once-overpowering fastball by the time he joined the Red Sox, he still had enough left in his arsenal to win more than 60 percent of his decisions during his time in Beantown, while capturing another four ERA titles. Relying heavily on off-speed pitches and guile, Grove won at least 14 games for the Red Sox five straight times, surpassing 20 victories once and 17 wins two other times. In the process, he reached the 300-win plateau for his career, leaving behind him a legacy that has prompted many baseball historians to identify him as the greatest left-handed pitcher who ever lived.

Born in Lonaconing, Maryland, on March 6, 1900, Robert Moses Grove received little in the way of a formal education while growing up in the nearby hills of Maryland and developing an early interest in baseball. While starring in sandlot ball around the Baltimore area during the second decade of the 20th century, Grove attracted the attention of Jack Dunn, the owner of the minor-league Baltimore Orioles who discovered Babe Ruth just a few years earlier. Seeing the tremendous potential in the 6'3", 190-pound left-hander, Dunn signed Grove to his first professional contract prior to the 1920 campaign. Frequently displaying a lack of control on the mound, Grove finished just 12–12 in his first year with the Orioles. However, after gaining better command of his pitches, he developed into the International League's top hurler, compiling marks of 25–10, 18–8, 27–10, and 27–6 over the course of the next four seasons, while topping the circuit in strikeouts each year.

Ordinarily, Grove's dominating performance at the minor-league level would have earned him a trip to the majors after only one or two seasons. But Dunn, who ran an independent operation with no major-league affiliation, repeatedly turned down offers for Grove until Philadelphia A's owner and manager Connie Mack finally convinced him to part with his star pitcher by offering $100,600 for his services—the highest amount ever paid for a player at the time.

After struggling somewhat as a 25-year-old rookie, Grove began to right himself in his sophomore campaign, leading the American League with a 2.51 ERA and 194 strikeouts, despite posting a record of just 13–13. He subsequently developed into the junior circuit's most dominant pitcher, winning no fewer than 20 games in each of the next seven seasons, leading the league in strikeouts another five times, and winning four more ERA titles. Grove posted at least 24 victories in five of those campaigns, having his two best seasons in 1930 and 1931, when he helped lead the Athletics to their second and third straight pennants by compiling a total of 59 wins. After capturing the pitcher's version of the Triple Crown in 1930 by going 28–5 with a 2.54 ERA and 209 strikeouts, Grove amazingly improved upon his performance the following year. En route to earning AL MVP honors, the hard-throwing left-hander finished 31–4, with a 2.06 ERA, 175 strikeouts, and 27 complete games. Grove's league-leading 2.06 ERA placed him more than two runs per game below the league average. Although the A's failed to win the AL pennant in either of the next two seasons, Grove continued to excel, combining for another 49 victories to complete a seven-year stretch during which he posted an amazing record of 172–54.

Easily baseball's most dominant pitcher during that seven-year period, Grove thoroughly intimidated opposing batters with his lengthy delivery and blazing fastball. Joe Cronin, who later managed and played with Grove in Boston, described what it felt like facing the tall left-hander during his peak seasons: "Just to see that big guy glaring down at you from the mound was enough to frighten the daylights out of you."

Detroit Tigers Hall of Fame second baseman Charlie Gehringer noted, "His [Grove's] fastball was so fast that by the time you'd made up your mind whether it would be a strike or not, it just wasn't there anymore."

Mickey Cochrane, who played against Bob Feller when the Cleveland Indians fire-baller entered the league a few years later, served as Grove's primary catcher in Philadelphia. The Hall of Fame receiver suggested, "Feller never saw the day when he could throw as fast as Grove. Lefty was bigger, more powerful, and had a smoother delivery."

Doc Cramer, who played with Grove in both Philadelphia and Boston, said of his longtime teammate, "He didn't have a curve. All he had was a fastball. Everybody knew what they were going to hit at, but they still couldn't hit him. He was fabulous."

Despite the incredible success Grove experienced in Philadelphia, he frequently tested the patience of his manager and teammates with his fiery temperament and fierce competitive spirit. Known to shred uniforms, kick buckets, and rip apart lockers after a loss, Grove absolutely hated to lose, and he didn't hesitate to blame his teammates if he felt they cost him a game. While going for an AL record-breaking 17th consecutive victory in 1931, Grove became infuriated when a substitute outfielder allowed the opposing team to score the winning run by misjudging a routine line drive.

The left-hander spent the next several years blaming starting left-fielder Al Simmons for taking the day off to visit a doctor.

After Grove won 24 games for Philadelphia in 1933, dwindling attendance forced Connie Mack to trade his star hurler to the Red Sox for two ordinary players and $125,000 on December 12, 1933. A sore arm limited Grove to 12 starts and an 8–8 record in his first year in Boston. No longer able to overpower opposing hitters as he once did, upon his return, Grove reinvented himself at 35 years of age. Adopting a new approach he referred to as "curve and control," Grove subsequently relied primarily on breaking pitches, changing speeds, and spotting his fastball to navigate his way past opposing lineups. Although he never again reached the same level of dominance, Grove proved to be an extremely effective pitcher for the Red Sox over the course of the next five seasons. He concluded the 1935 campaign with a record of 20–12 and a league-leading 2.70 ERA. Grove followed that up by posting 17 victories in each of the next two seasons. He also led the league with a 2.81 ERA and six shutouts in 1936. Grove then compiled records of 14–4 and 15–4 in 1938 and 1939, respectively, winning the final two of his record nine ERA titles.

In discussing the change in philosophy he employed during his time in Boston, Grove explained, "I actually was too fast to curve the ball while with Baltimore and Philadelphia. The ball didn't have enough time to break because I threw what passed for a curve as fast as I threw my fastball. I couldn't get enough twist on it. . . . Now that I'm not so fast, I can really break one off and my fastball looks faster than it is because it's faster than the other stuff I throw." Grove added, "A pitcher has time enough to get smarter after he loses his speed."

Connie Mack agreed, stating, "Grove was a thrower until after we sold him to Boston and he hurt his arm. Then he learned to pitch."

In addition to becoming more of a thinker on the mound, Grove mellowed somewhat after joining the Red Sox. Yet, he still displayed at times the fierce temper for which he became so well noted during his time in Philadelphia, providing the greatest example of his dark side during a July 21, 1935, contest against Detroit. With Grove holding a 4–3 lead over the Tigers in the top of the ninth inning, Red Sox manager Joe Cronin ordered him to intentionally walk Hank Greenberg with two outs and a runner on second base. After reluctantly complying, Grove surrendered three consecutive singles to Tiger batsmen, giving Detroit a 6–4 lead heading into the bottom of the ninth. Leaving the field, Grove threw his glove into the stands, ripped off his uniform, and smashed one of Cronin's bats on his way to the clubhouse, where he continued his tirade. Grove finally regained his composure several minutes later when he discovered that fellow Red Sox pitcher Wes Ferrell delivered a pinch-hit, three-run homer in the bottom of the frame, thereby making a winner out of him. Grove showed his appreciation to Ferrell by silently rolling a bottle of wine over to him.

After posting seven victories in both 1940 and 1941 en route to reaching the 300-win mark for his career, Grove elected to announce his retirement. He ended his career with a record of 300–141, for an exceptional winning percentage of .680. He also compiled an ERA of 3.06, completed 298 of his 457 starts, and threw 35 shutouts. Pitching exclusively during an offensive-minded era, Grove posted the second-best adjusted ERA of all-time, with only Pedro Martinez compiling a lower mark. During his time in Boston, Grove went 105–62, with a 3.34 ERA, 119 complete games, and 15 shutouts.

After retiring from baseball, Grove returned to his hometown of Lonaconing, Maryland, where he became a friendly townsman who learned to

Courtesy Boston Public Library, Leslie Jones Collection

control his once-fierce temper. After being elected to the Baseball Hall of Fame in 1947, Grove eventually settled in Norwalk, Ohio, where he lived peacefully until May 22, 1975, when he passed away at the age of 75.

Taking into consideration the era during which Grove pitched and the level of dominance he reached during that period, noted author and baseball historian Bill James suggests, "What argument, if any, could be presented against the proposition that Lefty Grove was the greatest pitcher who ever lived?"

RED SOX CAREER HIGHLIGHTS

Best Season

Grove won four ERA titles while pitching for the Red Sox, and he also led the league with six shutouts in 1936. Nevertheless, he had his best all-around season in Boston in 1935, when he finished 20–12, with 23 complete games, 273 innings pitched, two shutouts, and a league-leading 2.70 ERA.

Memorable Moments/Greatest Performances

Grove actually pitched one of his best games for the Red Sox in a losing cause, shutting out the Washington Senators for 12 innings on September 2, 1940, before finally surrendering a run in the bottom of the 13th. The 40-year-old left-hander allowed eight hits and struck out five during the 1–0 loss.

Demonstrating a propensity for starting off the season quickly during his time in Boston, Grove spoiled the Yankees' home opener on April 17, 1936, allowing just two Lou Gehrig singles during an 8–0 victory over the eventual world champions. Four years later, on April 16, 1940, he similarly baffled Washington's lineup in the season opener at Griffith Stadium, allowing just two hits during a 1–0 Red Sox win.

Grove also put together two rather impressive streaks during his time in Boston, with the first coming early in 1936, when he surrendered just one earned run over 48 innings of work. On May 3, 1938, Grove won a 4–3 decision over the Detroit Tigers, beginning a record 20-game winning streak at home. He didn't lose again at Fenway Park until May 12, 1941.

Grove posted perhaps his most memorable win as a member of the Red Sox on July 25, 1941, defeating the Cleveland Indians at Fenway Park by a score of 10–6 for the 300th and final victory of his career.

NOTABLE ACHIEVEMENTS

- Won 20 games once (1935)
- Won 17 games twice (1936 and 1937)
- Posted winning percentage in excess of .750 twice (1938 and 1939)
- Compiled ERA below 3.00 three times
- Completed more than 20 games three times
- Threw more than 250 innings three times
- Led AL pitchers in ERA four times; winning percentage once; shutouts once; and WHIP twice
- Ranks among Red Sox all-time leaders in complete games (5th) and innings pitched (10th)
- Holds record for highest career winning percentage (.764) by a left-hander at Fenway Park
- Five-time AL All-Star (1935–1939)
- Member of Major League Baseball's All-Century Team
- Number 23 on *Sporting News*'s 1999 list of Baseball's 100 Greatest Players
- Elected to Baseball Hall of Fame by members of BBWAA in 1947

Mel Parnell

Courtesy Boston Public Library, Leslie Jones Collection

A consistent winner during his time in Boston, Mel Parnell disproved the theory that left-handers cannot pitch successfully at Fenway Park. Employing a hard-breaking slider that kept the ball in on the hands of right-handed batters, Parnell compiled a record of 71–30 in his home ballpark, en route to posting an overall mark of 123–75 in his 10 years with the Red Sox. Particularly effective from 1948 to 1953, Parnell went 109–56 over that six-year stretch, surpassing 20 victories twice, and winning 18 games two other times. He further endeared himself to Red Sox fans during that period by performing especially well against the New York Yankees, defeating Boston's foremost rivals 15 times between 1949 and 1953.

Born in New Orleans, Louisiana, on June 13, 1922, Melvin Lloyd Parnell attended Peters High School in New Orleans, where he spent most of his time on the ball field playing first base. Although Parnell preferred not to pitch because he wanted to play every day, he sometimes took the mound during batting practice at the behest of his coach in order to better prepare the team for opposing southpaws. Parnell, who earned the nickname "Dusty" due to his tendency to keep the ball low, rarely pitched in actual games. However, his coach surprised him on one occasion by asking him to take the mound for a crucial contest. Parnell responded by striking out 17 opposing batters, convincing a Red Sox scout in attendance to subsequently sign him to a contract.

After spending two years in the minor leagues, Parnell served in the Army Air Forces during World War II. Upon his release from active duty, Parnell returned to the minors, where he spent the entire 1946 campaign before joining the Red Sox for the first time in 1947. The 24-year-old left-hander had a rather uneventful rookie season, appearing in only 15 games and making just five starts. However, he earned a regular spot in Boston's starting rotation the following year, compiling a record of 15–8 and finishing among the league leaders with 16 complete games and an ERA of 3.14.

Parnell developed into a star in 1949, leading all AL hurlers with a record of 25–7, 27 complete games, and 295 innings pitched. He also finished second in the league with a 2.77 ERA, en route to earning All-Star honors for the first of two times and a fourth-place finish in the league MVP voting.

Parnell's magnificent performance helped dispel the previously held notion that left-handed pitchers could not succeed at Fenway Park due to the ballpark's odd configuration that featured the "Green Monster" in left field. Instead, Parnell managed to thrive at home, revealing the technique he used against right-handed batters when he stated, "You have to keep the hitters' elbows close to their body and cut down on their power." He further explained that the "Green Monster" didn't trouble him nearly as much as the lack of foul territory at Fenway, since foul flies rarely resulted in outs.

In discussing the success Parnell experienced in his home ballpark, former Red Sox third baseman Frank Malzone stated, "He really knew how to pitch at Fenway Park. They would say that lefties couldn't pitch at Fenway, but Mel had great success there because he was such a smart pitcher."

Parnell followed up his 25-win campaign by posting 18 victories in each of the next two seasons, before slumping to a record of 12–12 in 1952.

However, he rebounded in 1953 with a mark of 21–8. He also placed among the league leaders with a 3.06 ERA, 136 strikeouts, five shutouts, and 241 innings pitched. Although the New York Yankees captured their fifth consecutive world championship that year, Parnell handled Boston's rivals quite well, going a perfect 5–0 against them, with four shutouts.

Unfortunately, arm problems plagued Parnell in each of the next three seasons, limiting him to only 44 starts from 1954 to 1956. A torn muscle in his pitching arm finally forced Parnell to announce his retirement at the conclusion of the 1956 campaign. With a career record of 123–75, Parnell won more games than any other left-hander in Red Sox history. Only Cy Young, Roger Clemens, and Tim Wakefield posted more victories in a Red Sox uniform. Parnell also ended his career with an ERA of 3.50, 113 complete games, and 20 shutouts. He ranks among the Red Sox all-time leaders in the last two categories as well.

Following his retirement, Parnell managed in the minor leagues for four seasons, spending three of those campaigns piloting teams in the Red Sox farm system. He later served as a member of Boston's radio and television broadcasting crew from 1965 to 1968, assuming a position behind the microphone when the Red Sox defeated the Minnesota Twins and won the American League pennant in 1967. After leaving baseball, Parnell retired to New Orleans, where he resided until he passed away at 89 years of age in 2012, following a long battle with cancer.

Upon learning of Parnell's passing, former Red Sox pitcher Ike Delock said, "Mel was one of the nicest guys I ever met in baseball, and one of the best left-handers to pitch for the Red Sox, and in Fenway Park. He always pitched batters inside and believed that was a big reason he was successful. He kept telling the rest of us pitchers we needed to do the same. He was a true gentleman and one of my best friends on the team."

Former Boston outfielder Sam Mele, who also played with Parnell in the minor leagues, said of his former teammate, "Mel was a fun-loving guy and quite a competitor. He could really pitch. It's a shame he didn't start that 1948 playoff game against Cleveland. He was warming up when the manager [Joe McCarthy] sent someone to the bullpen and said he was switching to Denny Galehouse. I always believed we would have been in the World Series if Mel started. He was really disappointed but didn't say a word."

"Mel died a peaceful death," his son, Mel Parnell Jr., stated. "He loved the Red Sox. They were a big part of his life, as well as for our whole family. Dad felt the Red Sox were always like a family, and all of us have been so thankful about how they treated him. When he was inducted into the Red Sox Hall of Fame, that was one of the great thrills for our family."

Mel Parnell (r) with catcher Sammy White
Courtesy Boston Public Library, Leslie Jones Collection

Parnell's son added, "He liked pitching against the Yankees. He always enjoyed beating the best."

CAREER HIGHLIGHTS

Best Season

Even though Parnell won 21 games and established career highs with five shutouts and 136 strikeouts in 1953, he clearly pitched his best ball for the Red Sox four years earlier. In compiling a career-best 2.77 ERA and leading the American League with 25 wins, 27 complete games, and 295 innings pitched in 1949, Parnell earned his lone selection to the *Sporting News* All-Star Team.

Memorable Moments/Greatest Performances

Parnell put together the longest winning streak of his career in 1950, posting nine consecutive victories before finally being defeated.

Parnell posted one of the biggest wins of his career on September 25, 1949, putting the Red Sox in a first-place tie with the Yankees with only six games remaining in the regular season by defeating New York's Allie Reynolds 4–1 at Fenway Park. Parnell allowed just four hits, en route to winning his 25th game of the season.

Parnell had one of his finest all-around games on May 23, 1951, shutting out the St. Louis Browns on only four hits, while collecting four hits himself and scoring three runs during a 12–0 Red Sox victory.

However, Parnell experienced his finest moment on July 14, 1956, when he pitched a no-hitter against the Chicago White Sox at Fenway Park—the first thrown by a Red Sox pitcher in 33 years. In discussing his 4–0 no-no against Chicago, Parnell said, "I never did reach a state of nervousness because I just didn't expect it to happen." Ironically, Parnell's extraordinary effort proved to be the final highlight of his career, since a torn muscle in his pitching arm forced him into premature retirement at the conclusion of the campaign.

NOTABLE ACHIEVEMENTS

- Won more than 20 games twice (1949 and 1953)
- Posted 18 victories twice (1950 and 1951)
- Posted winning percentage in excess of .700 twice (1949 and 1953)
- Compiled ERA below 3.00 once (2.77 in 1949)
- Completed more than 20 games twice (1949 and 1950)
- Threw more than 200 innings six straight times (1948–1953)
- Led AL pitchers in wins once; complete games once; innings pitched once; and assists once
- Threw no-hitter vs. Chicago White Sox on July 14, 1956
- Ranks among Red Sox career leaders in wins (4th); shutouts (6th); innings pitched (5th); complete games (6th); and games started (5th)
- Won more games (123) than any other left-hander in Red Sox history
- Finished fourth in 1949 AL MVP voting
- 1949 *Sporting News* All-Star Selection
- Two-time AL All-Star (1949 and 1951)

2 9

Frank Malzone

Courtesy Mears Online Auctions

An outstanding all-around third baseman, Frank Malzone endeared himself to Boston fans for 11 seasons with his steady hitting and stellar play at the hot corner. The American League's premier defensive third baseman prior to the arrival of Brooks Robinson, Malzone captured the first three Gold Gloves awarded to junior circuit third sackers, earning the honor each year from 1957 to 1959. Playing for mostly dreary teams during his time in Boston, Malzone proved to be one of the club's few bright spots, earning a spot on the American League All-Star team eight times between 1957 and 1965, and leading all league third basemen in double plays a record five straight times at one point. A solid hitter as well, Malzone knocked in more than 90 runs three times while playing for the Red Sox.

Born in the Bronx, New York, on February 28, 1930, Frank James Malzone traveled a long and arduous road to the major leagues. After attending Gompers High School in the Bronx, Malzone signed with the Red Sox as an amateur free agent in 1947. He subsequently struggled his first few years in the minor leagues, before missing all of 1952 and 1953 while serving in the military during the Korean War. Looking back at the early stages of his career, Malzone said, "I was in the minor leagues for quite a while before I got an opportunity to play in the big leagues. I was in the army for two years in '52 and '53, and, when I got back, they put me in Triple-A and wanted to see if I could still play."

Malzone demonstrated that he still had the ability to play when he returned from the army in 1954, prompting the Red Sox to finally call him up late in 1955. However, after making Boston's roster the following spring, Malzone earned a return trip to the minors by batting just .165 in his 27 games with the big club. He eventually righted himself, though, returning to Boston in 1957, when he finally laid claim to the team's starting third base job at 27 years of age. Malzone considered the 1957 campaign to be a pivotal one in his career, stating years later, "In '57 I got the chance to play third base, and that was my first full year with the Red Sox. It was a big opportunity for me. I was at a stage in my career where I was either going to make it or be a career minor leaguer, or go into baseball as a coach. Things turned out for me."

Malzone ended up having an outstanding rookie season, hitting 15 home runs, driving in a career-high 103 runs, batting .292, and leading all players at his position in putouts, assists, and double plays, en route to winning the first of three straight Gold Gloves. At one point during the season, he tied an American League record for third basemen by amassing 10 assists in one game. Malzone's strong all-around performance earned him his first All-Star selection and a seventh-place finish in the league MVP voting.

Malzone followed up his exceptional rookie campaign with solid years in both 1958 and 1959, during which time he learned to take better advantage of Fenway Park's "Green Monster" in left field. After hitting 15 home runs, knocking in 87 runs, scoring 76, and batting .295 in the first of those years, he hit 19 homers, drove in 92 runs, scored a career-high 90 runs, accumulated 34 doubles, and batted .280 in 1959. Malzone made the All-Star team and won the Gold Glove Award both years, making him the last American League third baseman to win a Gold Glove prior to Brooks Robinson's extraordinary 16-year run.

Although Malzone continued to post solid numbers in 1960 and 1961, he experienced something of a drop-off in overall offensive production. However, he returned to top form in 1962, hitting a career-high 21 homers, knocking in 95 runs, and batting .283. He had one more quality season in 1963, hitting 15 home runs, driving in 71 runs, and batting .291, before age began to catch up with him the following year. After hitting only 13 homers, driving in just 56 runs, and batting only .264 in 1964—easily his poorest offensive performance since first becoming a regular in 1957—Malzone began to share playing time at third base with the left-handed hitting Dalton Jones the following year. Released by the Red Sox at the end of 1965, Malzone signed as a free agent with the California Angels. He ended his career as a part-time player on the West Coast, retiring at the conclusion of the 1966 campaign after being released by the Angels. Malzone ended his career with 133 home runs, 728 runs batted in, 647 runs scored, 1,486 hits, a .274 batting average, a .315 on-base percentage, and a .399 slugging percentage. He compiled the vast majority of those numbers while playing for the Red Sox.

Following his playing career, Malzone rejoined the Red Sox organization, assuming numerous roles, but serving the team primarily as a scout. After scouting for the organization for 35 years, Malzone eventually transitioned into the role of special assignment instructor. The Red Sox inducted him into their Hall of Fame in 1995 for his contributions to the franchise, both on and off the field. Malzone also joined several other former Red Sox players in the organization's 2004 World Championship celebration, riding in the "legends" duck boat during the championship parade. Malzone lived to see the Red Sox win another two World Series, before dying of natural causes at 85 years of age on December 29, 2015.

Upon learning of Malzone's passing, Carl Yastrzemski said, "When I first came to the big leagues in 1961, Frank was the guy who took me under his wing. I struggled when I first came up, and he took care of me and stayed with me. He was a real class guy, a very caring guy and I owe him a lot. You aren't going to find too many people like him."

Dwight Evans also expressed his sadness over Malzone's loss, stating, "I've known him a long time, ever since I came up. I took a liking to him. He had a good way about him, and I had some great conversations with him. He would always try to get me inside information on another team, and in Spring Training, all he would do is work with me on certain things. Balls down the line, fly balls, ground balls, to my left side, my right side." Evans added, "He may not have been one of the coaches on the team, but he was a coach for me, instructing me on the finer parts of the game. He would even throw me batting practice if I needed it. In some ways, Frank was like a big brother. I loved him as a man and as a mentor. He will be sorely missed."

Courtesy Of Boston Public Library, Leslie Jones Collection

RED SOX CAREER HIGHLIGHTS

Best Season

Malzone had his three best seasons in 1957, 1959, and 1962. As a rookie in 1957, he hit 15 home runs, scored 82 runs, batted .292, and established career highs with 103 RBIs, 185 hits, and five triples. In the last of those campaigns, he hit a career-high 21 homers, knocked in 95 runs, scored 74 others, batted .283, and collected 175 hits. But Malzone had his best all-around year in 1959, when he hit 19 home runs, drove in 92 runs, batted .280, and established career highs with 90 runs scored, 34 doubles, a .437 slugging percentage, and an OPS of .760, en route to earning All-Star honors and a 14th-place finish in the league MVP voting. Malzone also won the last of his three Gold Gloves by leading all AL third basemen in assists and double plays.

Memorable Moments/Greatest Performances

Malzone made his first major-league start a memorable one, going 6 for 10, with six consecutive hits, against Baltimore during a September 20, 1955, doubleheader.

Malzone had his biggest day at the plate on August 15, 1961, going a perfect 5 for 5, with two home runs, three RBIs, and two runs scored during an 8–0 Red Sox win over the Cleveland Indians.

Yet, when asked what he considered to be his greatest accomplishment as a major-league ballplayer, Malzone chose neither of those performances, instead relating the following incident:

> During one of the All-Star Games I played in [1959], I faced Hall of Famer Don Drysdale of the Dodgers. I had never faced him before, but I knew he pitched fast and hard. So, what's the first pitch he throws at me?—A hanging curveball. I hit it right out of the park. So, hitting a homer against Don Drysdale would have to be my greatest achievement in my Major League Baseball career.

NOTABLE ACHIEVEMENTS

- Hit more than 20 home runs once (21 in 1962)
- Knocked in more than 100 runs once (103 in 1957)
- Finished with more than 30 doubles four times (1957–1960)
- Led AL in games played and at-bats once (1958)
- Led AL third basemen in double plays five times; assists three times; putouts once; and fielding percentage once

- First player to lead all players at his position in his league in games played, putouts, assists, double plays, and fielding percentage in the same season.
- Ranks 11th all-time on Red Sox in hits (1,454).
- 1963 *Sporting News* All-Star selection
- Eight-time AL All-Star
- Three-time Gold Glove winner (1957–1959)

Mike Greenwell

Courtesy Boston Red Sox

Mike Greenwell never quite lived up to the high expectations Boston fans set for him early in his career. Expected to reach the same level of greatness previously attained by Ted Williams, Carl Yastrzemski, and Jim Rice, who immediately preceded him in left field for the Red Sox, Greenwell proved to be something of a disappointment to the "Fenway Faithful." Featuring a classic left-handed swing, Greenwell raised hopes in Beantown by batting well over .300 in each of his first five seasons, en route to earning a fourth-place finish in the AL Rookie of the Year voting in 1987 and a second-place finish in the MVP balloting the following year. However, after hitting 22 home runs and driving in 119 runs in 1988, Greenwell never again hit more than 15 homers or knocked in more than 95 runs in any single campaign. Nevertheless, he remained an extremely consistent player throughout his career, compiling a lifetime batting average in excess of .300, and giving the Red Sox solid, if unspectacular, play in left field, before differences with team management hastened his departure from Boston.

Born in Louisville, Kentucky, on July 18, 1963, Michael Lewis Greenwell grew up in Florida, where he acquired the nickname "Gator" for his penchant for wrestling alligators. Greenwell attended North Fort Myers High School, after which he signed with the Red Sox when they selected him in the third round of the 1982 amateur draft. He subsequently spent virtually all of the next five seasons in the minor leagues, receiving brief call-ups from the Red Sox toward the end of both the 1985 and 1986 campaigns.

Even though Greenwell demonstrated the ability to hit major-league pitching almost as soon as he arrived in Boston, the team's crowded outfield situation seemed destined to relegate him to a backup role. However, after making the Red Sox roster in spring training of 1987, Greenwell gradually earned the starting job in left field when injuries prevented Jim Rice from taking the field much of the time. Making the most of his opportunity, Greenwell posted a batting average of .328, hit 19 homers, and knocked in 89 runs, in only 125 games and 412 official at-bats. He followed that up with an exceptional 1988 campaign in which he hit 22 home runs, drove in 119 runs, scored 86, and batted .325. In addition to forcing Rice into the role of full-time DH, Greenwell's outstanding performance earned him All-Star honors for the first of two times and a second-place finish to Oakland's Jose Canseco in the league MVP voting.

Fast becoming one of Boston's most popular players, Greenwell began drawing comparisons to some of the team's all-time greats, with his smooth left-handed swing being likened to that of Ted Williams. Of course, such comparisons proved to be extremely premature, with Greenwell lacking the "Splendid Splinter's" keen batting eye and overall hitting prowess. He also didn't possess as much power at the plate as either Carl Yastrzemski or Jim Rice—the other two Boston left fielders to whom he often found himself compared. Although Greenwell continued to perform extremely well in subsequent seasons, he found it impossible to placate Red Sox fans, who expected so much more of him.

Greenwell posted solid numbers again in 1989, with 14 home runs, 95 runs batted in, 87 runs scored, and a .308 batting average. He followed that up with two more good years, compiling batting averages of .297 and .300 in 1990 and 1991, respectively, before a knee injury limited him to only 49 games and a .233 batting average in 1992. Healthy again in 1993, Greenwell hit 13 home runs, drove in 72 runs, scored 77, and batted over .300 (.315) for the final time in his career. He spent three more years in Boston, being reduced to a part-time role in 1996, when his close relationship with his teammates and manager Kevin Kennedy began to draw the ire of general manager Dan Duquette.

After holding a press conference to discuss his muddled contract situation, and seeing his friend Kennedy fired by Duquette for supposedly losing control of the team, Greenwell stated, "He [Kennedy] could not have stopped what I said or Roger [Clemens] said. Dan [Duquette] provoked that. He's all about power. He wants to be the only voice. . . . If he wants to fire Kevin, fine. That's his decision. But to put the blame on me and Roger is bull."

Choosing to leave the Red Sox at the end of the season after failing to come to terms with them on a new contract, the 33-year-old Greenwell said, "I'm not by any means saying I'm retiring, because I'm not. If the right situation is out there, I'll play. I'll play with some enthusiasm and a new challenge."

He added, "I'm not leaving upset, and I'm not leaving disappointed. My emotions are mixed, but as far as being happy, I'm happy. I'm proud of what I've done here. I hope I've given a reason for people to talk and come to the ballpark. If I've done that, it was worth it."

Greenwell left Boston with career totals of 130 home runs, 726 RBIs, 657 runs scored, 1,400 hits, and 275 doubles. He also batted .303, compiled a .368 on-base percentage, and posted a .463 slugging percentage.

Greenwell subsequently signed a $2.5 million deal to play for the Japanese Hanshin Tigers in 1997. However, after missing virtually all of spring training with an injured back, he fractured his left foot with a foul tip only days after he returned to the team, prompting him to announce his retirement. Greenwell returned to the United States, where he used the money the Tigers paid him to build an amusement park in Florida. Years later, he also began racing trucks, becoming a professional truck racer in 2006. Having given up that pastime in 2010, Greenwell retired to his 890-acre ranch in Alva, Florida, where he grows fruits and vegetables.

Shortly after he left Boston, Greenwell expressed his feelings about the time he spent in Beantown, and the manner in which the Red Sox decided to replace him in left field with Wil Cordero, stating:

It's weird. I still feel like I belong there. I still feel like I could put up numbers as good as the guy that's out there now. It's different if there's some young, up-and-coming star, but, when they bring in someone, I think that bothers you a little bit. . . . That seemed to be in their plans from the day they got him, and that kind of bothered me. I didn't realize it until the end of the year that, no matter what I did, I wasn't going to be back because I had the ear of the players and the ear of the media. That bothered some people.

Greenwell added, "Cordero is a good athlete, but it ain't as easy as it looks, and the fans will let him know that. I used to always hear [from the

Courtesy Boston Red Sox

fans], 'Jimmy would have had it,' or 'Yaz would have had it,' or 'Ted would have had it.' Maybe over the course of the year, he'll hear 'Mike would have had it.'"

CAREER HIGHLIGHTS

Best Season

Greenwell had an exceptional rookie year in 1987, hitting 19 home runs, knocking in 89 runs, scoring 71 others, accumulating 31 doubles, and establishing career highs with a .328 batting average, a .570 slugging percentage, and a .956 OPS. But he appeared in only 125 games, making the ensuing campaign easily his finest overall season. In addition to hitting 22 homers, scoring 86 runs, and amassing 39 doubles in 1988, Greenwell placed in the league's top five with 119 RBIs, a .325 batting average, 192 hits, eight triples, 313 total bases, 87 walks, a .416 on-base percentage, and a .531 slugging percentage. Only a steroid-filled Jose Canseco prevented Greenwell from earning AL MVP honors.

Memorable Moments/Greatest Performances

Greenwell made his first major-league hit a memorable one, giving the Red Sox a 4–2 victory over the Toronto Blue Jays on September 25, 1985, with a two-run homer in the top of the 13th inning.

Greenwell had one of his greatest days at the plate on September 14, 1988, hitting for the cycle during a 4–3 Red Sox win over the Orioles at Fenway Park.

On September 1, 1990, Greenwell accomplished the rare feat of hitting an inside-the-park grand slam, doing so during a 15–1 home win over the Yankees.

Yet, Greenwell accomplished his greatest feat on September 2, 1996, when he established a major-league record by knocking in all nine of his team's runs during a 9–8, 10-inning Red Sox win over the Mariners in Seattle. He went four for five during the contest, with a double and two homers, including a seventh-inning grand slam.

NOTABLE ACHIEVEMENTS

- Hit more than 20 home runs once (22 in 1988)
- Knocked in more than 100 runs once (119 in 1988)
- Batted over .300 seven times, topping the .320 mark on three occasions
- Surpassed 30 doubles five times
- Compiled on-base percentage in excess of .400 twice
- Posted slugging percentage in excess of .500 three times
- Led AL left fielders in assists three times and double plays twice
- Finished second in 1988 AL MVP voting
- Hit for cycle vs. Baltimore Orioles on September 14, 1988.
- 1988 Silver Slugger winner
- 1988 *Sporting News* All-Star selection
- Two-time AL All-Star (1988 and 1989)
- 1986 AL champion

Reggie Smith

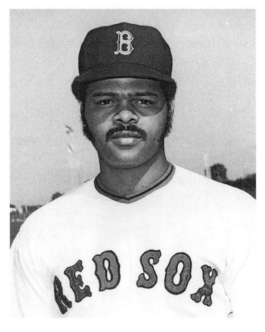

Courtesy Boston Red Sox

Labeled unfairly as a malingerer and an agitator, Reggie Smith spent seven turbulent seasons in Boston, frequently finding himself at odds with the hometown fans and media. Falsely accused of exaggerating the severity of his injuries at times, maligned by fans and the press for failing to live up to the exorbitantly high expectations they set for him, and persecuted for merely speaking his mind, Smith felt very much like an outsider during his time in Boston. Yet, he continued to produce on the field, establishing himself as one of the American League's finest all-around players in his years with the

Red Sox. A true "five-tool player" until knee problems slowed him down later in his career, the switch-hitting Smith hit for power and average from both sides of the plate, possessed outstanding speed, fielded his position well, and had one of the strongest throwing arms in the game. Smith hit more than 20 home runs five times for the Red Sox, batted over .300 three times, stole more than 20 bases once, and led all AL outfielders in putouts and assists once each. And, even though the fans and media in Boston often ridiculed him, his teammates held him in high esteem, typically describing him as someone who relentlessly learned to do new things, and who strived to be great at everything he did. John Curtis, who played with Smith in both Boston and St. Louis, said, "I will always remember Reg as one of the most complete players I ever saw. . . . I know he labored under the weight of everyone's expectations. In Boston, the sportswriters would wonder aloud why Reg wasn't playing up to his demonstrated abilities. . . . He once told me that the worst word in the English language was 'potential.'"

Born in Shreveport, Louisiana, on April 2, 1945, Carl Reginald Smith grew up in Los Angeles after moving there with his family as a child. Although Smith had a strong desire to go to college, his family's financial situation prompted him to sign with the Minnesota Twins as an amateur free agent in 1963, shortly after he graduated from Compton's Centennial High School, where he earned All-California honors in both baseball and football. Smith spent one year in Minnesota's farm system before being claimed by the Red Sox when the Twins left him unprotected in the draft. Originally signed as a shortstop, Smith moved to the outfield while ascending through Boston's farm system, finally arriving in Toronto in 1966, where he played for future Red Sox manager Dick Williams on Boston's top minor-league club. Although Smith earned Williams's favor by winning the International League batting title with a mark of .320, he made an even greater impression on his manager with his powerful throwing arm. Williams later said, "Smith had one hell of an arm, even for a shortstop. He could throw like the devil. He had such a strong arm, [then Red Sox manager] Billy Herman wanted to make him a pitcher. He was my center fielder and he could really play. At that time, he was just learning how to switch hit." Williams added, "He was a hell of a player. He was moody then, but I had a good time with Reggie."

Called up briefly to the majors at the end of 1966, Smith earned a permanent roster spot the following year when Williams took over as Red Sox manager. Smith claimed the starting center field job early in the season, after which he earned a second-place finish in the AL Rookie of the Year voting by hitting 15 home runs, driving in 61 runs, scoring 78, batting .246, and finishing third among all league outfielders in putouts. Batting leadoff for the American League champions throughout much of the campaign, Smith supplied most of the speed at the top of the batting order, leading the Red Sox with 16 stolen bases.

Smith posted similar offensive numbers in 1968, once again hitting 15 homers and scoring 78 runs, while knocking in 69 runs and stealing 22 bases. However, he raised his batting average to .265, topped the circuit with 37 doubles, and led all AL outfielders in putouts, en route to earning his only Gold Glove. He followed that up with three straight outstanding seasons, making the All-Star team for the first time in 1969, when he hit 25 home runs, drove in 93 runs, scored 87, and finished second in the league with a .309 batting average. After hitting 22 homers, batting .303, and scoring a career-high 109 runs in 1970, Smith homered 30 times, knocked in 96 runs, scored 85, batted .283, and led the league with 33 doubles and 302 total bases in 1971—a season in which he spent a considerable amount of time in right field, as well as center.

However, even as he ascended into stardom, Smith grew increasingly disenchanted with the atmosphere in Boston. As the last major-league team to integrate, the Red Sox under owner Tom Yawkey had built a reputation as a somewhat prejudiced organization. Therefore, Smith, being one of the first African American players with star potential brought up through the team's farm system, often encountered racism on his rise to the top. Teammate John Curtis suggested, "Race relations in the clubhouse actually weren't that bad. It was the front office where all the bigotry was festering. I don't recall any of my teammates making a racist remark about Reggie while I was in Boston."

Curtis also discussed the negative attitude that many Bostonians held toward Smith and other people of color when he said, "He [Smith] said some people in the bleachers would throw batteries, heated coins, and other projectiles at him. He also told me about a night when some hooligans drove up to his house and emptied the garbage cans he'd placed by the driveway all over his front lawn. That's when I began to understand that Boston was a different town for him than it was for me."

Certainly, Smith's inability to reach the level of greatness originally predicted for him when he first joined the Red Sox at age 21 caused many of the fans to express their anger toward him. But Smith further exacerbated the situation by speaking his mind publicly, telling a reporter on one occasion that he agreed with former Celtics star Bill Russell that Boston was among the more racially segregated cities in the United States, and subsequently pointing out specific areas of racism. Smith's candor ended up making life extremely difficult for him in Boston, as explained by Howard Bryant in his 2002 book *Shut Out*: "There was no way, Smith thought, that he could not enter the fray. . . . He was expected to produce winning baseball for the home fans, although some were the very people who sought to deny him rights as a person. He did not handle this conflict well, and he waged what was at times a constant war with the home fans at Fenway."

Smith also gradually came to loathe the cliquish atmosphere that existed on the Red Sox during his years with the club, stating in a 1978 *Sports Illustrated* article entitled "His Old Self Is on the Shelf," "It was ridiculous. I sometimes wondered whether we were a ball club or a social club. I got along well with Carl Yastrzemski. Consequently, those who disliked him disliked me. There were three or four cliques. There was the Yaz group, the Ken Harrelson group, the Jim Lonborg group and, later, the Conigliaro group, which was not only a clique but a family. People would throw parties just so they could not invite the guys they disliked. Then the other guys would throw their own parties and not invite the ones who didn't invite them."

Smith spent two more tumultuous years in Boston before he reached a point of no return with the Red Sox in 1973. Misdiagnosed by Boston's team physician, who prescribed just a cortisone injection and a few days' rest for his seriously injured left knee, Smith instead chose to sit out several weeks, causing him to incur the wrath of the front office and the Boston fans, who subsequently began serenading him with choruses of "Goodbye Reggie; goodbye Reggie; goodbye Reggie; we're glad to see you go." The fact that another examination by a doctor at the Tufts New England Medical Center revealed a ligament tear in Smith's knee failed to sway public opinion in the least.

On the heels of that episode came a well-publicized run-in with pitcher Bill "Spaceman" Lee, who Smith accused of failing to protect his teammates by pitching inside to opposing hitters. After Smith called Lee "gutless" for allowing Red Sox batters to be thrown at without retaliation, a battle between the two men ensued, resulting in a one-punch knockout of Lee. More negative publicity followed, causing the embattled outfielder to welcome the trade that sent him and pitcher Ken Tatum to the Cardinals for outfielder Bernie Carbo and pitcher Rick Wise at season's end. Looking back at his final days in Boston, Smith said, "It was time for me to leave when the Red Sox traded me. The clubhouse in Boston was a very antagonistic atmosphere. The reporters were stars in their own right, and there were unrealistic expectations put on the team every year. In addition, I had always felt I was a National League player trapped in the American League. This was my style of play—the running, the way pitchers challenged you with the fastball. The National League also had more established stars back then."

Smith spent the next two and a half years in St. Louis, making the NL All-Star team in 1974 and 1975, and earning an 11th-place finish in the league MVP voting in the first of those campaigns by hitting 23 home runs, knocking in 100 runs, and batting .309. In discussing Smith, former Cardinals teammate Bob Forsch said years later, "It was FUN being on the same team as he was. One, he was a POWER hitter and switch hitter. . . . He was a big guy, very strong, very muscular. Hard to believe he was that agile. He was very muscular for an outfielder. . . . Plus he also had one of the best outfield arms of anybody. And he was smart as well as strong—he never threw to the wrong base, and he kept the double play in order, which, to a pitcher, is BIG."

Concerned that they might not be able to re-sign him when he became eligible for free agency at the end of the year, the Cardinals dealt Smith to the Los Angeles Dodgers midway through the 1976 campaign. Smith remained in Los Angeles through 1981, playing for three pennant-winning teams and one world championship ball club during his time there. He earned another three All-Star selections while playing for the Dodgers, finished fourth in the NL MVP voting twice, and, in 1977, joined Steve Garvey, Ron Cey, and Dusty Baker in becoming the first quartet of teammates to surpass 30 home runs in the same season.

After being plagued by injuries his final three seasons with the Dodgers, Smith joined the Giants as a free agent in 1982. He spent his final year in the major leagues in San Francisco, before going to Japan for two years, where he closed out his playing career in 1984. Upon his retirement, Smith ranked second only to Mickey Mantle in home runs by a switch-hitter. Over the course of his career, he hit 314 home runs, knocked in 1,092 runs, scored 1,123 others, amassed 2,020 hits, batted .287, compiled a .366 on-base percentage, and posted a .489 slugging percentage. His Red Sox numbers include 149 homers, 536 RBIs, 592 runs scored, 1,064 hits, a .281 batting average, a .354 on-base percentage, and a .471 slugging percentage.

Following his retirement, Smith returned to the Dodgers, where he served first as a coach under Tommy Lasorda, and, later, as a minor-league instructor, player development official, and, finally, batting instructor for the major-league club. After leaving the Dodgers in 1999, he served as a coach on the U.S. baseball team that won gold at the 2000 Olympics and the 2006 U.S. entry in the World Baseball Classic. Smith currently runs a baseball academy in Encino, California, where he trains youth players.

Although Smith spent most of his career being thought of as "the other Reggie," former teammate John Curtis considered Smith to be a better all-around player than the more flamboyant and self-promoting Reggie

Courtesy Boston Red Sox

Jackson. Curtis, who pitched against both men, said, "On the basis of talent, I'd take Smith over Jackson any day. I played with both of them, and I wouldn't hesitate to take Smith's overall game over Jackson's showmanship."

RED SOX CAREER HIGHLIGHTS

Best Season

Smith had his three best seasons for the Red Sox from 1969 to 1971, posting outstanding numbers in each of those years. Although he batted .303 and established career highs with 109 runs scored and 176 hits in 1970, he compiled better overall numbers in each of the other two seasons. A strong case could be made for 1969 since Smith hit 25 homers, knocked in 93 runs, scored 87, batted .309, and posted an OPS of .895—the highest mark he compiled in any of the three seasons. However, Smith posted extremely comparable numbers in 1971, concluding the campaign with 30 homers, 96 RBIs, 85 runs scored, a .283 batting average, and a league-leading 33 doubles and 302 total bases. Even though his OPS of .840 fell 55 points short of the mark he compiled two years earlier, Smith made a greater overall impact in 1971 since he started 159 games, as opposed to 138 in 1969.

Memorable Moments/Greatest Performances

Smith hit home runs from both sides of the plate in the same game a total of six times, doing so on three occasions as a member of the Red Sox. He accomplished the feat for the first time on August 20, 1967, leading the Red Sox to a 12–2 victory over the California Angels in the process. Smith also homered from both sides of the plate during a 15–4 win over the Milwaukee Brewers on July 2, 1972, and during a 9–7 loss to the Detroit Tigers on April 16, 1973. Smith also hit for power in the 1967 World Series, homering twice and compiling a .542 slugging percentage against the St. Louis Cardinals.

Smith had arguably his two greatest days at the plate for the Red Sox shortly before the 1969 All-Star break. The hot-hitting outfielder extended his hitting streak to 21 games by going seven for nine, with a homer, two doubles, four RBIs, and four runs scored during a July 11 doubleheader sweep of the Baltimore Orioles. After Smith's streak ended the following day, he went 5 for 5, with two doubles, two RBIs, and two runs scored during a 7–6 win over the Yankees on July 15.

....
NOTABLE ACHIEVEMENTS
....

- Hit more than 20 home runs five times, topping 30 homers once (30 in 1971)
- Scored more than 100 runs once (109 in 1970)
- Batted over .300 three times
- Surpassed 30 doubles three times
- Stole more than 20 bases once (22 in 1968)
- Compiled slugging percentage in excess of .500 twice
- Led AL in doubles twice and total bases once
- Led AL outfielders in putouts once and assists once
- 1968 Gold Glove winner
- 1970 *Sporting News* All-Star selection
- Two-time AL All-Star (1969 and 1972)
- 1967 AL champion

Harry Hooper

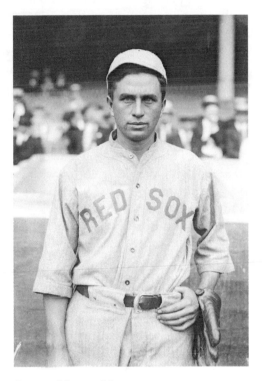

Courtesy Library of Congress

A steady leadoff hitter and exceptional defensive outfielder, Harry Hooper spent virtually all of his 12 years in Boston being overshadowed by more spectacular players such as Tris Speaker and Babe Ruth. But, by the time Hooper left the Red Sox at the conclusion of the 1920 campaign, he had established himself as the franchise's all-time leader in triples (130) and stolen bases (300). He also distinguished himself by being the only man to play on four Red Sox World Championship teams. Through it all, Hooper remained one of baseball's most dignified and intelligent players, earning the respect of his teammates with his calm demeanor and profound understanding of the game.

Born in Bell Station, California, on August 24, 1887, Harry Bartholomew Hooper began his formal baseball career shortly after he left his family's farm in August of 1902. Enrolling at the high school attached to Saint Mary's College of California, Hooper subsequently displayed a natural affinity for the game while playing for his high school team, starring both in the field and at the bat, en route to earning a contract with Sacramento of the California League upon his graduation. Yet, even as he continued to impress the various representatives of major-league clubs that watched him perform, Hooper moved inexorably toward obtaining the degree in engineering he craved, eventually graduating with honors from Saint Mary's College. Still planning to pursue a career as a civil engineer when he met with Red Sox owner John Taylor late in 1908, Hooper changed his plans when Taylor offered him a $2,800 contract for the 1909 season.

A natural right-handed hitter and thrower while at Saint Mary's, the 5'10", 168-pound Hooper began experimenting with switch-hitting after he joined the Red Sox at the start of the 1909 campaign. He finally decided to hit left-handed full time in order to shorten by a couple of steps his trip down to first base once he left the batter's box. While transitioning from one side of the plate to the other, Hooper ended up batting .282 in his 81 games as a rookie.

Hooper earned the starting job in right field the following year, appearing in 155 of Boston's 158 games. Although he batted just .267 and knocked in only 27 runs, the 22-year-old outfielder scored 81 runs, led the league with 34 sacrifice hits, and placed among the leaders with 40 stolen bases and 62 walks. He also displayed his strong and accurate throwing arm by leading all AL outfielders with 30 assists.

Hooper evolved into one of the junior circuit's best leadoff hitters the following year, concluding the 1911 campaign with a .311 batting average, 93 runs scored, 38 stolen bases, and a .399 on-base percentage. He also continued his outstanding play in right field, amassing another 27 assists, in combining with Tris Speaker and Duffy Lewis to form what came to be known as the "Million Dollar Outfield."

Although Hooper's batting average slipped to .242 in 1912, he proved to be an integral member of a Red Sox team that captured the American League pennant, finishing second on the club with 98 runs scored, 12 triples, 29 stolen bases, and 66 walks. He subsequently elevated his play against the New York Giants in the World Series, batting .290, compiling an on-base percentage of .361, and making several key plays in the field.

Even though the Red Sox failed to repeat as AL champions in 1913, Hooper had one of his finest seasons, batting .288, scoring 100 runs, and stealing 26 bases. His overall numbers fell off somewhat in each of the next two seasons. Nevertheless, Hooper came up big once again in the 1915 World Series, leading the Red Sox to a five-game win over the Phillies by hitting two homers, driving in three runs, scoring four others, and batting .350. Meanwhile, he continued to excel in right field, compiling 23 assists in each of those two campaigns, en route to accumulating 150 of the 455 assists Boston's much-heralded outfield amassed from 1910 to 1915. Hooper also did an outstanding job of playing Fenway Park's difficult sun field, inventing along the way the famous rump slide used to snare short flies and stop with his body those he found himself unable to reach.

Hooper remained in Boston five more years, playing for two more World Series champions, and performing particularly well in 1920, when he batted .312, posted a .411 on-base percentage, scored 91 runs, and finished third in the league with a career-high 17 triples. During that time, Hooper also wisely suggested to Red Sox manager Ed Barrow that he move young Babe Ruth to the outfield on those days he didn't pitch in order to take full advantage of his tremendous slugging ability and crowd appeal.

The 1920 campaign proved to be Hooper's last in Boston. After holding out for more money as a means of expressing his dissatisfaction with team management for trading away many of the club's best players, Hooper found himself dealt to the Chicago White Sox for Shano Collins and Nemo Liebold. With the Dead Ball Era having ended, Hooper subsequently posted some of the best offensive numbers of his career in his five remaining seasons with the White Sox. In addition to batting over .300 three times, he finished in double-digits in home runs for the only three times in his career, scored more than 100 runs twice, and compiled an on-base percentage in excess of .400 on two occasions. Hooper retired at the conclusion of the 1925 campaign with career totals of 75 home runs, 817 RBIs, 1,429 runs scored, 2,466 hits, 160 triples, 389 doubles, and 375 stolen bases. He also batted .281, compiled a .368 on-base percentage, and posted a .387 slugging percentage over the course of 17 major-league seasons. Hooper's Red Sox numbers include 30 home runs, 497 runs batted in, 988 runs scored, 1,707 hits, 130 triples, 246 doubles, 300 stolen bases, a .272 batting average, a .362 on-base percentage, and a .367 slugging percentage. In addition to holding franchise records for most triples and stolen bases, Hooper ranks among the team's all-time leaders in hits, walks, runs scored, total bases, games played, plate appearances, and at-bats.

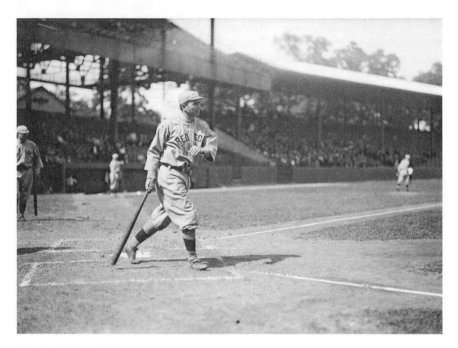

Courtesy Library of Congress

Following his retirement, Hooper returned to California, where he spent many years working in real estate. He also managed briefly in the minor leagues, spent two years coaching Princeton's baseball team, and served as U.S. postmaster for 24 years. Hooper passed away at the age of 87 on December 18, 1974, following a stroke, just three years after the members of the Veteran's Committee elected him to the Baseball Hall of Fame. Although the wisdom of Hooper's induction has since been questioned by many, his onetime teammate Smoky Joe Wood sang his praises when he said, "If there was any one characteristic of Harry Hooper's, it was that he was a clutch player. When the chips were down, that guy played like wildfire."

RED SOX CAREER HIGHLIGHTS

Best Season

With a livelier ball being used in the American league in 1920, Hooper posted his best offensive numbers during his time in Boston. In addition to compiling his highest batting average (.312), on-base percentage (.411), and slugging percentage (.470), he scored 91 runs, walked 88 times, hit seven home runs, collected 30 doubles, and stroked a career-high 17 triples. Hooper also performed well in 1911 (.311 average, 93 runs scored, 38 steals) and 1913 (.288 average, 100 runs scored, 26 stolen bases). Nevertheless, the feeling here is that Hooper played his best ball as a member of the Red Sox during the war-shortened campaign of 1918. Appearing in only 126 games, Hooper batted .289, finished second in the league with 13 triples and 26 doubles, and also ranked among the leaders with 81 runs scored, 137 hits, 24 stolen bases, 75 walks, 192 total bases, 40 extra-base hits, a .391 on-base percentage, and a .796 OPS. He also led all American League right-fielders with 221 putouts, while finishing second among players at his position with 16 assists.

Memorable Moments/Greatest Performances

Though not known for his home-run hitting prowess, Hooper displayed power at the plate from time to time. On May 30, 1913, he became the first player to lead off both games of a doubleheader with a home run. Only Rickey Henderson and Brady Anderson have accomplished the feat since.

Hooper flexed his muscles again in Game 5 of the 1915 World Series, helping the Red Sox clinch the world championship by becoming just the second player to hit two home runs in one World Series game (both homers actually bounced into the stands). Hooper's second round-tripper came in the top of the ninth inning, giving the Red Sox a series-clinching 5–4 victory over the Phillies.

Hooper also performed heroics in the Fall Classic with his glove. He helped Boston defeat New York in the final game of the 1912 World Series by robbing Giants second baseman Larry Doyle of a home run with a spectacular, bare-handed catch against the right-field fence. In the next day's *Boston Globe*, teammate Tris Speaker called Hooper's catch "the greatest, I believe, that I ever saw." Asked years later at an old-timers' game if he remembered Hooper, Doyle replied, "How in hell can I ever forget him!"

Hooper turned in another fielding gem in the opening contest of the 1916 World Series, helping the Red Sox preserve a 6–5 win over Brooklyn by making an outstanding catch from a sitting position, rising quickly, and throwing home to double-up Zack Wheat at the plate.

NOTABLE ACHIEVEMENTS

- Batted over .300 twice (1911 and 1920)
- Scored 100 runs once (100 in 1913)
- Finished in double-digits in triples nine times
- Topped 30 doubles once (30 in 1920)
- Stole more than 20 bases nine times, surpassing 30 steals twice and 40 thefts once (40 in 1910)
- Compiled on-base percentage in excess of .400 once (.411 in 1920)
- Led AL with 34 sacrifice bunts in 1910
- Led AL outfielders with 30 assists in 1910
- Led AL right-fielders in fielding percentage three times; putouts three times; and assists once
- Holds Red Sox career records for most triples (130) and most stolen bases (300)
- Ranks among Red Sox career leaders in hits (9th); walks (6th); runs scored (9th); total bases (10th); games played (7th); plate appearances (7th); and at-bats (7th)
- Ranks among Major League Baseball's all-time leaders in outfield assists (6th) and double plays turned by an outfielder (5th)
- Four-time AL champion (1912, 1915, 1916, and 1918)
- Four-time world champion (1912, 1915, 1916, and 1918)
- Elected to Baseball Hall of Fame by members of Veteran's Committee in 1971

Jason Varitek

Courtesy Keith Allison

Jason Varitek failed to compile the type of gaudy offensive numbers posted by virtually every other position player included in these rankings. Varitek never came close to knocking in 100 runs, and he scored as many as 70 runs in just two of the 10 years he served as Boston's starting catcher. He also batted over .280 just three times. And, even though Varitek spent his entire career with the Red Sox, he ranks among the team's all-time leaders in just two offensive categories, holding down the ninth spot in both doubles and extra-base hits. However, Varitek's contributions to the Red Sox extended far beyond his offensive production. An outstanding leader and exceptional handler of pitchers, Varitek gave Boston another coach on the field in many ways, providing guidance to the members of the Red Sox pitching staff, and inspiring his teammates with his selfless approach to the game. In discussing Varitek, former Red Sox outfielder Johnny Damon said, "He taught me how to be a leader and showed me how to be a champion. . . . It was an honor and a pleasure to have been his teammate." Meanwhile, Curt Schilling stated, "In my 23 years of professional baseball, I never played with or against a more selfless and prepared player than Jason Varitek."

Born in Rochester, Michigan, on April 11, 1972, Jason Andrew Varitek grew up in Florida, where he attended Lake Brantley High School in Altamonte Springs. After playing third base and catcher for his high school team, Varitek decided to continue his education when the Houston Astros selected him in the 23rd round of the 1990 amateur draft, enrolling at Georgia Tech University. Varitek subsequently earned various honors while playing for the Yellow Jackets baseball team, serving as a member of the 1992 U.S. Olympic team, and being named *Baseball America's* 1993 College Player of the Year. After being selected by the Seattle Mariners with the 14th overall pick of the 1994 amateur draft following his graduation, Varitek signed with the St. Paul Saints in the independent Northern League before agreeing to terms with the Mariners. By doing so, he delayed his entrance into Seattle's farm system until 1995. Varitek spent virtually all of the next three years in the minors, being dealt to the Red Sox, along with fellow prospect Derek Lowe, for reliever Heathcliff Slocumb midway through the 1997 campaign. The Red Sox called him up briefly in late September, with Varitek singling in his only trip to the plate.

After earning a roster spot in spring training, Varitek spent most of 1998 splitting time behind home plate with Scott Hatteberg. Appearing in 86 games, Varitek hit seven homers, drove in 33 runs, and batted .253. He established himself as Boston's starting catcher the following year, concluding the campaign with 20 home runs, 76 RBIs, 70 runs scored, a batting average of .269, and a career-high 39 doubles. Varitek's offensive production fell off somewhat in 2000, but he appeared to be well on his way to his finest season in 2001, before he broke his right elbow diving for a pop bunt during an 8–1 win over the Tigers on June 7.

Varitek returned to Boston's lineup in 2002 to hit 10 homers, knock in 61 runs, and bat .266. Yet, even though he posted relatively modest offensive numbers, pitchers enjoyed throwing to him because he prepared himself for every contest, studying the strengths and weaknesses of opposing batters, as well as the tendencies of his own pitchers. Before long, Varitek's hard work, dedication, and keen insight became his defining attributes, making him one of the team's most respected players and clubhouse leaders. Red Sox reliever Mike Timlin later expressed his admiration for Varitek when he stated, "His first care was that his teammates succeeded even before himself. I have never seen a player so prepared for every game."

Varitek developed into more of an offensive threat in 2003, when he began the finest three-year stretch of his career. In helping the Red Sox finish a close second in the AL East, Varitek hit 25 home runs, drove in 85 runs, and batted .273, en route to earning All-Star honors for the first time. He followed that up by hitting 18 homers, knocking in 73 runs, and batting a career-high .296 in 2004, before hitting 22 homers, driving in 70 runs, and batting .281 in 2005—a season in which he won his only Gold Glove and Silver Slugger. The Red Sox named Varitek captain during that time, according him that honor in December 2004. They also signed him to a four-year, $40 million contract, making him one of the highest-paid receivers in the game.

Varitek's offensive production subsequently began to decline, with him never again hitting more than 17 home runs, knocking in more than 68 runs, or batting any higher than .255. Yet, even as his batting average dropped below .230 and his playing time continued to diminish his final few seasons, Varitek remained a key contributor to the success the Red Sox experienced, working with the team's pitching staff, and sharing his insights with his fellow receivers. Varitek also helped solidify his place in Red Sox history on July 18, 2006, when he appeared in his 991st game behind home plate, breaking in the process Carlton Fisk's club record. The Red Sox honored him later in the year, when he became the first receiver in team history to catch 1,000 games. Varitek also holds the distinction of catching a major-league record four no-hitters over the course of his career.

Varitek became strictly a backup during the second half of 2009 after the Red Sox acquired All-Star Victor Martinez just prior to the July 31 trade deadline. He continued in that capacity his final two seasons, retiring at the conclusion of the 2011 campaign after spending much of his time tutoring young receiver Jarrod Saltalamacchia. Varitek ended his career with 193 home runs, 757 RBIs, 664 runs scored, 1,307 hits, 306 doubles, a .256 batting average, a .341 on-base percentage, and a .435 slugging percentage. With a total of 1,488 games caught, he appeared in more games behind home plate than any other receiver in Red Sox history.

Upon learning of Varitek's retirement, former Red Sox closer Jonathan Papelbon stated, "He showed me how to be a player with honesty, hard work, and integrity without ever having to say one word."

Mike Lowell said, "Tek was, hands down, one of the best teammates I ever had . . . he was a true captain in every sense of the word."

Longtime teammate Tim Wakefield added, "Although his leadership will be missed, his legacy in Red Sox history will be forged forever."

Derek Jeter of the rival Yankees also praised Varitek, stating, "I've always admired the way Jason played the game, and I appreciated the opportunity I had to get to know him throughout the years."

Following his retirement, Varitek assumed the role of special assistant to the general manager in Boston. Upon assigning that position to Varitek, Red Sox general manager Ben Cherington stated that the former catcher would be involved in areas such as "major league personnel decisions, evaluations, and mentorship and instruction of young players."

CAREER HIGHLIGHTS

Best Season

Varitek had the most productive season of his career in 2003, when he batted .273 and established career highs with 25 home runs and 85 RBIs. He posted solid numbers again two years later, concluding the 2005 campaign with 22 homers, 70 RBIs, 70 runs scored, and a .281 batting average. Yet, Varitek had his finest all-around season in 2004, when he hit 18 homers, knocked in 73 runs, scored 67 others, and reached career highs in hits (137), stolen bases (10), batting average (.296), on-base percentage (.390), and OPS (.872). He also led all AL receivers in putouts and committed only two errors, en route to compiling a career-best .998 fielding percentage.

Memorable Moments/Greatest Performances

Varitek had the greatest day of his career on May 20, 2001, when he led the Red Sox to a 10–3 victory over Kansas City by going 4 for 4, with three home runs and seven RBIs. He also performed exceptionally well against the Yankees in the 2004 ALCS, batting .321, with two homers, seven RBIs, and five runs scored.

However, Varitek will perhaps be remembered most for his involvement in a bench-clearing brawl that took place during a game between the Red Sox and Yankees on July 24, 2004. With the Yankees comfortably ahead in the nationally televised contest, Red Sox pitcher Bronson Arroyo hit Alex Rodriguez with a pitch, prompting the controversial slugger to gesture toward him. Varitek quickly interceded, exchanging words with Rodriguez, shoving his glove into his face, and wrestling with him, until both benches emptied. The incident seemed to light a fire under the Red Sox, who, after storming back to win the game by a score of 11–10, went on to post the best record in baseball from that point on. Sometimes regarded as the turning point in Boston's season, the melee helped spur the Red Sox on to win their first World Series in 86 years.

NOTABLE ACHIEVEMENTS

- Hit more than 20 home runs three times
- Surpassed 30 doubles five times
- Posted slugging percentage in excess of .500 once (.512 in 2003)
- Led AL catchers in putouts three times
- Ranks among Red Sox career leaders in doubles (10th); extra-base hits (10th); and games played (10th)
- Ranks first all-time among Red Sox catchers in games caught (1,488)
- Caught more no-hitters (4) than any other catcher in major-league history
- Hit three home runs in one game vs. Kansas City Royals on May 20, 2001
- 2005 Gold Glove winner
- 2005 Silver Slugger winner
- Three-time AL All-Star (2003, 2005, and 2008).
- Two-time AL champion (2004 and 2007)
- Two-time world champion (2004 and 2007)

Kevin Youkilis

Courtesy Keith Allison

Known for his grittiness, determination, intensity, and unusual batting stance, Kevin Youkilis evolved into one of the American League's toughest outs and most reliable defensive players during his time in Boston. A three-time AL All-Star and 2007 Gold Glove winner, Youkilis batted over .300 in three of his six full seasons with the Red Sox, while also hitting more than 25 home runs twice, driving in more than 100 runs once, and scoring more than 90 runs three times. His keen batting eye, patience at the plate, and ability to foul off good pitches also enabled him to compile an on-base percentage in excess of .400 on three occasions. A sure-handed fielder as well, Youkilis twice led players at his position in fielding percentage, at one point establishing a new major-league record for errorless chances at first base. Youkilis accomplished all he did for the Red Sox despite possessing somewhat limited athletic ability and a physique that caused his high school coach to call him "roly-poly," his college coach to refer to him as "pudgy," and the Red Sox scout who recruited him to label him as a "thicker-bodied guy." As Jackie MacMullan wrote for the *Boston Globe* in October 2009, "He [Youkilis] does not look like an MVP candidate; more a refrigerator repairman, a butcher, or the man selling hammers behind the counter at the *True Value* hardware store."

Born on March 15, 1979, to a Jewish father and a mother who converted to Judaism, Kevin Edmund Youkilis claims as his birthplace Cincinnati, Ohio, where he grew up idolizing Sandy Koufax. After playing first base, shortstop, third base, and the outfield for nearby Sycamore High School, Youkilis received a scholarship offer to attend the University of Cincinnati. While in college, Youkilis played mostly third base, excelling to such a degree that he earned Second-Team All-America honors in both his junior and senior years. In addition to compiling a batting average of .366 in his four years at Cincinnati, Youkilis ended up setting school records for most career home runs (56) and walks (206), and highest slugging percentage (.627) and on-base percentage (.499). Brad Meador, associate head coach at Cincinnati, later said, "He had a great eye . . . he hardly ever struck out looking. When he did, you knew the ump missed the call."

Nevertheless, Youkilis lasted until the eighth round of the 2001 amateur draft, when the Red Sox finally selected him with the 243rd overall pick. When asked what he liked about Youkilis, former Boston scout Matt Haas told *Sports Illustrated* in 2009, "At first glance, not a lot. He was unorthodox. He had an extreme crouch—his thighs were almost parallel to the ground. And he was heavier than he is now. But, the more I watched him, the more I just thought, 'Throw the tools out the window. This guy can play baseball.'"

Red Sox VP of player personnel Ben Cherington later noted, "Teams didn't appreciate performance as much then as they do now. His college performance was off the charts. . . . Now, teams appreciate what that means. There's no way he'd last that long now."

Youkilis clearly demonstrated that the scouts underestimated his ability once he entered Boston's farm system, earning Red Sox Minor League Player of the Year honors in both 2001 and 2002. Splitting the 2003 campaign between Portland in the Eastern League and Triple-A Pawtucket, Youkilis reached base safely in 71 consecutive games at one point, prompting John Sickels to write for ESPN:

> Youkilis is an on-base machine. He never swings at a bad pitch, and is adept at working counts and out-thinking the pitcher. Unlike some guys who draw lots of walks, Youkilis seldom strikes out. He makes solid contact against both fastballs and breaking pitches. Youkilis' swing is tailored for the line drive, and he may never hit for much home run power. But he hits balls to the gaps effectively, and could develop 10–14 home run power down the road. Youkilis does not have very good speed, though he is a decent base-runner. His defense at third base draws mixed reviews. His arm, range, and hands all rate as adequate/average. He doesn't kill the defense at third base, but he doesn't help it much either, and is likely to end up at first base down the road.

Youkilis's ability to reach base throughout his minor-league career earned him the nickname "the Greek God of Walks" in the book *Moneyball: The Art of Winning an Unfair Game*. It also prompted the Red Sox to give him a long look at third base in 2004, before sending him back down to Pawtucket to make room on the roster for Ramiro Mendoza. In his first 72 games in the major leagues, Youkilis hit seven homers, drove in 35 runs, scored 38 times, and batted .260. He appeared in another 44 games for the Red Sox the following year, batting .278 and compiling an on-base percentage of .400, before earning a permanent roster spot at the start of the 2006 campaign.

Although he also saw some action at third base and left field in his first full season, Youkilis spent the vast majority of his time at first base, doing a solid job at his new position by placing among the league leaders in assists and fielding percentage. He also made significant contributions to Boston's offense, hitting 13 home runs, driving in 72 runs, scoring 100 times, amassing 42 doubles, walking 91 times, batting .279, and compiling a .381 on-base percentage, despite struggling during the season's second half with plantar fasciitis and a problematic abdominal muscle. Youkilis had another good year in 2007, homering 16 times, knocking in 83 runs, scoring 85 times, batting .288, posting a .390 on-base percentage, and earning Gold Glove honors by going the entire year without committing an error at first base (although he made 3 errors in his 13 games at third base). In discussing what he perceived to be his primary role on the team, Youkilis noted,

"Fighting off pitches, fouling off pitches, laying off pitches, making it so the opposing pitcher can't breathe; that's my job."

Meanwhile, Red Sox manager Terry Francona observed, "He's taking more of what the pitchers give him, using the whole field. He's going to work the count about as good as any hitter in baseball. Last year, if he got a two-strike breaking ball, he might swing and miss. This year, he's fouling it off, or taking it to right field."

Having established himself as one of the integral members of Boston's starting lineup, Youkilis also felt more comfortable displaying the tremendous intensity he took with him to the field each day. In explaining his approach to the game, Youkilis told Ian Browne of MLB.com, "I think I try to pride myself on playing the game right. Of course, there are some people that don't like the way you go about your business. What I've found is you can't please everybody. There are people out there that work some hard jobs and like guys that play hard, and that's what I'm going to do; I'm going to play hard. I play with a lot of passion. This is my life and something I take very seriously. I don't take the game for granted."

Youkilis's high level of intensity caused him to clash with teammate Manny Ramirez during a game at Fenway Park in early June of 2007, with the two players having to be separated by teammates in the Red Sox dugout after Ramirez reportedly took a swing at Youkilis. Commenting on the fray afterwards, manager Terry Francona said, "We had a lot of testosterone going tonight." Asked about the incident the following year, Youkilis stated, "We have two different approaches to the game. Winning and losing isn't life and death to Manny."

While the Red Sox ended up parting ways with Ramirez one year later, Youkilis went on to have the two finest seasons of his career, earning All-Star honors in both 2008 and 2009. After hitting 29 home runs, driving in 115 runs, scoring 91 times, and batting .312 in the first of those campaigns, he homered 27 times, knocked in 94 runs, scored 99 others, and batted .305 the following year. Youkilis finished third in the AL MVP voting in 2008, and sixth in 2009.

The success Youkilis experienced those two seasons prompted Red Sox executive VP Theo Epstein to say, "Statistically, if you consider 2008 and 2009, you could make the case there has been no better player in the league."

Youkilis continued to perform at an extremely high level in 2010, before a right thumb abductor muscle tear cut his season short on August 2. He concluded the campaign with 19 home runs, 62 RBIs, 77 runs scored, a

.307 batting average, a .411 on-base percentage, and a .564 slugging percentage in 102 games and 362 official at-bats.

The arrival of first baseman Adrian Gonzalez and the departure of third sacker Adrián Beltré prompted the Red Sox to move Youkilis back to the hot corner in 2011. While Youkilis handled the transition well, leading all AL third basemen with a .967 fielding percentage, injuries once again cut into his playing time, limiting him to 120 games, 17 home runs, 80 RBIs, and a batting average of just .258.

After experiencing philosophical differences with new Red Sox manager Bobby Valentine, who questioned his motivation and physical ability to succeed, Youkilis found himself splitting time at third base with rookie Will Middlebrooks early in 2012. After Youkilis hit just four homers, drove in only 14 runs, and batted just .233 in 42 games with the club, the Red Sox traded him to the Chicago White Sox on June 24 for pitcher Zach Stewart and utility man Brent Lillibridge. Youkilis left Boston with career totals of 133 home runs, 564 RBIs, 594 runs scored, 961 hits, and 239 doubles, a batting average of .287, a .388 on-base percentage, and a .487 slugging percentage.

Although Youkilis proved to be a productive hitter for the White Sox during the second half of the 2012 campaign, hitting 15 home runs and knocking in 46 runs, he compiled a batting average of just .236 in 80 games. Granted free agency at season's end, Youkilis subsequently signed a one-year deal with the Yankees, for whom he appeared in only 28 games before having to undergo season-ending surgery to repair a herniated disk in his back. Concerns over his health and diminishing offensive production prevented Youkilis from receiving an acceptable offer from any major-league club when he once again became a free agent at the end of 2013, prompting him to eventually sign a one-year, $4 million deal with the Rakuten Golden Eagles of the Japanese Pacific League. In explaining Youkilis's decision, his agent Joe Bick said, "In the final analysis, he [Youkilis] said, 'the right thing for my family and me is to go do this. It will be a wonderful life experience.'"

Limited by injuries to only 21 games in 2014, Youkilis chose to announce his retirement at seasons's end, after which he accepted a position with the Chicago Cubs, for whom he currently serves as a scout and development consultant.

RED SOX CAREER HIGHLIGHTS

Best Season

Youkilis had an outstanding year for the Red Sox in 2009, concluding the campaign with 27 home runs, 94 RBIs, 99 runs scored, a .305 batting average, a .548 slugging percentage, and a career-high .413 on-base percentage. However, he posted slightly better overall numbers one year earlier, when he scored 91 runs, compiled a .390 on-base percentage, and established career highs with 29 homers, 115 RBIs, 43 doubles, 168 hits, 306 total bases, a batting average of .312, and a slugging percentage of .569, en route to earning a third-place finish in the league MVP voting.

Memorable Moments/Greatest Performances

Youkilis made his major-league debut a memorable one, homering in his second at-bat against 1996 Cy Young Award winner Pat Hentgen in Toronto on May 15, 2004. Following the contest, an ecstatic Youkilis proclaimed, "This one will go down probably as the greatest day of my life."

Youkilis also began the 2007 postseason in unforgettable fashion, homering against the Angels in the first inning of Game 1 of the ALDS. After the Red Sox swept the Angels in three straight games, Youkilis helped lead them to a seven-game victory over the Cleveland Indians in the ALCS by hitting three home runs, driving in seven runs, scoring 10 times, and posting a batting average of .500 by collecting 14 hits in 28 times at bat.

Youkilis put together a pair of impressive streaks during his time in Boston—one with the bat, and the other with the glove. He hit safely in 23 consecutive games from May 5, 2007, to June 2, 2007, batting .426 (43–101), with six home runs, 13 doubles, and 21 RBIs. At one point during the streak, Youkilis collected at least two hits in nine straight games, tying Jim Rice's team record in the process. Meanwhile, Youkilis established new major-league records for first basemen by going 238 games and 2,002 chances without committing an error—a streak that began early in 2006 and ended on June 7, 2008.

Yet, Youkilis accomplished perhaps his greatest feat on August 22, 2009, just one day after learning that his friend and former minor-league teammate Greg Montalbano had succumbed to testicular cancer at the age of 31. After dedicating his next game to his friend's memory and inscribing "GM" in marker on his cap, Youkilis led the Red Sox to a 14–1 pounding of the Yankees by going 3 for 5, with two home runs, a double, and six RBIs. As he crossed home plate after each home run, he looked up and pointed to the sky. Following the contest, an emotional Youkilis said, "That was for him. There are some crazy things that have happened in my life. You . . . feel like there's somebody out there somewhere pushing balls out for you, and doing great things."

NOTABLE ACHIEVEMENTS

- Hit more than 20 home runs twice
- Knocked in more than 100 runs once (115 in 2008)
- Batted over .300 three times
- Scored 100 runs in 2006
- Surpassed 30 doubles five times, topping 40 mark twice
- Compiled on-base percentage in excess of .400 three times
- Posted slugging percentage in excess of .500 three times
- Led AL first basemen with 1.000 fielding percentage in 2007
- Led AL third basemen with .967 fielding percentage in 2011
- Finished third in 2008 AL MVP voting
- 2008 AL Hank Aaron Award winner
- 2007 Gold Glove winner
- Three-time AL All-Star (2008, 2009, and 2011)
- Two-time AL champion (2004 and 2007)
- Two-time world champion (2004 and 2007)

Rico Petrocelli

Courtesy D.B. Sports Memorabilia

Employing a short, compact right-handed swing perfectly suited for Fenway Park, Rico Petrocelli managed to become a Red Sox fan favorite even though he grew up in Brooklyn, New York rooting for the hated Yankees. Spending his entire career in Boston, Petrocelli hit 210 home runs as a member of the Red Sox, surpassing 25 homers on three occasions, and establishing a new American League record for shortstops (since broken) by hitting 40 round-trippers in 1969. Petrocelli also knocked in more than 100 runs once, drew more than 90 bases on balls twice, and compiled an on-base percentage in excess of .400 once. A solid fielder as well, Petrocelli led all AL shortstops in fielding percentage twice, before moving to third base, where he topped all players at his position in fielding percentage once more.

Born in Brooklyn on June 27, 1943, Americo Peter Petrocelli developed his love for baseball at an early age. Growing up during the 1950s, when three major-league teams still called the city of New York home, Petrocelli often attended games at Ebbets Field and Yankee Stadium, where he rooted for Mickey Mantle and his beloved Yankees. Outstanding in both basketball and baseball, Petrocelli earned all-scholastic honors in both sports while attending Brooklyn's Sheepshead Bay High School. A pitcher and power-hitting outfielder in high school, Petrocelli moved to shortstop after signing with the Red Sox as an amateur free agent following his graduation in 1961. He spent the next three years advancing through Boston's farm system, earning a brief call-up at the end of 1963 before being returned to the minors for more seasoning at the start of the ensuing campaign.

Petrocelli began experimenting with switch-hitting in his final year of minor-league ball, but he abandoned the idea at the suggestion of Red Sox hitting coach Pete Runnels shortly after the team named him its starting shortstop early in 1965. Urged by Runnels to pull the ball as much as possible in order to take full advantage of Fenway Park's short left-field wall, Petrocelli developed a compact swing that enabled him to consistently drive pitches toward the "Green Monster." After hitting only 13 homers and knocking in just 33 runs as a rookie, Petrocelli hit 18 home runs and drove in 59 runs in 1966.

However, as Petrocelli began to mature as a player, his relationship with Red Sox manager Billy Herman gradually deteriorated. Herman displayed little patience toward the moody and insecure Petrocelli, making life extremely difficult for the young shortstop. It wasn't until Red Sox management relieved Herman of his duties late in 1966 that Petrocelli truly began to reach his potential. With new Red Sox skipper Dick Williams asking Petrocelli to serve as leader of the team's inexperienced infield at the start of 1967, the 23-year-old shortstop had the finest season of his young career, helping Boston capture the AL pennant by raising his batting average 21 points, to .259. He also hit 17 homers and knocked in 66 runs, en route to earning All-Star honors for the first time.

With a chronic elbow problem that Petrocelli first developed in high school troubling him throughout the 1968 campaign, he missed 39 games, finishing the year with only 12 home runs, 46 runs batted in, 41 runs scored, and a batting average of just .234. After spending most of the subsequent off-season exercising his upper body and altering his diet, the 6-foot, 180-pound Petrocelli returned to the Red Sox stronger and healthier than ever in 1969. In easily his finest season, Petrocelli hit 40 home runs, knocked in 97 runs, scored 92, batted .297, and compiled a .589 slugging percentage. He also displayed far more patience at the plate, walking a total of 98 times. Free of pain in his right (throwing) elbow for the first time, Petrocelli excelled in the field as well, committing only 14 errors, en route to leading all players at his position with a .981 fielding percentage, which remains a Red Sox record for shortstops. Petrocelli's exceptional all-around play earned him All-Star honors for the second time and a seventh-place finish in the AL MVP voting. He followed that up with another big year in 1970, hitting 29 home runs, knocking in a career-high 103 runs, scoring 82 times, and batting .261.

A consummate team player, Petrocelli agreed to move to third base when the Red Sox acquired Gold Glove shortstop Luis Aparicio from the Chicago White Sox prior to the 1971 season. Working feverishly during spring training to learn his new position, Petrocelli ended up exceeding all expectations, setting a major-league record for third basemen by going 77 straight games without an error, making only 11 miscues all year, and leading all AL third sackers with a .976 fielding percentage. He also had a solid year at the plate, hitting 28 homers, driving in 89 runs, scoring 82, batting .251, walking 91 times, and compiling a .354 on-base percentage. Although Petrocelli's offensive numbers fell off somewhat the following year (15 home runs; 75 RBIs; .240 average), he continued his stellar play at the hot corner, committing only 13 errors, leading all league third basemen in double plays, and placing second among players at his position in putouts and fielding percentage.

Petrocelli spent four more years in Boston, battling injuries and health problems that prevented him from ever again performing at optimum proficiency. A recurrence of his earlier elbow injury limited him to only 100 games in 1973, forcing him to undergo surgery during the subsequent off-season. Although Petrocelli returned to the Red Sox lineup to post solid numbers in 1974, a September 15 beaning by Milwaukee's Jim Slaton sidelined him for the final two weeks of the campaign. Petrocelli never fully recovered from the beaning, developing a severe inner-ear imbalance that affected his hitting the remainder of his career. Yet, even though he batted just .239 and hit only 7 home runs in 1975, Petrocelli provided veteran leadership to a Red Sox club that captured the American League pennant.

Nevertheless, after he posted a batting average of just .213 in 85 games the following year, the Red Sox decided to release him prior to the 1977 regular season. Petrocelli subsequently announced his retirement, ending his career with 210 home runs, 773 runs batted in, 653 runs scored, 1,352 hits, a .251 batting average, a .332 on-base percentage, and a .420 slugging percentage. He ranks in the Red Sox all-time top-10 in home runs, RBIs, and walks (661). Meanwhile, only Ted Williams hit more grand slams than Petrocelli's nine.

Following his retirement, Petrocelli remained close to the game by writing a regular column in the *Boston Herald* that followed the progress of the Red Sox. He also became involved in sports talk radio, spent one year serving as color commentator for Red Sox radio broadcasts, and later became a minor-league manager. After leaving the game for good, Petrocelli became a successful businessman, heading the Petrocelli Marketing Group, which sells customizable promotional products and shirts, and running Petrocelli Sports, Inc., which focuses on speaking engagements, celebrity bookings, and sports memorabilia.

CAREER HIGHLIGHTS

Best Season

Even though Petrocelli hit 29 home runs and knocked in a career-high 103 runs in 1970, he clearly had his finest season in 1969, when he drove in 97 runs and established career-high marks in home runs (40), runs scored (92), hits (159), doubles (32), walks (98), batting average (.297), on-base percentage (.403), and slugging percentage (.589). Petrocelli's 40 homers set a new AL record for shortstops, surpassing the mark of 39 previously reached by Boston's Vern Stephens in 1949. Meanwhile, his .589 slugging percentage placed him second in the league to Oakland's Reggie Jackson. Petrocelli also excelled in the field, tying a then-record for fewest errors by a shortstop by committing only 14 miscues. At one point during the season, he went 44 consecutive games without making an error.

Memorable Moments/Greatest Performances

Petrocelli performed extremely well during the latter stages of Boston's "Impossible Dream" season of 1967, helping the Red Sox overcome an early 2–0 deficit to the Indians on September 20 by hitting a two-run homer off Cleveland ace Sam McDowell. Petrocelli's blow provided much of the impetus for the Red Sox to eventually win the contest by a score of 5–4. He also helped make history in Game 6 of the World Series by joining Carl Yastrzemski and Reggie Smith in hitting consecutive home runs in the fourth inning of Boston's 8–4 victory that evened the Fall Classic at three games apiece. Petrocelli also homered earlier in the contest.

Petrocelli again demonstrated his ability to perform well under pressure in the 1975 World Series. Although the Red Sox ended up losing to Cincinnati in seven games, Petrocelli batted .308 and drove in four runs.

On September 29, 1969, Petrocelli established a new American League record for shortstops by hitting his 40th home run of the year against the Washington Senators' Jim Shellenback at RFK Stadium.

Petrocelli had another big day on May 28, 1971, when he homered twice and knocked in three runs against eventual AL MVP Vida Blue to lead the Red Sox to a 4–3 win. Adding to the intrigue surrounding the contest was the fact that Blue entered the game with a record of 10–1, while Boston starter Sonny Siebert boasted a mark of 8–0.

Petrocelli had one of his most productive days at the plate on June 21, 1972, when he helped lead the Red Sox to an 11-inning, 10–9 win over the Texas Rangers by knocking in six runs, four of which came on a grand slam home run.

Yet, the seminal moment of Petrocelli's career occurred during the last game of the 1967 regular season, when he caught Rich Rollins's pop-up to record the final out of Boston's 5–3 victory over the Minnesota Twins. The win ended up putting the Red Sox in the World Series for the first time in 21 years.

NOTABLE ACHIEVEMENTS

- Hit more than 20 home runs three times, topping 40 homers once (40 in 1969)
- Knocked in more than 100 runs once (103 in 1970)
- Surpassed 30 doubles twice
- Compiled on-base percentage in excess of .400 once (.403 in 1969)
- Posted slugging percentage in excess of .500 once (.589 in 1969)
- Led AL with 10 sacrifice flies in 1970
- Led AL shortstops in fielding percentage twice
- Led AL third basemen in fielding percentage and double plays once each

- Holds Red Sox single-season record for highest fielding percentage by a shortstop (.981 in 1969)
- Ranks second all-time on Red Sox with nine career grand slams
- Ranks among Red Sox career leaders in home runs (10th); RBIs (9th); walks (10th); games played (9th); plate appearances (10th); and at-bats (10th)
- 1969 *Sporting News* All-Star selection
- Two-time AL All-Star (1967 and 1969)
- Two-time AL champion (1967 and 1975)

Tony Conigliaro

Courtesy Richard Albersheim

One of the most promising careers in Major League Baseball all but ended on August 18, 1967, when California Angels right-hander Jack Hamilton hit Boston Red Sox slugger Tony Conigliaro in the face with a pitch, fracturing his left cheekbone, dislocating his jaw, and severely damaging his left retina. Only 22 years old at the time, Conigliaro had already hit 104 home runs for the Red Sox, becoming in the process the youngest American League player ever to reach the 100-homer plateau. By topping the junior circuit with 32 round-trippers two seasons earlier, Conigliaro also established himself as the youngest home run champion in league history. Conigliaro showed tremendous determination by returning to the Boston lineup some 18 months later, earning 1969 AL Comeback Player of the Year honors by hitting 20 home runs and driving in 82 runs. He amazingly followed that up with arguably the finest statistical season of his career in 1970. However, the success Conigliaro experienced those two seasons turned out to be short-lived, with the internal damage caused by his earlier beaning eventually proving too much to overcome. Suffering from impaired vision, Conigliaro sat out three of the next five seasons, appearing in a total of only 95 games during that time, before finally announcing his retirement at just 30 years of age. The tragic events surrounding Conigliaro's career caused Red Sox fans to spend the next several years wondering what might have been.

Born in Revere, Massachusetts, on January 7, 1945, Anthony Richard Conigliaro attended St. Mary's High School in Lynn, Massachusetts, where he first began to draw the attention of major-league scouts with his strong throwing arm and home run hitting prowess. Despite receiving offers from several other clubs following his graduation, Conigliaro elected to sign with his hometown team, inking a $20,000 deal with the Red Sox in 1962 while still only 17 years old. Conigliaro spent the next two years working his way up the Boston farm system, before joining the big club at the start of the 1964 campaign.

Still only 19 years old when he arrived in Boston, Conigliaro made an immediate impression on Red Sox manager Johnny Pesky, who inserted the young outfielder into his starting lineup. Taking note of the right-handed hitting Conigliaro's aggressiveness at the plate, Pesky later said, "He was fearless of the ball. He would just move his head, like [Ted] Williams did. A ball up and in, Tony would just move his head. He thought the ball would never hit him."

Williams also admired Conigliaro's hitting style, telling him, "Don't change that solid stance of yours, no matter what you're told."

Since Conigliaro crowded home plate as much as anyone in the league, he often found himself being plunked by opposing pitchers. The first such instance took place on May 24, 1964, when Moe Drabowsky hit him on the left wrist, causing a hairline fracture. Conigliaro, though, ended up missing only four games. He proved to be less fortunate later in the year when a Pedro Ramos pitch broke his arm, forcing him to sit out more than a month. Nevertheless, Conigliaro had a solid rookie campaign, compiling a

.290 batting average and finishing with 24 homers, 52 RBIs, and 69 runs scored, despite appearing in only 111 games.

Although a broken left wrist caused Conigliaro to miss three weeks of the ensuing campaign, he again posted solid numbers, driving in 82 runs, scoring 82, batting .269, and leading the league with 32 home runs. He followed that up with another good year in 1966, batting .265, scoring 77 runs, and placing among the league leaders with 28 homers, 93 RBIs, and a .487 slugging percentage.

In addition to performing well on the playing field over the course of his first three seasons, Conigliaro handled himself quite well off it, establishing a reputation as a teenage heartthrob. The 6'3" handsome star attracted a considerable amount of attention from local girls, as well as young ladies on the road. Dick Williams, who took over as Red Sox manager in 1967, attempted to curtail Conigliaro's extracurricular activities by assigning a veteran player to room with him on the road. However, Williams later wrote in his autobiography, "I never saw him [Conigliaro]. Not late at night, not first thing in the morning, never. I was providing veteran influence to a suitcase."

Yet, "Tony C.," as he came to be known, was all business on the ball field, earning the respect of his teammates with his ability to perform well under pressure. Speaking of the right fielder in *Forever Fenway*, Red Sox pitcher Jim Lonborg stated, "He was one of the best clutch hitters I ever saw. In our minds, if we ever wanted someone to come to the plate and drive in a run, you would love to see Tony Conigliaro come up to the plate and be that man."

Still, Conigliaro's teammates also remained concerned over the young slugger's tendency to crowd home plate. Red Sox second baseman Mike Andrews told Bob Ryan in an August 18, 2013, *Boston Globe* article entitled "Tony Conigliaro Would Have Been an All-Time Great," "I was always concerned about the way he 'froze' at the plate. I guess I shouldn't say 'froze.' It's more the way he wouldn't give in. You know, I had been wearing an earflap helmet that year [1967]. I may have been the first. I had been trying to get him to use one, but unfortunately he didn't."

Meanwhile, the book *The 1967 Impossible Dream Red Sox*, reveals that, on August 17, 1967, Ted Williams warned Conigliaro's close friend Ed Penney, "Tony is crowding the plate. He's much too close. Tell him to back off. It's serious time now. The pitchers are going to get serious." Williams reminded Penney before he said goodbye to him later that evening, "Tell Tony what I said. Don't forget to tell Tony what I told you."

Penney relayed Williams's message to Conigliaro, but the latter unfortunately didn't heed his warning. The Red Sox played the California Angels at Fenway Park the very next day, and, after singling in his first at-bat, Conigliaro stepped to the plate in the bottom of the fourth inning to face Angels pitcher Jack Hamilton for the second time. Rico Petrocelli describes the events that followed in his book, *Tales from the Impossible Dream Red Sox*:

> Tony set himself in the batter's box, crowding the plate as always, while I knelt in the on-deck circle. I always believed there was a spot where Tony couldn't see the inside pitch. If you threw it to the right spot, he'd hit that ball nine miles. But then there was this blind spot, a little more inside. Sometimes he moved too late to get out of the way, and sometimes he never moved at all.
>
> I saw Hamilton's first pitch coming in and knew it was head high. But Tony didn't start to react until the last fraction of a second. Instinctively he threw up his hands to protect his head, but not nearly in time. The ball crashed into the side of his face with a sharp crack that I swear could have been heard clearly all over that noisy ballpark. It sounded like the ball hit his helmet, so my immediate reaction was relief that the ball had struck plastic instead of flesh. But the sound was probably his cheekbone breaking. In his desperate scramble to get out of the way of the ball, Tony had dislodged his helmet, and the ball struck him flush in the left side of his face, just below the eye socket.

Petrocelli further elaborated in *Forever Fenway*: "He didn't move or react until the very last second, and, by that time, it was too late. He got it right off the side of the face—in the temple in fact—and, when he was down, I could see his face swell up, just like blowing a balloon up, and you could see the blood rushing into that area."

Lying near home plate with his cheekbone shattered and his left eye completely shut, Conigliaro later said, "I thought I was going to die. Death was constantly on my mind."

Although Conigliaro escaped with his life, he never fully recovered from the beaning, sitting out the next 18 months with severely impaired vision. His Red Sox teammates tried to reassure him that they never would have captured the 1967 AL pennant had it not been for his contributions earlier in the year. (Conigliaro earned All-Star honors by hitting 20 home runs, knocking in 67 runs, and batting .287.) George Scott took it one step further, stating, "I've said it a million times, if Tony had been in the lineup, we would have won [the World Series]. He was one of those guys. Reggie Jackson was a big-game player. Tony was that kind of player."

Conigliaro's fracture healed, but a hole remained in his retina that could not be repaired. Yet, even though he never fully regained his vision, it improved to the point that he mounted a comeback in 1969. Appearing in 141 games, Conigliaro hit 20 homers, knocked in 82 runs, and batted .255. He improved upon those numbers significantly the following season, batting .266 and establishing career highs with 36 home runs, 116 runs batted in, and 89 runs scored. Conigliaro's miraculous performance enabled him to win the Hutch Award, presented annually to the active MLB player who "best exemplifies the fighting spirit and competitive desire" of Fred Hutchinson by persevering through adversity.

Unfortunately, Conigliaro's vision began to deteriorate late in the season, prompting the Red Sox to trade him to the California Angels at the end of the year. Barely able to see out of his left eye by the start of the ensuing campaign, Conigliaro batted just .222 during the season's first half, before announcing his retirement. Although he attempted another comeback with the Red Sox in 1975 after his vision improved once again, Conigliaro retired for good after posting a batting average of just .123 in 69 plate appearances. He ended his career with 166 home runs, 516 runs batted in, 464 runs scored, 849 hits, a batting average of .264, an on-base percentage of .327, and a slugging percentage of .476, compiling virtually all those numbers while playing for the Red Sox.

Following his retirement, Conigliaro moved to San Francisco, where he became a sportscaster at a local television station. Longing for a return to Boston, he flew back to his hometown on January 3, 1982, to interview for a job as the analyst for Red Sox games on cable television. However, he suffered a massive heart attack just a few days later while being driven back to Logan Airport by his brother Billy. Having lapsed into a coma before he ever reached the emergency room at Massachusetts General Hospital, Conigliaro never regained consciousness, spending the remainder of his life at his parents' home in Nahant, Massachusetts, before being moved to a nursing home in nearby Salem, where he passed away eight years later, on February 24, 1990. He was only 45 years old. In 1990, the Red Sox instituted the Tony Conigliaro Award, which is presented annually to the major-league player who best overcomes obstacles and adversities through the attributes of spirit, determination, and courage that were considered trademarks of Conigliaro.

RED SOX CAREER HIGHLIGHTS

Best Season

Conigliaro amazingly posted the best numbers of his career in 1970, three years after he suffered his near-fatal beaning. In addition to finishing fourth in the AL with 36 home runs, he placed second in RBIs (116) and eighth in slugging percentage (.498). Making Conigliaro's statistics even more impressive is the fact that he compiled them with only limited vision. Upon his return to the Red Sox, he learned that he couldn't see the ball if he looked directly at the pitcher. However, Conigliaro learned to use his peripheral vision to see the ball better, picking it up by looking a couple of inches to the left.

Memorable Moments/Greatest Performances

Unfortunately, the most vivid memory most people have of Conigliaro centers around the events that took place on that fateful afternoon of August 18, 1967. Nevertheless, "Tony C." provided Red Sox fans with a number of thrills. Conigliaro homered in his very first at-bat at Fenway Park, helping the Red Sox win their 1964 home opener 4–1 over the White Sox by turning on the first pitch he saw from Chicago's Joe Horlen and driving it over the "Green Monster" in left field.

Although the Red Sox lost both ends of a doubleheader to the A's on July 27, 1965, Conigliaro had a big day at the plate, going four for eight, with three home runs and six runs batted in. After homering twice in the opener, Conigliaro hit a grand slam in the nitecap.

Conigliaro hit one of the biggest home runs of his career on June 15, 1967, giving the Red Sox a 2–1 victory over the Chicago White Sox by delivering a two-out, two-run homer in the bottom of the 11th inning.

Conigliaro played his most memorable game for the Red Sox on April 8, 1969, when he made his long-awaited return from his 1967 beaning on Opening Day in Baltimore. Appearing in his first game in 18 months, Conigliaro gave the Red Sox a brief 4–2 lead over the Orioles with a dramatic two-run homer in the top of the 10th inning. After the Orioles came back to tie the contest with two runs of their own in the bottom of the frame, Conigliaro scored the game-winner on a sacrifice fly by Dalton Jones in the top of the 12th inning.

Courtesy Legendary Auctions

NOTABLE ACHIEVEMENTS

- Hit more than 30 home runs twice
- Knocked in more than 100 runs once (116 in 1970)
- Compiled slugging percentage in excess of .500 three times
- Led AL in home runs once (32 in 1965)
- Youngest player ever to lead his league in home runs
- Youngest American League player to reach 100 home runs
- 1969 AL Comeback Player of the Year
- 1970 Hutch Award winner
- 1967 AL All-Star
- 1967 AL champion

Johnny Damon

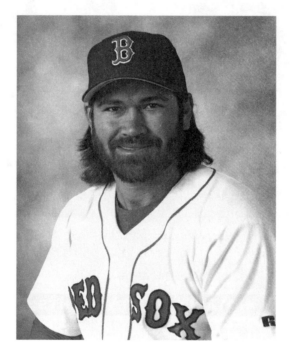

Courtesy Boston Red Sox

One of the self-proclaimed "Idiots" that helped lead the Red Sox to the greatest comeback in major-league history and their first world championship in 86 years, Johnny Damon spent four years in Boston, establishing himself as one of the team's clubhouse leaders and most indispensable players. Whether lightening the mood in the Red Sox locker room with his relaxed, carefree attitude or inspiring his teammates with his hustle and aggressive style of play on the field, Damon contributed greatly to the success the Red Sox experienced from 2002 to 2005. Batting leadoff for the Sox throughout most of that period, Damon scored more than 100 runs each season, batted over .300 twice, and stole more than 30 bases twice, en route to earning two AL All-Star nominations and one *Sporting News* All-Star selection. Although he lacked a strong throwing arm, Damon also excelled in the outfield, where he used his great speed to track down fly balls and compensate for the defensive shortcomings of left fielder Manny Ramirez. In the end, Damon's all-around contributions to the Red Sox helped them win at least 93 games in each of his four seasons with the club, enabling them to advance to the playoffs three times and win one world championship in the process.

Born in Fort Riley, Kansas, on November 5, 1973, Johnny David Damon spent his earliest years living as an "Army brat," moving with his Thai mother and American father, a staff sergeant in the U.S. Army, from one overseas military base to another, before his father left the Army and settled the family in the Orlando area shortly before young Johnny began school. After suffering through a difficult childhood during which he found himself plagued by a speech impediment, Damon began to blossom as a teenager, becoming a straight-A student, track star, and baseball and football hero at Dr. Phillips High School in Orlando. Despite being rated as the top high school prospect in the country by *Baseball America* as a senior, Damon briefly toyed with the idea of attending college on a football or track scholarship, before he finally elected to pursue a career in baseball when the Kansas City Royals selected him in the first round of the 1992 amateur draft, with the 35th overall pick.

Damon spent the next three years advancing through Kansas City's farm system, before the talent-starved Royals summoned him to the big leagues in early August of 1995. Appearing in 47 games over the final seven weeks of the campaign, the 21-year-old Damon batted .282, stole seven bases, drove in 23 runs, scored 32 others, and hit the first three home runs of his major-league career. Damon earned a starting job in Kansas City's outfield the following year, after which he established himself as one of the team's mainstays over the next few seasons. Splitting his time between center field and left from 1996 to 2000, Damon never batted any lower than .271, surpassing the .300 mark on two occasions. He also scored more than 100 runs three times and stole more than 30 bases twice. Damon had his best season for the Royals in 2000, when he hit 16 home runs, knocked in 88 runs, batted a career-high .327, placed among the league leaders with 214 hits, 42 doubles, and 10 triples, and topped the circuit with 136 runs scored and 46 stolen bases. Convinced that they would be unable to re-sign him when he became eligible for free agency at the end of 2001, the Royals subsequently included Damon in a three-team deal they completed with the A's and Devil Rays on January 8, 2001, that sent the speedy outfielder to Oakland. Although Damon's offensive production fell off somewhat in his one year in Oakland, he ended up signing a four-year, $31 million contract with the Red Sox at season's end.

Joining a Red Sox squad that won only 82 games the previous year, Damon paid immediate dividends on the huge investment by batting .286, scoring 118 runs, amassing 178 hits, stealing 31 bases, and leading the league with 11 triples. His strong performance helped the Red Sox improve their record to 93–69, earning him in the process the first All-Star selection of his career and the respect of everyone associated with the ball club.

Star shortstop Nomar Garciaparra said of his new teammate, "When you have that type of leadoff guy, who can get on and steal a base, it puts pressure on the pitcher."

Red Sox coach Ron Jackson stated, "People don't realize that he's the guy who makes it all happen here."

Meanwhile, General Manager Theo Epstein said, "You can't believe how hard he plays."

Opposing manager Joe Torre also expressed his admiration for Damon, saying, "The Red Sox have never boasted any speed. They've mainly been a one-dimensional offense, with a history of waiting for that one big inning. Johnny gives them speed, which makes them that much tougher."

Damon proved to be somewhat less productive in his second season in Boston, concluding the 2003 campaign with a batting average of .273 and 103 runs scored. Nevertheless, he assumed a greater role in the Red Sox clubhouse, helping to improve their growing sense of camaraderie by serving as one of the most prominent figures in their movement toward an anti-establishment image. After featuring a conservative, clean-cut look at his previous stops, Damon eventually embraced the new image that his Red Sox teammates cultivated, becoming the poster boy for it with his long hair and thick beard that very much caused him to take on the appearance of a caveman.

With the Red Sox having allowed themselves to be beaten down psychologically by the arch-rival New York Yankees in seasons past, Damon proclaimed early in 2004 that he and his teammates intended to stop using their brains. Nicknaming themselves the "Idiots," the Red Sox subsequently spent most of the season conducting themselves like children, engaging in clubhouse pranks and other mischievous behavior. Damon joined Kevin Millar and David Ortiz as the lead pranksters, with Damon's practice of doing naked pull-ups before each game becoming legendary.

Still, in spite of their laid-back attitude and casual approach off the field, the Red Sox proved to be all business between the white lines, with Damon revealing the intensity with which he played when he said, "I play the game like it's going to be my last." He added, "I want to be the best leadoff hitter of our time."

The 6'2" Damon added 15 pounds of muscle prior to the start of the 2004 campaign, enabling him to become more of a power threat at the plate. Serving as Boston's offensive catalyst throughout the season, the lefty-swinging Damon established new career highs with 20 homers and 94 RBIs, finished second in the league with 123 runs scored, batted .304, and stole 19 bases. He also performed well during the postseason, batting .467 against Anaheim in the ALDS, homering twice and driving in seven runs against New York in the ALCS, and hitting a homer, knocking in two runs, and scoring four times during Boston's four-game sweep of St. Louis in the World Series.

Playing most of 2005 with a sore shoulder he injured when he ran into a wall in May, Damon hit only 10 home runs. Yet, he still managed to knock in 75 runs, score 117 times, collect 197 hits, steal 18 bases, and finish fourth in the league with a .316 batting average. He also led all AL outfielders with 394 putouts. But, with the Red Sox suffering a three-game sweep at the hands of the Angels in the ALDS, they refused to offer Damon more than a three-year contract when he became a free agent at season's end, prompting the 32-year-old outfielder to sign a four-year, $52 million deal with the hated Yankees.

On February 8, 2006, one month after signing with the Yankees, Damon took out a full-page ad in the *Boston Globe* in which he thanked Red Sox fans for supporting him. Yet the "Fenway Faithful" found it difficult to forgive Damon for going to New York, especially after he stated early in 2005, "There's no way I can go play for the Yankees, but I know they're going to come after me hard. It's definitely not the most important thing to go out there for the top dollar, which the Yankees are going to offer me. It's not what I need."

Damon ended up performing extremely well for the Yankees over the next four seasons, surpassing 20 homers and 100 runs scored twice, stealing more than 20 bases three times, batting over .300 once, and helping them win their 27th world championship in 2009. After becoming a free agent again at the end of the 2009 campaign, Damon signed with the Tigers,

Courtesy Boston Red Sox

with whom he spent just one year, posting a .271 batting average and scoring 81 runs. From Detroit, he moved on to Tampa Bay, where he spent the 2011 season, before signing with Cleveland at season's end. Damon retired after the Indians released him on August 9, 2012. He concluded his career with 235 home runs, 1,139 RBIs, 1,668 runs scored, 2,769 hits, 522 doubles, 109 triples, 408 stolen bases, a .284 batting average, a .352 on-base percentage, and a .433 slugging percentage. Damon batted over .300 five times, scored more than 100 runs ten times, and stole at least 25 bases ten times. In his four years with the Red Sox, he hit 56 home runs, knocked in 299 runs, scored 461 times, amassed 730 hits, collected 136 doubles and 29 triples, stole 98 bases, batted .295, compiled a .362 on-base percentage, and posted a .441 slugging percentage.

Although Damon spent the final seven years of his career playing for other teams, he stated after leaving the Red Sox, "I love Boston, and I always will. I'll always have terrific memories and great fans here."

RED SOX CAREER HIGHLIGHTS

Best Season

Damon had an outstanding year for the Red Sox in 2005, when he earned the only *Sporting News* All-Star selection of his career by hitting 10 homers, driving in 75 runs, stealing 18 bases, and finishing among the league leaders with 117 runs scored, 197 hits, and a .316 batting average. But he posted slightly better overall numbers the season before, concluding the 2004 campaign with 20 home runs, 123 runs scored, 189 hits, 19 stolen bases, a .304 batting average, a career-high 94 RBIs, a .380 on-base percentage, and a .477 slugging percentage. Damon's OPS of .857 represented easily the highest mark he compiled as a member of the Red Sox, trailing only the .877 that he posted for the Royals in 2000, his final year in Kansas City.

Memorable Moments/Greatest Performances

Damon put together one of the longest hitting streaks in Red Sox history in 2005, hitting safely in 29 consecutive games before seeing his streak come to an end on July 18.

On June 27, 2003, Damon tied a major-league record by becoming just the second player to get three hits in one inning, reaching base on a single, double, and triple in the first inning of a 25–8 mauling of the Florida Marlins. He finished the game with five hits, three RBIs, and three runs scored. Damon had another huge day on April 7, 2004, going 5 for 5, with a double, stolen base, two RBIs, and two runs scored during a 10–3 win over the Orioles in Baltimore.

Still, when Red Sox fans think of Damon they are most likely to reflect back on his outstanding 2004 postseason performance. After batting .467, scoring four runs, and stealing three bases during Boston's three-game sweep of Anaheim in the ALDS, Damon struggled throughout most of the ALCS, collecting just three hits in 29 at-bats in the first six games against New York. However, after being told by his teammates prior to Game 7 that it was his time to shine, Damon led the Red Sox to victory by going three for six, with two home runs and six RBIs. His second-inning grand slam against reliever Javier Vazquez put the Red Sox ahead 6–0, all but cementing their unprecedented comeback, as they went on to clinch the AL pennant by cruising to a 10–3 victory. Damon's six RBIs established a new ALCS single-game record. He also contributed greatly to Boston's four-game sweep of St. Louis in the World Series, batting .286, leading all players with four runs scored, and setting the tone for the Red Sox 3–0 win in the series clincher by leading off the contest with a home run.

NOTABLE ACHIEVEMENTS

- Batted over .300 twice
- Scored more than 100 runs four times, surpassing 120 runs scored once (123 in 2004)
- Hit 20 home runs in 2004
- Finished in double-digits in triples once (11 in 2002)
- Surpassed 30 doubles four times
- Stole more than 30 bases twice
- Led AL with 11 triples in 2002
- Led AL outfielders in putouts once and fielding percentage once
- Led AL center fielders in putouts twice
- Holds share of major-league record with three hits in one inning (vs. Florida on June 27, 2003)
- 2005 *Sporting News* All-Star Selection
- Two-time AL All-Star (2002 and 2005)
- 2004 AL champion
- 2004 world champion

Mike Lowell

Courtesy of Keith Allison

Initially considered to be merely a throw-in by the Marlins in the deal that sent Josh Beckett to Boston and Hanley Ramirez to Florida, Mike Lowell ended up spending five seasons with the Red Sox, establishing himself during that time as one of the team's leaders and most outstanding clutch performers. Admired and respected by all of his teammates for his professionalism and strong work ethic, Lowell helped lead the Red Sox to three playoff appearances and one world championship in his five years in Beantown, earning World Series MVP honors in 2007, when he batted .400

during Boston's four-game sweep of Colorado in the Fall Classic. A solid hitter, Lowell hit more than 20 home runs twice, knocked in more than 100 runs once, and batted over .300 once for the Red Sox, en route to earning one All-Star nomination and one top-five finish in the league MVP voting. An exceptional fielder as well, Lowell led all AL third basemen in putouts and fielding percentage once each, concluding his career with the second-highest fielding percentage among players at his position in major-league history. Making Lowell's accomplishments even more impressive is the fact that he overcame cancer early in his career, shortly after the Yankees traded him to the Marlins prior to the 1999 campaign.

Born in San Juan, Puerto Rico, on February 24, 1974, Michael Averett Lowell grew up in Miami, Florida, after moving there with his family at the age of four. Short and skinny as a teenager, Lowell saw very little playing time for Christopher Columbus High School's baseball team in his one year there, prompting him to transfer to Coral Gables Senior High School for his final two years. Excelling at second base and shortstop for Coral Gables, Lowell earned a scholarship to Miami's Florida International University, where he eventually grew to 6'4" and added some much-needed weight. Even though he displayed very little power at the plate during his college career, Lowell earned All-Conference honors as a second sacker three times, prompting the Yankees to select him in the 20th round of the 1995 amateur draft.

Lowell spent the next four years in New York's farm system, gradually developing into more of a power threat, while also learning how to play third base. He made his first major-league appearance late in 1998, playing in eight games for the eventual world champions, and collecting four hits in 15 at-bats, for a .267 batting average. With Scott Brosius holding down the third base job, the Yankees elected to trade Lowell to Florida for three midlevel pitching prospects on February 1, 1999. However, during a routine physical conducted just a few weeks later, doctors discovered a suspicious lump in Lowell's groin area that they diagnosed as testicular cancer. Forced to undergo surgery and radiation therapy, the 25-year-old Lowell spent the next three months recuperating, before finally returning to the playing field at the end of May.

Displaying a tremendous amount of fortitude, Lowell ended up posting decent numbers as a rookie in 1999, batting .253, hitting 12 homers, and driving in 47 runs, in only 97 games and 308 official at-bats. He established himself as Florida's starting third baseman the following season, beginning an outstanding five-year run during which he averaged 25 home runs and 95 runs batted in. Lowell surpassed 20 home runs four times and 100 RBIs twice during that period, having his best season for the Marlins in 2003, when he helped lead them to the world championship by hitting 32 homers and knocking in 105 runs, en route to earning NL All-Star honors for one of three times and an 11th-place finish in the league MVP voting.

Even though Lowell won the only Gold Glove of his career in 2005, the season proved to be a disappointing one for him at the plate. In easily his worst big-league season, he hit just eight homers, knocked in only 58 runs, and batted just .236. Believing that the 31-year-old third baseman had already seen his best days, and, with budding star Miguel Cabrera eager to take over at the hot corner, the Marlins elected to include Lowell and his hefty salary in the seven-player trade they completed with the Red Sox on November 24, 2005, that also sent Josh Beckett and Guillermo Mota to Boston for top prospects Hanley Ramirez and Anibal Sanchez, among others.

Lowell gave the Red Sox exceptional defense at third base in his first year in Boston, committing only six errors in the field in 153 games, and leading all players at his position in putouts. He also experienced an offensive resurgence, concluding the campaign with 20 home runs, 80 runs batted in, 79 runs scored, a batting average of .284, and a career-high 47 doubles. Lowell followed that up with the finest season of his career in 2007. In addition to hitting 21 homers, he placed among the league leaders with 120 RBIs, 191 hits, and a .324 batting average, en route to earning All-Star honors and a fifth-place finish in the league MVP balloting. Lowell's outstanding all-around performance prompted Red Sox captain Jason Varitek to proclaim, "He [Lowell] is our MVP."

Lowell's work ethic, coolness under pressure, and fluency in both Spanish and English allowed him to become one of Boston's clubhouse leaders. Red Sox manager Terry Francona said of his third baseman, "He's a leader . . . a professional . . . a pro's pro."

Lowell demonstrated his ability to perform well in the clutch throughout the 2007 postseason, helping the Red Sox capture their second world championship in four years by hitting two homers, driving in 15 runs, and batting .353. A free agent after he claimed World Series MVP honors, Lowell subsequently accepted the three-year, $37.5 million contract the Red Sox offered him.

A torn hip labrum that required surgery at the end of the year limited Lowell to 113 games in 2008. Nevertheless, he managed to post solid numbers, finishing the season with 17 homers, 73 RBIs, and a .274 batting average. With the Red Sox reducing his playing time again the following year in an effort to keep him healthy, Lowell concluded the 2009 campaign with

17 homers, 75 RBIs, and a .290 batting average. After undergoing surgery again at season's end, this time to repair an injured right thumb, Lowell assumed a backup role with the team in 2010, filling in at first and third base, and also serving as a part-time DH and pinch-hitter. He announced his retirement at the end of the year, finishing his career with 223 home runs, 952 RBIs, 771 runs scored, 1,619 hits, a .279 batting average, a .342 on-base percentage, and a .464 slugging percentage. In his five years with the Red Sox, Lowell hit 80 home runs, knocked in 374 runs, scored 293 times, accumulated 650 hits, batted .290, compiled a .346 on-base percentage, and posted a .468 slugging percentage.

Since retiring from the game, Lowell has served as an analyst on the MLB Network, appearing on that station's *MLB Tonight* program.

RED SOX CAREER HIGHLIGHTS

Best Season

Lowell had the best season of his career in 2007, when he hit 21 home runs, scored 79 runs, amassed 37 doubles, established career highs with 120 RBIs, 191 hits, a .324 batting average, and a .378 on-base percentage, and posted an OPS of .879 that represents easily the highest mark he compiled in his five years with the Red Sox. Performing particularly well after the All-Star break, Lowell batted .350 during the season's second half. Meanwhile, his total of 120 RBIs represents a franchise record for a Red Sox third baseman.

Memorable Moments/Greatest Performances

Lowell hit arguably the most dramatic home run of his career on August 3, 2010, leading the Red Sox to a 3–1 win over Cleveland by hitting a two-run shot in the bottom of the second inning, on the very first pitch he saw after spending nearly two months on the disabled list.

Still, Lowell will always be remembered most fondly by Red Sox fans for his fabulous performance throughout the 2007 postseason. After batting .333 against the Angels in the ALDS, he helped Boston overcome a 3–1 deficit to Cleveland in the ALCS by homering once, knocking in eight runs, and once again hitting .333. Lowell came up big again in the World Series, leading the Red Sox to a four-game sweep of the overmatched Colorado Rockies by homering once, driving in four runs, scoring six others, and batting .400. His seventh-inning leadoff homer in Game 4 provided the winning margin in the series clincher, further solidifying his position as MVP of the Fall Classic.

NOTABLE ACHIEVEMENTS

- Hit more than 20 home runs twice
- Knocked in more than 100 runs once (120 in 2007)
- Batted over .300 once (.324 in 2007)
- Surpassed 30 doubles twice, topping 40 doubles once (47 in 2006)
- Compiled slugging percentage in excess of .500 once (.501 in 2007)
- Led AL third basemen in putouts once and double plays once
- Holds Red Sox single-season record for most RBIs by a third baseman (120 in 2007)
- Holds second-highest fielding percentage among third basemen in baseball history
- Finished fifth in 2007 AL MVP voting
- 2007 World Series MVP
- 2007 AL All-Star
- 2007 AL champion
- 2007 world champion

Billy Goodman

Courtesy Mears Online Auctions

Known for his defensive versatility, Billy Goodman played every position on the diamond except pitcher and catcher over the course of his 16-year major-league career. Although he spent the vast majority of his time playing either first or second base in his 10-plus years in Boston, Goodman also saw a significant amount of action at third base, left field, and right field, performing well wherever the Red Sox placed him. An outstanding hitter as well, Goodman compiled a lifetime batting average of .300, posting a mark of .306 as a member of the Red Sox, and winning the American League batting title in 1950 with an average of .354. He also displayed a keen batting eye, enabling him to compile an outstanding .376 on-base percentage during his career. Yet, due largely to his tremendous versatility, Goodman served as a full-time member of Boston's starting lineup for only three seasons, filling in wherever the Red Sox needed him in the other seven campaigns.

Born in Concord, North Carolina, on March 22, 1926, William Dale Goodman attended Winecoff High School in Concord, where he starred in basketball, football, and his first love, baseball. He began his professional career shortly after he graduated, signing with the Atlanta Crackers of the Southern Association in 1944, at just 18 years of age. After one year in Atlanta, Goodman temporarily left baseball to serve in the U.S. Navy during World War II. He returned to the Crackers in 1946, posting a batting average of .389 that prompted the Red Sox to purchase his contract at season's end.

Goodman earned a spot on the Red Sox roster coming out of spring training, but, after batting just .182 in extremely limited duty over the season's first two months, he returned to the minor leagues, joining the American Association's Louisville Colonels. Goodman manned virtually every position on the field while at Louisville, making an extremely favorable impression on Red Sox general manager Eddie Collins, who likened him to Jimmy Dykes, one of the most versatile players of the 1920s. Collins, known for his high standards, described Dykes as "the best until the kid [Goodman] came along."

Meanwhile, Larry Woodall, a former coach and, later, a scout for the Red Sox, proclaimed, "Goodman can make a monkey out of a scout. He doesn't look as if he can do anything right when you first see him. You have to watch him for a while before you realize that he can't do anything wrong."

Having performed exceptionally well at Louisville throughout the remainder of 1947, Goodman returned to the Red Sox the following year to establish himself as the team's starting first baseman. Appearing in 127 games as a rookie, the left-handed hitting Goodman knocked in 66 runs, scored 65 others, batted .310, and compiled a .414 on-base percentage. He continued to man first base for the Red Sox in 1949, concluding the campaign with 56 RBIs, a .298 batting average, and an on-base percentage of .382, despite missing several games in August due to a fungus condition he originally contracted in the Navy that weakened and blistered his hands and legs.

Goodman started off the 1950 season well, batting .333 through the end of April. However, he sustained a chip fracture to his ankle in a collision at first base on April 30, forcing him to miss the next few weeks.

Slugging Walt Dropo assumed first-base duties in his absence, laying claim to the starting job by displaying considerably more power than the slap-hitting Goodman. Upon his return, Goodman filled in wherever the Red Sox needed him, seeing time in the outfield and at all four infield positions. Although he ended up appearing in only 110 games and accumulating just 485 plate appearances, Goodman posted the best numbers of his young career, knocking in 68 runs, scoring 91, and winning the batting title with a mark of .354. His outstanding performance earned him a second-place finish to New York's Phil Rizzuto in the AL MVP voting.

Goodman continued to man several positions over the course of the next six seasons, although he spent the vast majority of his time at second base, taking over as the club's regular second sacker after Bobby Doerr announced his retirement at the conclusion of the 1951 campaign. Wherever he played, though, he did a solid job. And, wherever the Red Sox put him in the field, he continued to hit. Goodman never batted less than .293 in any of his six remaining seasons in Boston, posting a mark in excess of .300 on three occasions. He also scored more than 90 runs two more times, while regularly walking more than twice as many times as he struck out. In fact, Goodman amazingly fanned a total of only 26 times in over 1,100 plate appearances from 1953 to 1954. He had his most productive season in 1955, when he batted .294, compiled a .394 on-base percentage, walked 99 times, and scored 100 runs.

Goodman's ability to reach base made him an outstanding leadoff or second-place hitter during his time in Boston, even though his lack of power often caused him to be overlooked in favor of some of the team's more colorful stars. As Al Hirshberg wrote in a 1951 *Saturday Evening Post* article, he was "not a glamorous slugger, not a colorful, flamboyant personality, not a magnet for autograph hounds." In fact, the 5'11", 150-pound Goodman was "built like an undernourished ribbon clerk . . . Billy Goodman neither looks nor acts like a baseball star. He just goes out every day and plays the game."

Dave "Boo" Ferriss, who spent four years playing with Goodman in Boston, said of his former teammate during a July 2007 interview, "Oh, he could hit. You know, he was a wiry guy; wasn't very big; not a long-ball hitter. He hit very few home runs, but he could swing a bat. And he was versatile. He was playing when I was coaching. I was very close to Billy. . . . He was like [Johnny] Pesky. He could spray that ball. He could hit. . . . You looked up and he was on base."

Bobby Doerr, who Goodman spent his first few years in Boston idolizing, spoke fondly of his onetime teammate, saying, "He was just a very,

very fine person, and a darn good ballplayer. He was like the perfect guy to be on a ball club because he could play so many different positions. If he was playing utility, he was great when he went into a game. . . . He played a good first base. He didn't have the power that first basemen generally have, but he was always on base and ran the bases well. He was a good fielder. . . . As a utility player, he was perfect in that way too. He could go in any time and do a good job."

Used sparingly by Red Sox manager Pinky Higgins early in 1957, Goodman collected just 1 hit in 16 at-bats before being dealt to the Baltimore Orioles for pitcher Mike Fornieles on June 14. Goodman spent the remainder of the year in Baltimore, before being included in a seven-player trade the Orioles completed with the Chicago White Sox during the subsequent off-season. After batting .299 as Chicago's primary third baseman in 1958, Goodman assumed a utility role in each of the next three seasons, failing to compile 300 at-bats or hit any higher than .255 in any of those campaigns. Released by the White Sox just prior to the 1962 season, Goodman signed with the expansion Houston Colt .45's, with whom he spent his final major-league season. He retired at the end of the year, ending his career with a .300 batting average, a .376 on-base percentage, a .378 slugging percentage, 591 runs batted in, 807 runs scored, 1,691 hits, and only 19 home runs. In addition to batting .306 during his time in Boston, Goodman compiled a .386 on-base percentage, scored 688 runs, and collected 1,344 hits as a member of the Red Sox.

Following his retirement, Goodman spent three years managing and coaching in the minor leagues, before returning to Boston as a "special scout" in 1966. He remained in Boston just one year, after which he spent his final 10 seasons in baseball serving as an instructor in the organizations of the Kansas City Athletics, the Atlanta Braves, and the Kansas City Royals. Goodman retired from the game in 1976 and subsequently became an antiques dealer in Sarasota, Florida, where he also spent much of his time playing golf, fishing, and gardening. He became ill with multiple myeloma in 1983 and passed away on October 1, 1984, at only 58 years of age.

RED SOX CAREER HIGHLIGHTS

Best Season

It could be argued that Goodman had his best year in 1955, when, appearing in a career-high 149 games, he batted .294, compiled a .394 on-base percentage, and established career highs with 100 runs scored, 176 hits, and 99 bases on balls. However, he clearly played his best ball for the Red Sox in 1950, when, despite appearing in only 110 games, he scored 91 runs, knocked in a career-best 68 runs, and posted easily the highest batting average (.354), on-base percentage (.427), and slugging percentage (.455) of his career, en route to earning a second-place finish in the league MVP balloting.

Memorable Moments/Greatest Performances

Goodman had perhaps his biggest day at the plate for the Red Sox on June 4, 1952, helping them defeat Cleveland 13–11 by going 5 for 5, with three RBIs, four runs scored, and a stolen base. He had another huge day on September 21, 1954, collecting seven hits in nine trips to the plate and scoring five runs during a doubleheader sweep of the Athletics in Boston.

Goodman didn't hit many home runs over the course of his career, but he usually made them count. His first homer proved to be a memorable one, coming against Detroit's Virgil Trucks with the bases loaded during an 8–1 Red Sox win at Briggs Stadium on July 29, 1948. Goodman hit another memorable home run on May 8, 1953, when he helped the Red Sox end a 13-game losing streak to the Yankees by homering off New York starter Johnny Sain in the bottom of the 11th inning. Goodman's blast gave the Red Sox a 2–1 victory over their tormentors.

NOTABLE ACHIEVEMENTS

- Batted over .300 five times, surpassing the .350 mark once (.354 in 1950)
- Scored 100 runs once (1955)
- Surpassed 30 doubles three times
- Compiled on-base percentage in excess of .400 twice
- Led AL with .354 batting average in 1950
- Led AL first basemen with .992 fielding percentage in 1949
- Finished second in AL MVP voting in 1950
- Two-time AL All-Star (1949 and 1953)

Pete Runnels

Pete Runnels (l) with Curt Gowdy
Courtesy Boston Public Library, Leslie Jones Collection

Much like Billy Goodman, his immediate predecessor on this list, Pete Runnels displayed a tremendous amount of versatility during his time in Boston, playing all four infield positions at one time or another. Primarily a shortstop his first few years with the Washington Senators, Runnels later moved to first and second base for the Senators, manning those same two positions in his five seasons with the Red Sox after they traded for him prior to the start of the 1958 campaign. Although he possessed only marginal range and quickness, Runnels had sure hands, allowing him to successfully field almost everything he reached. As a result, he led all American League first basemen in fielding percentage in 1961, just one year after he topped all AL second sackers in the same category. Also very much like Goodman, the left-handed hitting Runnels possessed very little power at the plate but had a solid line-drive swing and a keen batting eye that enabled him to annually finish among the league leaders in batting average and on-base percentage. Particularly effective once Ted Williams took him under his wing, Runnels batted over .300 five straight times for the Red Sox, capturing two batting titles, and finishing a close second to his tutor on a third occasion.

Born in Lufkin, Texas, on January 28, 1928, James Edward Runnels acquired the nickname "Pete" from his family, who called him "Little Pete" after his father. Growing up in the logging town of Lufkin, about 120 miles northeast of Houston, Runnels often found it difficult to nurture his love for baseball, instead spending most of his time playing football and basketball while attending Lufkin High School. Yet, even though he only played sandlot ball in the summer, Runnels developed a passion for baseball, continuing to play his favorite sport after he joined the Marines following his graduation from high school in 1945.

After spending three years in the service, Runnels attended just one semester at Rice University before he decided to pursue a career in Major League Baseball. He received a rough initiation into the pro game, though, failing a tryout with the St. Louis Cardinals in 1949. Runnels subsequently signed with the Chickasha, Oklahoma, club of the Class D Sooner League, performing so well in the minors over the course of the next two seasons that the Senators purchased his contract for $12,500. Assigned to Washington's Triple-A affiliate in Chattanooga, Tennessee, Runnels compiled a .356 batting average through the first few months of the 1951 campaign, prompting the hitting-starved Senators to summon him to the big leagues at midseason. Appearing in 78 games at shortstop the remainder of the year, Runnels committed 18 errors, batted .278, and scored 31 runs.

Runnels remained at shortstop for the Senators the next three seasons, playing steady, if unspectacular, defense and gradually developing into one of the team's better offensive players. After compiling batting averages of .285, .257, and .268 from 1952 to 1954, Runnels posted marks of .284 and .310 the next two seasons, while splitting his time between first and second base. In addition to batting .310 in 1956, Runnels established new career highs with eight homers, 76 RBIs, 179 hits, and 29 doubles.

Runnels followed up his finest season with his worst, batting just .230 in 1957. His poor performance prompted the Senators to trade him to the Red Sox at the conclusion of the campaign for first baseman Norm Zauchin and promising young outfielder Albie Pearson.

The 30-year-old Runnels experienced a rebirth in Boston. Tutored by none other than Ted Williams, Runnels learned to be more selective at the plate. Williams also instructed the 6-foot, 170-pound Runnels to cut down on his swing so that he might take better advantage of his new home ballpark by driving the ball more to the opposite field. Williams's advice paid huge dividends for Runnels and the Red Sox, with the lefty-swinging infielder quickly developing into one of the league's best contact hitters. Taking over as Boston's regular second baseman in 1958, Runnels earned a 10th-place finish in the AL MVP voting by ranking among the league leaders with 103 runs scored, 183 hits, 32 doubles, 87 walks, a .322 batting average, and a .416 on-base percentage. Runnels's .322 average placed him a close second in the league to teammate Williams, who topped the circuit with a mark of .328.

A true sportsman and gentleman, Runnels always maintained that he considered the 1958 batting race to be the highlight of his career, stating on one occasion, "I enjoyed [Ted] Williams' 1958 catching me [for the batting crown] on the final day more than the later titles of 1960 and 1962 because of the great competition. Wasn't he capable!"

Meanwhile, Williams later admitted that he would not have minded in the least if Runnels finished ahead of him in the batting race, confiding, "I was thinking in my heart, 'I hope he wins it. I'm not going to give it to him, but I hope he wins it.' Runnels had never won a batting championship, and I had won five. We weren't in the pennant race. It certainly wouldn't make much difference to me at that point. I wasn't getting the kick out of it I had the year before."

Certainly Runnels's calm and gentle demeanor contributed somewhat to the philanthropic attitude the "Splendid Splinter" held toward him. Williams likely also appreciated Runnels's ability to get on base ahead of him. Generally hitting second in the Red Sox batting order, immediately ahead of his tutor, Runnels accorded Williams numerous opportunities to drive in runs. After hitting .322 in 1958, Runnels posted marks of .314 and .320 the next two seasons, capturing the batting title in 1960, Williams's final year in Boston. Runnels also compiled an on-base percentage in excess of .400 in each of those years, concluding the 1959 campaign with 95 runs scored as well. He continued his outstanding hitting after Williams retired, batting .317 in 1961, and edging out Mickey Mantle for the batting title the following year with a mark of .326.

Runnels also offered the Red Sox a considerable amount of versatility in the field. After spending most of his time at second base his first three years in Boston, Runnels moved to first base his final two seasons. He saw some action at the other two infield positions as well.

Yet, in spite of the success Runnels experienced in Boston, he expressed interest in leaving shortly after the Houston Colt .45's became Major League Baseball's first entry in his home state of Texas in 1962. The Red Sox complied with Runnels's wishes, trading him to Houston for outfielder Roman Mejias prior to the 1963 campaign. Runnels played one full season in Houston, batting .253 in 1963, before being released by the club on May 19, 1964, after he hit just .196 in 22 games. Runnels subsequently announced his retirement, ending his career with 49 home runs, 630 RBIs, 876 runs scored, 1,854 hits, a .291 batting average, a .375 on-base percentage, and a .378 slugging percentage. While with the Red Sox, he hit 29 homers, knocked in 249 runs, scored 407 others, accumulated 825 hits, batted .320, compiled a .408 on-base percentage, and posted a .427 slugging percentage. A model of consistency during his time in Boston, Runnels batted somewhere between .314 and .326 in each of his five seasons with the Red Sox.

Following his retirement, Runnels returned to the Red Sox as a coach, serving in 1965 and 1966, before leaving the game for good. He subsequently returned home to Pasadena, Texas, where he expanded his outside business interests. In addition to owning a gas station and a sporting goods store, he operated Camp Champions, a summer camp program in Marble Falls, Texas. A fine golfer, Runnels often said that he would love to exit this life after driving a tee shot onto a green. Sadly, this came to pass on May 20, 1991, just three days after he suffered a heart attack while playing golf. Runnels was only 63 years old.

RED SOX CAREER HIGHLIGHTS

Best Season

Runnels won the AL batting title with a mark of .320 in 1960, even though a stomach ulcer plagued him for much of the year. Nevertheless, he posted better overall numbers in 1958 and 1962, finishing those two seasons with remarkably similar statistics. Runnels batted .322, collected 183 hits, accumulated five triples and 32 doubles, hit eight homers, drove in 59 runs, compiled a .416 on-base percentage, and posted a .438 slugging percentage in 1958. Four years later, he batted .326, amassed 183 hits, collected 5 triples and 33 doubles, hit 10 home runs, knocked in 60 runs, compiled a

.408 on-base percentage, and posted a .456 slugging average. But Runnels scored 23 more runs in 1958 than in 1962, crossing the plate a career-high 103 times. He also finished in the league's top five in six offensive categories. Meanwhile, he ranked in the top five in only two categories in 1962. All things considered, Runnels had his finest season in 1958.

Memorable Moments/Greatest Performances

Although Runnels hit only 49 home runs his entire career, he helped the AL defeat the NL 9–4 in the second All-Star game of 1962 by delivering a pinch-hit homer.

Runnels had the greatest day of his career on August 30, 1960, when he tied a major-league record by amassing nine hits during a doubleheader sweep of the Detroit Tigers. Runnels went 6 for 7 in Boston's 5–4 opening game victory, delivering Frank Malzone with the winning run in the bottom of the 15th inning with an RBI double. Runnels's six safeties tied the AL mark for the most hits in one game. He continued his hot-hitting in the nitecap, collecting three hits in four at-bats during Boston's 3–2, 10-inning win.

NOTABLE ACHIEVEMENTS

- Batted over .300 five times, surpassing the .320 mark three times
- Scored more than 100 runs once (103 in 1958)
- Surpassed 30 doubles three times
- Compiled on-base percentage in excess of .400 four times
- Two-time AL batting champion (1960 and 1962)
- Led AL first basemen with .995 fielding percentage in 1961
- Led AL second basemen with .986 fielding percentage in 1960
- Ranks among Red Sox career leaders in batting average (5th) and on-base percentage (6th)
- 1958 AL Comeback Player of the Year
- Five-time AL All-Star

George Scott

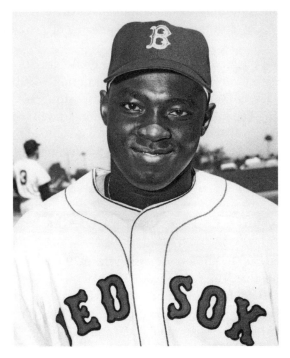

Courtesy Boston Red Sox

One of the more colorful players to call Fenway Park home, George Scott actually had two tours of duty in Boston. Scott spent his first six big-league seasons with the Red Sox, serving primarily as their starting first baseman from 1966 to 1971, before being dealt to the Brewers prior to the 1972 campaign. He spent the next five years in Milwaukee but later returned to Boston, where he played another two and a half years, before moving on to Kansas City and, finally, New York. Even though Scott had arguably his two most productive seasons for the Brewers, Boston fans continue to think of him as one of their own, embracing his quirky personality that prompted him to refer to his home runs as "taters" and his glove as "Black Beauty." A powerful right-handed batter, Scott hit more than 30 home runs twice during his career, once as a member of the Red Sox. He also knocked in more than 100 runs and batted over .300 twice. One of the finest fielding first basemen of his time, Scott also won eight Gold Gloves for his exceptional defensive work, earning six in succession at one point.

Born in Greenville, Mississippi, on March 23, 1944, George Charles Scott grew up in poverty, losing his father at the age of two and picking cotton as a young boy to help support his family. In discussing his early life, Scott said, "That's all we knew. The reason you did that, all of that money was turned over to your parents to make ends meet. Nothing can be worse than getting up at four in the morning waiting for a truck to pick you up to go pick and chop cotton from six or seven in the morning until five or six in the afternoon."

Still, Scott always found time for sports, excelling in baseball, football, and basketball as a teenager. After starring in all three sports while attending Coleman High School in Greenville, Scott signed with the Red Sox as an amateur free agent for $8,000 in 1962 even though, by his own admission, he preferred football and basketball to baseball. In explaining his decision, Scott revealed, "I got tired of watching my mom struggle. I didn't have the mind that I could go to college and see my mother struggle for another four or five years."

Scott spent the next four years playing all over the infield in the minor leagues, before an exceptional 1965 campaign during which he won the Triple Crown with Pittsfield of the Double-A Eastern League prompted the Red Sox to invite him to spring training the following year. Scott ended up earning the starting job at first base in 1966, beating out fellow prospect Tony Horton in the process. He subsequently got off to a hot start, ranking among the league leaders in home runs, RBIs, and batting average through mid-May. Scott's strong showing during the early stages of the campaign prompted future Hall of Famer Rick Ferrell, who watched him during spring training and the first few weeks of the season, to proclaim, "In all my years in baseball, I have never seen a player have a debut like Scott. He's amazing."

However, opposing teams soon began to figure out how to pitch to Scott, who later said, "What happened is the pitchers and teams adjusted on me, and I didn't adjust to them quick enough. After the All-Star break, they started throwing me a lot of change-ups and curve balls, and I didn't make the adjustment. I don't even know whether I was capable of making the adjustment at that time. All the leagues I had come up through, they threw me a lot of fastballs and I could hit that fastball."

Although Scott finished the year with 27 home runs and 90 RBIs, he also batted just .245 and struck out a league-leading 152 times. Nevertheless, he played relatively well over the course of his first major-league season, leading all AL first basemen in putouts and double plays, making the All-Star team, and finishing third in the Rookie of the Year voting.

Scott improved upon his overall performance the following year, helping the Red Sox win the pennant by hitting 19 home runs, driving in 82 runs, finishing fourth in the league with a .303 batting average, reducing his strikeout total to 119, and once again topping all players at his position in putouts and double plays, en route to earning the first Gold Glove of his career and a 10th-place finish in the AL MVP balloting. Yet, the 6'2", 215-pound Scott experienced difficulties with new Red Sox manager Dick Williams, who benched his first baseman once for swinging at bad pitches and chastised him on numerous occasions for being overweight. In discussing Scott with reporters shortly after the Red Sox dropped the Fall Classic to St. Louis, Williams stated, "I would have hated to put him on the scales during the World Series because I know his weight was way up again. But, George knows that when he lets his weight go up, he will pay for it."

At the same time, though, Williams praised Scott for his fielding ability, saying, "Until I saw George Scott, I thought Gil Hodges was the greatest defensive first baseman I ever saw. But Scott changed my mind."

Scott, in fact, possessed rare fielding ability, especially for a man his size. Blessed with soft hands and exceptional instincts around first base, he made playing his position look easy, doing an extraordinary job of scooping low throws and fielding ground balls. Former Red Sox second baseman Mike Andrews told the *Boston Globe* years later, "I've never to this day seen anyone play first base like that. He was just like a big cat over there, and he saved me a lifetime full of errors. It was like you had a million-dollar insurance policy that you had taken out, and all you had to do was get the ball started over there somewhere and he could reach it."

Scott and Williams continued to experience a somewhat contentious relationship the next two seasons, with the manager frequently expressing his dissatisfaction with his first basemen's bulging waistline. In fact, after Scott suffered through a horrendous 1968 campaign during which he hit only 3 home runs, drove in just 25 runs, and batted an anemic .171, Williams shifted him to third base the following year. Although Scott rebounded somewhat, hitting 16 homers, knocking in 52 runs, and batting .253, he didn't begin to enjoy the game again until the more even-tempered Eddie Kasko assumed the managerial reins from Williams prior to the 1970 campaign.

Able to relax more with Kasko at the helm, Scott allowed his affable nature to surface, adopting the nickname "Boomer" for the sound the ball made when it made contact with his bat, and referring to his home runs as "taters." Years later, Scott told the *Clarion-Ledger* of Jackson, Mississippi, "Anything over 450 feet, I'd call it a long tater. A short tater was one that barely got over the wall." Scott showed improvement on the field as well, batting .296 in 1970, and hitting 24 homers, knocking in 78 runs, and winning his third Gold Glove the following year.

Nevertheless, seeking to improve their team speed, the Red Sox included Scott in a 10-player trade they completed with the Milwaukee Brewers on October 10, 1971, that netted them 1969 stolen-base champ Tommy Harper. Scott thrived in Milwaukee, surpassing 20 homers in three of the next five seasons, topping 100 RBIs twice, batting over .300 once, and winning five straight Gold Gloves. He had his two best years for the Brewers in 1973 and 1975, hitting 24 home runs, knocking in 107 runs, scoring 98 others, and batting a career-high .306 in the first of those campaigns, before leading the league with 36 homers, 109 RBIs, and 318 total bases two years later.

The Red Sox elected to reacquire Scott prior to the 1977 season, trading Cecil Cooper to Milwaukee for him and outfielder Bernie Carbo on December 6, 1976. Scott played well for the Red Sox his first year back, earning All-Star honors by hitting 33 home runs, knocking in 95 runs, and scoring 103. But, after initially looking forward to returning to Boston, Scott eventually grew disenchanted with the franchise with which he began his career, commenting years later, "I was very excited about going back. I don't think the Red Sox were that excited about having me back."

As one of the first black players to come up through the Red Sox farm system, Scott felt the team treated him unfairly at times during his first tour of duty with the club, occasionally displaying a lack of sensitivity toward him. He believed that little changed during his absence, with the front office continuing to favor some players over others. After injuries limited Scott's offensive production in 1978, the Red Sox traded him to Kansas City early the following year when he got off to another slow start. Scott split the remainder of the season between the Royals and the Yankees, before retiring at the end of the year. He finished his career with 271 home runs, 1,051 runs batted in, 957 runs scored, 1,992 hits, a .268 batting average, a .333

on-base percentage, and a .435 slugging percentage. During his time in Boston, he hit 154 homers, knocked in 562 runs, scored 527 others, accumulated 1,088 hits, batted .257, compiled a .326 on-base percentage, and posted a .421 slugging percentage.

After leaving the major leagues, Scott spent the next few seasons playing and managing in the Mexican League. He later became a full-time manager in Independent League Baseball from the mid-1980s to 2002, ending his baseball career managing the Berkshire Black Bears of the Northern League in 2002. All the while, Scott waited for a call that never came from either the Red Sox or Major League Baseball that would have accorded him the opportunity to serve as an instructor, a coach, or a manager. During that time, he became a diabetic, failing to properly manage his weight, which eventually ballooned to more than 400 pounds. Scott finally lost his battle, dying from his illness at the age of 69, on July 28, 2013.

Upon hearing of Scott's passing, the Red Sox released a statement through team historian and vice president/emeritus Dick Bresciani, that read, "In losing George Scott, we have lost one of the most talented,

Courtesy Boston Red Sox

colorful, and popular players in our history. He had great power and agility, with a large personality and a large physical stature. He could light up a clubhouse with his smile, his laugh, and his humor—and he was the best defensive first baseman I have ever seen. We will miss him, and we send our condolences to his family."

RED SOX CAREER HIGHLIGHTS

Best Season

Scott had his most productive offensive season for the Red Sox in 1977, when he hit 33 home runs, knocked in 95 runs, batted .269, and scored a career-high 103 runs. But, after clubbing 25 homers by the All-Star break, he hit just eight more the rest of the year. Scott displayed far more consistency at the plate in 1967, when he hit 19 home runs, drove in 82 runs, scored 74, and batted .303. His .373 on-base percentage surpassed the mark he posted in 1977 by nearly 40 points, enabling him to compile a slightly higher OPS (.839 to .837). Furthermore, while the "Boomer" finished in the league's top 10 in only three offensive categories in 1977, he placed among the leaders in seven different departments a decade earlier, finishing third in hits (171) and triples (7), fourth in batting average, sixth in RBIs and total bases (263), seventh in on-base percentage, and eighth in slugging percentage (.465). Scott's solid all-around year earned him a 10th-place finish in the AL MVP voting. He also captured Gold Glove honors, something he failed to do in 1977, when he committed a career-high 24 errors.

Memorable Moments/Greatest Performances

Scott hit the most memorable home run of his career early in his rookie season of 1966, delivering a titanic blast against Hall of Fame left-hander Whitey Ford at New York's Yankee Stadium on April 26. Facing Ford in the top of the third inning with two men out and no one on base, Scott drove a ball into the upper deck in left field, some 500 feet from home plate. Ford later recalled that Scott's homer was one of the longest he ever surrendered, suggesting that only Frank Howard and Walt Dropo hit ones that traveled as far. Asked by Ford to estimate the length of Scott's drive had its flight not been interrupted by the seats it struck in left field, Mickey Mantle replied with a laugh, "Well, to pick a round number, you could say 550 feet and not be exaggerating."

Scott hit another memorable home run in the next-to-last game of the 1967 regular season, giving the Red Sox a 3–2 lead over the Twins in the bottom of the sixth inning by hitting a solo shot into the center field bleachers against Minnesota reliever Ron Kline. The Red Sox went on to win the game 6–4, setting up a winner-take-all scenario for the season finale. Scott, in fact, came up big for Boston several times late in the year, batting .344 over the final eight games of the regular season.

NOTABLE ACHIEVEMENTS

- Hit more than 20 home runs three times, surpassing 30 homers once (33 in 1977)
- Scored more than 100 runs once (103 in 1977)
- Batted over .300 once (.303 in 1967)
- Compiled slugging percentage of .500 once (.500 in 1977)
- Led AL first basemen in putouts and double plays twice each
- Three-time Gold Glove winner
- Two-time AL All-Star (1966 and 1977)
- 1967 AL champion

4 2

Jon Lester

Courtesy Keith Allison

A study in courage and perseverance, Jon Lester overcame cancer to eventually establish himself as one of the best left-handed pitchers in baseball. After surviving his life-threatening ordeal in 2007, Lester posted at least 15 victories for the Red Sox in five of the next six seasons, en route to compiling one of the highest winning percentages in franchise history. During that time, the hard-throwing left-hander also earned three All-Star selections and two top-five finishes in the Cy Young voting. An exceptional postseason performer as well, Lester helped the Red Sox capture two world championships, with his brilliant pitching in the 2013 World Series leading Boston to a six-game victory over St. Louis.

Born in Tacoma, Washington, on January 7, 1984, Jonathan Tyler Lester attended Bellarmine Prep, a Catholic High School in Tacoma, where he excelled in baseball, football, and basketball. Although Lester's strong left arm and powerful 6'4", 200-plus-pound frame made him a standout in all three sports, baseball remained his first love, prompting him to sign with the Red Sox after they selected him in the second round of the 2002 amateur draft with the 57th overall pick. Lester spent just one year in the minor leagues before his name began to surface in trade talks, first for Alex Rodriguez, and, later, for Josh Beckett. However, the Red Sox firmly believed that Lester had the ability to succeed at the major-league level, causing them to exclude him from any such deals. Boston scouting director Jason McLeod later said of the young left-hander, "The first time I saw him pitch, I called Theo Epstein and said, 'Whatever you do, don't trade Jon Lester.'" Minor-league manager Todd Claus also felt strongly about Lester, later stating, "I've always maintained from the first day I saw him he's one of the best prospects in the minor leagues I've ever seen."

After struggling somewhat in his first two years in the minors, Lester improved dramatically in 2005 when he added a cutter and a changeup to his curve and 94 mph fastball. Spending the entire year with Portland in Class-AA, Lester ended up winning Eastern League Pitcher of the Year honors. Although Lester began the 2006 campaign at Triple-A Pawtucket, injuries to various members of Boston's starting rotation prompted the Red Sox to summon him to Beantown in early June. The 22-year-old southpaw subsequently compiled a record of 7–2 and an ERA of 4.76 in his 15 starts with the Red Sox, turning in the finest performance of his young career on July 18, when he tossed eight innings of one-hit ball in defeating Kansas City 1–0.

Unfortunately, doctors discovered only six weeks later during an exam for a sore back caused by a minor fender-bender that Lester suffered from anaplastic large cell lymphoma—a treatable form of cancer. Earlier symptoms of the illness included a loss in weight and night sweats. However, after chemotherapy, Lester overcame his malady and was declared cancer-free in December. Looking back at the ordeal, teammate Jason Varitek suggested, "It mentally took him from a young man to an adult."

It subsequently took Lester considerable time to gain back the weight he lost, build up his velocity, and regain command of his pitches. However, after spending most of 2007 in the minor leagues, Lester returned to Boston late in the year, going 4–0 in his 11 starts. Commenting on Lester's return, manager Terry Francona stated, "Learning how to pitch in the major leagues in the middle of a pennant race isn't an easy thing to do, but I think he handled it really well." The Boston Baseball Writers' Association of America paid tribute to Lester by voting him the 2007 Tony Conigliaro Award. He also received the 2008 Hutch Award.

Lester developed into arguably Boston's most reliable starting pitcher the following year, when he finished 16–6, with a 3.21 ERA and a league-leading two shutouts, including a May 19 no-hitter against the Kansas City Royals. He remained the team's most dependable starter in the three seasons that followed, posting an overall mark of 49–26 from 2009 to 2011, while compiling an ERA below 3.50 all three years. Lester also evolved into more of a strikeout pitcher during that time, fanning 225 batters in both 2009 and 2010. His 19 victories and 3.25 ERA in the second of those campaigns earned him a spot on the AL All-Star Team and a fourth-place finish in the Cy Young balloting.

Yet, even though Lester pitched well in 2011, compiling a record of 15–9, he found himself embroiled in controversy as the season drew to a close when it surfaced that at least three Red Sox pitchers, including himself, regularly ate fried chicken and drank beer in the clubhouse on those days they weren't scheduled to pitch. With the Red Sox posting a record of only 7–20 during the month of September en route to finishing out of the play-offs, team management addressed the situation by replacing Terry Francona as manager with Bobby Valentine.

Valentine and the Red Sox proved to be a poor match, with Boston finishing only 69–93 in 2012. Lester similarly struggled, going just 9–14, with a career-high 4.82 ERA. However, the Red Sox and Lester both returned to top form under new manager John Farrell in 2013, with the left-hander helping his team post the American League's best record during the regular season by finishing 15–8, with a 3.75 ERA. Lester then pitched brilliantly throughout the postseason, going a combined 4–1 with a sub-2.00 ERA in the playoffs and World Series, in leading the Red Sox to their third world championship in 10 years. Nevertheless, with Lester scheduled to become a free agent following the conclusion of the 2014 campaign, the Red Sox elected to trade him and outfielder Jonny Gomes to the Oakland Athletics for Yoenis Céspedes and a competitive round 2015 draft pick just prior to the July 31 trade deadline after he compiled a record of 10-7 and an outstanding 2.52 ERA for them during the season's first four months. Lester left Boston having posted a career record of 110-63, along with a 3.64 ERA, a WHIP of 1.287, and 1,386 strikeouts in 1,519 1/3 innings pitched.

Lester ended up spending just two months in Oakland, winning six of his 10 decisions with the Athletics, before agreeing to a six-year, $155 million deal with the Chicago Cubs at season's end. After going just 11-12 with a 3.34 ERA in his first year in Chicago, Lester returned to top form the following season, earning a runner-up finish in the N.L. Cy Young voting and helping the Cubs capture their first world championship in more than 100 years by compiling a record of 19-5 and an ERA of 2.44 during the regular season, before winning three of his four postseason decisions. He followed that up with another solid performance this past season, posting a mark of 13-8, en route to improving his career record to 159-92. Lester has also compiled a career ERA of 3.51, a WHIP of 1.242, and a total of 2,041 strikeouts in 2,184 1/3 innings pitched.

RED SOX CAREER HIGHLIGHTS

Best Season

Lester pitched exceptionally well in 2008, compiling a record of 16–6, with a career-best 3.21 ERA and a league-leading two shutouts. Nevertheless, he clearly had his best season in 2010, when he finished 19–9, with a 3.25 ERA and 225 strikeouts, en route to earning his only top-five finish in the Cy Young voting. Lester finished second in the American League in wins, third in strikeouts, and ninth in earned run average. Meanwhile, his WHIP of 1.202 was the best of his career.

Memorable Moments/Greatest Performances

After making 17 starts in the minor leagues following his illness, Lester made his emotional return to the Red Sox on July 23, 2007, a successful one, allowing the Indians two runs on five hits over six innings, in defeating Cleveland 6–2. He pitched even better in his first start at Fenway three weeks later, allowing Tampa Bay just one run on two hits over seven innings. Although Lester left the contest trailing by a score of 1–0, the Red Sox pushed across two runs in the bottom of the ninth inning to come away with a 2–1 win. Lester also came up big in that year's World Series, getting the win in Game 4 by shutting out Colorado on only three hits before being relieved with two men out in the sixth inning. Although the Rockies rallied late against Boston's bullpen, the Red Sox held on for a 4–3 series-clinching win.

Lester pitched the most memorable game of his career on May 19, 2008, when he no-hit the Kansas City Royals at Fenway Park. Lester walked two batters and struck out nine during the 7–0 victory, with Jacoby Ellsbury saving his no-hitter by making a diving catch in center field to end the fourth inning. Following the contest, Red Sox manager Terry Francona, who earlier in the day attended his son's commencement ceremony at the

University of Pennsylvania, told Sean McAdam at ESPN.com, "This probably isn't fair to say, but I feel like my son graduated and my son threw a no-hitter. It's probably selfish on my part to even say something like that. But I think it's obvious how we feel about this kid."

Lester attempted to duplicate his earlier feat just a little over one year later when he worked six and one-third perfect innings against the Texas Rangers on June 6, 2009, before surrendering a one-out double to Michael Young in the top of the seventh inning. Lester ended up going the distance, allowing the Rangers just one run and two hits, and striking out 11, in defeating Texas 8–1.

Lester turned in another brilliant effort on May 10, 2013, when he allowed just one man to reach base during a 5–0 complete-game win over the Blue Jays. Only a sixth-inning double down the left field line by Toronto shortstop Maicer Izturis stood between Lester and perfection.

Lester also pitched magnificently during Boston's run to the world championship, allowing just two runs and three hits over 7 ⅔ innings in defeating Tampa Bay 12–2 in Game 1 of the ALDS, before surrendering three runs in his two starts against Detroit, in splitting his two decisions in the ALCS. He subsequently defeated St. Louis twice in the World Series, winning Games 1 and 5, and allowing the Cardinals just one run and nine hits in 15 ⅓ total innings of work.

NOTABLE ACHIEVEMENTS

- Has won at least 15 games five times
- Has compiled a winning percentage in excess of .700 three times
- Has thrown more than 200 innings five times
- Has struck out more than 200 batters twice (2009 and 2010)
- Led AL pitchers with 2 shutouts in 2008
- Threw no-hitter vs. Kansas City on May 19, 2008
- Ranks among Red Sox career leaders in strikeouts (5th); winning percentage (7th); and games started (7th)
- Finished fourth in 2010 AL Cy Young voting
- 2008 Hutch Award winner
- Two-time AL All-Star (2010 and 2011)
- Two-time AL champion (2007 and 2013)
- Two-time world champion (2007 and 2013)

Tim Wakefield

Courtesy Keith Allison

One of the longest-tenured players in Red Sox history, Tim Wakefield spent 17 years in Boston after beginning his career with the Pittsburgh Pirates. During that time, the right-handed knuckleball specialist started more games (430) and threw more innings (3,006) than any other pitcher ever for the Red Sox. Wakefield also ranks second to Roger Clemens in strike-outs (2,046) and third in wins (186), behind only Clemens and Cy Young.

Cast aside by the Pirates, Wakefield accomplished all he did in Boston even though he didn't throw his first pitch for the Red Sox until after his 28th birthday.

Born in Melbourne, Florida, on August 2, 1966, Timothy Stephen Wakefield attended Eau Gallie High School, after which he enrolled at Florida Institute of Technology. While attending Florida Tech, Wakefield starred at first base for the Panthers' baseball team, setting single-season school records for most home runs (22) and RBIs (71). Subsequently drafted as a first baseman by the Pittsburgh Pirates when he graduated in 1988, Wakefield soon found himself transitioning to the mound after a scout told him he lacked the skills necessary to succeed as a position player at the major-league level. Stating at the time, "I just want to be able to say I tried everything I could to make it," Wakefield began experimenting with the knuckleball, which eventually became his signature pitch.

Wakefield spent the next four years honing his pitching skills in Pittsburgh's farm system, before finally making his debut with the Pirates on July 31, 1992, by striking out 10 batters during a complete-game win over the St. Louis Cardinals. Wakefield continued to excel for the Pirates over the season's final two months, helping them advance to the playoffs by compiling a record of 8–1 and an ERA of 2.15, en route to earning a third-place finish in the NL Rookie of the Year voting. However, after subsequently defeating the Braves twice in the 1992 NLCS, Wakefield took a step backwards the following year, concluding the 1993 campaign with a record of 6–11 and an inordinately high 5.61 ERA. The Pirates returned Wakefield to the minor leagues at season's end, after which he spent most of 1994 pitching for their Triple-A affiliate in Buffalo, before being released on April 20, 1995.

Following Wakefield's release, the Red Sox acted quickly, signing the 28-year-old right-hander to a contract just six days later. Wakefield spent the first few weeks of the campaign at Triple-A Pawtucket, working with Phil and Joe Niekro, who encouraged him to use the knuckleball as his out pitch. Having perfected the knuckler, Wakefield joined the Red Sox by mid-May, after which he became their most reliable starter the remainder of the year, posting a record of 16–8 and an ERA of 2.95. His outstanding performance earned him a third-place finish in the Cy Young balloting and *Sporting News* American League Comeback Player of the Year honors.

Wakefield pitched less effectively for the Red Sox in each of the next three seasons, compiling an overall record of 43–36, while posting an ERA well in excess of 4.00 each year. Nevertheless, he managed to win 17 games for the Boston club that lost to Cleveland in the 1998 ALDS.

Although Wakefield saw some action as a starter as well, he spent most of the next four seasons working out of the bullpen, posting an overall mark of 32–38 from 1999 to 2002. He pitched his best ball for the Red Sox during that four-year stretch in 2002, going 11–5 with a 2.81 ERA. After being returned to the starting rotation in 2003, Wakefield remained a regular member of Boston's starting staff for the next several years, finishing in double-digits in wins in six of the next seven seasons. He posted a record of 16–12 at 39 years of age in 2005, before equaling his career high with 17 victories two years later, in helping the Red Sox capture their second world championship in four seasons. In 2009, the 42-year-old Wakefield became the second-oldest player to be named to the All-Star team for the first time, earning a spot on the AL roster by posting a league-best 11–3 record by the All-Star break. On July 3, he also surpassed Roger Clemens for the most starts in franchise history. However, injuries to his calf and lower back ended up sidelining him for much of the season's second half, causing him to finish the year with a record of only 11–5.

Wakefield spent two more years in Boston, working as both a starter and a reliever, and passing Clemens along the way for the most innings pitched by a Red Sox hurler. On May 11, 2011, he pitched one and one-third innings in relief against the Toronto Blue Jays, making him, at 44 years, 282 days, the oldest player ever to appear for the Red Sox. Some four months later, on September 13, he posted the 200th and final victory of his career, doing so after eight unsuccessful attempts. Wakefield retired at season's end with a career record of 200–180, an ERA of 4.41, and 2,156 strikeouts in 3,226 innings pitched. In his 17 years with the Red Sox, he went 186–168, with a 4.43 ERA and 2,046 strikeouts in 3,006 innings of work.

Following his retirement, Wakefield served briefly as a studio analyst for Red Sox coverage on NESN television, before accepting a position as a special assignment instructor in baseball operations within the Red Sox organization in April of 2013. He also is part owner of a restaurant in Pembroke, Massachusetts, called Turner's Yard.

RED SOX CAREER HIGHLIGHTS

Best Season

Wakefield won 17 games for the Red Sox in 1998 and 2007, and he also posted 16 victories in 2005. He also had a very solid year in 2002, when, splitting his time between starting and relieving, he went 11–5, with a 2.81 ERA and a career-best 1.053 WHIP. Yet, Wakefield pitched his best ball for the Red Sox in his very first year with them, going 16–8 with a 2.95 ERA in 1995. He also threw a career-high six complete games, en route to earning a 3rd-place finish in the Cy Young voting and a 13th-place finish in the MVP balloting.

Memorable Moments/Greatest Performances

Wakefield tied a major-league record on August 10, 1999, when he struck out four batters in the ninth inning of a 9–6 victory over the Kansas City Royals.

Wakefield ironically pitched perhaps his finest game for the Red Sox in a losing cause, dropping a 1–0 decision to Randy Johnson and the Yankees on September 11, 2005. Wakefield went the distance in the contest, striking out a career high 12 batters, and allowing just 3 hits to New York, one of which was a first-inning homer by Jason Giambi.

Wakefield turned in another exceptional effort on April 15, 2009, when he carried a no-hitter into the eighth inning against Oakland, before allowing the A's two runs and four hits over the final two frames of an 8–2 Red Sox victory. Taking the mound just one day after Boston's bullpen worked more than 11 innings of relief, Wakefield told manager Terry Francona prior to the game, "I understand the circumstances, and I just wanted you to know: Whatever happens, don't take me out; let me keep going." Wakefield's complete-game win at 42 years of age made him the oldest Red Sox pitcher to go the distance.

Wakefield also pitched extremely well against the Yankees in the 2003 ALCS, defeating Mike Mussina in Games 1 and 4 by scores of 5–2 and 3–2. After allowing just two runs and two hits over six innings in the opener, he surrendered only one run on five hits over seven innings in Game 4. Unfortunately, Wakefield's earlier successes ended up being overshadowed by his failure in Game 7. After entering the decisive contest with the score tied 5–5 in the 10th inning and retiring the side in order, Wakefield gave up a home run to Aaron Boone on his first pitch in the 11th, enabling the Yankees to advance to the World Series. The veteran right-hander subsequently displayed his class by apologizing to the fans of Boston after the game.

NOTABLE ACHIEVEMENTS

- Won at least 16 games four times
- Compiled ERA below 3.00 twice (1995 and 2002)
- Threw more than 200 innings five times
- Holds Red Sox career records for most games started (430) and innings pitched (3,006)
- Ranks among Red Sox career leaders in wins (3rd); strikeouts (2nd); and pitching appearances (2nd)
- Finished third in 1995 AL Cy Young voting
- 1995 AL Comeback Player of the Year
- 2009 AL All-Star
- Two-time AL champion (2004 and 2007)
- Two-time world champion (2004 and 2007)

Duffy Lewis

Courtesy Library of Congress

The third member of Boston's "Million Dollar Outfield," which played together from 1910 to 1915, Duffy Lewis did an expert job of patrolling left field for the Red Sox for eight seasons, proving to be particularly adept at playing the steep incline in front of Fenway Park's left-field wall. Possessing excellent range and an outstanding throwing arm, Lewis consistently ranked among the American League's leading outfielders in putouts and assists, compiling more than 20 assists in six of his eight years with the Red Sox. A solid line-drive hitter as well, Lewis batted over .300 twice and knocked in 109 runs in 1912, when he finished second in the junior circuit in that category for the first of two straight times. Lewis also placed second in the league in home runs once and doubles twice, amassing more than 30 two-baggers in five consecutive seasons at one point. Yet, Lewis built his reputation primarily on his defense, playing left field at Fenway Park so well that the incline in front of the wall came to be known as "Duffy's Cliff."

Born in San Francisco on April 18, 1888, George Edward Lewis acquired his lifelong nickname "Duffy" from his mother's maiden name. Lewis learned how to play baseball while growing up in a rough area of San Francisco, where he experienced one of the worst natural disasters in U.S. history—the infamous San Francisco earthquake that took place on April 18, 1906, his 18th birthday. Lewis first began to develop a reputation while playing at Saint Mary's College, where his short right-handed swing and exceptional quickness captured the attention of major-league scouts. After one year at Saint Mary's, Lewis signed with the Alameda team in the California League, spending one and a half years there before joining the Pacific Coast League's Oakland Oaks midway through the 1908 campaign. Lewis remained in Oakland until the end of 1909, when Red Sox owner John L. Taylor signed him to his first major-league contract.

Still only 21 years old when he arrived at Hot Springs, Arkansas, for his first spring training with the Red Sox, Lewis found it difficult to accept the harsh treatment accorded to rookies at that time. Confident and outspoken, Lewis confronted veterans on the team when they attempted to limit his time in the batting cage, prompting his new manager, Patsy Donovan, to fine and bench him at one point. The young outfielder's unwillingness to yield to players with more seniority agitated Tris Speaker as much as anyone, causing a somewhat contentious relationship to develop between the two men that lasted throughout their many years as teammates.

Yet, Lewis did not permit his many distractions to prevent him from earning a starting job in his first year in the league. Appearing in all but seven of Boston's regular season contests, Lewis had a solid rookie season, finishing second in the AL with eight home runs, driving in 68 runs, batting .283, and placing third among league outfielders with 28 assists. He followed that up with an even better sophomore campaign, batting a career-high .307, accumulating another 27 assists in the outfield, and finishing among the league leaders with seven homers and 86 RBIs. Lewis subsequently helped the Red Sox capture the pennant in 1912 by batting .284 and establishing career highs with 109 runs batted in and 85 runs scored.

The Red Sox didn't fare nearly as well in 1913, finishing just fourth in the junior circuit. And, as it became increasingly evident they would not be earning a return-trip to the World Series, the combative nature of the relationship that existed between Lewis and Speaker reached its peak. With Speaker continually knocking Lewis's cap off his head in an effort to reveal the latter's rapidly receding hairline, Lewis threw his bat at his teammate, hitting him in the shins hard enough that Speaker had to be assisted from the field. Nevertheless, the two men did not allow their personal differences to affect their play on the field. While Speaker ended up batting .363, Lewis posted a mark of .298, drove in 90 runs, and amassed a career-high 12 triples. Meanwhile, both men continued to excel on defense, forming two-thirds (along with Harry Hooper) of one of the best defensive outfields in baseball history. In 1913 alone, Boston's starting outfield combined for an amazing 84 assists, with 29 of those being credited to Lewis. Although Speaker drew a considerable amount of acclaim for his extraordinary defense in center field, Hooper considered Lewis to be the best of the three "at making the backhand running catch at balls hit over his head." And Lewis did a superb job of navigating Fenway Park's extremely tricky left field, which, when the ballpark opened in 1912, featured a 10-foot embankment just in front of the wall.

In discussing his mastery of the territory he covered for six seasons, Lewis explained to a sportswriter, "I'd go out to the ballpark mornings and have somebody hit the ball again and again out to the wall. I experimented with every angle of approach up the cliff until I learned to play the slope correctly. Sometimes it would be tougher coming back down the slope than going up. With runners on base, you had to come off the cliff throwing." The slope remained part of the terrain in left field until 1933, when Fenway Park received a thorough facelift.

Although Lewis received less credit for his hitting, he presented opposing pitchers with a solid right-handed bat, using his compact swing to drive balls to both gaps, thereby collecting a significant number of extra-base hits. Generally batting fourth in Boston's lineup, right behind Speaker, Lewis finished among the league leaders in two-baggers eight times. He also ranked among the leaders in RBIs on seven occasions.

After posting solid numbers from 1914 to 1916, Lewis batted over .300 for the second time in his career in 1917, compiling a mark of .302. He subsequently missed the entire 1918 campaign while serving as player-manager of a naval baseball team at Mare Island, California, during World War I. Following his discharge from the service, the Red Sox included him in a seven-player trade they completed with the Yankees that also sent pitchers Dutch Leonard and Ernie Shore to New York. Lewis spent two years in New York, before being dealt to the Washington Senators at the conclusion of the 1920 campaign. After batting just .186 in 27 games with the Senators over the first two months of the 1921 season, the 33-year-old Lewis joined Salt Lake City of the Pacific Coast League. He spent the next seven years serving as a player-manager at the minor-league level before retiring prior to the 1928 season.

During his 11-year major-league career, Lewis hit 38 homers, knocked in 793 runs, scored 612, collected 1,518 hits, 68 triples, and 289 doubles, batted .284, compiled a .333 on-base percentage, and posted a .384 slugging percentage. In his eight years with the Red Sox, he hit 27 home runs, drove in 629 runs, scored 500 others, accumulated 1,248 hits, 62 triples, and 254 doubles, batted .289, compiled a .340 on-base percentage, and posted a .395 slugging percentage.

Following his retirement, Lewis served as a coach for the Boston Braves from 1931 to 1935, after which he became the team's traveling secretary,

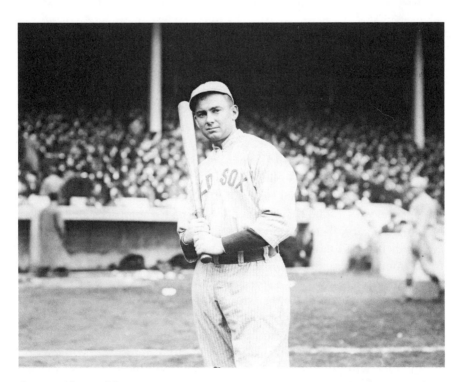

Courtesy Library of Congress

a position he held until 1961, nearly a decade after the Braves relocated to Milwaukee. Lewis lived another 18 years, passing away in Salem, New Hampshire, on June 17, 1979, at 91 years of age.

RED SOX CAREER HIGHLIGHTS

Best Season

Lewis had his most productive season for the Red Sox in 1912, helping them capture the American League pennant by hitting six homers, collecting nine triples and 36 doubles, batting .284, and establishing career highs with 109 runs batted in and 85 runs scored. Appearing in all 154 games for the Red Sox, Lewis also finished fifth among AL outfielders with 301 putouts and 23 assists.

Memorable Moments/Greatest Performances

Lewis got one of the more memorable hits of his career in the epic September 6, 1912, pitching matchup between Walter Johnson and Smoky Joe Wood, driving in Tris Speaker with the game's only run on an opposite field double. Lewis's safety enabled Wood to keep his consecutive game winning streak alive.

Lewis played perhaps his finest all-around game for the Red Sox on September 23, 1916, leading his team to a 5–3 win over Cleveland by going 5 for 5, with two triples and two runs scored. He also made two spectacular catches in left field, turning the second of those grabs into a double play.

A standout performer in both the 1915 and 1916 World Series, Lewis batted .444, homered once, and knocked in five runs in the first of those Fall Classics, helping the Red Sox defeat the Philadelphia Phillies in five games. After winning Game 3 with an RBI single off Hall of Fame pitcher Grover Cleveland Alexander in the bottom of the ninth inning, Lewis drove home the winning run in Game 4 with a double. He also made game-saving catches in both contests. Lewis followed that up by blasting a long drive that bounced into the center field bleachers for a game-tying home run in the series finale. His exceptional play throughout the series prompted the *Boston Globe*'s Tim Murnane to write, "The all-around work of the modest Californian never has been equaled in a big Series." Lewis also performed well in the 1916 Fall Classic, collecting six hits in 17 at-bats for a .353 batting average, with a triple and two doubles.

NOTABLE ACHIEVEMENTS

- Batted over .300 twice (1911 and 1917)
- Knocked in more than 100 runs once (109 in 1912)
- Finished in double-digits in triples once (12 in 1913)
- Surpassed 30 doubles five times
- Stole more than 20 bases once (22 in 1914)
- Led AL with 31 sacrifice bunts in 1912
- Holds Red Sox career record with 219 sacrifice bunts
- Three-time AL champion (1912, 1915, and 1916)
- Three-time world champion (1912, 1915, and 1916)

Ellis Kinder

Ellis Kinder (l) with Billy Hitchcock
Courtesy Boston Public Library, Leslie Jones Collection

Nicknamed "Old Folks" due to his relatively late arrival to the major leagues, Ellis Kinder made up for lost time in his eight years with the Red Sox. After spending his first three seasons working mostly as a starter, Kinder proved to be the American League's top reliever over the course of the next five campaigns, leading the junior circuit in saves and appearances twice each. Along the way, Kinder established himself as one of the few pitchers in baseball history to win or save a combined total of at least 200 games, while also spending at least a third of their career serving primarily as a starter.

Born in Atkins, Arkansas, on July 26, 1914, Ellis Raymond Kinder spent nearly a decade in the minor leagues before finally earning a trip to the majors in 1946. Already past his 31st birthday when he joined the St. Louis Browns following a stint in the military during World War II, Kinder spent most of his rookie campaign working out of the bullpen, compiling a record of 3–3 and a 3.32 ERA. Moved into the starting rotation the following year, Kinder finished 8–15 with a 4.49 ERA for the lowly Browns.

Traded to the Red Sox along with utility infielder Billy Hitchcock for three nondescript players and $65,000 on November 18, 1947, Kinder subsequently thrived in Boston. After going 10–7 and compiling a 3.74 ERA for his new team in 1948, the 34-year-old right-hander developed into one of the league's top starters the following year. In addition to posting a record of 23–6, Kinder placed among the league leaders with a 3.36 ERA, 138 strikeouts, 19 complete games, and 252 innings pitched. He also topped the circuit with six shutouts and a .793 winning percentage, en route to earning a fifth-place finish in the AL MVP voting and *Sporting News* Pitcher of the Year honors.

Although Kinder experienced much less success when the Red Sox elected to split his time between the starting rotation and the bullpen the following year, he pitched relatively well, compiling a record of 14–12, throwing 11 complete games, and placing among the league leaders with nine saves. Desperate for bullpen help, the Red Sox converted Kinder into a full-time reliever in 1951, after which he established himself as the league's top closer. Topping the circuit with 63 relief appearances, Kinder finished 11–2, with a 2.55 ERA and a league-leading 14 saves. After slumping somewhat the following year, Kinder posted exceptional numbers again in 1953, concluding the campaign with a record of 10–6, a sparkling 1.85 ERA, and a league-leading 27 saves, which tied the major-league record at that time. Kinder's 69 relief appearances also established a new AL mark (since broken).

Catcher Mickey Owen, who spent his final season in Boston, suggested that Kinder's short windup and quick release were the things that made him so successful, stating that the pitcher delivered the ball quicker than "anybody I ever saw; he got rid of the ball so rapidly the batter didn't have a chance to tune himself to Kinder." Kinder's superb changeup, which frequently made batters look foolish, also proved to be a key to his success.

Kinder spent two more years in Boston, continuing to pitch well for the Red Sox even after he reached 40 years of age. After posting eight wins and

15 saves in 1954, he won five games, saved 18 others, and compiled an ERA of 2.84 the following year.

Placed on waivers by the Red Sox following the 1955 campaign, Kinder subsequently joined the St. Louis Cardinals. He split the 1956 season between the Cardinals and Chicago White Sox, retiring early in 1957 after being released by the White Sox. Kinder concluded his career with a record of 102–71, an ERA of 3.43, and 102 saves. In his eight years with the Red Sox, he compiled a record of 86–52, posted an ERA of 3.28, and saved 93 games—the fourth most in team history.

A hard drinker and fast liver, Kinder developed liver disease later in life, leading to his premature passing at only 54 years of age in 1968. He died in Jackson, Tennessee, after undergoing open-heart surgery.

RED SOX CAREER HIGHLIGHTS

Best Season

Kinder pitched exceptionally well out of the bullpen in 1953, posting 10 victories, compiling an outstanding 1.85 ERA, and leading the league with 27 saves. Nevertheless, there can be no doubting that he had the finest season of his career in 1949, when he rivaled teammate Mel Parnell as the American League's best pitcher. In addition to finishing second in the circuit to Parnell with 23 wins, Kinder ranked among the league leaders with 19 complete games, 252 innings pitched, and 138 strikeouts. Meanwhile, his six shutouts and .793 winning percentage led all AL hurlers.

Memorable Moments/Greatest Performances

Kinder defeated the White Sox almost singlehandedly on August 6, 1950, when, in addition to limiting Chicago to two runs, he hit a grand slam home run and knocked in six of Boston's nine runs. Kinder's homer during the 9–2 complete-game victory proved to be the only one of his career.

Kinder turned in another extraordinary effort against the White Sox on July 12, 1951, throwing 10 innings of scoreless relief during a 17-inning, 5–4 Red Sox win. Kinder worked the final 10 frames, striking out five and allowing only five hits, in earning the victory.

Yet, Kinder pitched perhaps the most memorable game of his career while nursing a terrible hangover. Facing the Yankees in a winner-take-all situation on the final day of the 1949 season, Kinder entered the contest having arrived at his hotel room in a bad way at 4:30 AM. In spite of his earlier transgressions, Kinder battled Yankee ace Vic Raschi pitch for pitch, allowing just one run and four hits to New York over the first seven innings. Unfortunately for the Red Sox, the floodgates opened after manager Joe McCarthy elected to pinch hit for Kinder in the top of the eighth. The Yankees subsequently scored four times against the Boston bullpen in the bottom of the frame, making a three-run rally by the Red Sox in the top of the ninth a case of too little too late. The 5–3 New York victory sent the Yankees to the World Series. Meanwhile, Kinder, who disagreed vehemently with McCarthy's decision to remove him from the contest, subsequently accused his teammates of choking, suggesting, as told by John Steadman in the *Baltimore Sun*, that they appeared to play the game with "a chicken bone caught in their throats."

NOTABLE ACHIEVEMENTS

- Won more than 20 games once (1949)
- Posted winning percentage in excess of .700 twice, topping the .800 mark once (1951)
- Compiled ERA below 3.00 four times, finishing with mark below 2.00 once (1949)
- Threw more than 200 innings twice (1949 and 1950)
- Saved more than 20 games once (27 in 1953).
- Led AL pitchers in winning percentage once; shutouts once; saves twice; and appearances twice
- Ranks fourth in Red Sox history with 93 career saves
- Finished fifth in 1949 AL MVP voting
- 1949 *Sporting News* All-Star Selection
- 1949 *Sporting News* Pitcher of the Year

4 6

Curt Schilling

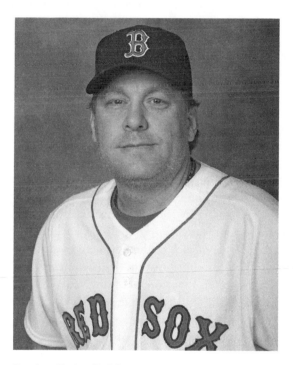

Courtesy Boston Red Sox

After originally being drafted by them nearly two decades earlier, Curt Schilling finally made his pitching debut for the Red Sox in 2004, at the age of 37. Traded to the Baltimore Orioles in July of 1988, Schilling spent the next 16 years with four other clubs, before he finally returned to the franchise that gave him his start in professional ball. The hard-throwing right-hander subsequently spent the final four years of his career in Boston, remaining fully healthy in only two of those campaigns. However, during that time, Schilling helped lead the Red Sox to a pair of world championships, compiling an overall postseason record of 6–1 in 2004 and 2007, en route to helping the Sox bring an end to "the Curse of the Bambino." The author of one of the most memorable pitching performances in playoff history, Schilling proved to be a key contributor to Boston's unprecedented comeback in the 2004 ALCS—one that saw the Red Sox overcome a three-games-to-none deficit against the New York Yankees. He continued his outstanding pitching in that year's World Series, working six strong innings against St. Louis in Boston's 6–2 victory in Game 2. Schilling's exceptional work on the mound helped end 86 years of frustration for Red Sox fans, clearly earning him a spot in these rankings.

Born in Anchorage, Alaska, on November 14, 1966, Curtis Montague Schilling attended Shadow Mountain High School in Phoenix, Arizona, after which he enrolled at Yavapai College in Prescott, Arizona. Selected by the Red Sox in the second round of the 1986 amateur draft, Schilling left school to begin his professional career in Boston's farm system. After spending the next two and a half years in the minor leagues, Schilling joined Brady Anderson in going to Baltimore when the Red Sox packaged both players for right-hander Mike Boddicker. Schilling made his major-league debut with the Orioles later in 1988, posting an unimpressive 0–3 record and 9.82 ERA in his four starts. Working almost exclusively in relief, Schilling continued to struggle in each of the next three seasons, even after Baltimore traded him to Houston prior to the 1991 campaign.

Following his failures in Houston, Schilling suffered the embarrassment of being chastised by his idol, Roger Clemens, for wasting his considerable physical talent. Accused by the Texas native of failing to take the game seriously, and of not taking full advantage of his wide assortment of pitches, which included an overpowering fastball, an exceptional split-finger fastball, and an above-average changeup, the 25-year-old Schilling decided to rededicate himself to his profession. Fully motivated for the first time in his young career after the Philadelphia Phillies acquired him just prior to the 1992 campaign, Schilling had his breakout season, finishing 14–11, with an outstanding 2.35 ERA. Although his ERA jumped to 4.02 the following year, Schilling compiled a record of 16–7 and struck out 186 batters, in helping the Phillies capture the 1993 National League pennant. After missing a considerable amount of time in each of the next three seasons with arm problems, Schilling evolved into one of the senior circuit's top hurlers in 1997, going 17–11, with a 2.97 ERA and a league-leading 319 strikeouts. He continued to excel in each of the next two seasons as well, posting a total of 30 victories, before his outspoken nature and criticism of Philadelphia's front office prompted the Phillies to trade him to Arizona midway through the 2000 campaign.

Schilling went only 5–6 for the Diamondbacks during the second half of 2000, posting a rather pedestrian 3.69 ERA in his 13 remaining starts. However, he experienced something of a renaissance the following year, pitching at a level he failed to reach even in his best years in Philadelphia. Vying with teammate Randy Johnson for supremacy among National League hurlers in each of the next two seasons, Schilling finished 2001 with a record of 22–6, an ERA of 2.98, 293 strikeouts, and a league-leading 257 innings pitched and 6 complete games. He followed that up in 2002 by going 23–7, with a 3.23 ERA, 316 strikeouts, and 259 innings pitched. Although Schilling finished second to Johnson in the NL Cy Young voting both years, *Sporting News* named him its Pitcher of the Year both times. Schilling also established himself as one of the sport's greatest big-game pitchers in 2001, compiling a perfect 4–0 record during the playoffs and World Series, along with a fabulous 1.12 ERA. The combined efforts of Schilling and Johnson enabled the Diamondbacks to capture their first and only world championship, earning each hurler a share of World Series MVP honors.

After being limited by arm problems to 24 starts and a record of only 8–9 in 2003, Schilling found himself headed back to Boston when the Red Sox acquired him for four players at the end of the year. Healthy again in 2004, Schilling went 21–6, with a 3.26 ERA and 203 strikeouts, en route to earning a second-place finish in the AL Cy Young balloting. More importantly, he helped lead the Red Sox to their first world championship in 86 years by going 3–1 during the postseason, despite being hampered much of the time by a severely injured ankle.

Recurring ankle problems forced Schilling onto the disabled list for much of 2005, limiting him to only 32 appearances and 11 starts. However, after winning only eight games and compiling an inordinately high 5.69 ERA that year, he returned in 2006 to finish 15–7, with a 3.97 ERA and 183 strikeouts. Although limited by shoulder problems to only 24 starts and 9 victories in 2007, Schilling managed to help the Red Sox capture their second world championship in four years by winning all three of his postseason decisions.

After signing a one-year deal with the Red Sox for the 2008 season, Schilling missed the entire campaign with a shoulder injury that eventually required surgery. Unable to make a full recovery from the procedure, Schilling officially announced his retirement on March 23, 2009, at 42 years of age. He ended his career with a record of 216–146, an ERA of 3.46, and

3,116 strikeouts in 3,261 innings of work. Over the course of 20 big-league seasons, Schilling won at least 15 games eight times, surpassing 20 victories on three occasions. He also struck out at least 300 batters three times and led his league in complete games four times, and wins, strikeouts, and innings pitched twice each. Schilling earned six All-Star selections and three second-place finishes in the Cy Young voting. Perhaps the finest big-game pitcher of his generation, he posted a career record of 11–2 in postseason play, along with an outstanding 2.23 earned run average. In his four years with the Red Sox, Schilling went 53–29, with a 3.95 ERA and 574 strikeouts in 675 innings of work.

In discussing his approach to pitching, and the success he experienced over the course of his career, Schilling stated, "It's command. Control is the ability to throw strikes. In the big leagues, everybody has control. Command is the ability to throw quality strikes. And, when you add preparation to command, good things will happen."

Courtesy Boston Red Sox

Since retiring from the game, Schilling has continued his charitable work for victims of amyotrophic lateral sclerosis (ALS). He also assumed a position with ESPN as a Baseball analyst in 2010 that he retained until early 2016, when a series of controversial political and social opinions he expressed on Twitter and Facebook prompted the network to relieve him of his duties. Until 2013, Schilling lived in Medfield, Massachusetts, in Drew Bledsoe's former home. However, the failure of his 38 Studios business, which he originally founded as Green Monster Games, forced him to put his 8,000 square foot home on the market with a listing price of $3 million.

RED SOX CAREER HIGHLIGHTS
Best Season

Schilling clearly had his best season for the Red Sox in 2004, when he finished 21–6, with a 3.26 ERA and 203 strikeouts in 227 innings pitched. Schilling's 21 victories and .778 winning percentage led the American League. Meanwhile, his 3.26 ERA placed him second in the league rankings. He also finished third among AL hurlers in strikeouts and innings pitched. Schilling's strong performance earned him his only All-Star selection and top-five finish in the Cy Young voting as a member of the Red Sox. He also finished 11th in the MVP balloting.

Memorable Moments/Greatest Performances

Schilling pitched his best game for the Red Sox on June 7, 2007, when he came within one out of throwing his first career no-hitter. With an earlier Boston error giving the A's their only previous base-runner, just a two-out line-drive single in the bottom of the ninth inning by Oakland's Shannon Stewart prevented the 40-year-old right-hander from tossing his first no-hitter. Schilling retired the next batter, though, giving him a 1–0, complete-game win.

Nevertheless, Schilling saved his most memorable performance for the 2004 postseason, earning a permanent place in the hearts of Red Sox fans with his heroic effort against the Yankees in Game 6 of the ALCS. After tearing the tendon sheath in his right ankle while defeating the Angels 9–3 in Game 1 of the ALDS, an injured Schilling started the opening contest of the ALCS. Clearly not himself that evening, Schilling lasted only three innings, surrendering six runs and six hits to New York, before being replaced by Curt Leskanic in the bottom of the fourth. In spite of his earlier setback, Schilling returned to the mound for Game 6, hoping to even the series at three games apiece. Even though he needed to have the tendon in his injured ankle stabilized repeatedly over the course of the contest, Schilling worked seven strong innings, allowing the Yankees just one run on four hits, en route to winning the game 4–2. With the sutures used to stabilize the tendon in his ankle causing Schilling's sock to become soaked with blood, the contest subsequently became known as "the Bloody Sock Game." Schilling's heroic performance forced a Game 7, which the Red Sox won, making them the first team in MLB history to overcome a three-games-to-none deficit. Pitching under the same conditions, Schilling also started and won Game 2 of the World Series, allowing the Cardinals one run on four hits over six innings, in leading the Red Sox to a 6–2 victory.

Schilling also pitched well for the Red Sox during the 2007 postseason, throwing seven shutout innings in a 9–1 victory over the Angels in the clinching game of the ALDS, defeating Cleveland in the sixth game of the ALCS to force a Game 7, and winning Game 2 of the World Series against Colorado.

NOTABLE ACHIEVEMENTS

- Won more than 20 games once (21 in 2004)
- Posted winning percentage in excess of .700 once (.778 in 2004)
- Struck out more than 200 batters once (203 in 2004)
- Threw more than 200 innings twice (2004 and 2006)
- Led AL pitchers with 21 wins and .778 winning percentage in 2004.
- Ranks among Red Sox career leaders in: winning percentage (6th); fewest walks allowed per nine innings pitched (2nd); most strikeouts per nine innings pitched (8th); and strikeouts-to-walks ratio (2nd)
- Finished second in 2004 AL Cy Young voting
- 2004 AL All-Star
- Two-time AL champion (2004 and 2007)
- Two-time world champion (2004 and 2007)

Derek Lowe

Courtesy Boston Red Sox

One of the most versatile pitchers in Red Sox history, Derek Lowe proved to be equally effective working as a starter or as a reliever over the course of his eight seasons in Boston, winning more than 20 games in 2002, just two years after he led the American League in saves. The first pitcher in baseball history to surpass 20 victories after earlier recording at least 40 saves in a season, Lowe also made history on April 27, 2002, when he threw the first no-hitter at Fenway Park in 37 years. However, when Boston fans think of Lowe, they are more likely to reflect back on his fabulous performance throughout the 2004 postseason that helped the Red Sox capture their first world championship since 1918. Lowe created a permanent place for himself in Red Sox lore that year by winning the clinching game of the ALDS, ALCS, and World Series, en route to compiling a perfect 3–0 record in the playoffs and World Series.

Born in Dearborn, Michigan, on June 1, 1973, Derek Christopher Lowe starred in four sports while attending Dearborn's Edsel Ford High School, excelling in baseball, basketball, soccer, and golf. After committing to attend Eastern Michigan University on a basketball scholarship, the 6'6" Lowe elected to postpone his college education when the Seattle Mariners selected him in the eighth round of the 1991 MLB Draft. Lowe spent the next several years in the minors, before the Mariners finally promoted him to their major-league roster in 1997. However, in desperate need of bullpen help, Seattle traded Lowe and catcher Jason Varitek to the Red Sox in late July for reliever Heathcliff Slocumb.

Although Lowe spent most of his time in Seattle's farm system working as a starter, the Red Sox decided to convert him into a full-time reliever shortly after he arrived in Boston. After compiling an overall record of only 3–11 as a spot-starter/long reliever in his first two years in Boston, Lowe began to thrive when the Red Sox placed him exclusively in the bullpen in 1999. Gradually establishing himself as the team's closer over the course of the campaign, Lowe finished the year with a record of 6–3, an ERA of 2.63, and 15 saves. He developed into one of baseball's top closers the following year, when he compiled a 2.56 ERA and led the American League with 42 saves.

Lowe pitched relatively well in 2001, saving another 24 games, even though he won only 5 of his 15 decisions. But he lost his closer's job when the Red Sox acquired Ugueth Urbina just prior to the trade deadline, forcing him to spend the remainder of the year working primarily as a setup man. After asking to be returned to the starting rotation at the beginning of the ensuing campaign, Lowe exceeded all expectations by finishing 2002 with a record of 21–8 and an ERA of 2.58, en route to earning a third-place finish in the league Cy Young balloting. Although he pitched less effectively the following year, compiling a very mediocre 4.47 ERA, Lowe managed to post a record of 17–7. He followed that up by going 14–12 with an unimpressive 5.42 ERA in 2004. Nevertheless, Lowe performed exceptionally well during the postseason, helping the Red Sox capture the world championship by winning all three of his decisions and compiling an ERA of 1.86 in his four appearances.

In spite of Lowe's heroics during the 2004 playoffs and World Series, the Red Sox allowed him to leave when he became a free agent at the end of the year. The 31-year-old right-hander subsequently signed with the Dodgers, with whom he spent the next four seasons. Lowe compiled an overall mark of 54 48 in his four years in Los Angeles, leading the National League with 16 victories in 2006. After becoming a free agent again at the end of 2008, Lowe signed another four-year deal, this time with the Braves. He pitched fairly well his first two years in Atlanta, posting 31 victories. However, the Braves elected to trade Lowe to the Cleveland Indians for minor-league reliever Chris Jones prior to the 2012 campaign after he finished just 9–17 the previous year. Lowe spent most of 2012 in Cleveland, before joining the Yankees when the Indians released him in August. He signed with Texas at the end of the year, but announced his retirement after being released by the Rangers on

Courtesy Boston Red Sox

May 23. Lowe ended his career with a record of 176–157, an ERA of 4.03, and 1,722 strikeouts in 2,671 innings of work. In his eight years with the Red Sox, he went 70–55, with a 3.72 ERA, 85 saves, and 673 strikeouts in 1,037 innings pitched.

RED SOX CAREER HIGHLIGHTS

Best Season

Even though Lowe had an outstanding year working out of the bullpen in 2000, leading the American League with 42 saves, he had his finest all-around season in 2002. In addition to finishing second among AL hurlers with 21 wins and a 2.58 ERA, he allowed only 166 hits in 220 innings, en route to compiling a career-best WHIP of 0.974. Lowe's exceptional performance earned him a third-place finish in the Cy Young voting and his lone selection to the *Sporting News* All-Star team.

Memorable Moments/Greatest Performances

Lowe pitched the greatest game of his career on April 27, 2002, when he no-hit the Tampa Bay Devil Rays at Fenway Park. Lowe struck out six batters and issued only one walk during the 10–0 win, allowing just one man to reach base. His extraordinary effort made him the first pitcher to toss a no-hitter at Fenway Park since Dave Morehead in 1965.

Lowe had hurled another gem just a few weeks earlier, in his first start of the year on April 5, when he allowed just one hit over seven innings in defeating the Orioles 3–0 in Baltimore.

Yet, Lowe will always be remembered most by Red Sox fans for his superb pitching throughout the 2004 postseason. After winning Game 3 of the ALDS against Anaheim with one scoreless inning of relief, he defeated the Yankees in Game 7 of the ALCS by allowing just one run and one hit over six innings of work, doing so on only two days' rest. Lowe then capped off his brilliant postseason by working seven scoreless innings against the Cardinals in Game 4 of the World Series, leading the Red Sox to a 3–0 win and a four-game sweep of St. Louis. Red Sox reliever Mike Timlin later told MLB.com, "That [winning Game 4 of the World Series] was classic Derek. He's not orthodox about the way he does things, but there is no doubt about the ability he has and the size of his heart."

NOTABLE ACHIEVEMENTS

- Won more than 20 games once (21 in 2002)
- Posted winning percentage in excess of .700 twice (2002 and 2003)
- Compiled ERA below 3.00 three times
- Threw more than 200 innings twice (2002 and 2003)
- Saved more than 40 games once (42 in 2000)
- Led AL pitchers with 42 saves in 2000
- Threw no-hitter vs. Tampa Bay on April 27, 2002
- First pitcher in history to win 20 games one year after recording at least 20 saves
- First pitcher in history to win 20 games after recording 40 saves in a season earlier in career
- Ranks sixth in Red Sox history with 85 career saves
- Finished third in 2002 AL Cy Young voting
- 2002 *Sporting News* All-Star selection
- Two-time AL All-Star
- 2004 AL champion
- 2004 world champion

Josh Beckett

....

Courtesy Keith Allison

Brash, cocky, and arrogant, Josh Beckett rubbed many people the wrong way during his time in Boston. In fact, Beckett ended up leaving Beantown a hated man after his immature and irresponsible behavior helped lead to manager Terry Francona's departure at the conclusion of the 2011 campaign. Nevertheless, the hard-throwing right-hander made significant contributions to the Red Sox during his six-plus years with them, posting an overall record of 89–58, earning three All-Star selections, and helping them capture the world championship in 2007, when he compiled a perfect 4–0 record in postseason play. Possessing outstanding stuff, superb control, and supreme confidence, Beckett had the ability to navigate his way past even the toughest opposing lineups, giving the Red Sox an excellent chance to emerge victorious every time he took the mound. Those very qualities helped make him one of the finest big-game pitchers of his time. Yet, the same swagger with which Beckett carried himself eventually led to his downfall, causing him to be labeled a clubhouse distraction, and prompting the Red Sox to part ways with him during the latter stages of the 2012 campaign.

Born in the tiny Houston suburb of Spring, Texas, on May 15, 1980, Joshua Patrick Beckett developed a love of baseball at an early age, idolizing fellow Texans Nolan Ryan and Roger Clemens as a young boy. Hoping to follow the same path as his two childhood heroes, Beckett starred on the mound for Spring High School's varsity baseball team, throwing a fastball in the low 90s by the time he entered his sophomore year. After being voted the Texas 5-A High School Player of the Year as a junior, Beckett earned High School Pitcher of the Year honors from *USA Today* by going 10–1, with a 0.46 ERA and 155 strikeouts in 75 innings in his senior year. The success Beckett experienced at such a young age helped instill in him the confidence for which he later became so well noted, prompting him to have the word "phenom" stenciled on one of his jackets.

Although major-league scouts found themselves being similarly impressed by Beckett's exceptional ability, the Tampa Bay Devil Rays, who held the rights to the first pick in the 1999 draft, selected high school outfielder Josh Hamilton instead after meeting with Beckett and finding him to be a bit too sure of himself for their liking. As a result, the 19-year-old right-hander instead went to the Florida Marlins with the second overall pick.

Beckett spent most of the next two years excelling in the minor leagues before Florida called him up in September of 2001. He subsequently made four starts for the Marlins over the season's final month, making a very strong impression by winning two of his four decisions, compiling a 1.50 ERA, and striking out 24 batters in 24 innings of work, while allowing opposing batters only 14 hits.

Although Beckett earned a regular spot in Florida's starting rotation the following spring, persistent problems with blisters on his pitching hand forced him onto the DL three times in 2002, limiting him to 21 starts and a record of only 6–7. Troubled by a sprained elbow during the early stages of the 2003 campaign, Beckett made only 23 starts for the Marlins, compiling a record of 9–8 and an ERA of 3.04, and striking out 152 batters in only 142 innings. Fully recovered, though, by the time the Marlins entered the playoffs as the

NL wild card, Beckett helped lead his team to an improbable run to the world championship by turning in two strong performances against the Yankees in the World Series. Working on just three days' rest both times, he allowed New York just two runs on eight hits in 16 innings of work, earning series MVP honors by winning the clinching Game 6 at Yankee Stadium with a complete-game, five-hit shutout.

Beckett's exceptional postseason pitching prompted Florida GM Dave Dombrowski to proclaim, "He's got a chance to be a premium pitcher for a long time."

Meanwhile, Marlins manager Jack McKeon gushed, "I've had a lot of young pitchers. Believe me, this guy here is, I'd have to say, by far the most outstanding young man I've had as far as mental toughness in the big leagues."

McKeon added, "He's got tremendous upside. I might have had to push him a little, but, basically, he deserves all the credit. This guy is going to be something special."

Beckett remained in Florida two more years, having his best season for the Marlins in 2005, when he finished 15–8, with a 3.38 ERA and 166 strikeouts. But, with the Marlins seeking to reduce their payroll and the Red Sox looking to bolster their starting rotation, the teams completed a trade on November 24, 2005, that sent Beckett, Mike Lowell, and veteran reliever Guillermo Mota to Boston for a package of prospects that included highly touted shortstop Hanley Ramirez.

The deal ended up being a good one for both teams, with Ramirez subsequently establishing himself as one of the National League's best young players and Beckett assuming the role of staff ace in Boston. After struggling somewhat in his first year, compiling an ERA of 5.01 despite winning 16 games, Beckett thrived in 2007 under new pitching coach John Farrell, who helped him vastly improve his control and suggested that he use his breaking ball more. In addition to finishing the campaign with a record of 20–7 and an ERA of 3.27, Beckett struck out 194 batters and walked only 40, thereby posting an exceptional strikeout-to-walk ratio of nearly 5 to 1. His outstanding performance earned him his first All-Star nomination and a second-place finish in the league Cy Young voting.

Commenting on his young teammate, Curt Schilling stated, "He's cocky. So am I. You have to be cocky to be good."

Third baseman Mike Lowell added, "He's a competitor. He has tons of confidence in his stuff, and he's unique in the sense that he has three legit pitches. Hard-throwing right-handers don't throw too many changeups to other right-handers. That's something special he has, plus a nasty curveball."

Beckett continued his outstanding pitching in the postseason, compiling a perfect 4–0 record and an ERA of 1.20, in leading the Red Sox to victories over the Angels in the ALDS, the Indians in the ALCS, and the Rockies in the World Series.

Although the 2007 campaign proved to be the high point of Beckett's time in Boston, he had two other very good years for the Red Sox. After going just 12–10 with a 4.03 in 2008, he earned All-Star honors for the second time the following year, when he finished 17–6, with a 3.86 ERA and a career-high 199 strikeouts. A lower back strain forced Beckett to sit out two months of the 2010 season, limiting him to 21 starts and a record of just 6–6. However, he pitched extremely well the following year, compiling a record of 13–7 and an ERA of 2.89.

Nevertheless, Beckett found himself being cast as the primary culprit when the Red Sox finished out of the playoffs in 2011 due to their poor performance over the season's final month. Crucified by the Boston media for being the noted leader of a group of Red Sox pitchers that typically ate fried chicken and drank beer in the clubhouse during games in which they were not scheduled to pitch, Beckett became increasingly unpopular in Beantown, having his commitment to the team questioned by the press, Red Sox fans, and team management alike. Things only worsened for him in 2012, when he compiled a record of 5–11 and an ERA of 5.23 over the first five months of the campaign. Beckett found himself embroiled in another controversy that year when he reportedly played several rounds of golf after being scratched from his scheduled start due to an injury. Seeking to rid themselves of his and other undesirable contracts, the Red Sox subsequently included Beckett in a nine-player trade they completed with the Dodgers on August 25 that also sent Carl Crawford, Adrian Gonzalez, and Nick Punto to Los Angeles. In addition to posting an overall record of 89–58 for the Red Sox, Beckett compiled an ERA of 4.17 and struck out 1,108 batters in 1,240 innings during his time in Boston.

Beckett has accomplished very little since leaving the Red Sox, winning two of his five remaining decisions in 2012, before suffering through an injury-marred 2013 campaign that included a bout with thoracic outlet syndrome, which caused him to feel numbness and a tingling sensation in his pitching hand that required surgery to repair. He finished the year with a record of 0–5 and an ERA of 5.19.

Looking back at his years in Beantown, Beckett said, "I'm happy that I got a chance to play in Boston, but I'm glad it's over."

In discussing the events that transpired during his final season with the Red Sox, Beckett stated, "It just got way too personal for me. It wasn't just like, 'Hey, you suck on the baseball field.' It was now, 'Hey, you're a bad person.' It was getting personal. It wasn't even about baseball anymore. It was definitely time to make a change. I think everybody from the front office to the players recognized that."

He added, "I think it almost ended up being like a pity party in the clubhouse. Nobody wants to hear shit like that. Nobody wants to hear the personal stuff. Everybody in the clubhouse can deal with, if someone has a bad game, then you can deal with that somebody is going to get picked on. But, when the team wins and you're still hearing about it, it's going too far. It was starting to affect the other guys. I don't want to be that guy. And it wasn't just about baseball anymore."

Beckett accomplished very little after he left the Red Sox, winning two of his five remaining decisions in 2012, before suffering through an injury-marred 2013 campaign that included a bout with thoracic outlet syndrome, which caused him to feel numbness and a tingling sensation in his pitching hand that required surgery to repair. After going 0-5 with a 5.19 ERA in 2013, Beckett performed much better over the first two months of the 2014 season, before a torn labrum in his left hip brought his season and career to a premature end. Announcing his retirement following the conclusion of the campaign, Beckett ended his career with a record of 138-106, an ERA of 3.88, a WHIP of 1.232, and 1,901 strikeouts in 2,051 total innings of work.

RED SOX CAREER HIGHLIGHTS

Best Season

Beckett pitched quite effectively for the Red Sox in 2009 and 2011, compiling a record of 17–6, an ERA of 3.86, and a career-high 199 strikeouts in the first of those campaigns, before going 13–7, with 175 strikeouts and an outstanding 2.89 ERA two years later. However, Beckett had his finest all-around season in 2007, when he finished 20–7, with a 3.27 ERA and 194 strikeouts. In addition to leading all AL pitchers with 20 wins, he posted the second-best winning percentage (.741) in the league, finished sixth in earned run average and WHIP (1.141), and placed seventh in strikeouts.

Memorable Moments/Greatest Performances

During an interleague game against the Phillies on May 20, 2006, Beckett became the first Red Sox pitcher in 35 years to hit a home run when he went deep against Philadelphia right-hander Brett Myers. Beckett homered again three years later, this time against Philadelphia's J. A. Happ.

Beckett turned in a number of exceptional pitching performances over the course of the 2009 campaign, with the first of those coming on Opening Day, when he struck out 10 and allowed just one run on two hits over seven innings, in defeating defending AL champion Tampa Bay 5–3. Beckett threw a pair of shutouts less than a month apart later in the year, blanking the Braves 3–0 on just five hits on June 20, before recording the 100th victory of his career with a 6–0, three-hit whitewashing of the Royals on July 12. He also engaged in a classic pitcher's duel with former Florida teammate A. J. Burnett on August 7, allowing the Yankees just four hits over seven scoreless innings in a game New York eventually won by a score of 2–0 in 15 innings.

Still, Beckett will be remembered most fondly by Red Sox fans for his magnificent pitching during the 2007 postseason. After shutting out the Angels on just four hits in Game 1 of the ALDS, he defeated the Indians twice in the ALCS, allowing them a total of only three runs on nine hits in 14 innings of work, en route to earning ALCS MVP honors. Beckett subsequently defeated Colorado by a score of 13–1 in the opening contest of the World Series, allowing the Rockies just one run on six hits over seven very strong innings, while amassing nine strikeouts.

NOTABLE ACHIEVEMENTS

- Won 20 games once (2007)
- Won at least 16 games two other times (2006 and 2009)
- Posted winning percentage in excess of .700 twice (2007 and 2009)
- Compiled ERA below 3.00 once (2011)
- Threw more than 200 innings three times
- Led AL pitchers with 20 wins in 2007
- Ranks among Red Sox career leaders in: strikeouts (6th); strikeouts-to-walks ratio (5th); and strikeouts per nine innings pitched (6th)
- Finished second in 2007 AL Cy Young voting
- 2007 *This Year in Baseball* Pitcher of the Year
- 2007 ALCS MVP
- Three-time AL All-Star (2007, 2009, and 2011)
- 2007 AL champion
- 2007 world champion

Jacoby Ellsbury

Courtesy Keith Allison

Although Jacoby Ellsbury likely will be vilified by Red Sox fans the rest of his playing days for leaving their team via free agency at the end of 2013 to join the hated New York Yankees, the "Fenway Faithful" can take solace in the fact that the speedy center fielder helped them win two world championships in his seven years in Boston. Despite missing a significant amount of playing time in two of his six full seasons in Beantown, Ellsbury managed to score more than 90 runs four times, bat over .300 three times, and steal more than 50 bases three times, establishing himself in the process as the third top base-stealer in Red Sox history. The owner of three of the top-five single-season stolen-base marks in club history, Ellsbury set a new franchise record in 2009, when he swiped 70 bags. A solid outfielder as well, Ellsbury compiled a perfect 1.000 fielding percentage in two seasons, en route to posting a career mark of .995 that places him third among all active outfielders.

The son of a full-blooded Native American (Navajo) mother and a father of English and German descent, Jacoby McCabe Ellsbury was born in Madras, Oregon, on September 11, 1983. An outstanding all-around athlete blessed with exceptional running speed and extraordinary leaping ability, Ellsbury excelled in baseball, football, and basketball while attending Madras High School. After Ellsbury batted .537 and stole 65 bases as a senior at Madras, the Tampa Bay Devil Rays selected him in the 23rd round of the 2002 amateur draft. However, he instead chose to accept a scholarship offer from nearby Oregon State University, where he went on to earn *Baseball America* first-team All-American and Pac-10 Conference Co-Player of the Year honors as a junior.

Ellsbury elected to turn pro after his third year at Oregon State, signing for a $1.4 million bonus with the Red Sox after they selected him in the first round of the 2005 amateur draft with the 23rd overall pick. He subsequently spent just two years in the minor leagues before the Red Sox called him up in late June of 2007 to replace an injured Coco Crisp in center field. Although Crisp's return to the starting lineup shortly thereafter made Ellsbury's first stay in Boston a brief one, the young outfielder left a lasting impression on Red Sox legend Johnny Pesky in just his third game when he scored all the way from second base on a wild pitch. Pesky later described Ellsbury's dash in the *Boston Globe* as "the greatest single play I've ever seen in all my years in baseball."

After being sent back down to Triple-A Pawtucket just a few days later, Ellsbury rejoined the Red Sox when rosters expanded on September 1. He spent the remainder of the year in Boston, living up to the hype that preceded him as one of baseball's top prospects by batting .353, hitting three homers, driving in 18 runs, scoring 20 times, and stealing nine bases, in only 33 games and 116 official at-bats. Although Ellsbury contributed little to the Red Sox during the American League playoffs, garnering a total of only 10 plate appearances against the Angels and Indians, he proved to be a huge factor in the World Series, starting all four games against Colorado and batting .438, with three RBIs and four runs scored.

Ellsbury built on the momentum he created late in 2007 by posting solid numbers the following year, concluding the 2008 campaign with a .280 batting average, 98 runs scored, and a league-leading 50 stolen bases, en route to earning a third-place finish in the Rookie of the Year voting. After replacing Crisp as the starter in center field during the season's second half, Ellsbury also did an outstanding defensive job, using his great speed to lead the team in outfield putouts, while going the entire year without committing an error.

Jason Bay, who took over in left field for the departed Manny Ramirez for the final two months of the campaign, marveled at Ellsbury's ability to cover ground in center, stating, "He's one of those guys who is athletic and fast, and he knows how to play the outfield. He's fun to watch, especially in right-center. There's a lot of room, and you really get to see him get after it."

Bay added, "Ells has that closing speed. When you're close to a ball and you can't get it, he can."

Meanwhile, Jason Varitek expressed his appreciation for Ellsbury's offensive contributions, saying, "He can create havoc on them bases. He's got a little Johnny Damon in him, with a little different swing. He'll just continue to get better as he plays this game longer."

Mike Lowell also noted, "Ellsbury has put a new dimension of pure speed and excitement into our game."

Ellsbury improved upon his numbers in virtually every offensive category in 2009, finishing the year with 60 RBIs, 94 runs scored, a .301 batting average, and a league-leading 10 triples and 70 stolen bases. His 70 steals established a new team record, surpassing the previous mark of 54 set by Tommy Harper in 1973. Ellsbury also had another exceptional defensive year, committing only two errors all season long and placing fourth among all AL outfielders in putouts, en route to earning Defensive Player of the Year honors in MLB.com's annual *This Year in Baseball* Awards.

Unfortunately, an early season collision with Red Sox third baseman Adrian Beltre resulted in hairline fractures to four of Ellsbury's left ribs the following year, limiting him to only 18 games. However, after instituting a new workout regimen during the subsequent offseason that focuses on muscle groups related to specific aspects of baseball, Ellsbury returned to the Red Sox in better shape than ever before at the start of 2011. Displaying the results of his improved conditioning, the 27-year-old outfielder turned in easily the finest season of his young career, concluding the campaign with 32 home runs, 105 RBIs, 119 runs scored, 212 hits, 46 doubles, 39 steals, a .321 batting average, a .376 on-base percentage, a .552 slugging percentage, and a league-leading 364 total bases. Ellsbury's exceptional performance earned him a spot on the AL All-Star team, a second-place finish to Detroit's Justin Verlander in the league MVP balloting, and AL Comeback Player of the Year honors.

The injury bug bit Ellsbury again in 2012, with his collision with Tampa Bay shortstop Reid Brignac while attempting to break up a double play resulting in a subluxation of his right shoulder. Able to appear in only 74 games over the course of the season, Ellsbury finished the year with just four homers, 26 RBIs, 43 runs scored, 14 stolen bases, and a batting average of .271. Despite playing the latter stages of the 2013 campaign with a swollen hand and a severely injured foot that earlier forced him to sit out nearly a month, Ellsbury had a solid all-around year, batting .298, scoring 92 runs, and leading the league with 52 stolen bases. He subsequently played extremely well during the playoffs and World Series, helping the Red Sox capture their eighth world title by compiling a .344 batting average, scoring 14 runs, and stealing six bases in 16 postseason contests.

Ellsbury's contributions to two championship teams notwithstanding, has been treated with disdain by the Fenway Faithful ever since he signed

Courtesy Keith Allison

a seven-year, $153 million contract with the New York Yankees just one month after he celebrated the Red Sox' 2013 World Series triumph with the rest of his teammates. Ellsbury left Boston with career totals of 65 home runs, 314 RBIs, 476 runs scored, 865 hits, and 241 stolen bases, a batting average of .297, an on-base percentage of .350, and a slugging percentage of .439.

While Ellsbury has played relatively well for the Yankees over the course of the last four seasons, he has been injured much of the time, preventing him from performing at the same level he reached during his time in Boston. After hitting 16 homers, driving in 70 runs, scoring 71 times, batting .271, and stealing 39 bases for New York in 2014, Ellsbury posted lesser numbers in each of the last three seasons, during which time he has gradually evolved into a part-time player. Ellsbury will enter the 2018 campaign with career totals of 104 home runs, 512 RBIs, 749 runs scored, 1,376 hits, and 343 stolen bases, a lifetime batting average of .284, an on-base percentage of .342, and a slugging percentage of .417.

RED SOX CAREER HIGHLIGHTS

Best Season

Although Ellsbury stole more bases and accumulated more triples in three other seasons, he established career highs in every other offensive category in 2011. In addition to leading the AL with 364 total bases and 83 extra-base hits, he finished third in the league in hits (212), doubles (46), and runs scored (119), fourth in stolen bases (39), fifth in home runs (32), batting average (.321), and OPS (.928), and sixth in RBIs (105) and slugging percentage (.552). Ellsbury also led all AL outfielders with 388 putouts and a perfect 1.000 fielding percentage. His fabulous all-around season earned him a second-place finish in the league MVP voting and his only Gold Glove and Silver Slugger Awards.

Memorable Moments/Greatest Performances

Ellsbury gave an early indication of his ability to perform well under pressure in Game 3 of the 2007 World Series, when he collected four hits, including three doubles. His pair of two-baggers off Colorado's Josh Fogg in the top of the third inning made him the first rookie to hit two doubles in the same inning of a World Series game.

Ellsbury used his great speed to nearly enter the record books, with his streak of 25 consecutive stolen bases that lasted from his rookie season of 2007 until May 18, 2008, falling just short of Tim Raines's major-league mark of 27 straight successful stolen base attempts. Shortly after his streak ended, Ellsbury swiped three bases against the Baltimore Orioles on May 30, becoming in the process the first Red Sox player to steal more than two bags in a game since Jerry Remy pilfered four bases on June 14, 1980. When Ellsbury stole home against Andy Pettitte and the Yankees on April 26, 2009, he also became the first Red Sox player to register a straight steal of home since Jeff Frye accomplished the feat 10 years earlier. On May 30, 2013, Ellsbury set a Red Sox team record when he stole five bases during a 9–2 victory over the Philadelphia Phillies at Citizens Bank Park.

Ellsbury also used his glove and bat to turn in some of his most memorable performances. On May 20, 2009, he tied a major-league record for outfielders by recording 12 putouts in a nine-inning game. Ellsbury also recorded the longest errorless streak by a Red Sox outfielder in history, going 232 games and 554 chances without committing an error before misplaying a ball hit by Jorge Cantú of the Florida Marlins on June 17, 2009.

Meanwhile, at the plate, Ellsbury had walk-off hits in consecutive games against the Cleveland Indians in early August of 2011, giving the Red Sox a 3–2 win on August 2 with a ninth-inning single off Vinnie Pestano, before homering off Joe Smith in Boston's final at-bat the very next day. However, he had his two best days that year against the arch-rival Yankees, hitting a three-run homer and driving in a career-high six runs against New York during Boston's 10–4 win on August 6, before hitting three home runs during a doubleheader split with the Yankees on September 25, with his three-run blast in the top of the 14th inning of Game 2 giving the Red Sox a 7–4 victory.

NOTABLE ACHIEVEMENTS

- Batted over .300 three times
- Hit more than 30 home runs once (32 in 2011)
- Knocked in more than 100 runs once (105 in 2011)
- Scored more than 100 runs once (119 in 2011)
- Surpassed 200 hits once (212 in 2011)

- Finished in double-digits in triples once (10 in 2009)
- Surpassed 30 doubles twice, topping 40 mark once (46 in 2011)
- Stole more than 50 bases three times, topping 70 mark once (70 in 2009)
- Posted slugging percentage in excess of .500 twice
- Led AL in stolen bases three times; triples once; total bases once; and plate appearances once
- Led AL outfielders in putouts once and fielding percentage twice
- Ranks third in Red Sox history with 241 stolen bases
- Holds Red Sox single-season record with 70 stolen bases in 2009
- Member of 30-30 club (2011)
- 2009 MLB.com's *This Year in Baseball* Defensive Player of the Year
- Finished second in 2011 AL MVP voting
- 2011 AL Comeback Player of the Year
- 2011 Gold Glove winner
- 2011 Silver Slugger winner
- 2011 AL All-Star
- Two-time AL champion (2007 and 2013)
- Two-time world champion (2007 and 2013)

Jim Lonborg

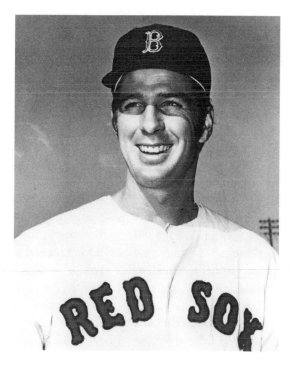

Courtesy Boston Red Sox

It might appear difficult at first to justify the inclusion of Jim Lonborg in these rankings since he had only one dominant season during his time in Boston. But, for that one season, Lonborg was arguably the best pitcher in baseball, serving as an integral member of the 1967 Red Sox club that shocked everyone by winning the American League pennant. While teammate Carl Yastrzemski captured most of the headlines with his fabulous performance over the course of the campaign, Lonborg proved to be nearly as important to the success of the team. Anchoring Boston's starting rotation throughout the year, the lanky right-hander led all AL hurlers with 22 wins, 246 strikeouts, and 39 starts. He also finished second in the league with 15 complete games and 273 innings pitched, en route to earning Cy Young and *Sporting News* AL Pitcher of the Year honors and a sixth-place finish in the league MVP voting. Unfortunately, Lonborg posted double-digit wins only once more for the Red Sox after injuring his leg in a skiing accident during the subsequent off-season. Nevertheless, I felt compelled to include him on this list since the Red Sox never would have won the 1967 American League pennant without him.

Born in Santa Maria, California, on April 16, 1942, James Reynold Lonborg grew up in nearby San Luis Obispo, where he spent much of his time rooting for the Dodgers after they moved from Brooklyn to Los Angeles in 1958. Focusing on baseball and basketball while attending San Luis Obispo High School, Lonborg subsequently enrolled at Stanford University, where he initially planned to pursue a career in medicine. However, he soon found himself being heavily scouted by the Baltimore Orioles, who offered him a contract after his junior year. Lonborg, though, elected to sign with the Red Sox for a much higher bonus offer of $25,000.

Desperate for pitching help, the Red Sox summoned Lonborg to the big leagues after the 22-year-old right-hander spent just one year in their farm system. After earning a spot in Boston's starting rotation during spring training, Lonborg ended up going 9–17 with a 4.47 ERA for a team that finished ninth in the American League in 1965, with a record of only 62–100. Nevertheless, the 6'5", 200-pound Lonborg displayed all the physical tools necessary to become a big winner, featuring in his repertoire an explosive fastball and an above-average curve. Although the Red Sox finished ninth in the standings again in 1966, they improved their record by 10 games. Lonborg followed suit, concluding the campaign with a record of 10–10 and an ERA of 3.86.

Asked by Boston management to work on his breaking ball in the Venezuela winter league during the subsequent off-season, Lonborg returned to the Red Sox a more polished pitcher at the start of 1967. He also became more aggressive on the mound, claiming the inside part of the plate for himself by throwing high-and-tight fastballs to opposing batters, at the urging of new pitching coach Sal Maglie, who developed a reputation as a "head-hunter" during his playing days. Even though Lonborg had to leave the team periodically between starts to fulfill his Army Reserve duties, he pitched exceptionally well throughout the year, aided by Tom Yawkey, who flew him in on a private plane to make certain he didn't miss any of his starts. Lonborg ended up posting an ERA of 3.16, leading all AL hurlers with a record of 22–9, 246 strikeouts, and 39 starts, and finishing second in the circuit with 273 innings pitched and 15 complete games. His outstanding performance earned him AL Cy Young honors and a sixth-place finish in the league MVP voting.

Pitching particularly well for the Red Sox down the stretch, Lonborg outdueled Minnesota's Dean Chance in the regular season finale to put his team in the World Series for the first time in 21 years. He then dominated the St. Louis Cardinals in Games 2 and 5 of the Fall Classic, allowing them a total of only four hits and one run, in tossing two complete-game victories. Unfortunately, Lonborg faltered in Game 7, when, working on only two days rest, he surrendered six earned runs in six innings during a 7–2 loss.

Shortly after signing a new contract with the Red Sox for 1968, Lonborg elected to go skiing at Lake Tahoe, California. Reflecting back on his decision years later, Lonborg stated, "There was nothing in my contract that said I couldn't ski, and I felt it was the main reason I had been so successful in '67—because I was in such great shape. But, looking back on it, I didn't have enough experience to know when it was time to go inside and say you've had enough for the day."

Lonborg ended up tearing two ligaments in his left knee during a December 23 mishap, forcing him to undergo surgery just four days later. After spending six weeks in a waist-high cast, he spent the remainder of the off-season working diligently to prepare himself for the upcoming campaign. Yet, in compensating for his knee during his training sessions, Lonborg unknowingly altered his pitching motion slightly, causing him to place added stress on his right shoulder. Muscle and tendon damage resulted, preventing Lonborg from ever again pitching at the same level he reached in 1967.

Lonborg later revealed, "They were able to diagnose it as rotator cuff problems, which they really didn't know how to treat back then. I had tons of cortisone shots, and I tried to come back too soon without building up my arm strength properly. It was just a case of youthful energy, and wanting to get back on the field."

Lonborg started a total of only 44 games from 1968 to 1970, compiling an overall mark of just 17–22 during that time. However, he began to show signs of returning to his old form in 1971, finishing the year with a record of 10–7 and tossing three complete games during the month of September. Looking back at that period of his career, Lonborg said, "Most everybody was hopeful that I would be able to get back to my initial form. I always felt very good around the clubhouse; my teammates were great, and the Red Sox were very patient with me. I did have flashes of the old stuff, but had not yet learned what it took for my body to heal properly."

A third consecutive third-place finish in 1971 finally caused the Red Sox to lose patience with Lonborg, prompting them to include him in a 10-player trade they completed with the Milwaukee Brewers on October 10, 1971, that sent Tommy Harper and Marty Pattin, among others, to Boston. Lonborg spent only one season in Milwaukee, compiling a record of 14–12 and a career-best 2.83 ERA for the Brewers in 1972, while also tossing 11 complete games. In spite of Lonborg's strong showing, he soon found himself packing for Philadelphia after the Phillies acquired him in a seven-player deal on October 31, 1972. Lonborg spent the next seven years in Philadelphia, ending his career there in 1979 after posting an overall record of 75–60. Although he never regained his hard sinking fastball, Lonborg developed a better slider and change-up and learned how to work the corners of the plate. He had his two best years for the Phillies in 1974 and 1976, posting 17 victories, compiling a 3.21 ERA, tossing 16 complete games, and throwing 283 innings in the first of those campaigns, before going 18–10 with a 3.08 ERA two years later. Lonborg announced his retirement after being released by the Phillies on June 16, 1979, ending his career with a record of 157–137, a 3.86 ERA, 90 complete games, and 15 shutouts. He compiled a record of 68–65 and an ERA of 3.94,

Courtesy Boston
Red Sox

threw 38 complete games, and tossed six shutouts while pitching for the Red Sox.

Following his retirement, Lonborg returned to school, attending UMass/Boston for one year, before spending the next three years at Tufts University Dental School. After honing his skills with several local dentists following his graduation, Lonborg eventually established his own practice in Hanover, Massachusetts—a small, quiet community between Boston and Cape Cod. He still works there today, living just a short drive away in the nearby town of Scituate.

RED SOX CAREER HIGHLIGHTS

Best Season

Was there ever any doubt? Lonborg had easily his finest season in 1967, when he finished 22–9, with a 3.16 ERA, 15 complete games, 2 shutouts, and a league-leading 246 strikeouts. He allowed only 228 hits in 273 innings of work, en route to posting a career-best WHIP of 1.138. Lonborg led all AL pitchers in three categories, placed second in two others, and finished third in another, earning in the process the Cy Young Award and spots on the *Sporting News* and AL All-Star teams for the only time in his career.

Memorable Moments/Greatest Performances

Lonborg experienced virtually all of his greatest moments with the Red Sox in his banner year of 1967, with the first of those coming on April 28, when he defeated Catfish Hunter and the A's by a score of 3–0. Lonborg allowed six hits and struck out a season-high 13 batters during the contest. He turned in another gem on July 9, shutting out the Tigers on just three hits over seven innings on a steamy night in Detroit. The 3–0 win by Lonborg, who lost 12 pounds during the contest, ended a five-game losing streak by Boston. The Red Sox began a 10-game winning streak just a few days later, putting themselves right in the thick of the pennant race. Lonborg defeated Catfish Hunter again on September 12, this time by a score of 3–1, notching his 20th victory of the year by throwing a complete-game eight-hitter, and helping his own cause by driving in the winning run with an eighth-inning triple.

Lonborg, though, saved his most memorable efforts for the end of the year, when his superb pitching almost brought the Red Sox their first world championship in nearly half a century. Facing the Twins on the final day of the regular season in what amounted to a winner-take-all affair, Lonborg squared off against Minnesota staff ace Dean Chance, a 20-game winner himself. Overcoming two early miscues by his teammates that gave the Twins a pair of unearned runs, Lonborg continued to hold Minnesota at bay until the Red Sox pushed across five runs in the bottom of the sixth inning. Lonborg ended up going the distance, allowing the Twins just seven hits and one earned run during a 5–3 Red Sox win that put them in the World Series. Making things even sweeter, Lonborg collected two hits during the contest. After he retired the final batter on a pop-up to shortstop Rico Petrocelli, Lonborg found himself being lifted onto the shoulders of George Scott and Mike Andrews. However, the pitcher's glee suddenly turned to fear as Red Sox fans stormed the field. Looking back, Lonborg recalled, "The crowd starting moving toward the right-field foul pole, and I was trying to get back to the dugout. A lot of articles of my clothing were starting to disappear; the moment of jubilation had passed, and now the moment of anxiety had started to set in." He added, "Initially, it [winning the pennant] was what you would dream about in Little League. The winning pitcher . . . being on the mound to win the pennant . . . everyone congratulating me. But, a few minutes later, you realize you're not going where you want to go. I was trying to get back in the dugout. Thank God for the Boston police, they were able to control the crowd. It was delirium."

Lonborg continued his extraordinary pitching against the Cardinals in the World Series, evening the Fall Classic at a game apiece by tossing just the fourth one-hitter in series history in Game 2—a 5–0 victory. Lonborg retired the first 19 batters he faced, before walking Curt Flood with one man out in the seventh inning. He subsequently carried his no-hitter into the eighth, when Julian Javier collected the only St. Louis safety by lining a two-out double to left field. After the Cardinals won the next two contests, Lonborg returned to the mound for Game 5, getting the Red Sox back in the series with a 3–1 complete-game victory. Lonborg surrendered just three hits to the Cardinals, allowing them to score their only run on a two-out homer by Roger Maris in the bottom of the ninth inning. Unfortunately, working on short rest didn't agree with Lonborg in Game 7, with the weary hurler dropping a 7–2 decision to Bob Gibson and the Cardinals.

NOTABLE ACHIEVEMENTS

- Won more than 20 games once (22 in 1967)
- Posted winning percentage in excess of .700 twice (1967 and 1970)
- Threw more than 250 innings once (273 in 1967)
- Struck out more than 200 batters once (246 in 1967)
- Led AL pitchers in wins once; strikeouts once; and games started once
- Won two games in 1967 World Series
- 1967 AL Cy Young Award winner
- 1967 AL *Sporting News* Pitcher of the Year
- 1967 *Sporting News* All-Star selection
- 1967 AL All-Star
- 1967 AL champion

Summary and Honorable Mentions: The Next 25

Having identified the 50 greatest players in Boston Red Sox history, the time has come to select the best of the best. Based on the rankings contained in this book, the members of the Red Sox all-time team are listed below. Our squad includes the top player at each position, along with a pitching staff that features a five-man starting rotation and a closer. Our starting lineup also includes a designated hitter. Also listed are the members of the second team.

FIRST TEAM STARTING LINEUP:

Player	Position
Tris Speaker	CF
Wade Boggs	3B
Jimmie Foxx	1B
Ted Williams	DH
Nomar Garciaparra	SS
Carl Yastrzemski	LF
Bobby Doerr	2B
Carlton Fisk	C
Dwight Evans	RF

FIRST TEAM PITCHING STAFF:

Player	Position
Pedro Martinez	SP
Roger Clemens	SP

Cy Young	SP
Babe Ruth	SP
Smoky Joe Wood	SP
Ellis Kinder	CL

SECOND TEAM STARTING LINEUP:

Player	Position
Dom DiMaggio	CF
Dustin Pedroia	2B
David Ortiz	DH
Jim Rice	LF
Mo Vaughn	1B
Joe Cronin	SS
Jackie Jensen	RF
Frank Malzone	3B
Jason Varitek	C

SECOND TEAM PITCHING STAFF:

Player	Position
Luis Tiant	SP
Lefty Grove	SP
Mel Parnell	SP
Jon Lester	SP
Tim Wakefield	SP
Derek Lowe	CL

Although I limited my earlier rankings to the top 50 players in Red Sox history, many other fine players have performed for the Fenway Faithful over the years, some of whom narrowly missed making the final cut. Following is a list of those players deserving of an honorable mention. These are the men I deemed worthy of being slotted into positions 51 to 75 in the overall rankings. The statistics they compiled during their time in Boston, and their most notable achievements as Red Sox are also included.

Jonathan Papelbon
Courtesy Keith Allison

51—Jonathan Papelbon (P, 2005–2011)

Red Sox Numbers: Record: 23–19, .548 Win Pct., 2.33 ERA, 219 Saves
Notable Achievements:
Saved more than 30 games six times, topping 40 saves once (41 in 2008)
Compiled ERA below 2.00 three times, posting mark below 1.00 once
     (0.92 in 2006).
Compiled more strikeouts than innings pitched six times
Posted WHIP under 1.000 four times
Holds Red Sox career record for most saves (219)
2007 Babe Ruth Award winner as MVP of World Series.
Four-time AL All-Star
2007 AL champion
2007 world champion

52—Jimmy Collins (3B, 1901–1907)

Red Sox Numbers: 25 HR, 385 RBIs, 448 Runs Scored, 881 Hits, 171 Dou-
     bles, 65 Triples, 102 SB, .296 AVG, .336 OBP, .423 SLG PCT
Notable Achievements:
Batted over .300 twice, topping the .320 mark both times
Scored 108 runs in 1901

Jimmy Collins
Courtesy Mears Online Auctions

Finished in double-digits in triples four times

Surpassed 30 doubles three times, topping 40 two-baggers once (42 in 1901)

Stole more than 20 bases once (23 in 1903)

Led AL third basemen in assists once; putouts twice; double plays once; and fielding percentage twice

Ranks 10th all-time on Red Sox with 65 triples

Two-time AL champion (1903 and 1904)

1903 world champion

Elected to Baseball Hall of Fame by members of Old Timers Committee in 1945.

53—Ellis Burks (OF, 1987–1992)

Red Sox Numbers: 94 HR, 388 RBIs, 446 Runs Scored, 791 Hits, 160 Doubles, 27 Triples, 95 SB, .280 AVG, .341 OBP, .455 SLG PCT

Ellis Burks
Courtesy Ted Straub

Notable Achievements:
Hit more than 20 home runs twice
Batted over .300 once (.303 in 1989)
Surpassed 30 doubles four times
Stole more than 20 bases three times
Led AL center fielders with 15 assists in 1987
Led AL center fielders with .994 fielding percentage in 1990
1990 Gold Glove winner
1990 Silver Slugger winner
1990 *Sporting News* All-Star selection
1990 AL All-Star

54—Dutch Leonard (P, 1913–1918)

Red Sox Numbers: Record: 90–64, .584 Win Pct., 2.13 ERA, 96 CG, 25
   Shutouts
Notable Achievements:
Surpassed 15 victories four times, winning as many as 19 games once (19–5
   in 1914)

Dutch Leonard
Courtesy Library of
Congress

Compiled winning percentage in excess of .700 once (.792 in 1914)
Compiled ERA below 3.00 six times, with mark of 0.96 in 1914 representing the lowest single-season ERA since 1900
Surpassed 20 complete games once (26 in 1917)
Threw more than 200 innings four times
Led AL in ERA and WHIP once each
Ranks among Red Sox career leaders in ERA (4th) and shutouts (5th)
Three-time AL champion (1915, 1916, and 1918)
Three-time world champion (1915, 1916, and 1918)

55—Buck Freeman (1B, OF, 1901–1907)

Red Sox Numbers: 48 HR, 504 RBIs, 403 Runs Scored, 879 Hits, 158 Doubles, 90 Triples, 59 SB, .286 AVG, .339 OBP, .442 SLG PCT
Notable Achievements:
Finished in double-digits in home runs three times
Knocked in more than 100 runs three times
Batted over .300 twice, surpassing the .330 mark once (.339 in 1901)
Amassed 20 triples in 1903
Finished in double-digits in triples three other times
Surpassed 30 doubles twice
Compiled on-base percentage in excess of .400 once (.400 in 1901)
Posted slugging percentage in excess of .500 twice (1901 and 1902)
Led AL in home runs once; RBIs twice; triples once; and total bases once
First player to lead both the NL (1899) and AL (1903) in home runs

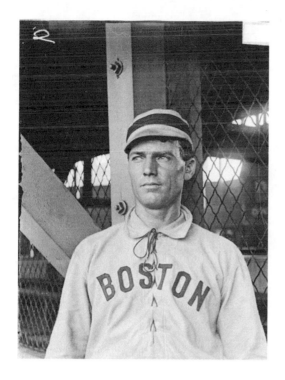

Buck Freeman

Ranks third in Red Sox history with 90 triples
Two-time AL champion (1903 and 1904)
1903 world champion

56—Larry Gardner (3B, 2B, 1908–1917)

Red Sox Numbers: 16 HR, 481 RBIs, 496 Runs Scored, 1,106 Hits, 151
    Doubles, 87 Triples, 134 SB, .282 AVG, .350 OBP, .377 SLG PCT
Notable Achievements:
Batted over .300 twice
Finished in double-digits in triples four times
Stole more than 20 bases twice
Finished second in AL with 19 triples in 1914
Led AL third basemen in assists once (312 in 1914)
Ranks among Red Sox career leaders in triples (5th) and steals (6th)
Three-time AL champion (1912, 1915, and 1916)
Three-time world champion (1912, 1915, and 1916)

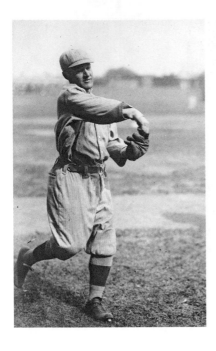

Larry Gardner
Courtesy Library of Congress

57—Doc Cramer (OF, 1936–1940)

Red Sox Numbers: 1 HR, 270 RBIs, 509 Runs Scored, 940 Hits, 146 Doubles, 44 Triples, 22 SB, .302 AVG, .349 OBP, .378 SLG PCT
Notable Achievements:
Batted over .300 four times
Scored more than 100 runs twice
Accumulated 200 hits in 1940
Finished in double-digits in triples twice
Surpassed 30 doubles three times
Led AL in hits once; sacrifice hits once; and at-bats twice
Led AL outfielders in putouts twice and double plays once
Led AL center fielders in assists once and fielding percentage once
Four-time AL All-Star

58—Rick Burleson (SS, 1974–1980)

Red Sox Numbers: 38 HR, 360 RBIs, 514 Runs Scored, 1,114 Hits, 203 Doubles, 21 Triples, 67 SB, .274 AVG, .326 OBP, .362 SLG PCT
Notable Achievements:

Doc Cramer
Courtesy Boston
Public Library,
Leslie Jones
Collection

Rick Burleson
Courtesy Boston Red Sox

Surpassed 30 doubles three times
Led AL with 721 plate appearances and 663 at-bats in 1977
Led AL shortstops in assists once; putouts twice; double plays once; and
    fielding percentage once
1979 Gold Glove winner
1977 *Sporting News* All-Star selection
Three-time AL All-Star (1977–1979)
1975 AL champion

59—John Valentin (SS, 3B, 2B, 1992–2001)

Red Sox Numbers: 121 HR, 528 RBIs, 596 Runs Scored, 1,043 Hits, 266
    Doubles, 17 Triples, 47 SB, .281 AVG, .361 OBP, .460 SLG PCT
Notable Achievements:
Hit more than 20 home runs twice
Knocked in more than 100 runs once (102 in 1995)
Scored more than 100 runs twice
Batted over .300 twice
Surpassed 40 doubles three times
Stole 20 bases once (1995)
Compiled on-base percentage in excess of .400 once (.400 in 1994)
Posted slugging percentage in excess of .500 twice
Led AL with 47 doubles in 1997
Led AL shortstops in assists once
Led AL third basemen in putouts once
Hit for the cycle on June 6, 1996
Hit three home runs in one game on June 2, 1995
Turned in unassisted triple play on July 8, 1994
1995 Silver Slugger winner

60—Dick Radatz (P, 1962–1966)

Red Sox Numbers: Record: 49–34, .590 Win Pct., 2.65 ERA, 102 Saves
Notable Achievements:
Won at least 15 games twice (1963 and 1964)
Saved more than 20 games four straight times (1962–1965)
Compiled ERA below 2.50 three times, posting mark below 2.00 once
    (1.97 in 1963)
Posted winning percentage in excess of .700 once (.714 in 1963)

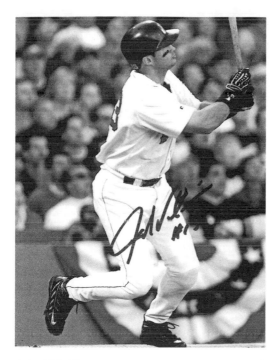

John Valentin
Courtesy Mainline Autographs

Threw more than 100 innings four straight times (1962–1965)
Compiled more strikeouts than innings pitched three times (1962–1964)
Led AL pitchers in saves twice (1962 and 1964)
Ranks among Red Sox career leaders in: saves (3rd); WHIP (tied-8th);
    and strikeouts per nine innings pitched (2nd)
Holds Red Sox single-season records for most wins (16) and strikeouts (181)
    by a reliever (1964)
Finished fifth in 1963 AL MVP voting
1964 Thomas A. Yawkey Red Sox MVP
Two-time *Sporting News* AL Fireman of the Year (1962 and 1964)
Two-time AL All-Star (1963 and 1964)

61—Bob Stanley (P, 1977–1989)

Career Numbers: Record: 115–97, .542 Win Pct., 3.64 ERA, 132 Saves,
    21 CG, seven Shutouts

Dick Radatz
Courtesy 1960s Baseball

Notable Achievements:
Posted double-digit wins five times, surpassing 15 victories twice
Saved more than 20 games twice, topping 30 saves once (33 in 1983)
Compiled ERA below 3.00 three times

BOB STANLEY

Bob Stanley
Courtesy Boston Red Sox

Posted winning percentage in excess of .700 twice, finishing with mark of .882 (15–2) in 1978

Threw more than 100 innings nine times, surpassing 200 innings once (217 in 1979)

Holds Red Sox career record for most pitching appearances (637)

Ranks among Red Sox career leaders in saves (2nd) and innings pitched (6th)

Holds Red Sox single-season record for most innings pitched by a reliever (168 in 1982)

Finished seventh in AL Cy Young voting twice (1978 and 1982)

Two-time AL All-Star (1979 and 1983)

1986 AL champion

62—Wes Ferrell (P, 1934–1937)

Red Sox Numbers: Record: 62–40, .608 Win Pct., 4.11 ERA, 81 CG, 9 Shutouts; 17 HR, 82 RBIs, .308 AVG, .384 OBP, .490 SLG PCT
Notable Achievements:

Won at least 20 games twice, posting 25 victories in 1935

Compiled winning percentage in excess of .700 once (.737 in 1934)

Surpassed 25 complete games three times, completing 31 games in 1935

Threw more than 300 innings twice (1935 and 1936)

Led AL pitchers in wins once; complete games three times; innings pitched three times; and games started twice

Batted .347 in 1935, with 7 home runs and 32 RBIs, in 150 at-bats

Hit two home runs in one game five times

Finished second in 1935 AL MVP voting

1937 AL All-Star

63—Mookie Betts (OF, 2014–Present)

Career Numbers: 78 HR, 310 RBIs, 349 Runs Scored, 609 Hits, 142 Doubles, 16 Triples, 80 SB, .292 AVG, .351 OBP, .488 SLG PCT
Notable Achievements:

Has hit more than 20 home runs twice, topping 30 homers once (31 in 2016)

Has knocked in more than 100 runs twice

Wes Ferrell (l) with Billy Werber
Courtesy Boston Public Library, Leslie Jones Collection

Has scored more than 100 runs twice
Has batted over .300 once (.318 in 2016)
Has topped 200 hits once (214 in 2016)
Has surpassed 40 doubles three times
Has stolen more than 20 bases three times
Has posted slugging percentage in excess of .500 once (.534 in 2016)
Led A.L. with 359 total bases and 672 at-bats in 2016
Finished second in A.L. with .318 batting average, 122 runs scored,
    and 214 hits in 2016
Has led A.L. right-fielders in: putouts twice; double plays once; and
    fielding pct. once
Has hit three home runs in one game twice (vs. Baltimore on May 31,
    2016 & vs. Arizona on August 8, 2016)
July 2016 A.L. Player of the Month
Finished second in 2016 A.L. MVP voting
2016 Silver Slugger winner
2016 Gold Glove winner

Mookie Betts
Courtesy Keith Allison

2016 Wilson Defensive Player of the Year
Two-time A.L. All-Star (2016 & 2017)

64—Billy Werber (3B, SS, OF, 1933–1936)

Red Sox Numbers: 38 HR, 234 RBIs, 366 Runs Scored, 575 Hits, 130 Doubles, 25 Triples, 107 SB, .281 AVG, .367 OBP, .425 SLG PCT
Notable Achievements:
Batted over .300 once (.321 in 1934)
Scored more than 100 runs once (129 in 1934)
Surpassed 200 hits once (200 in 1934)
Finished in double-digits in triples once (10 in 1934)
Surpassed 30 doubles three times, topping 40 mark once (41 in 1934)
Stole more than 20 bases three times, swiping 40 bags in 1934
Led AL in stolen bases twice and plate appearances once
Led AL third basemen in assists once and putouts once
Tied for ninth in Red Sox history with 107 stolen bases

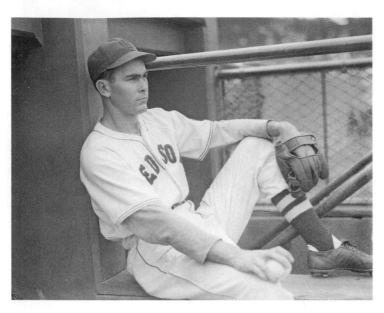

Tex Hughson
Courtesy Boston Public Library, Leslie Jones Collection

Trot Nixon
Courtesy Joe Donovan

65—Tex Hughson (P, 1941–1944, 1946–1949)

Career Numbers: Record: 96–54, .640 Win Pct., 2.94 ERA, 99 CG, 19
   Shutouts
Notable Achievements:
Won at least 20 games twice
Won 18 games another time
Compiled winning percentage in excess of .700 three times
Compiled ERA below 3.00 four times
Surpassed 20 complete games three times.
Threw more than 250 innings three times
Led AL pitchers in wins once; winning percentage once; complete games
   twice; innings pitched once; strikeouts once; and WHIP once
Ranks among Red Sox career leaders in shutouts (tied-7th) and complete
   games (10th)
Finished sixth in 1942 AL MVP voting
1942 *Sporting News* All-Star selection
Three-time AL All-Star (1942–1944)
1946 AL champion

66—Trot Nixon (OF, 1996, 1998–2006)

Red Sox Numbers: 133 HR, 523 RBIs, 547 Runs Scored, 912 Hits, 204
   Doubles, 28 Triples, 29 SB, .278 AVG, .366 OBP, .478 SLG PCT
Notable Achievements:
Hit more than 20 home runs three times
Scored 100 runs in 2001
Batted over .300 twice
Surpassed 30 doubles twice
Compiled slugging percentage in excess of .500 three times
Led AL right fielders in double plays twice and fielding percentage once
2004 AL champion
2004 world champion

67—Bill Lee (P, 1969–1978)

Red Sox Numbers: Record: 94–68, .580 Win Pct., 3.64 ERA, 64 CG, 7
   Shutouts

Notable Achievements:
Won 17 games three times
Compiled winning percentage in excess of .800 once (.818 in 1971)
Compiled ERA below 3.00 twice
Completed more than 15 games three times
Threw more than 250 innings three times
Led AL pitchers in assists once
Ranks 10th all-time among Red Sox pitchers with 321 appearances
1973 AL All-Star
1975 AL champion

68—Jim Tabor (3B, 1938–1944)

Red Sox Numbers: 90 HR, 517 RBIs, 393 Runs Scored, 838 Hits, 162 Doubles, 27 Triples, 64 SB, .273 AVG, .324 OBP, .431 SLG PCT

Bill Lee
Courtesy Boston Red Sox

Jim Tabor
Courtesy Boston Public Library, Leslie Jones Collection

Notable Achievements:
Hit more than 20 home runs once (21 in 1940)
Knocked in more than 100 runs once (101 in 1941)
Surpassed 30 doubles once (33 in 1939)
Posted slugging percentage in excess of .500 once (.510 in 1940)
Led AL third basemen in: assists once; putouts once; and double plays once
Hit four home runs and knocked in 11 runs in a doubleheader vs. the A's
    on July 4, 1939
Hit three home runs in one game vs. Philadelphia on July 4, 1939
Tied ML record by hitting two grand slams in one game on July 4, 1939

69—Troy O'Leary (OF, 1995–2001)

Red Sox Numbers: 117 HR, 516 RBIs, 490 Runs Scored, 954 Hits, 209
    Doubles, 37 Triples, 12 SB, .276 AVG, .331 OBP, .459 SLG PCT
Notable Achievements:
Hit more than 20 home runs twice

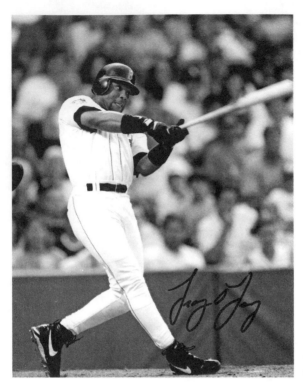

Troy O'Leary
Courtesy Mainline Autographs

Dave "Boo" Ferriss
Courtesy Pristine Auction

Knocked in more than 100 runs once (103 in 1999)

Batted over .300 twice

Surpassed 30 doubles five times

Led AL left fielders in putouts once

Hit first grand slam in Red Sox postseason history on October 11, 1999, in Game 5 of ALDS vs. Cleveland

Hit two home runs and knocked in seven runs vs. Indians in Game 5 of 1999 ALDS

70—Dave "Boo" Ferriss (P, 1945–1950)

Career Numbers: Record: 65–30, .684 Win Pct., 3.64 ERA, 67 CG, 12 Shutouts

Notable Achievements:

Won more than 20 games twice

Compiled winning percentage in excess of .700 twice

Compiled ERA under 3.00 once (2.96 in 1945)

Surpassed 25 complete games twice

Threw more than 250 innings twice

Led AL pitchers with .806 winning percentage in 1946

Ranks third all-time on Red Sox in career winning percentage (.684)

Finished fourth in 1945 AL MVP voting and 7th in 1946 balloting

Two-time *Sporting News* All-Star selection (1945 and 1946)

1946 AL All-Star

1946 AL champion

71—Rick Ferrell (C, 1933–1937)

Red Sox Numbers: 16 HR, 240 RBIs, 221 Runs Scored, 541 Hits, 111 Doubles, 17 Triples, 7 SB, .302 AVG, .394 OBP, .410 SLG PCT

Notable Achievements:

Batted over .300 twice (1935 and 1936)

Surpassed 30 doubles once (34 in 1935)

Compiled on-base percentage in excess of .400 once (.406 in 1936)

Led A.L. catchers in assists once; putouts twice; fielding percentage once; and caught-stealing percentage once

Tied for eighth all-time on Red Sox with .394 on-base percentage

Four-time AL All-Star (1933–1936)

Rick Ferrell
Courtesy Boston Public
Library, Leslie Jones
Collection

Elected to Baseball Hall of Fame by members of Veteran's Committee in 1984

72—Jimmy Piersall (OF, 1950, 1952–1958)

Red Sox Numbers: 66 HR, 366 RBIs, 502 Runs Scored, 919 Hits, 158 Doubles, 32 Triples, 58 SB, .273 AVG, .340 OBP, .397 SLG PCT
Notable Achievements:
Scored more than 100 runs once (103 in 1957)
Surpassed 40 doubles once (40 in 1956)
Led AL with 40 doubles in 1956 and 19 sacrifice hits in 1953
Led AL outfielders in putouts twice; double plays once; and fielding percentage once
Led AL center fielders in assists once; double plays twice; and fielding percentage twice
Led AL right fielders in putouts once and double plays once
Finished ninth in 1953 AL MVP voting
1958 Gold Glove winner
Two-time AL All-Star

Jimmy Piersall (r) with
Ted Williams
Courtesy Boston Public
Library, Leslie Jones
Collection

73—Bill Mueller (3B, 2003–2005)

Red Sox Numbers: 41 HR, 204 RBIs, 229 Runs Scored, 437 Hits, 106 Doubles, 9 Triples, 3 SB, .303 AVG, .378 OBP, .474 SLG PCT
Notable Achievements:
Batted over .300 once (.326 in 2003)
Surpassed 30 doubles twice, topping 40 mark once (45 in 2003)
Posted slugging percentage in excess of .500 once (.540 in 2003)
Led AL with .326 batting average in 2003
Hit two grand slams in one game vs. Texas on July 29, 2003
Hit three home runs in one game vs. Texas on July 29, 2003
2003 Silver Slugger winner
2003 *Sporting News* All-Star selection
2004 AL champion
2004 world champion

74—Dennis Eckersley (P, 1978–1984, 1998)

Red Sox Numbers: Record: 88 71, .553 Win Pct., 3.92 ERA, 64 CG, 10 Shutouts
Notable Achievements:

Bill Mueller
Courtesy Mainline
Autographs

Dennis Eckersley
Courtesy Legendary
Auctions

Won 20 games in 1978
Won 17 games in 1979
Compiled winning percentage in excess of .700 twice
Compiled ERA under 3.00 twice
Threw more than 200 innings three times
Finished fourth in 1978 AL Cy Young voting
1982 AL All-Star
Elected to Baseball Hall of Fame by members of BBWAA in 2004

75—Xander Bogaerts (SS, 3B, 2013–Present)

Career Numbers: 51 HR, 283 RBIs, 360 Runs Scored, 684 Hits, 131 Doubles, 11 Triples, 41 SB, .283 AVG, .339 OBP, .409 SLG PCT
Notable Achievements:
Has hit more than 20 home runs once (21 in 2016).
Has batted over .300 once (.320 in 2015)
Has scored more than 100 runs once (115 in 2016)
Has surpassed 30 doubles three times
Finished second in A.L. with .320 batting average and 196 hits in 2015
Two-time Silver Slugger winner (2015 & 2016)
2016 A.L. All-Star
2013 A.L. champion
2013 world champion

Xander Bogaerts
Courtesy Keith Allison

Glossary

ABBREVIATIONS AND STATISTICAL TERMS

AVG. Batting average. The number of hits divided by the number of at-bats.

CG. Complete games pitched.

CL. Closer.

ERA. Earned run average. The number of earned runs a pitcher gives up, per nine innings. This does not include runs that scored as a result of errors and is calculated by dividing the number of runs given up, by the number of innings pitched, and multiplying the result by 9.

HITS. Base hits. Awarded when a runner safely reaches at least first base upon a batted ball, if no error is recorded.

HR. Home runs. Fair ball hit over the fence, or one hit to a spot that allows the batter to circle the bases before the ball is returned to home plate.

IP. Innings pitched.

OBP. On-base percentage. Hits plus walks plus hit by pitches, divided by plate appearances.

OPS. On-base plus slugging percentage. The sum of a player's on-base percentage and his slugging percentage.

RBI. Runs batted in. Awarded to the batter when a runner scores upon a safely batted ball, a sacrifice, or a walk.

RUNS. Runs scored by a player.

SB. Stolen bases.

SLG PCT. Slugging percentage. The number of total bases earned by all singles, doubles, triples, and home runs, divided by the total number of at-bats.

SO. Strikeouts.

SP. Starting pitcher.

WHIP. Walks plus hits per innings pitched. Walks plus hits, divided by innings pitched.

WIN PCT. Winning percentage. A pitcher's number of wins divided by his number of total decisions (i.e., wins plus losses).

Sources

BOOKS

DeMarco, Tony, et al. *The Sporting News Selects 50 Greatest Sluggers*. St. Louis, MO: Sporting News, 2000.

Shalin, Mike, and Neil Shalin. *Out by a Step: The 100 Best Players Not in the Baseball Hall of Fame*. Lanham, MD: Diamond Communications, 2002.

Thorn, John, and Pete Palmer, eds., with Michael Gershman. *Total Baseball*. New York: HarperCollins, 1993.

Williams, Ted, with Jim Prime. *Ted Williams' Hit List*. Indianapolis, IN: Masters Press, 1996.

VIDEOS

Forever Fenway: 75 Years of Red Sox Baseball. Major League Baseball Productions, 1987.

The Greats of the Game—Ted Williams. Major League Baseball Productions, 1985.

Sports Century—Carl Yastrzemski. ESPN, 2003.

Sports Century: Fifty Greatest Athletes—Ted Williams. ESPN, 1999.

INTERNET WEBSITES

The Ballplayers, online at BaseballLibrary.com (http://www.baseballlibrary.com/baseballlibrary/ballplayers).

Biographies, online at Hickoksports.com (http://www.hickoksports.com/hickoksports/biograph).

Historical Stats, online at MLB.com (http://www.mlb.com/stats.historical/individual stats player).

MLB Awards, online at MLB.com (http://www.mlb.com/awards/mlb_awards/mvp_history).

The Players, online at Baseballanswers.com (http://www.baseballanswers.com/topic/stan-musial).

The Players, online at Baseballink.com (http://www.baseballink.com/baseballink/players).

The Players, online at Baseball-Almanac.com (http://www.baseball-almanac.com/players).

The Players, online at Baseball-Reference.com (http://www.baseball-reference.com/players).

The Teams, online at Baseball-Reference.com (http://www.baseball-reference.com/teams).

TSN-All-Stars, online at BaseballChronology.com (http://www.baseballchronology.com/Baseball/Awards/TSN-AllStars.asp).